An Ear to the Ground:
Presenting Writers from 2 Coasts

AN Ear to the Ground:

Presenting Writers from 2 Coasts

**Edited by
Scott C. Davis**

 Cune

An Ear to the Ground: Presenting Writers from 2 Coasts
Seattle, 1997. Special thanks to Neal Bastek, Bjorn Benson, Mari Lynch Dehmler, Steven Schlesser, Holly L. Thomas.

Copies of *An Ear to the Ground* are available: In paperback for $19.95 plus $2.50 shipping and handling within the United States. ($1.50 shipping and handling for each additional book.) In hardcover for $29.95 plus $3.00 shipping and handling within the United States. ($2.00 for shipping and handling for each additional hardcover book.)

Individuals: To order, call (800) 789-7055; email to Cune @ AOL.com; or send a check to Cune, P.O. Box 31024, Seattle, WA 98103. Washington State residents add 8.2 % sales tax.
Bookstores: Available from Bookpeople, Baker & Taylor, Pacific Pipeline.

Cune is a project of the Allied Arts Foundation. Make tax-deductible contributions to "Cune Project/Allied Arts" and mail to Cune at the above address. For information about Cune books, send a 32 cent stamp to the above address. To schedule Cune authors for readings or interviews, call (206) 789-7055. Contact Cune by fax: (206) 782-1330; or email: Cune @AOL.com. Visit our online magazine at http://www.cunepress.com/cune.

 Cune

The Local/International Series
Cune is an online magazine and literary press based in Seattle. We operate as an artists and writers cooperative and publish "local writers of international significance." Our name is derived from "cuneiform."

Cune Press and *An Ear to the Ground* are a project of the Allied Arts Foundation. Thank you Allied Arts.

Books by writers from *An Ear to the Ground:* The following titles are published by Cune Press or are sold in Cune's catalogue.
Currently in print:
Burning Stone by Zoë Landale (poetry; Ronsdale).
Colour of Winter Air by Zoë Landale (poetry; Sono Nis).
Grace & Desolation by Sean Bentley (poetry).
Lost Arrow and Other True Stories by Scott C. Davis (nonfiction).
Love & Memory by Jamal Gabobe (poetry).
Paul Celan: Poet, Survivor, Jew by John Felstiner (nonfiction; Yale).
Publishing Lives: Interviews with Independent Book Publishers in the Pacific Northwest and British Columbia edited by Jerome Gold (nonfiction; Black Heron Press).
The Soul of Our Culture by Scott C. Davis (nonfiction).
To Paint Her Life: Charlotte Salomon in the Nazi Era by Mary Lowenthal Felstiner (nonfiction; University of California Press).
The World of Patience Gromes: Making and Unmaking a Black Community by Scott C. Davis (nonfiction; Kentucky).
A Writer Called "X" by Scott C. Davis (nonfiction).
Forthcoming in 1997:
Seeking the Heart of the Syrian People by Scott C. Davis (nonfiction).
In the Jar of Our Senses by Doug Nathan (poetry, recipes).
A Study in Failure by Steven Schlesser (nonfiction).
the never field by Nathalie Handal (poetry; Post-Apollo).

A Note to the Reader

An Ear to the Ground presents essays by emerging writers from the East and West Coasts of North America. The theme is "local truth."

Most of the writers in *An Ear to the Ground* have never before been published in book form. Their essays represent a variety of styles and sensibilities. The idea is to broaden the audience for good writing. I do not suppose that every piece will appeal to every reader. Neither are essays intended to be definitive literary statements. *An Ear to the Ground* is designed as a salon. Essays, portraits, profiles, and bios are intended as conversation. I hope that each reader will come away with two or three writers whom he or she especially enjoys and will look up the longer work of these writers. Or, will send letters to encourage essayists to continue to write and publish.

Three essays are by guest writers Horton Foote, Arun Gandhi, and Václav Havel—chosen because their philosophies characterize the philosophy of this book and of Cune Press.

An Ear to the Ground has been cooperatively published. It is a response to recent developments in the publishing industry. For details, see the "Afterword."

—Scott C. Davis

Writers from 2 Coasts

Contents

6

Miriam Frances Abety

Battle of the T-shirts

I was born with curly jet-black hair and eyes. "You're a Cuban," my father would tell me, "who was born in the US by accident." My mother, a redhead from the countryside of Oriente, Cuba, came to New York to escape the monotony of a small agrarian town. She would dash from the kitchen, ladle in hand and yell, "You are *Americana.*" As a teen and young adult, I never knew what nationality to claim. Now I identify myself as Cuban.

A few years ago, my friends Rolando and José and I walked into a Publix supermarket. We bought supplies consisting of wine, cheese, Cuban bread, and grapes for our ritual *Café-con-leche* Sunday, in which we read and critique each other's work. *Café-con-leche*, "Coffee-with-milk," is the name I came up with for our writing group. I felt that the name reflected our cultural relationship in the community and with each other. Two of us are Cuban born, one is not; two of us grew up in Miami and felt rootless for many years, one did not; two of us are gay, one is not; two of us are men, one is not; two of us have liberal views when it comes to dialogue with Cuba, one does not. When we are together, we add rich flavor to each other's lives.

It was near noon, and the *vigilante* summer sun torched my arms, burned my nose, and vexed my eyes. I had forgotten my sunglasses so I compensated by squinting. We passed the shopping carts and headed for the ATM. I observed the silhouette of a muscular man just ahead. He walked alongside two smiling men, smaller than he. My friends poked me to let me know the one with wavy hair and Fabio frame, the *papi* or cute one, was observing me. The sun's intense light hovered just above him like an aura. I squinted to get a better view and noticed his bright smile. I smiled back. We Latins are very friendly, you know. "Well, Miriam," said my friend Rolando, "it looks like we've found you a date and you won't have to spend the weekend cleaning your house, after all."

"Are you kidding?" José said, "he's obviously looking at me."

I didn't pay attention to José. My eyes tried to automatic focus, like the lens of a modern camera. My lenses, however, were manual, and did not cooperate. I got closer and, naturally, so did the man. He must have been as nearsighted as I, for when we were close enough to read each other's T-shirts, we reacted like aggressive animals ready to defend our territory. We stood firm, about two feet away from each other, two stiff alley cats ready for combat.

One of us wore a T-shirt that had a picture of Nelson Mandela and the caption, "*The Miami Herald* Welcomes Nelson Mandela to Miami." The other one wore a *gusano* (worm) T-shirt. In Miami's Cuban community, a *gusano* is symbolic. You see, when the mass exodus of Cubans from the island in the late 1960s flooded Miami, Castro called the exiles *gusanos,* cowards. The caption of the T-shirt read, "*Gusano o muerto. Nunca dialogo.*" A worm or dead. Never dialogue. To understand why these two T-shirts can bring two Cubans to challenge each other, much like the shoot outs at the O.K. Corral, one must understand the conservative Cuban community's dislike for Mandela.

Nelson Mandela has expressed sympathy toward Cuba's Fidel Castro. In Miami, if you associate yourself with Castro or even approve of dialogue, you are automatically categorized as a communist. You are a natural enemy to a *gusano,* no matter what. In Miami's Cuban community, politics are black and white; no room for hues of gray. You either are, or you're not, on the "right" side—the extreme right.

Here we were, high noon and ready for the Battle of the T-shirts. We Cubans are very emotional, you know. He stared at my shirt, I at his. Not everything is so clear cut, I wanted to say. Our two sets of friends sized each other up. José is Audrey Hepburn thin, Rolando average build. One of the *papi's* friends was Jackie Gleason fat, the other, average build. This inevitable altercation would leave three people in bad shape, the Café-con-leche team, that is.

My opponent looked down at me. I looked up at him and raised my eyebrows. "Any questions?" my eyebrows asked. For a moment I felt that he was going to spit at me. He moved a little bit forward, then his friends grabbed him. My friends grabbed me.

"*Vamos*," the fat one on the other side said.

The *papi* walked closely in front of me. I could smell his breath, café-con-leche. He looked at me, I stared at him as defiantly as a cornered mouse, he winked, and asked "Mandela?"

"He's South Africa's José Marti," I said, knowing he'd understand. José Marti was the legendary Cuban patriot/poet who fought for independence from Spain.

The *papi* motioned me to walk into the store where the ATM was located. Cubans are very polite, you know. We entered.

"Well," José said, "maybe he was interested in me after all."

Profile

Once Miriam Frances Abety and I went to a reading at Books and Books, a Spanish-style building in the heart of Coral Gables that is every local writer's Mecca. Miriam was wearing her black "Against Animal Testing" T-shirt, and her long, curly auburn hair was all over the place. I dressed more appropriately for the reading; a plaid shirt with cut off sleeves and jeans with holes in the knees. The bookstore was flooded with the usual writing students, writing wannabes, and writers like myself.

Allan Gurganis read from his new book *White People*. While he read, Miriam and I bickered in whispers, arguing, as always, about how I feel about writers who join academia and dilute writing by making it structured. Afterwards, we left, blaming each other for missing the content of the evening. We went to Miriam's house. She played her favorite Cuban singer, La Lupe, a singer the likes of Nina Simone with the civility of Janis Joplin. We drank Robert Mondavi white zinfandel and "clinked" our glasses, our peacemaking. She read a story to me she had been working on. "So the literary mood permeates," she said. She read her short story about a middle-aged woman whose preppy daughter comes to visit and who disapproves of her mother's lifestyle. In page after page, written with ink from the heart, and a spicy touch of madness, I was engaged with a writer who is full of life, as life is full of her.

To be a single mother, a career woman, a graduate student in a doctoral program in psychology and a master's program in creative writing, a social activist, and a prolific writer, simultaneously, requires an unusual and powerful alchemy. Miriam never fails to amaze, irritate, and anger with her prose.

—José Toledo

Bio

Miriam Frances Abety

Place of residence: Miami.

Birthplace: Manhattan.

Day job: Therapist in domestic violence program.

Education: M.S. in psychology. Completing Ph.D. and M.F.A. in creative writing.

Awards: First prize, *New Times* Hurricane Andrew Writing Contest. Second round finalist, Steven Spielberg's Screenwriting Fellowship. Voted Best Sister of Flagettes in High School.

Current projects: *The Son of the Wagonman*—a novel. *Like a Miami Flamingo*—a memoir from which this essay is excerpted.

Favorite book: The last one I read that inspired me.

Beliefs: Vegetarian and animal rights activist.

Recognition: Thanks Sami, for being the best daughter and friend any woman could have. I'm really proud of you!

❋

Jocelyn M. Ajami

A Different Path

According to the Tao Te Ching, "a good traveler has no fixed plans and is not intent upon arriving." When people look at me they are convinced that I am Italian, Greek, or even Romanian. Actually, I was born in Caracas, Venezuela of Arab parents, who were both Christian. I attended a strict Catholic school where I was surrounded by cheerful nuns. I thought of myself as Latin American until I was a teenager and realized that *hummus* and *caraotas con arroz* (black beans and rice) were not part of the same cultural banquet. I now think of myself as Hispanic, Arab, North American. Tomorrow I may become something else. I view ethnicity as a work-in-progress.

I ended up in Boston by a quirk of fate and it is here, in my most recent hometown, that I discovered Islam. I am not Muslim, but through my studies of Moorish architecture I developed a cultural appetite for all things "Islamic." My religious views, however, come from a totally different source. Growing up Catholic, I had a wonderful brush with Christianity and no reason to rebel. But I have always been spiritually greedy, and so the all-inclusiveness of the Tao Te Ching drew me to it because it accommodates all religious paths. Through the Tao, I could more deeply explore the wonders of Islam, particularly the unique aesthetic of Islamic geometric art which has influenced my own notion of abstraction. Much of my work as a painter and as a filmmaker is devoted to exposing the stereotypes of Islam in the Western press while communicating its tenets. As a writer, I take courage from the prophet's own words: "The ink of the scholar is more precious than the blood of the martyr."

Profile

I met Jocelyn M. Ajami in 1989 at Dave's Cafe, on Newbury Street in Boston's Back Bay. I had just moved from Nantucket where I had spent three years gathering myself and writing fiction. The move to Boston meant a return to a business lifestyle, and I was craving the conversation of artists and writers, so accessible to me on Nantucket.

Dave's was a small, street-side cafe, and I overheard Jocelyn talking: "The painting I'm doing is just killing me." She looked great, so I said, "Hello."

I found that, like myself, Jocelyn is an inveterate "cafeist." She finds inspiration and interchange at cafes, creative differences, and cross-fertilization. Whether she juxtaposes glass and rope in a painting, or documents on video a village where Jews and Arabs invent a way of life together, Jocelyn employs her artist's sensibility.

Now, in 1996, Dave's has been replaced by a Sushi bar, but Jocelyn and I remain great friends. She is still killing herself over the next project, and she still looks great.

—William J. Martin

Bio

Jocelyn M. Ajami
Place of residence: Boston.
Day jobs: Painter. Filmmaker. Teacher.
Education: B.A. in French. M.A. in studio art and art history.
Serial publication: *Aramco*—essays.
Awards: Leadership Foundation Fellowship, from the International Women's Forum. Merit Finalist Award, Houston International Film Festival, for *Oasis*. Honorable mention, American Film and Video Festival, for *Jihad*.
Current project: *Gypsy Heart*—a film on flamenco dance.
Favorite book: *Tao Te Ching* by Lao Tzu.
Belief: Taoist.
Craving: Bread, bread, bread.

Lucy Aron

Butterfly Love

The fritillary, a pale orange butterfly with dull black spots, fluttered and flailed in the web outside my window as the spider watched from an upper corner. A moment later, a second fritillary appeared and began darting frantically around the periphery of the web. It charged towards the web, then wheeled off, back towards it, and away again. Its dance of indecision suggested a creature suspended between the conflicting impulses of self-preservation and self-sacrifice.

Was the second butterfly the mate of the first? And did the frenzied display reflect concern? Empathy? Love? Butterfly love. An absurd phrase. Entomologists assure us that invertebrates do not love. Their physical bonding is devoid of emotional content. They lack the complex attachments of the more highly evolved species and behave, so we are informed, in strict accordance with the mandates of their genetic code. They have no gene for compassion.

Or do they?

If the behavior of the second butterfly was not a demonstration of caring, why didn't it simply fly away as soon as it sensed peril? Why did it keep gravitating back towards the captured butterfly, as though wanting to rescue it?

I was torn between my own contradictory impulses. Should I just watch, dismayed yet transfixed by the unfolding drama, or demolish the web and liberate the butterfly? Though I knew the spider was merely fulfilling its biological imperative, I identified with the butterfly as it struggled against the lethal strands. I felt a reflexive empathy—weak against strong, victim against aggressor, prey against predator.

Yet I am a predator. I don't eat red meat or fowl, but I do eat fish. I don't actually kill fish, but the act of consumption renders me a co-conspirator in their demise. I destroy snails in my garden. I kill fleas and ticks on my dog, and flies and mosquitoes in the house. I rationalize, with a twinge of discomfort, that these are defensive gestures against potential vectors of disease.

Why, then, was I distressed at the prospect of a butterfly's death? Was I responding not to death, but to the dying process, a reflection of my own anxieties? Or to the butterfly's gossamer beauty? And which considerations ought to determine such life and death decisions—here and elsewhere? Aesthetics, evolutionary status, abundance, size, charm, service, or entertainment value?

I don't know. I've sought a philosophy which would teach me how to make peace with life's contradictions, to accept its relentless shades of gray—to cherish rather than allow them to confuse and bedevil me. A philosophy that resonates with my innermost, if incomplete, vision of truth. Appalled by the arrogance, rapacity, and short sightedness of Western culture, I have chosen an eclectic blend of Zen Buddhism, Taoism, and Native American thought. Their cosmologies are disparate, yet I'm inspired by the balance they embody—between head and heart, yin and yang—and by their fierce reverence for life.

Still, facile answers elude me. What does reverence for life mean in the crucible of day-to-day existence? All inanimate stuff of the planet, according to many non-Western belief systems, is as alive as any finch or daffodil. We must destroy in order to provide food, clothing, shelter. But destroy what, and how much? Which animals? Which plants?

In many Native Americans traditions, one takes from the earth only with a profound sense of gratitude, and always gives back to it. When picking herbs to use medicinally or ceremonially, the Mohawks never remove the largest or healthiest members—those that are essential to the perpetuation of the plant community. And when possible they sow seeds back into the ground from the parent plant. My existence affects the natural world. I can only hope to affect it as consciously and tenderly.

The second butterfly seemed to understand that there was a critical line. If crossed, there would be no crossing back. Ultimately, the butterfly was unwilling to take that final step. Ultimately, I, too, was unwilling to interfere between the spider and its captive. My role wasn't to judge their private *pax de deux* but to acknowledge, with awe, the spider's dance as vital as the butterfly's to the universal pageantry.

Despite my biases. Despite my unease about what Whitman called "you bitter hug of mortality." Despite my butterfly love.

Profile

Lucy Aron

I imagine that a wonderful railroad car was traveling through the world and stopped on the side of a mountain because that was the perfect place. For meditation and thought. For planting an orange grove. For listening to coyotes sing in the canyon and hearing the fish swim in the ocean.

That's where Lucy Aron lives with her husband and two golden retrievers, a library of books, a hot tub, and a garden of snapdragons and purple sage. She is a pianist and can listen to music for hours at a time. She loves Glenn Gould. She is not totally unlike him.

—Barbara Sachs

Bio

Lucy Aron

Place of residence: Santa Barbara, California.

Education: B.A. in music, University of California at Berkeley.

Anthology: *Where the Heart Is: A Celebration of Home.*

Serial publications: *Cleveland Plain Dealer. Orange Coast Magazine.*

Awards: First prize Santa Barbara Arts Fund Individual Artist Awards for Nonfiction (1995). Second place in Dog Obedience Class.

Current project: Book about work and community.

Favorite book: *A Fine and Private Place* by Peter Beagle.

Beliefs: Quaker with Buddhist tendencies, aspiring mystic, and devout fool.

Cravings: Pavich jumbo flame seedless raisins.

Barbara Nimri Aziz

"Move Over"

"Move Over" is the title of a poem by Mohja Kahf. And for me it is a statement that Western feminists need to hear. It is time for Western feminists to step aside and let women from other parts of the world speak. Why is it that feminists who serve as book editors and conference organizers urge me to talk about my victimization at the hands of my brother, husband, or another Arab man? Why won't they hear me explain the injustices of Western actions, for example, in the Gulf War? These women, perhaps more than my Arab brother, are an obstacle to my true liberation.

Do you remember the opening passages of Maxine Hong Kingston's *The Woman Warrior*, or Alice Walker's *The Color Purple*, or Nawal el-Saadawi's *The Hidden Face of Eve*? I cannot forget them, and you, too, may remember how each opens with a powerful scene of a woman being abused. Either she is raped, or driven to suicide, or violated in some other way. A coincidence? "Abused Third World Women." Is such a portrayal a fair reflection of reality, or a pre-judgment? By selecting these themes, can publishers of our work influence our voice?

The books I note, and many more like them, were celebrated in the West, especially by feminists. As a result, they appear in many world literature courses and are a must on any women's studies college reading list. Even high school teachers assign these books. Think about receptive young readers eager to learn about the wider world. Often these stories are the first image young people have of Asians, Africans, or Arabs.

Why do so many stories about third world women portray us as victims? I only began to ask myself this question very late in the game because it took me years to break through the conditioning and to say, "Wait a minute. Is this really what I am?" Finally, when I did speak out, Western feminists responded that, "The world must understand what hardships you face." Moreover, they maintain, "These sufferings bond women worldwide. These stories arouse interest where, before, there was none at all. We take pity on you."

Why do we need bonds of suffering to unite us? And why do stories of our suffering seem to dominate what is published, and thereby what is known about us? I am speaking not only about Asian, African, and Arab women but also about those of us identified as Hindu, Muslim, African-American, Nicaraguan, or Bosnian—all so-called third world women.

In the United States, the power centers are the Congress, the judiciary, corporate boards, the clergy—Muslim, Christian, Buddhist, and Jewish—the military, and the press. All these remain entrenched male domains. Before the Western feminist movement began in the 1970s, scholars, journalists, and activists gave little thought to the power of our patriarchy here. Then feminists began to expose social inequities and call for a balance. There were some changes, and some women entered places where they had once been excluded. Yet gains were limited.

So I can't help wondering: is it possible that, because of their frustration over limited success at home, feminists have shifted their attention to women worldwide? Are these women distorting the third world situation to create a winning argument for themselves at home—to make it appear they are really better off, after all? And why the focus on the abuse of third world women at the hands of their patriarchal systems? What about the exploitation of third world women by international corporations, by arms suppliers from the industrial world?

The Arab or Muslim woman is a prime example of the edgy relationship that third world women have with Western women. Recall Taslima Nisrine, the lately celebrated writer in Bangladesh. She was publicly denounced in some circles within Bangladesh because she had criticized some interpretations of the Qur'an. Newspapers worldwide rushed to report how rampaging hoards of Muslim men were out to kill her. What a boon for Western feminists! They could expose the excesses of Islam, and its abuse of women, especially those who aspire to be freethinkers. In the end, Western women offered Nisrine and other Muslim women little real assistance. (Nisrine herself, I was told, was aware that she might be exploited by Western women if she called for their help.) Before this, Nisrine's writing hadn't interested American readers, and her work was not translated into English. But once she fit the stereotype promoted by feminists—sure enough, a collection of her work is being translated for publication by a major house in the United States. Meanwhile, the American public was left with the impression of another ugly incident from the "undeveloped, extremist" third world.

Let's come back to the roles of American women. Where are American women effective today? Few women, regrettably, have risen to positions of power in the Senate or in corporate America. One place they seem to be more influential is the local media and publishing. Feminists have a major impact on what is published about women in the world and thereby on what is taught about other societies in schools and colleges.

The Arab or Muslim woman finds herself defined by experts in women's studies. Repeatedly we find the same simplistic presentations. First, we are perceived as weak. Second, we are seen as victim. Third, our oppressor is typically a male relative. Fourth, we appear uneducated and incapable of managing without outside help—namely support, publicity, and ministering from those already educated and liberated, the capable Western women. Fifth, the Arab or Muslim woman is caged and needs to be released. Everything is set up for the arrival of a fairy godmother.

The pattern I speak about is very real, and I believe that it is by design. It is not a conspiracy in itself. It is rather a natural spin-off of arrogance. These women often exhibit the same patronizing attitude for which they fault the men of their own society. Remember their complaints of how they were criticized by men for their oversensitivity and weakness? Aren't they making the same accusation toward Arab and Muslim women? Western women assume that they are somehow historically better placed to take global leadership of women's issues—that they evolved ahead of others to an advanced stage of social and sexual enlightenment.

The assumptions of Western women are unfounded. There is also a racist element in their attitude. We have repeatedly tried to correct this. But the many objections voiced by women worldwide are unrecorded in the West. Americans and Europeans simply fail to hear third world women when we call out to them, "Wait a minute! We do not all feel the way such and such an author reports we feel. What about my brother? What about my father? What about the strong among us?"

Meanwhile, to verify these Western claims, a select group of third world authors are trotted from one TV round table to another, from one feminist conference to the next, and featured in magazine stories on a regular basis. Take the example of Arab women and the Egyptian writer, Nawal el-Saadawi. Careful research by Amal Amireh, presented at the 1995 Middle East Studies Association conference, pointed out that current editions of el-Saadawi's work in English have been altered to overemphasize violence to women and demonstrate apparent intolerance in Islam. Perhaps against her own wishes, el-Saadawi has found her work used by others to try to illustrate the general oppression of Islam toward women.

The best known books about Arab and Muslim women are, in any case, not by Arab authors, but by American women. Anne Mahmoody's book *Not Without My Daughter* has been made into a successful film. More recently, in the wake of the Gulf War, we have *Price of Honor,* by Jan Goodwin, and *Nine Parts of Desire,* by Geraldine Brooks. Goodwin and Brooks (both journalists) draw on the research of Arab women scholars, and therefore bring an "insider" authority to their claims.

As third world women, we must not be intimidated. We must ask: Why this fascination, this curiosity, this obsession with the lives of Arab and Muslim women, almost to the exclusion of other subjects? And what happens to our male writers?

We have many male novelists of the caliber of Nobel laureate Naguib Mahfouz. Yet few are published abroad and most remain unknown outside the Arab world. Many find themselves overlooked in favor of Arab women writers who are, perhaps, less accomplished. And, when Arab male writers are sought out, it is less for their humanistic creative work and more for their analyses of Middle East political events. But that's another story.

In the end, let us recognize that Western feminism, including its academic dimension, has its cultural context and its political agenda. The women who embrace us and pander to us as victims must step back. Then they must learn to take our strength with our weakness.

Profile

I met Barbara Nimri Aziz in March 1994 in the offices of WBAI Radio in Manhattan. As a Pacifica community radio station, WBAI's studio has a well worn, utilitarian atmosphere. Together with its sister stations, WBAI is the last bastion of really free speech in the country—a milieu into which Aziz fits perfectly, although she's been here only since 1989.

Aziz earned a doctorate in anthropology and for almost two decades conducted research in the Himalayas, India, and China. Now she is a working freelance print journalist. And she also serves as senior producer at WBAI. Her program *Tahrir* (liberation) features Arab and Arab-American thinkers, writers, and artists and is one of the few outlets of Arab thought in this country. Spare time? There's canoeing and hiking. And also literature. In 1992 Aziz founded RAWI, INC.—Radius of Arab-American Writers. (In Arabic *al-rawi* means storyteller.) This unique, budding organization pulls together the country's best Arab literary talent. Will Arab-American culture break out? In all, the signs are good. But on this gray, wet day in March, Barbara Nimri Aziz saw things differently.

"Can I tape our interview?" I asked.

"No," she said. Aziz looked at me. I was your average white guy, undoubtedly biased, not to be trusted. "First," Aziz continued, "let me ask you some questions." She ripped into me pretty good, one question after another: "What are you looking for?" she asked. "Trying to confirm the usual stereotypes? Do you want to know how my father or my brother oppressed me?" She was combative.

We were sitting in a scruffy producer's common room furnished with sound-deadening peg board. From the on-air monitor I could hear a talk show host discussing racial stereotypes. Aziz's battle also had to do with racism—in this case, deep-rooted prejudice toward her people. "I am invited to scholarly conferences," she said, "and, as long as I talk about the weaknesses and flaws in Arab culture, I am welcomed. But what of the real issues and the personal side of our lives? What of the hypocrisy that we Arabs and Muslims in the West must face at every turn? When I want to speak this truth, the microphone is turned off. By that I mean I am only occasionally invited to talk on these subjects. But I must participate, and so I work in alternative media such as WBAI."

Logic, vision, conviction. An impressive woman, indeed. A woman who seemed to draw strength from the dim light of WBAI's low budget digs. We talked for an hour longer. Barbara calmed, but nothing friendly. Afterward, we walked out together. On the street corner, in the daylight, Barbara was reduced to human stature. I wanted to give her a hug—this was the Patty Hearst syndrome, I knew, the desire to be loved by one's captors, not a good move at all. So I turned and walked away.

By the next time we spoke, Aziz had decided to trust me. She was businesslike, gracious. This was the Aziz that RAWI members knew. But take my word. Beneath the surface of this rational, professional woman is immense feeling. She seems to think that her ideas are not an intellectual game: the lives of many people depend upon what she says. How was it that, in my earlier interview, I was allowed to see inside?

"I was upset that day," said Aziz.

—Scott C. Davis

Bio

Barbara Nimri Aziz
Place of residence: New York City.
Birthplace: Canada.
Grew up in: Canada, India, and the Middle East.
Day jobs: Radio broadcaster for Pacifica Radio. Freelance writer.
Education: Master's and Ph.D. at University of London, England.
Serial publications: *The Christian Science Monitor. Natural History. Aramco World.*
Director and cofounder: Radius of Arab-American Writers, a network of writers of Arab descent. (RAWI, P.O. Box 620 Prince St. Station, New York, NY 10012. Email for Barbara Nimri Aziz: aziz@escape.com.)
Current projects: Two manuscripts-in-progress. The first is titled: *Between Two Rivers: The Story of an American Woman's Journey in Iraq.* The second is a book about three Nepali women activists.

Favorite book: *Madness and a Bit of Hope,* poems by Safiya Henderson Holmes (Writers and Readers Publishing Company).
Belief: Arab nationalism.
Cravings: Good radio drama and birds singing in the evening.

jonetta rose barras

A Search for Integrity

Growing up in segregated New Orleans, my grandmother impressed upon me that we were not financially wealthy. She stressed, however, that even the richest person was stricken with unalterable poverty if her word could not be trusted, if she lacked integrity.

This axiom is the filter through which I look at society and judge many of our leaders. Recently a friend and I were hard pressed to come up with a list of ten Americans who, in our opinion, possess integrity—something more than honesty. Integrity, as defined by Stephen Carter, Professor of Law at Yale, requires three things: first, discerning what is right and what is wrong; second, acting on what has been discerned, even at personal cost; and third, saying openly that one's actions are based on this understanding of right and wrong. My friend and I frustrated ourselves flicking off names. Most didn't meet the Carter litmus test.

I have come to understand integrity, like leadership, as an awesome responsibility. This thought brought me to the front door of Nation of Islam Leader Louis Farrakhan. As the primary organizer of the October 16, 1995, Million Man March in Washington, D.C., Minister Farrakhan promised black America a new spirit and a new movement. In particular he made this promise to the nearly one million African-American men who answered his call for atonement and reconciliation. But what he has delivered thus far has been posturing and rhetoric, sans atonement.

Let's be clear. In the face of great opposition from my female colleagues, who accused Farrakhan of discriminating against women, I supported the Million Man March as an all-male gathering. Yet, as I listened that day to speech after speech, I waited patiently for the atonement which march leaders had promised. Specifically, for atonement toward African-American women who have been forced to stand at the forefront of the movement for black equality and economic parity. There were pledges, charges, and counter-charges, but no atonement arrived.

Now comes the latest injury. In his 1996 trip to Libya, Iran, and other destinations Farrakhan has taken the success of the Million Man March and pimped it across the globe. Apparently he hoped to demonstrate a political potency that before the Million Man March had been questioned.

It isn't surprising that Farrakhan would travel throughout Africa to find comfort in the homes of notorious African and Middle Eastern leaders—in Nigeria and Iraq. And his friendship with Libya's Mu'ammar al-Qadhafi isn't new. The two men have managed a mutual admiration society for years. (Let's not forget that Qadhafi helped finance the Nation of Islam's previous foray into the cleaning products industry back in the early 1980s.) What is disgraceful is Farrakhan's use of the Million Man March as a bridge to these men, who have killed their own in the name of Allah and national security. What's really at work with his African trip is the worst kind of capitalism— the kind that purports to serve the poor or the needy when, in fact, its only intent is to fill its coffers. Some capitalists simply can't conceal their mercenary traits.

Farrakhan says he wants to use the wealth of these foreign countries to benefit deteriorating African-American communities in the United States. There is great wealth here in America, and in the black community, which spends more than $200 billion each year. It's more useful, more practical, and just plain right for Farrakhan to start in his own backyard, tapping middle and upper income African-Americans to support economic development in blighted urban centers. This, after all, is what the Islamic leader promised to do with the cash collected at the march.

Some people will question my attack on Farrakhan. They will say he has every right to travel to Africa and meet with whomever he wants. They will say he doesn't owe the public anything. But this is exactly the point of integrity and leadership. Farrakhan's controversial trip abroad cast a shadow over an otherwise positive event. He should have understood his new found role in representing, even unofficially, African-Americans.

Farrakhan's African trip was a tear in the cloth of integrity. I can't ignore it. My grandmother's hand still rests on my shoulder. I am forced to attempt a repair whenever I discover it. Farrakhan came to black America seeking redemption and forgiveness; he received that. He stirred the hope of one million black men and an equal number of African-American women and a sprinkling of whites. He called for a finer, more positive image of black males and black male leadership. African-Americans placed their faith in Farrakhan and the sincerity of his message that day in October. Should we desire leaders of integrity? That's not too much to expect.

Profile

jonetta rose barras (jon ete roz bar ez) *n.* 1. A Southern belle, well mannered in feminine charm. 2. As relentless in pursuit of a story as she is poised and confident. 3. Tenacious and contrarian. 4. A lovely walking paradox who can kill, but sweetly.

jonetta moved into my life about a year ago—in the first months of 1995, a couple of years after we began publishing the *Quarterly Black Review of Books*. We had taken space in Manhattan's Soho District—an old manufacturing area, hardwood floors, loft space, lots of brick: you'd have to know Soho to appreciate it. We had organized our office and were getting the early issues of QBR out the door, but it was a tough go.

Enter jonetta. Mind you, the door was only slightly ajar, but jonetta's enthusiasm carried the day. How did she know what we needed? jonetta wrote reviews for us and helped in practical ways, but her largest contribution was concept. She set a tone for our reviews: critical yet accessible. She gave our writing emotional timbre. jonetta saw the reason for QBR. To her it wasn't "one more thing." It was a cause. It performed an essential function.

jonetta changed us. Did she do this consciously? Perhaps not—she operates so much out of heart. I'm sure it had everything to do with her giving nature. Needless to say, she is a well-balanced spirit, well-weighted in both talent and intellect, sensitivity and compassion. jonetta is a woman you want in your corner, for every possible reason. What more can I say?

—Max Rodriguez

Bio

jonetta rose barras
Place of residence: Washington, D. C.
Birthplace: New Orleans.
Day jobs: Writer, editor, columnist.
Education: Trinity College.
Books: *the corner is no place for hiding. Dawn.*
Serial publications: *New Republic* and *Washington Post*—essays.
Current projects: *Losing My Virginity*—a collection of essays. *Last Days of Sacrificia Dupree*—a novel.
Favorite book: *One Hundred Years of Solitude* by Gabriel Garcia Marquez.
Belief: The power of love and the human potential to alter any negative force.
Craving: Time, more time.

James Bash

Alleys—A Reminiscence

Portland, Oregon is a city bereft of alleys. Streets and avenues are every-where, but the unpaved, uneven, and pock-marked alley is almost nowhere to be found. It's as if an anti-alley league swept through town and convinced the city fathers to make these unnamed, one-lane streets illegal. But in doing so they deprived Portland of a mainstay of America's urban landscape.

An alley is like a good butler who makes his services available when you need them; otherwise, he blends into the background. The electric poles, sewage connections, and gas and water lines are located in alleys of many towns and cities. And when these utilities need to be repaired, the workers and their vehicles don't have to block the street in front of your house. If your garage entry is from the alleyway, you don't have to lose precious space in the front yard to a double-wide driveway. In fact, you don't have to have a fancy garage door because guests can't see it from the sidewalk.

I miss alleys. I grew up in towns where alleys became an extension of your backyard. An alley was the perfect place to leave your junker, an old barbecue, and a couple of rust-laden folding chairs. If you tore out an old toilet from your remodeled bathroom, you could deposit it in the alley for the garbage men to pick up, rather than leave it near the front sidewalk for the neighborhood to inspect.

As a teenager in Wilbur, Washington, I would cut through several alleys on the way to school. I shared my favorite shortcuts with dogs and cats, which wandered about that small town in search of their friends and enemies. Together we kept the original meaning of alley intact, because in medieval France *allée* meant "walking street."

Our house had a burn barrel in the alleyway. We put our used paper, cardboard, and plastic packaging in that ancient container, which had lost its original color and acquired the orange-red tones of a hardened life. After lighting the contents we had to watch for a short while in case the wind might catch a scrap of burning paper and toss it on some dry grass. The sight of flames leaping in the barrel could spark my mind, but the smell of plastic wrap always made my nose hairs curl.

The hoop on the neighbor's garage didn't pose any particular problems to a game of basketball, but the alley sure did. Before I could dribble, I had to smooth the gravel as well as I could by dragging my shoe over the surface and casting aside the larger stones. Ruts and potholes could affect the strategy of the game. Alley players try to work with inside knowledge of the court, and rocky ones have their advantages.

Most alleys that I've seen are packed with gravel, and it still amazes me how weeds and bits of grass can poke their way through. The sound of car tires over crushed rock is one that you rarely hear in a big city unless you have an alley. To a child, waiting for a parent to return home, the crunchy sound can be comforting.

I once lived in an apartment that fronted an alley in Parkland, Washington. The actual mailing address included one-half in it—something like 114½ G Street. The place was nicely furnished but failed to impress one coed who just couldn't believe that I lived in an alley. To her, as to most suburban Americans, an alley is a dark, unkempt, sinister place. Alleys conjure images of broken streetlights, cobblestones, the Mafia, and the poor.

Those who think alleys have to be grimy should visit the historic section of downtown Philadelphia and wander along Elfreth's Alley, which advertises itself as "the oldest continuously inhabited street in the United States." Many of its narrow rowhouses date from the 1720s and are still used as residences. With this sort of start, America should have become a nation of alleys.

I asked a city engineer about the dearth of alleys in P-town. "The city was designed without alleys," he said, "because landowners wanted to make more profits. No one wanted to give away precious land for an alleyway."

Unfortunately, P-town succumbed to the mundane pressures of money, so we don't have the Gasoline Alleys and Tin Pan Alleys that other cities are measured by. We do have a number of bowling alleys. Maybe I can overcome my melancholy by starting a team called the Alley Cats. We could develop gravelly voices and exhibit untamed and uneven play.

Profile

James Bash is a good man with an original twist. Take, for example, his Christmas caroling. Where other carolers gather in homes or go from door to door in well-to-do neighborhoods, James carols the shut-ins of Northwest Portland. He gets permission from the various landlords to gain access for an evening. Then he invites fellow church members and friends to carol.

The buildings we enter are nearly all four-story and five-story square-windowed cubes of soot-blackened brick. The musty halls are walled in flat yellow and floored in dull worn green and black linoleum, like the insides of a tired 1950s high school. The ritual is the same each time: buzz ourselves in, ride the elevator to the top, loudly sing five or six carols to the echoing hall with as much harmony as we can, shout "Merry Christmas," and head for the stairs and the next hallway below. If we pause for a moment we can hear muffled words: "Thanks!" and "Merry Christmas to you too!" Sometimes, if we look back, we can see doors opening and heads appearing.

This began in 1988 and the ritual continues, with James the leader today just as he was then. Over the years the tenants have gotten braver and fonder of us. They open their doors to the singing now, and often join in. Without James, this event could not be as it is. It could exist, certainly. But the openhearted zest and tenderness of these outings come straight from him.

James lives with his wife Kathy in Portland, appreciated by those who read him, cherished by those who know him.

—Victor Chapman

Bio

James Bash
Place of residence: Portland, Oregon.
Birthplace: Bellevue, Ohio.
Grew up in: Pacific Northwest.

Day job: Technical writer at Sequent Computers.

Education: B.A., Pacific Lutheran. Graduate work at University of Iowa and University of Vienna, Austria.

Current projects: Short stories. Articles for the *NW Neighbor* newspaper. Singing with the Portland Symphonic Choir and the Oregon Symphony Orchestra. Organizing the NordFest Folk Festival in Portland.

Worst houseguests: Two Russians. We had signed up for two Estonian singers, but we got two Russian men. Each weighed over 200 pounds. Their previous employment? They had trained mercenaries in Angola and Lebanon. Now they sold oil and gasoline on the Estonian black market. What were they? Russian mafia.

Worst drinking experience: Trying to match the Russians in glass after glass of vodka—not recommended, even in your own home.

Favorite books: *Imperial Masquerade* and *Money and Class in America* by Lewis H. Lapham (Grove/Atlantic).

Belief: Christian. I belong to a Lutheran Church.

Cravings: Classical music. Singing.

Window espresso: In the summer, my next-door neighbor comes right up to our kitchen window to get a cup of latte. We also have a bird feeder nearby, which we keep well-stocked. Heck, it's great to have a happy neighborhood.

Sean Bentley

Night Train to Pisa

It was the middle of the Gulf War. The already ugly Americans were especially despised abroad, and not only by Muslims. Yanks were staying home in droves, for fear of terrorism of one sort or the other, bombs, kidnapping, hijacking, random shootings. My wife, Robin, and I, who had been planning for a year to travel to Europe—the first time for me, at the advanced age of thirty-seven—were only spurred on by the highly reduced airfares. Americans are xenophobes, we thought, paranoiacs. It wasn't like we were going to the Middle East. That sort of thing didn't happen to *us.*

The night was chilly and wet, and we were at the Gare de Lyons, to ride the overnight train from Paris to Pisa. A young man in somewhat punky clothes approached me and asked, in Italian, whether I was Italian. Only several hours later would I remember him, and think: Perhaps he knew something. Perhaps he was screening his countrymen, keeping them off the doomed train. For now, I simply replied *no* (one of my few foolproof Italian phrases), and we boarded.

Just past midnight I was awakened by our rolling into the Dijon station: the changing sounds and motions of the train, garish platform lights, various accents reverberating down the corridors. Compartment doors opened and closed, baggage trundled along, conductors called out in French. Peering out the window, we wondered where these people were going and why so late. Some, by their light dress, were locals, and some clearly foreigners, with much luggage.

Soon the train clacked into darkness, slowly accelerating to about fifty miles an hour. We were grateful that we still had our small compartment to ourselves—that dreaded sharing of space, such as it was, with strangers. By morning we'd be in Italy. We had a big day ahead, many connections to make.

Then we came to a stop. I opened my eyes, let up the shade, and looked out the window again. Moonless night filled the window except for a faint illumination like phosphorescence, thrown on the siding from our cabin's lamp. We were nowhere—among fields, apparently. In the distance, two pale headlight beams crept across the horizon, between the star-like pinpricks of lights from a house or two. Were we at a crossing? Why should we stop like this? The train remained silent. We sat and sat.

Eventually other passengers became restless. Their murmur snapped me alert. Even in peacetime, many media-saturated Americans picture European trains as being under a constant siege of communists, Palestinians, Nazis, pirates, gypsies, God knows what—pick your prejudice—all bearing automatic weapons and searching out Yankees, Jews, young women, or even worse, *random* hostages. Between us Robin and I fit the first three categories, not to mention the fourth. Still, I resisted this; we were not in some country where soldiers might pour onto the train at any time, stereotypically asking for papers and then dragging us away. Were we?

To make matters worse, the power soon went off. We sat in the dark. Normally I adopt the common stance of "it can't happen here" (knowing that it often can, and usually does). But perhaps that bravado, that whistling in the dark, can serve as a beginning of true fearlessness. Robin, scrunched against the window, wrapped in a small blanket, was certain enough of our safety to try to sleep. I didn't sleep. I listened for clues.

Maybe all the stay-at-home Yanks were right. It's well and good to fantasize (by looking at Gothic architecture, or hearing, as we had, accordion music coming archetypically from an apartment in a Parisian lane) that time has stood pastorally still in Europe, but one tends to over-romanticize. Anyway, the past was no less dangerous than the present.

Finally footsteps—the terrorist's?—tramped down the corridor in our direction. An English passenger nabbed the person, asked why we were stopped. "*Un accident,*" was the cryptic reply "in the next car." "Authorities" were being summoned from Dijon, an hour's wait was expected (we'd already sat for twenty minutes). I was reassured, but only slightly. Who had spoken? There could still be someone with an Uzi, holding hostages, I imagined. The train staff wouldn't want a panic. Though it only prolonged the mystery, I was not about to investigate, not wanting to get my head blown off.

At length the power came back on. This seemed a good sign. However, it failed again after a couple of minutes. Perhaps, I hoped, they were trying to conserve their batteries. This happened twice, an interesting way to measure time, like slow-motion water torture. At last we started creeping along— but back toward Dijon. The wheels squealed, the train groaned as it negotiated gentle curves. What could this mean?

At about 1:30, over an hour after first stopping, we rolled lugubriously into a switching yard I'd seen at the outskirts of Dijon, empty trains and extra cars lined up and dark as crates in a huge haunted warehouse. Here, unbelievably, we stopped once more. Again we waited. Were they swapping cars? Rerouting the train? After a bit, creaks and clunks signaled a move, and we pulled forward. At last! I thought, let's get on the road. And then with a jerk we stopped, hope restored and dashed yet again. Another long and enigmatic lull.

Then once more we continued forward, increasing speed (ah!) and passing a small station house, which had been lit but empty not long before. Now in the dim light of a street lamp, we saw by the tracks a man in a gray suit, walking back toward town. He carried a doctor's black bag with silver buckles. A doctor. A safe icon, recognizable, apolitical. Two men stood before the station house in serious talk, while others inside appeared to be filling out papers, hunched over a small table, bright lamp-glow on their faces. We were back on our way, papers unasked for, lineage unquestioned, bodies untouched. The night train to Pisa had claimed, though mysteriously, only one victim, and he was not us.

Profile

When I first met Sean Bentley in September 1979, he went by the alias of Lenny E. Beast. We were in Parrington 223B on the University of Washington campus where his father had held poetry workshops for nearly two decades. Beast, wearing his Captain America T-shirt, read "The Man with

Meadows in Both Halves of Him, Living with It," written during a recent cross-country trip.

Since then Sean has turned me on to writers Albert Goldbarth, Colin Wilson, and H.P. Lovecraft; and I have turned him on to Glenlivet, Oban, Cragganmore, and other such golden elixirs from the highlands and lowlands of Scotland. I'm not sure who got the better deal, but they definitely go together.

Two instances stand out of life imitating art: On a journey we took to the Oregon coast during a powerful wind storm, Sean buried himself in a giant pile of seafoam; and one night in the Canadian Rockies, near the Athabascan glacier north of Banff, he took a burning stick from our fire and traced Picassoesque images against the frigid dark which hung glowing green in the air longer than we thought possible.

It is this spontaneous joy and beauty that make Sean's writing so compelling. His latest book, *Grace & Desolation*, pulls together the last six years of his life, which have seen the death of his father and the birth of his son.

—Herb Payton

Bio

Sean Bentley
Place of residence: Bellevue, Washington.
Birthplace: Seattle.
Day job: Senior Technical Editor, Microsoft Corporation.
Education: B.A., University of Washington.
Books: *Into the Bright Oasis. Instances. Grace & Desolation.*
Current project: Essay on being a second-generation artist.
Favorite book: *A Sympathy of Souls* by Albert Goldbarth.
Craving: To travel abroad.

Sylvia Benzaquen

Visiting Kibbutz Hanita, 1971

Many years ago, when I was still opening my eyes to the world, something happened, a small incident that I remember very clearly. It taught me that humans beings, whatever you hear, are essentially kind and good.

After finishing high school, every child strongly believes that he or she owns the planet. In this belief I was not different from others my age who grew up in a wonderful country named Venezuela.

Venezuela in the 1960s was one of the best places in the world. Oil was given to us in a full hand, the entire country was like a big party continuously celebrating prosperity. My parents knew that the boom would not last. To prepare me for life after the party was over, they proposed that I spend a year before college far from home, on a continent of my choosing.

So it was that I flew to Israel and began studies at Haifa University. One day I received a postcard from a Venezuelan friend named Ruben. He was living in Kibbutz Hanita, learning Hebrew and Judaism, following through on his decision to become a Jew. Ruben wanted me to visit him. Ronit, a fellow student, advised me about the danger of traveling to his kibbutz. "It is very insecure," she said. "He is living on the line that divides Israel from Lebanon."

I grew up playing with the children of a Lebanese family who lived in my building. They were fine people, very friendly. "I'm going to visit my friend for the weekend," I said.

Ronit was upset. "You're out of your mind," she said. Ronit was from Colombia and felt responsible for me, a fellow South American. In clear Spanish she explained: "The area where you are planning to go is full of terrorists who infiltrate through Lebanon. And most of the attacks are aimed at the Kibbutz Hanita where your friend is living. Don't put your life in danger."

"I've got to go," I said. "My friend Ruben is lonely and homesick."

"In that case," Ronit, said. "I'm coming with you. You're not going to get killed alone."

A couple of days later, Ronit and I were traveling north on a bus. At some point near Lebanon, we were supposed to change to a local. I was happy and excited. Ronit was shaking.

We got to Quiriat Shemona late at night, and all passengers left the bus. When the bus was empty, the driver turned to us. "OK girls, this is my last stop," he said. He was young and strong, handsome and polite. Black hair, blue eyes, white skin, smiling lips.

"What's the best way to the kibbutz?" we asked.

"There's no way before tomorrow morning," he said. "The last bus left fifteen minutes ago."

"What?" we answered together. "There must be a way."

"Do you understand Hebrew?" the driver continued, "or should I explain myself in plain English? There is no way you can get there now. The first bus leaves at six o'clock in the morning, and I'm the driver."

"Could we wait inside this bus?"

"No, ladies. For security reasons, I have to close the bus and park it in a special area."

"Could you then show us a park or another place where we could spend the night? We have no money to pay for a hotel."

"Girls, if I leave you sleeping in the park, tomorrow morning I will find two bodies. Terrorists are all over this area. If you want, however, I will take you to my house, and tomorrow morning I will drive you on my first route to the kibbutz."

My friend and I looked at each other and then discussed the offer, speaking in Spanish so he wouldn't understand, We were both innocent virgins who had the privilege, until then, of a very happy and easy life in our countries. We were between two very simple realities. Would we be murdered by a terrorist, or raped by a Jew?

A little later we entered the house of that young driver. His wife opened the door, and did not seem surprised to see her husband with two strangers. This was not the first time he had taken lost tourists to spend the night in their home. We were starving. The driver's wife gave us dinner, opened the living room sofa bed, and put on new sheets. Soon we were both asleep.

Ronit and I arose at five o'clock in the morning, and breakfast was waiting for us. We took showers, walked to the bus, and left heading north. On the way the driver told us about his experiences as a soldier. "I took many pregnant Lebanese women to Israeli hospitals to give birth to their children," he said. "These woman sit at the frontier and cry in pain until Israeli soldiers take them. And they are grateful—they love Israelis. Today they repay us by telling us about impending rocket attacks, so that we can run to the shelters until the danger is gone."

When we reached Kibbutz Hanita, the driver did not leave us until we found Ruben, my Venezuelan friend.

I remember my visit to Ruben and Kibbutz Hanita as though it were yesterday. The couple who adopted us for the night—I never saw them again. I was young, and they taught me something important. They taught me to trust humanity. I wish them well.

Profile

Sylvia Benzaquen.

I'm landing in Caracas, Venezuela, with my boyfriend. I am filled with excitement, trepidation, and wonderment about this foreign country and the prospect of meeting my future husband's family. Immediately embraced by Sylvia, my future sister-in-law, I begin to feel at ease. Though she hardly speaks English, and I hardly Spanish, we surpass the language barrier and become fast friends . . . sisters.

It is no surprise that Sylvia graduated as a journalist and made journalism her life's work. A romantic and a dreamer, she instinctively speaks in metaphor, as if she is writing an essay or a poem against the backdrop of a tropical paradise. Born in Tangier, Morocco, Sylvia grew up in Argentina and Venezuela. Fresh out of college, she worked in television for three years:

production, copy writing. At the end, for a couple of months, she did her own talk show featuring live interviews with local authors. In 1980 she left the country to travel, then came back to work as a journalist, and finally took a job as an editor with *El Universal,* the largest newspaper in South America, where she served as editor of *Estampas,* the Sunday magazine.

In 1983 Sylvia worked as a correspondent for *Revista Variedades,* a Caracas-based weekly magazine. In 1985, Sylvia decided to make New York her home. She continues to stay in touch with her hometown by writing a weekly column for a local Caracas newspaper where she notes her thoughts, feelings, and impressions of the moment. Her warmth and devotion make her home a natural stopping place for friends and family the world over.

—Joy Benzaquen

Bio

Sylvia Benzaquen
Place of residence: New York.
Birthplace: Tangier, Morocco.
Grew up in: Argentina and Venezuela.
Day job: Freelance journalist.
Serial publications: New York City correspondent for *Nuevo Mundo Israelita* (Caracas). *Revista Estampas, El Universal* (Caracas).
Book: Biography of Venezuelan painter Amparo Rojas.
Current projects: A movie script and a novel.
Favorite book: *The Exemplary Novels of Miguel de Cervantes Saavedra* by Miguel de Cervantes Saavedra.
Belief: Jewish.
Craving: I pray for world peace.

Peggy Bird

The Fabric of Our Lives

Cotton. The fabric of our lives. That's what the ad says. My sewing room says otherwise. I had decided that the room needed yellow walls. But before I could paint, I had to clean. After weeks of mental preparation I was finally ready. I gathered plastic garbage bags, a mug of coffee, and classic rock tapes and descended the steps to my sewing room. The first task was sorting through the fabric I had stashed away, just in case. As in—just in case you have to clothe the population of a small town from materials on hand. The preliminary sort produced three piles: projects I intended to make, pieces for the quilt ladies, and I'm-not-sure.

Then came the hard work: reducing the size of the stash. The first pile was small and done quickly. Pile two was not small but went fast, too. Pile three was neither small nor fast. Which of the pieces of cloth heaped around me could I shed? The green and blue patterned wool I bought in Wales? Granted, that was 1971. I wanted it for a miniskirt to wear with knee high leather boots and a poor boy turtleneck I'd bought in London that fall. Since then, time and my young figure have slipped away from me. The purple Ultra-Suede I bought with Margaret? It was expensive. I've always been afraid to cut it but I can still envision a vest. The extra ten yards of lace from Meg's wedding? I didn't want to run out when I was making pew markers. There was half a silk skirt—the first project Becky and I did together. We got to be friends faster than we could sew. And loose woven wool with a man's vest pattern tucked into the folds. Elizabeth's boyfriend. What was his name?

I found what I needed for the crazy quilt pillow top I was making as the ring bearer's pillow in a daughter's upcoming wedding. I also found a swatch of embroidery on banana cloth cut from a shirt my husband had worn when he lived in the Philippines, embroidered linen, a handkerchief, and spidery lace once owned by grandmothers, and the sash from a sister's tea dress.

I stroked and rearranged pile three several times before I gave up and decided to store it in the garage while I painted my sewing room. "The fabric of my life isn't cotton," I thought. "It's wool and Ultra-Suede, silk, lace, banana cloth, linen. Cotton's there someplace but so's polyester."

The fabric of my life isn't one fiber or one strand. Like the ring bearer's pillow, my life is pieced from different fabrics, oddly shaped, unmatched— held together by thread and careful stitching.

Profile

Summer at the Oregon coast 1994: bright, breezy days and cool, star-flecked nights. The constant, heavy-breathing surf. And we're all indoors, sitting in attention at our desks, alert, a little nervous.

I'm the teacher. So what? I'm nervous, too. I have fifteen adult students; one is twenty-four, one is seventy-three. A lawyer, an accountant, a real estate agent. They all want to be writers, and I haven't the faintest idea if they can write their way out of a paper bag.

I learn quickly enough. These guys could write their way out of Houdini's straightjacket. We hastily construct a circle of tables, escaping the desks, and the one who sits in the middle of the circle every day, without a hint of reserve, is Peggy Bird. Peggy reminds me of my mother in all the important ways. She is a seemingly conventional woman of a certain age, pragmatic, blunt, gruffly maternal. I watch her and think "Her love is tough love."

Day by day, the radical inside emerges. She has insights. Quick solutions, secret lusts. Dangerous dreams. She writes and writes all week, and a year later she comes back and writes some more, and keeps writing. She has claimed for her territory the power of the mundane, the terror of the daily—ordinary miracles. She isn't going to quit, and if I were you, I'd get out of her way.

—Sallie Tisdale

Bio

Peggy Bird
Place of residence: Vancouver, Washington. Spends time each year with family in Philadelphia.
Birthplace: Philadelphia.
Grew up in: Pennsylvania and the Pacific Northwest.
Day job: Meeting facilitator.
Education: R.N., Hospital of the University of Pennsylvania. B.S., Portland State University.
Serial publication: *Georgetown Magazine*—essay.
Awards: Columbia Scholastic Press Award. "Best Girl" Title—courtesy of Jas Whitehill Baziuk.
Current project: A correspondence between two young women in 1870.
Favorite books: Whatever is on my bedside table, which at the moment includes *Eloise* by Kay Thompson, *Liar's Club* by Mary Karr, *Fire at Eden's Gate* by Brent Walth, and *The Forest House* by Marion Zimmer Bradley.
Beliefs: I believe much of what I learned in catechism class at Holy Spirit Lutheran Church, most of what my daughter told me about her teenage years, and all of the words of "Amazing Grace."
Cravings: The usual—love, chocolate, peace, respect, Starbucks frappachino, and, occasionally, a Philadelphia sticky bun.

Robert J. Brake

North Dakota:
It's the Place Ya Gotta See

When my Anchorage tour bus driver bragged, "I've been to forty-nine states," I didn't ask which state he'd avoided. I knew. It's my home state—North Dakota, the foot-of-the-heap state everyone avoids. Perplexed, I decided to call my old high school pal Alvin, a North Dakota maven who graduated in the top seventy-five percent of his class.

"Al, how come North Dakota gets such a bum rap?"

"I dunno," he mused. "You can get a divorce, a vasectomy, or a nosejob, and nobody lays a guilt trip on ya. But tell 'em you like North Dakota and they think yer a pervert. I jest don't understand. North Dakota's like heaven, without dyin'!"

"How's that?"

"Well," he reflected, "ya know, we got a lotta good-hearted Catliks and Lutherns, mainly Republicans. Famous people, too. Lawrence Welk, Eric Sevareid, Roger Maris, Louis L'Amour, Maxwell Anderson."

"But all those celebrities are dead," I said, "and many states have Catholics and Lutherans. Tourists think North Dakota's really flat, cold, and boring. What about that?"

"OK, so she's a little flat," he conceded. "But not like Nebraska! I tried rollin' a marble across North Dakota from Fargo, and she spun off Killer Curve at Medina. Besides," he added, "what with all those lakes in Minnesota and mountains in Montana, tourists need a little relief."

"Well," I persisted, "what about the cold weather?"

"Hell," he snapped, "It's colder in Fairbanks and Frostbite Falls. Besides, it keeps us on our toes. Sometimes, in the cold weather, we even read books and talk to each other."

"I'll buy that, Al," I confessed. "But what about the boring bit?"

"Easy," he gushed. "We have tons of fun here. We picnic and polka, fish illegally at night, and go to tractor pulls—you know, lots of excitin' stuff."

"What about stress, Al?"

"What stress?"

"You know. From pollution, crime, traffic congestion, and crowding."

"We don't have much pollution," he insisted, "except when yer down-wind from the alfalfa mill. Crime? Hey, what's to steal? Maybe some crab apples once in a while. Traffic messes? Rare. Except maybe when we get a fertilizer spill down at the three-way. Crowding? Impossible. We only got nine people a mile here. We're America's most rural state, and damn proud of it!"

"OK," I confessed. "I'm impressed. But Al, what's really special about North Dakota?"

"Look at what we got," he bragged. "The windiest city in America—Fargo at 14.4 mph average. The only American city named Beach. The Red River flowin' 540 miles—north. And Rugby—the geographical center of North America. Hey, we gotta lot to brag about, Bobbo."

"OK, Al, I'm impressed," I admitted. "North Dakota has a lot to offer tourists. But so do other states. How do you compare with them?"

"Easy," he chortled. "We're smarter than some. Kansas once passed a law to round *pi* from 3.14159265 down to three. Now, that's dumb. Alaska? Hey, they don't even have an official state motto. We got three! Sioux State, Peace Garden State, and Flickertail State. Rhode Island prison inmates had to get a law passed to change their underwear once a week. North Dakota convicts get fresh shorts two-three times. And Kentucky? Who'd live in a state where they got a law requiring everybody to bathe at least once a year? North Dakotans bathe monthly, need it or not."

"'Enough said, Al," I replied. "You've done your homework and, in some small ways, North Dakota seems great compared with other states. But, seriously now, what's the really big attraction of living in North Dakota?"

"Look, Bob, it's peaceful here. Nice people, quiet, almost worry-free, and damn good neighbors ta boot! We laugh, play, cry, and work like anybody else. We're normal, ordinary folk."

"Al, lots of Americans fail to understand or appreciate North Dakota. What's your biggest gripe about them?"

"They ain't been here, but they still think we're all a buncha over-seventy geezers and mortuary bait with something wrong with our butts, hobblin' down Main Street sprinklin' weed killer and goin' to the bingo parlor. They think our kids are a buncha hayseeds who get off checkin' out corpses sittin' on our park benches. While there ain't always a lot to do, we're not jest waxworks farmers sittin' around, staring at black-and-white TVs with our wives and five kids. All kind of nice folks live here and they like and respect each other. Maybe we don't smell the roses like you guys in Oregon, but we can smell the sunflowers and look at amber waves of grain and that stuff. We jest live in a different kind of paradise."

That different-kind-of-paradise angle reeled me in. So I thanked Al and started to hang up when he blurted out one more tourist tip.

"Bobbo, ya gotta see the world's largest buffalo at Jamestown. Sixty tons of concrete—'nuf to pave a county road!"

That did it! This prodigal son is gonna get back to North Dakota to rediscover his roots. Excuse me. I'm packing!

Profile

Robert J. Brake is known to his close friends and family as "Oobear." Although he claims "folks back home" in North Dakota call him "Bobbo," he is too audacious and eclectic for me to find this handle credible.

A true stylist, Robert employs comedic elements in everything he does. After three decades of university teaching, he thinks of himself as a performer—meticulously staging events in the classroom to cajole students into learning. Humor, play, and participation are the tools of this gifted teacher. Yet rarely is his style understood by peers.

Although he has written and published scores of academic pieces, Robert's greatest love is writing and reading humor. Most admired are S.J. Perelman, Woody Allen, and Garrison Keillor.

In Keillor's *Book of Guys*, men are portrayed as *goofy guys at heart*. "Bobbo" is one goofy guy and Robert has made an art of it.

—Janice Sethne

Bio

Robert J. Brake

Place of residence: Portland, Oregon.

Birthplace: Jamestown, North Dakota.

Day job: Professor of Business, Concordia University, Portland.

Education: B.S., North Dakota State University. M.A., University of South Dakota. Ph.D., Michigan State University.

Serial publications: Numerous articles on business topics.

Awards: Outstanding Young Teacher. Best Lecturer. Business Communicator of the Year.

Current project: A book about lessons learned from teachers.

Favorite book: *Book of Guys* by Garrison Keillor.

Cravings: An overwhelming desire to be someone else and a modest ambition to save mankind.

Katherine Burger

Running into Guatemala

A few years ago a romantic relationship ended for me. I felt bruised and out of sorts with the world. "Why not visit me in Guatemala?" suggested my peripatetic friend Sarah Gates. All I knew about Guatemala was that an undeclared war between its rightist army and leftist peasants was in progress and that the country seemed to be an endless source of one-paragraph filler items in *The New York Times*, viz.: "Bus plunges over a precipice in Guatemala; thirty-seven killed . . . 416 injured." In my present mood Guatemala seemed an appropriate vacation destination.

Sarah said to fly courier—"They buy your luggage space and use it for some kind of secret but presumably legal cargo, and you and your carry-on luggage fly half fare."

I went to a courier service in downtown Manhattan called "Now Voyager." The walls displayed huge stills from that movie: Paul Henried staring goony-eyed at Bette Davis, two cigarettes stuck in his mouth. That's what romance will do to you.

The Now Voyager clientele was comprised of bouncy young people who wanted to get away from it all—to Paris, Madrid, Casablanca, Rio. "I want to go to Guatemala," I announced. Well, they informed me, this was my lucky day: there was one round trip ticket available this month, leaving tomorrow, coming back in twelve days. If I chose to accept, a man would contact me during my Miami layover, arrange for my flight to Guatemala

City, and give me a baggage claim that I would then relinquish to my Guatemala contact, a Señor Caraballo. I began to feel marginally excited, as if I were in a Bette Davis movie, an amalgam of "Now Voyager" and "Watch on the Rhine." Did I want to sign on? I did. Did I need shots, a visa, a green card? No, I was assured, just my passport.

I left New York on a cold January morning and flew to Miami. A morose young Hispanic man came up to me in the Miami Airport and gestured that I should follow him. "*Sí,* Now Voyager," he admitted grudgingly, so I accompanied him to the Aviateca Airlines counter, where the two agents seemed to know my laconic friend, welcoming him with overt hostility. They accepted my ticket with exaggerated reluctance, then examined it intently. In due course they found something about it they didn't like. This made them happy. My contact became even more morose. The three of them proceeded to argue in Spanish about my ticket for the rest of my four hour layover. Tempers flared, tempers subsided. Tiny cups of espresso were flung back like shots of whiskey. Arms were waved, phone calls made, a twenty dollar bill appeared and was passed back and forth over the counter like a shuttlecock.

"What's going on?" I kept asking, "What's wrong?" The morose man shrugged me off. The only thing he said was "If you do get to Guatemala tonight—if—don't take a taxi. *Peligroso.*" I knew this word. Posters in the New York City subways advise that the "*via del tren subterráneo es peligrosa.*" "But why is it dangerous?" I asked. The morose young man wouldn't elaborate, except to say that he would stay in a hotel if he were me—if I got to Guatemala at all, that is.

Finally, reluctantly, at the last possible moment, the agents behind the counter issued a new ticket. I ran down the corridor to the Aviateca gate, my carry-on luggage banging against my legs, and barely made the flight.

Part of my agreement with Now Voyager was that I would be a fit representative for them, which meant no bad behavior, such as drinking. But when the Aviateca stewardess offered me a glass of good French wine, compliments of the Airline, I figured what the hey, I was over the hurdles.

It was ten o'clock at night when I deplaned in Guatemala City. It was hot. I had had two, maybe three glasses of wine on the plane and was feeling no pain. I had to meet Señor Caraballo in the customs room, hand over my baggage claims ticket, and find a taxi. I had studied my Spanish/English phrase book and memorized the appropriate phrases. I was on track, floating in a complacent haze.

I got in line with the other disembarked passengers. They were filing past a checkpoint, through gates, then across a vast empty room and out into the tropical night. I presented my passport to the uniformed official, but he seemed to want something more. I rifled through my phrase book but nothing I came up with—"good morning," "hotel," "menu"—seemed to appease him. The man behind me began to get restless. He was German, dressed head to toe in a rainbow of *tipica*—the characteristic and ubiquitous woven fabric of Guatemala.

"He says you need a tourist card. You can't get into ze country vissout a tourist card. Stand aside, plis."

I didn't have a tourist card. No one had told me I needed a tourist card. "Just a passport," they'd assured me in New York. I could have purchased a tourist card in Miami for two dollars, sometime during the four hour layover, but no one there saw fit to advise me that it might be a good, nay, a necessary item to have on hand. The offices here in Guatemala were closed for the night. Sorry, but they couldn't let me into the country without a tourist card.

"Stand aside, plis," the German returnee repeated. I stood aside, in shock. The rest of the passengers—sun-seeking blonde hippies from Northern Europe—flowed past me, flourishing their tourist cards, and disappeared into the night.

I was left alone with the keeper of the gate. He gestured to two soldiers. They came over, unshouldering guns so big they needed both hands and wide leather shoulder straps to support them. "Wait here. Don't move from here," the official said, and walked off. The soldiers watched me intently. I didn't move. I didn't even breathe deeply. Minutes sped by like turtles on downers. The airport emptied. Lights went off in the huge waiting room. At the other side of that vast room, beyond the gates and barriers, I could see the customs room. I imagined Señor Caraballo giving up and leaving, the taxis leaving. I imagined spending the night in the airport, with my soldier buddies. I imagined Sarah fretting all night then going to the town phone and calling my apartment, the American Counsel, my mother. After ten or fifteen long minutes the soldiers started arguing with each other, gesturing at me. Then they left.

I was alone. Anxiety bloomed in me like a dark, malignant flower.

I picked up my bags and ran. Through the gates and across the big room, I ran into Guatemala. Actually, I ran into the customs room. There were several men there, lounging and chatting. They all wore white cotton short-sleeved shirts and dark pants. They stared at me. "Pardon," I said in my best Spanish, "*Dónde está Señor Caraballo*?" A tall, courtly looking, handsome, shining man stepped forward, his face full of concern.

"I am Señor Caraballo," he said, "You are Katherine Burger? I had almost given up on you. Is something wrong? Can I help?"

He came back with me to the immigration office. The soldiers and the immigration official had returned with reinforcements. More officials and more soldiers had been summoned to deal with me, and they seemed rather agitated that I wasn't there to be dealt with. Señor Caraballo talked to them, his hands moving as if he were soothing a nervous horse. There was a lengthy discussion. The officials asked me questions—about my visit, my political inclinations, my job, my grandparents' jobs—and I endeavored to answer them. Señor Caraballo translated and soothed.

"I'm sorry, señorita," he said at last, "They won't let you into the country unless you leave your passport here. You can pick it up tomorrow, when you come to purchase your tourist card."

"I will help you get a taxicab," my champion said.

"*Muy gracias*," I answered. "But I'm going to Antigua tonight."

He shrugged. "I'm sorry. You could stay at a hotel."

But Sarah—who had no phone—was expecting me; I was already past due. And it seemed easier to negotiate a taxi ride than a hotel, although by now all of the taxi-finding/fare negotiating phrases I'd memorized had deserted me. I could see myself asking for a pen for my aunt instead.

I surrendered my passport to the officials and followed Señor Caraballo across the big room to the glass doors. We stepped outside. The night was hot and close, a complete change from the January New York I'd left behind at the start of this long day.

"You shouldn't have told them that you're a writer," Señor Caraballo chided me gently. "They think that is political."

"But I'm not a journalist."

"All writing is political," he answered. If the guns hadn't convinced me, I knew now that I was no longer in Kansas.

There were only two taxis left in the parking lot, each one brokered by a small boy. The boys hung on Señor Caraballo's sleeves, imploring him, each touting the merits of his taxi cab and its driver and disparaging the competition. Señor Caraballo spoke with each boy, then ushered me into the cab of choice. We shook hands.

"Enjoy your stay in my country," he said.

The driver was silent, and the road climbed almost immediately. In a few minutes we were cresting above Guatemala City. It spread out below us, a bowl of light, bigger and brighter than I'd imagined. And then we were driving between steep embankments which eclipsed the lights, up switchbacks, through dark, unseen, mountainous countryside. There were no other cars on the road; we seemed to have the entire country to ourselves.

I now had the leisure to sit back and think about—OK, obsess about—the morose Miami man's warning: *peligroso*. Were there *banditos* in the hills? Guerrillas? Renegade soldiers? Would the driver himself slit my throat and take my traveler's checks? But all he had said was, "*Peligroso, muy peligroso.*"

I was relieved when a sign said: Antigua 2 km. A short time later we entered a colonial Spanish town: white stucco; tile roofs; plazas with fountains; narrow, cobbled streets. Everything was closed up tight; there were few lights, fewer people. With a shock I realized that the plazas I was seeing were the same plaza, over and over again. Was my driver circling around and around the town like this while making up his mind to rob me? Looking for a dark deserted street to accomplish same? Looking for his *compadres* in crime?

But the driver conveyed to me that he couldn't find the address. "OK," I thought, "we're lost; nothing to worry about. He is a nice guy, after all; give him the benefit of the doubt." Then he stopped the cab in the proverbial dark, deserted street. Panic surged though me. "This is it! Where did I pack my Swiss Army knife?"

But then the driver got out of the cab and peered at the number on the side of a white adobe building. He grinned at me triumphantly and pounded on the huge metal door. I got out of the cab and found the name under the doorbell: Sarah Gates. Chaos condensed into the known and loved. I rang the bell, then pounded on the door myself in an excess of sheer good feeling, like a gorilla proclaiming, "I am!" against its chest.

I suddenly realized that I hadn't thought of my ex-boyfriend and my chronic bad mood for hours now. I was in an exotic country, on the verge of who-knows-what new experiences. The world seemed once again full of romance and adventure, and by God I was ready.

Profile

Katherine Burger is a New Yorker who traveled to the West and did time at Evergreen, a college in Olympia, Washington known for its advanced ideas. In those days, 1974, she was a poet and rock climber and hung around with Tom Sleigh, a tall, emaciated Evergreen student-poet who, when his girlfriend ditched him, stood on the dock and watched her ride off on a ferry boat which left a "spermy wake."

I was pursuing a notion of chastity if not celibacy, no wakes for me, spermy or otherwise. So Katherine and I began an affectionate, chaste relationship that has lasted ever since. Back then we were trying to figure out how to make it as writers. One Saturday we drove from Seattle in my '65 Mediterranean blue missing-the-front-passenger-seat vw bug on a tour of Whidbey Island, Camano Island, and the Skagit flats (the delta of the Skagit River). The object of our circle tour was Fishtown, the last vestige of traditional salmon fishery on the Skagit, a collection of shacks on stilts in the marsh water connected by wooden ramps.

We were looking in particular for Tom Robbins, whose book *Another Roadside Attraction* had come out three years earlier and won raves among local readers. Tom had taken the literary hermit approach, fleeing a cultural center for the sticks. In Tom's case, he moved from Ballard, Seattle's Norwegian ghetto, to LaConner, the Victorian art colony on the Swinomish Slough, and then to Fishtown—or so I had heard. On the way into Fishtown we drove a narrow, private road, passing signs: No Trespassing; Absolutely No Trespassing; Trespassers Shot. We forged ahead, and, after winding through the woods above the Skagit we came to a clearing with a turnaround, a view of the mighty river, and one last sign: Trespassing $10.

Kathy and I never did find Tom Robbins, but it didn't matter because there was another approach. Instead of leaving Seattle to become a hermit on the Skagit, a person could leave this provincial cultural center for a national center, a mega-place, the heart of the literary universe.

A year later, when I was in Manhattan, Kathy took me to see her father, literary agent Knox Burger, in his Greenwich Village office. I met Kathy's mother, a writer and sculptor who gave me the news on the book-length manuscript that she was currently circulating among Manhattan publishers. Kathy talked of her friendship with Malcolm Braly—a West Coast guy who survived San Quentin, moved to New York, and became our nation's foremost prison novelist.

I visited the 1838 Federal style townhouse where Kathy grew up and where Jane E. Jacobs rented a work room when she was writing her classic study, *The Death and Life of Great American Cities.* Kathy and I took long quick-paced walks across Manhattan and did an especially thorough tour of the Village, passing cafes where, years before, Dylan Thomas drank, Bob Dylan sang, and James Agee talked all night.

I knew that the Village had been William Faulkner's Paris, the place where he found theory to structure his down-home subject. I knew that Faulkner's reputation had been made, not in Mississippi, but in Greenwich Village. I also knew that another Southerner, James Agee, had come here and Robert Penn Warren had holed up over in New Haven. I was from the West—a place just as obscure as the South had been before Southern writers found Greenwich Village. I thought that the Village was an opportunity for me, and Kathy was my link to this place.

Years passed. In the end, Tom Sleigh took the academic approach, went on to become a prof at Dartmouth and a published poet. Kathy became a playwright and moved into the apartment in the attic of her family home where she lived between stints at writer's colonies, the odd out-of-town acting tour, and occasional trips to big mountains. For some reason I stayed in Seattle, halfway between Fishtown and Greenwich Village.

Kathy and I kept in touch, and every so often we compared notes. Kathy was having more success than I. She was hired to write a screenplay about Maud Gonne, her poetry and plays were read, performed, published. She took roles in Off Off Off Broadway productions. Now she works winters as a child wrangler at the Metropolitan Opera, a great job which does not involve data entry. In the summers she manages the Byrdcliffe Art Colony in Woodstock, New York. In 1995 Kathy's play *Morphic Resonance* had a reading at The Ensemble Studio Theatre's Octoberfest and has had some nibbles by other theatre companies. "I live on hope," Kathy says. After all of these years, in my estimation, the world of arts and letters has failed to do justice to this woman.

—Scott C. Davis

Bio

Katherine Burger
Places of residence: New York City and Woodstock, New York.
Birthplace: New York City.
Grew up in: Greenwich Village and rustic cabins in New England.
Day jobs: Winter—child wrangler at the Metropolitan Opera (in charge of the children's chorus). Summer—Manager of the Byrdcliffe Art Colony in Woodstock. (Byrdcliff: a residency program for writers and visual artists. Contact: The Woodstock Guild, 34 Tinker Street, Woodstock, New York 12498. Voice: 914-679-2079.)
Education: Oberlin College and Evergreen State College.
Plays: *Way Deep,* published by Samuel French, and about a dozen productions.
Awards: Fellowships at several art colonies including the Millay Colony. Finalist in the Chesterfield Screenplay writing competition.
Current project: Illustrating a book I've written.
Beliefs: Animism and yoga.
Craving: Sushi.

Lance Carden

Coaster Connoisseur

I may never set foot in one again, but I'm still boosterish about roller coasters.

When I grew up in southwest Oklahoma, my father wouldn't let me on a coaster. It was a protective instinct. He had suffered a terrible experience up in Oklahoma City during the Depression. Someone succeeded in coaxing him onto a roller coaster without warning. Expecting it to be child's play, he lost eyeglasses and an overcoat on the first plunge. When the car returned him to the loading zone, Dad was apparently so frozen with fear he couldn't move or even speak. Attendants told him it was time to get off, but he just stared straight ahead. Giving up, they sent him off for another ride.

It was only this summer that I really learned about coasters. I came to understand that, beyond its "scream machine" dimension, a coaster ride can be enjoyed intellectually and aesthetically. And that's why I went to ride Cyclone.

Most of the folks you hear screaming overhead at amusement parks don't know what they're experiencing. They don't realize that the twentieth century has perfected an art form that began with relatively crude fifteenth and sixteenth century Russian ice slides. The modern coaster combines the simplicity of those rides with the technology of a trolley and the manipulation of a magician.

Once launched, the movement of a coaster is impelled solely by gravity and momentum. Only so much speed is possible, depending on the total "drop" of the coaster from its highest to its lowest point.

Coaster builders exact maximum excitement by anticipating the riders' experience and taking full advantage of staged effects. For instance, it's no coincidence that cars are usually cranked up from the starting platform to the first drop at a tantalizingly slow pace, giving passengers plenty of time to size up their seemingly precarious position.

You know how the cars in front of you disappear when they plunge? This makes you think the tracks go straight down. That is certainly not the case. The angle of the drop is usually forty-five to fifty degrees. The awesome first drop of Cyclone at Coney Island is reportedly fifty-three degrees.

You know how the cars whip back and forth next to those tinker toy structures that support the tracks? Seeing a coaster's wooden ribs flash by your face makes you think you're moving faster than you are.

Wind is important, too. Windshields wouldn't greatly affect the actual speed of a coaster, but they could significantly reduce riders' perceptions of speed. You know how a coaster never seems to slow down? It's because designers create diversions—a sharp curve or a dark tunnel wherever the cars' flagging momentum might be noticed. Even on a slow coaster, a tight curve can be hair raising.

I took my first coaster ride in August at Agawam Park outside Springfield, Massachusetts. The big Cyclone at Agawam doesn't open until noon, but the relatively benign Thunderbolt accepts passengers at 11:00 AM. To ride Cyclone, children have to be at least fifty-four inches tall. For Thunderbolt, a mere four feet will suffice.

I felt foolish, standing in line for twenty minutes with a group of giggling school kids. All the more so because it was a hot, humid day, and steam heat seemed to roll off the treeless tarmac. But my friends, a pair of coaster zealots, insisted on taking the very first ride.

They tried to hop on the last car—which offers the most thrills—but we were told to fill the cars from front to back, according to our place in line. To my relief, we wound up in the middle. As we fastened safety belts, there was a lot of nervous laughter. Someone shouted, "Raise your hands when you go over the top!"

To my consternation, Ian and Peter did exactly that. Every time the coaster came to a precipice, they held their hands above their heads and shouted with joy. No one could have pried my hands from the lap bar! The very first drop terrified me, and I started screaming bloody murder. Nonetheless, I still expected to recover my wits and enjoy the rest of the ride. But things only got worse. Fear turned to panic. I couldn't stop screaming. I can't describe the coaster's rapid contortions; it was all a blur. But I do know that I wanted off that contraption more than anything in the world. When it finally stopped, I was exhausted.

"How was it?" Peter asked.

"Terrible," I replied. "Did you like it?"

"Not much, really."

"Oh?"

"Not much of a coaster—too tame."

"You're kidding?"

"What'd you think?"

"It terrified me!"

After a quick conference, we decided that Peter and Ian would go for another ride on Thunderbolt, while I tried to recover. I cooled off with a giant ice cream cone, but I couldn't calm down, in part because I was still determined to ride Cyclone.

The portion of the park dominated by Cyclone's undulating latticework was blocked till noon by a miniature train. When it finally chugged away, most of the crowd sprinted the length of a football field to line up for tickets. I let Peter and Ian compete for the first ride. I was in no hurry.

When it was my turn to board Cyclone, I was grateful to be alone. I didn't try to be nonchalant. This time, I was going to be psychologically prepared. And I think I was, until a young man on the public address system cautioned all passengers to secure any "loose objects." I felt for my spectacles. They seemed to fit snugly, but I remembered my father's ride.

As the cars began to slowly ratchet their way up to the first precipice, I took the glasses off and held them in my right fist. But I wanted my hand free to hold on to the bar. I couldn't make up my mind what to do. There was no pocket in my T-shirt. My jeans were too tight.

Finally, just as the lead cars began to disappear from view, I thrust the glasses between my legs and forgot them. It was survival time!

A ride on Thunderbolt, I found out, does not prepare you for Cyclone. You might as well train for the Indy 500 by taking a ride on the swan boats in Boston Public Garden. Cyclone goes up much farther and down much faster than Thunderbolt. Even more discombobulating are the sudden hairpin turns, not so much because centrifugal forces fling you about—which they do, of course—but because the cars shake and rattle so furiously you think they'll fly apart.

When Cyclone finally rattled to a stop, my glasses were gone, which was only a minor concern. I was glad to be alive.

Back on the steaming midway, Peter and Ian assured me that Cyclone was a dog compared to the truly great coasters. I didn't care. I was in a daze, thinking of Dad—and suddenly grateful for the weather. At least I hadn't lost an overcoat!

Profile

I got to know Lance Carden in November 1988. I was on an author tour but didn't have a publicist and couldn't get interviews scheduled very tightly. In Boston I got two good interviews but spent most of my time with Lance freewheeling through Boston and Cambridge. He arranged a reading for me at the Boston Forum, a social service center in the Back Bay, and later we crashed a Sunday afternoon soiree held by Mel King, the towering African-American politico and intellectual. While we ate Mel's seafood stew, Mel held forth in his kitchen, every bit as regal as an African king.

In Cambridge, I looked up Brenda Walcott, the African-American poet and dramatist, who was living hard and poor but still had her dignity. She was getting ready to leave the city for Martha's Vineyard and sold me a copy of her sixteen-page booklet of poems: *Slave of a Slave.* Brenda had three tickets to an underground theatre production, so Lance joined us for the play. Afterwards, we met the cast at a local diner and talked and ate until two in the morning. When Lance and I tried to find a way home: no subway cars, no buses, no cabs. At last we reached Boston, but how to get to Lance's digs in Jamaica Plain? And what was the point? Lance had a key to the Boston Forum. We slept in our clothes on secondhand sofas.

The next time I got to Boston was December 1994. I had started Cune and was paying courtesy calls on book reviewers. Lance and I met in Davis

Square, in Somerville, a stop or two up the line from Harvard Square. There we waited in the Someday Cafe, a Seattle-style coffee house that is divided into two storefront rooms a few feet apart—which is how we almost missed Lee Mintz, my old freshman roommate from Grove House at Stanford. Lee had been an expert on Haiti in his Stanford days and a practitioner of karate before it became popular. Lee was a Jew, and I think karate was his way of taking revenge on Hitler, so to speak.

Lance and Lee and I sat at a large table in the corner of room number two, the cafe's living room, and we were talking but Lance didn't say much, just his sly, tight grin. Lance doesn't carry fat on his body, so his grin is very thin. Lee was filling us in on the history and philosophy of human culture and, every so often when he took a breath, I blurted out a few truisms about the need for writers to band together and form their own presses. Or maybe it was the other way around.

Then Katherine Powers arrived. I didn't know her, but she was a friend of Paul Aaron's. Paul is a guy from a Brandeis think tank who knows everyone from Jonathan Raban to Patrick Seale. So Katherine was new, but promised that we could recognize her because of her fierce, Irish eyes. Her eyes *were* fierce. She is a freelance writer, the daughter of a famous Irish novelist, and she reviews books for the *Globe*. She spends most of her waking hours reading literature: "I'm unbelievably lucky," she said. She and Lee sized each other up while I talked about book publishing. Lance kept his sly grin going, looking to me, then to Lee and Katherine when they stopped sizing and took hold of the publishing question. Both Lee and Katherine more or less liked my ideas. But they needed to rework them to make them palatable. Lee went off on a long, brilliant riff on the film industry, citing parallels to publishing.

Katherine excused herself, she was reading that evening. But Lance had hardly done more than give her his smile. I wanted to stop her for a minute and help her appreciate the ticking that I knew was going on in Lance's mind but she was in a hurry and Lance wasn't helping much. That's Lance. Totally unconcerned about what people—even book reviewers—think of him. After Katherine left, Lance and Lee and I went down the block to the India restaurant, which had a big sign over the door. "Authentic Indian Cuisine," it announced in yellow, vaguely Sanskrit letters on a blazing red background. This place had tablecloths and no other guests. I ate curried chicken over rice and listened while Lance and Lee tussled with the question of African-American schools in Cincinnati just before and after the Civil War.

For several years now Lance has been writing a book about Boston's African-American community—including some fascinating stuff on Malcolm X. He couldn't care less about schmoozing and networking. He is a thinker and writer, attuned to the moment by moment emergence of ideas.

—Scott C. Davis

Bio

Lance Carden

Place of residence: Jamaica Plain, Massachusetts.

Birthplace: Oklahoma City.

Grew up in: Lawton, Oklahoma.

Day job: Monitor Radio.

Education: M.F.A. in creative writing, University of Oregon.

Book: *Witness, an Oral History of Black Politics in Boston 1920–1960*, Boston College (1989).

Serial publication: *The Christian Science Monitor.*

Current project: An interpretive history of blacks in Boston.

Favorite book: *A Bend in the River* by V.S. Naipaul.

Kenneth Carroll

Searching For Common (sense) Ground

*"Black anti-Semitism and Jewish anti-Black racism are real,
and both are as profoundly American as cherry pie."*

—Cornel West, 1993

"You're a *Black Jew*," said my five-year-old brother, angry over my refusal to share my candy with him. His slur was a common one used in our biracial Washington, D.C. neighborhood, and, while it angered me, it couldn't change the fact that I had a full pack of Now or Laters and that he was candyless. Unable to take the candy from me or buy himself a pack, he was reduced to invectives.

"Na-na, na-na-na," I responded.

Sometimes I look back at the appearance of former Nation of Islam spokesman, Khallid Muhammed at Howard University in fall 1993. In the controversy surrounding Muhammed there was something frighteningly similar to my brother's juvenile insult and my equally juvenile response. Young blacks—angered, frustrated and envious of Jewish power—used the controversy to insult Jews, who responded with assertions of rising black anti-Semitism. What angered me more than the foolish rancor of the controversy, with its childish and hysterical language, was its unleashing of vapid, opportunistic demagogues.

This controversy had little to do with Jews. It had much more to do with the black quest for control of D.C. and those roguish individuals who, like preacher-pimps, wait to exploit that need. A climate of raw despair exists in D.C.'s black community. The federal government is reclaiming control it earlier gave to local citizens under "home rule." We have high unemployment, endemic violence, inadequate housing, substandard health care, and a criminally incompetent city government. Add to this the current attack on affirmative action and the stunted vision of current black leadership, and you have a desperation as palpable as D.C.'s brutally humid summers. Against this backdrop, blacks are re-examining historically solid relationships with whites, including those with unions and progressive Jews. The history of Jewish participation in the civil rights movement in years past, however glorious, is not sufficient to save today's victims: my incarcerated nephew, my addicted sister, or my chronically unemployed brother. In fact Jews, like other whites, have exploited blacks. As a young man in D.C.'s housing projects, I remember the community's ambivalence toward Jewish merchants who provided essential goods, yet overcharged for substandard merchandise. But no one in my neighborhood was stupid enough to suggest, as do the current black demagogues, that Jews were the root of our problem.

Khallid Muhammad and our local demagogue-lites were given TV coverage and newspaper headlines simply for uttering anti-Semitic slogans. They assured their followers that victims of white supremacy cannot be themselves racist or anti-Semitic (just as Jewish demagogues assured themselves that they cannot be racist because of the Holocaust). I have been roundly attacked in D.C. for simply questioning these intellectual oafs and their equally idiotic (and racist) social theories, which usually involve melanin or genetics.

The danger black anti-Semitism presents to Jews pales in comparison to the danger faced by a D.C. community poised precariously on the threshold of the next century. We lost precious moments in our struggle during the Khallid Muhammad controversy. Demagogues lead us away from the real issues. We must address the sharing of American wealth and power. Progressive black struggle requires the principled alliance of all fair-minded people as we work to repair our fractured capital city. Still, we reserve the right to determine the course of our struggle and reject the idea of blind alliance. Only intelligence and vigilance can eliminate the evils of racism and anti-Semitism. Progressive African-Americans and Jews in D.C. are already beginning the process of finding common ground and common sense in this moment of distrust. History and destiny leave us no choice.

Profile

It's amazing how Kenneth Carroll at times reminds me of an offensive lineman and then, as quickly as he can recite a poem, he resembles a deacon . . . one of God's best men. Carroll is a man who was baptized by black nationalism and, like Malcolm X, is now able to see his soul in the mirror of others. In Washington, D.C., he is at the center of much of the city's literary activity. It's a good thing the guy isn't a Muslim or he would be organizing a million poets to read in front of the Capitol. Watch out for his fiction. Carroll can be a conjurer and weaver of tales. Folks say his life is fast becoming folklore, and my name is BrerBert.

—E. Ethelbert Miller

Bio

Kenneth Carroll
Place of residence: Washington, D.C.
Birthplace: Washington, D.C.
Day jobs: Writer's Corp. Freelance writer.
Education: University of D.C.
Anthology: *In Search of Color Everywhere.*
Serial publications: *Washington Post. One Magazine.*
Awards: Literary Friends of Washington Award.
Current project: A non-gangsta retrospective of growing up in the notorious Montana Terrace housing projects of D.C.
Favorite book: Anything written by Ernest Gaines.
Belief: African spirituality.
Craving: Coltrane albums.
Favorite folks: Joy Hunter, Thomas Carroll, Estella L. Carroll.

José Casarez

The Fall

My older brother Miguel Angel has the long twisted toes that run on my mother's side of the family. He is better looking than me. Mother's friends remind me of this when they come to visit. Mom loves him more. "Flaco horroroso!" she calls me. The horrible skinny one. That's me.

When will I be as big as Miguel? He eats two peanut butter and jelly sandwiches every day when he comes back home from school. Is that the secret?

I'm going to run away to another family as soon we get back from Disneyland this spring. I'll stay with my friend Robbie who has cable and HBO. *His mother lets him stay up as long as he wants. She has only hit him once in his whole life.*

I am the middle child of three. Each of us is two years apart. It's hard to say how old I was when I realized that my mother didn't love me. Was it at age nine? Was I in the third grade? When the wooden spoon came down on my wrist, when she pulled my ear for some now forgotten reason, then I was sure. I might have deserved it at the time, but I can't remember that too clearly. A child's choices are simple—fear or rage. For me, fear was always something more difficult to deal with. Rage came easily and still does—but now, after twenty years, for different reasons.

As a child, Miguel Angel wanted to be a pilot. He had model airplanes, and even without them he could imagine flight by holding a pencil in his hand and watching it move through the air in front of his face. Sometimes, if he took too long in the bathroom, I would barge in and find him playing with a pencil, watching it fly as he sat on the toilet.

I was born in May under the sign of Taurus; I'm the bull in temper and disposition. So my brother was the Angel and I was the Bull.

My mother never hesitated to tell me how stubborn I was and that I could argue over anything. "*Vas a ser abogado*," she would say. I did not become a lawyer. She was wrong about that.

Newark, California is on the southeast side of the San Francisco Bay. Here, my brother and I would walk together in the morning to H.A. Snow Elementary School. As soon as we were around the first corner I would cross the street—we would continue the rest of the trek on different sides. I would speed up, then slow down, trying to provoke Miguel Angel into a race. Who would get to school first? This was all that mattered in the morning on the way to school when I was nine.

Sometimes, we would begin to walk rapidly, neither actually wanting to run; we waddled like ducks, eyeing each other regularly, moving with determined and rigid bodies, our paper bag lunches swinging in hand. He would smile. I was completely serious.

This waddling was enough most mornings. One cold day in January, however, when Miguel Angel turned his head and smiled, I moved faster, he answered, and soon we broke into a gallop: the race was on. I crossed the street as soon as I could to be on his side, the school side, the side where the race would end. Running ahead of me, Miguel Angel glanced back for a moment. He smiled happy. He was free.

The houses blur. Miguel Angel is laughing, moving to some rhythm in space. Time slows with speed. I'm behind, watching his back bounce in front of me. He is close. Just a little more and I can win. Cold morning touches our ears. Penny change for the nickel milk carton rattles in our pockets. The wind moves through our hair, past our bodies, now changing, evolving, streaking through the frozen landscape. His form is long, his bell bottoms move like flags in the wind. Houses, trees, telephone poles stand still.

I ran faster, and he slowed slightly. His heels were right in front of me. Was he teasing me, giving me a chance to pass him, to win? I did not wait to find out. I pushed myself to within a few inches of his heels, kicked out my foot and hooked his ankle, knocking his two large feet together and sending twisted toes atangle. I tripped him in a simple act. "*Eres malo, siempre has sido malo.*" Mom was right. I was bad.

The flight was over. Miguel Angel had fallen. The ground received him with no love. He fell, dropping his lunch bag, hands lowered instinctively to save his face. His elbows bent as his full weight came onto his hands and knees. His body slid a few inches on the pavement. Miguel Angel had lost a shoe and his toes poked out of a torn sock.

I'm the bull waiting impatiently, circling slowly. My breath rises in the winter air. I can feel my heart. It races cold. I stop to watch the changes in Miguel Angel's body. What color is the soul before pain arrives? His face is flushed and confused. Then I see the butterflies approach. They come delicate and sure from a place deep underground. Pain always lives in darkness. They enter the soles of Miguel Angel's feet, flying rapidly through his body. In a position of prayer, head lowered, shoulders sunken, Miguel Angel rises from the ground. He raises his head and opens his mouth to release the winged creatures. They exit in a steady flow toward heaven.

I see red. The color of my ears when I'm angry. The color on my face now from running. It's the color of Christmas, Valentine's Day. The color of my heart. I know blood. I know anger. This color appears, and I'm not afraid.

I faced Miguel Angel. His knees were bleeding through the holes in his pants. He examined his hands. The Angel's face was deformed, twisted like a tree on the beach rejected by the sea. I felt no pity.

Miguel Angel looked down at his palms and began to pick gravel from the wounds, lips turned down. His sobbing grew, then he looked up. "You fell," I said. He gathered his shoe and lunch bag, then turned and walked.

Memory and time forge a place of redemption. I look back on my race with Miguel Angel, and I want to be the one who tumbles, or to remember it as an accident. Neither Bull nor Angel was ever meant to fall to the earth.

Profile

There is a shuttle that runs from the University of California at San Diego (UCSD) main campus in La Jolla to downtown San Diego, and it was on this shuttle that I met José Casarez in 1991. The two-person seats are awkwardly narrow, high in the back, and covered in blue vinyl. This design almost guarantees that you end up sitting on top of the person next to you and, if not that, sliding into this person at every turn. Conversation is unavoidable. I was married at the time and working as a scenic artist at the Mandel Weiss theatre at UCSD. He was in his last year as an undergraduate in sociology. Our relationship grew through a series of chance meetings, always after long absences, in yoga classes on campus, or on the streets of the Hillcrest-Northpark neighborhood. Once he was walking his bike home with a flat tire, and we ended up crossing the same intersection of Fifth and University in opposite directions.

In 1995 I'd lost contact with José and moved to Los Angeles. Later I discovered that José—after having returned from a trip to Europe—was headed to Los Angeles to begin graduate work at the University of Southern California film school. Now we're neighbors in Hollywood, and he's foster parent to my cat, Angelina.

We began cooking plantains, beans and rice, eggplant bartha, and other vegetarian delicacies together back in our days as shuttle mates. José has become a special confidant over many shared meals. I think he likes home cooking too much to really devote his life to the film industry. Still, I'm wishing him the best as a writer and filmmaker, and hoping that he'll always have time to cook and chat with me—and to feed Angelina.

—Amy Thornberry

Bio

José Casarez
Place of residence: Hollywood.
Birthplace: Fremont, California.
Day jobs: Filmmaker. Third and fourth grade elementary school teacher.
Education: B.A. in Sociology, UC Davis. M.F.A. candidate at USC School of Cinema and Television.
Current projects: Director of photography on *Inchallaa* (from Arabic *inshallah*, God willing), a USC student film. Short stories and screenplays.
Favorite book: *House on Mango Street* by Sandra Cisneros.
Cravings: Strawberries, Indian food, having my hair shampooed, avocados, homemade flour tortillas.

Adrian Castro

Ofun Twice, Again

II II
0   0
II II
0   0

The work will be in the realm of the imagination
as plain as the sky is to a fisherman.

—William Carlos Williams,
"Spring and All"

Omodé
tó iku—

murmured el negro viejo after his spirit mounted someone's head (Egungun). The spirit from another era, tiempo de la colonia, tiempo de *senseribó*, de los negros Kongo, negros Lukumí (Egungun). He said he knew the story—

Perhaps these were the last words he ever heard before the new pact was made. They said it would be of utmost importance for him to observe the taboo of not blowing out candles. The candle would be the measure, the vehicle of communication between Iku & himself—blowing the flicker would sever the dialogue. There would come a day when he would see through mystical vision a candle burning at someone's bedside. As an herbalist and diviner he could not heal that person. Iku would need that life, probably so that another one can be born somewhere else.

There was actually a time, maybe this is still going on, when a person's *ori inu* (that is, literally the "head inside," the entity within that says "do this" or "do that," that says "follow this path" or "follow that") would choose where and when it was going to be born, to whom, who would be the patron deity/Orisha, what course his life would follow, and finally when will he breathe his last sigh. This of course would be contingent on what kind of destiny, what kind of head the *ori inu* chose—*oriré* or *ori buruku*, good or bad head. But then sometimes a head chooses to be born and to die soon after and born and die and continue this cycle—the head of an *abiku*.

There was actually a time, maybe this is still going on, when before burying the *abiku*, someone (El Niño's parents, priests presiding over his ritual), would clip a piece of ear from El Niño's corpse or cut half his pinky. The idea was to identify him as *abiku* when he returned. If he had such markings his history, the paths he's traversed, the heads he's petitioned, would be known. The proper amuletos can be prepared, the taboos observed. Somewhere along the lines though, the *ori inu* in conjunction with his Orisha & Egun/ancestors must all make a pact with Iku.

El Niño actually wants to live.

> The Pact:
> 1.
> The candle will be our medium for dialogue
> We must always
> be on speaking terms
> 2.
> When you see the candle by the bedside burning
> it will be my message to you
> Do Not Touch!
> 3.
> You will heal through herbs &
> the words I give you to
> spray unto the solution

4.
Never dress in black
I may mistaken you for
someone ready to die
5.
As much as possible
do not speak wickedly or damn anyone
6.
As much as possible
stay away from funerals
I like to work alone
Death is death's work *(Iku n'iku che)*
7.
Egun will be my messenger
8.
You may also petition me
through that white staff
you know the one—
with bells & snail shells
You also know the chant
9.
Do not be tempted by possessions & titles
If you have patience
I will make possible
those you actually
will need
10.
Remember this pact
and I will give you health & long life *(aiku)*.

All this was negotiated just prior to his birth. He probably kneeled before the Owner of the Sky while Iku, his patron Orisha & many Egun sat watching with fly whisks in hand and full regalia (after all, one of their own was about to embark on his journey to the human world). The *ilé aìyé*.

He probably placed in circular fashion inside a big calabash all his choices, probably whispered into the gourd a slow *"Ashé tó iba Eshu."* We say probably because one thing is for sure, El Niño does not remember the details, in fact no one does (except the deities & Iku). No one remembers the details of their creation. No one remembers the destiny, the mission they chose, their personal Orisha and, most importantly, the date of their last breath.

Memory & continuity. Keeping el hilo de la conversación. Never losing the wavy & fragile link that keeps you grounded to your root. The dialogue with spirits that may tap your left shoulder and all that. But no one remembers. No one remembers. Esto sí es trágico.

In order to recall the details of what went on in the other world, to map his destiny, El Niño must be taken for divination. And even then one session won't do it. The story will get revealed as his life turns each page and changes rhythm and the oracle is cast several more times. So they took El Niño to the diviner Edikán's house. After pouring libations & reciting the necessary *ayuba* prayers—greeting the creator, the ancestors, the divination, earth, wind, river, ocean, jungle & crossroad Orishas, Edikán cast the divining chain/*ópele* used by the *babalawo*. A picture began to emerge. He said the Orishas & Egun, collectively called *ara orun* or citizens of the other world, have given us certain verses & stories to deliver messages regarding the rhythms of our lives. He said eventually El Niño will be initiated into the Orisha priesthood. He said El Niño's patron deity is Oshun but he will always have an affinity with Ogun & Obatalá. But most prominent is his close relationship with Egun, that is, the ancestors, Iku's messengers. He said it would be through a kinship with Egun that he would accomplish his most difficult tasks: even the arts of divination. He will be a mouthpiece for Egun.

Edikán said El Niño has a predisposition to a vivid imagination. Because of this there are and will be mysterious phenomena happening to him like visions & dreams of secret songs. He will not regard them as strange.

He said El Niño should be taught even at a young age the rigors of an herbalist. He should be taught at least how to recognize certain trees & plants, the healing properties of the most commonly used herbs, their harvesting times, how they mix and with what substances. All this will eventually lead to an encyclopedic knowledge not only of their healing properties but of their ability to alter the invisible rhythms that underlie most things.

Edikán said there will be certain resguardos that must be prepared so as to begin bridging the gap between the Orishas, Iku, Egun & himself. Even though El Niños's inner head/*ori inu* chose a good destiny in the other world, such destiny must be aligned with his physical head/*ori* in *this* world. It will be Orishas & Egun that will focus his life and help him fulfill the destiny he chose in the other world. He said beginning with the feet El Niño must be securely fastened to the earth so as not to depart too soon for the other world. (You see there is always the detail of Iku being overprotective. The relationship is like playing with a leopard—even an affectionate jab with its paw will cause a scar.) The head will also have to be ritually prepared and fed with bits of white fruit among other ingredients and thus given a firm root stability—"para que su cabeza no esté en el aire," he said.

We were witness to this event. We heard what needed to be done. There was actually a time, maybe this is still going on, when people consulted with the spirit world, the other world, on such occasions as the third month after birth. We collected the ingredients that would shape his destiny and began to assemble them. Much of them were from the river, the jungle & of course the cemetery. We heard what needed to be done.

Ara Orun are hip to the images & subtle rhythms that stories & verses evoke. The same images & subtle rhythms running through our lives. Edikán said that barring some details of modernity, this life would follow a certain ancient story pertaining to the divination—

Ofun is like this/
Ofun *ni jé bé*—

The page continues to turn. The rhythm, the rhythm will come from dreams.

In this essay I have not italicized Spanish. I have, however, italicized Lukumí. This word denotes a language, a culture, and a religion. As I was growing up in southwest Miami in the 1970s, Lukumí or Santería religion was around me, on the periphery. When I went to college I became more curious about the religion intellectually and culturally. I started writing. At first I was writing very different stuff, mostly Beat-influenced poetry. By the time I left college, however, I was using Lukumi culture and aesthetics in my writing. It was a vehicle of self-expression. After graduation I spent a lot of time around the Lukumi community and studied the cultural history more in detail. My interest deepened, and I decided to make a personal commitment. Now I am an initiated priest (babalosha *is the Lukumi term). There are large Lukumi communities in Miami and New York and smaller growing communities in Chicago and Los Angeles. For your information, a couple of definitions:*

Yoruba: a tribe from the African West Coast (now Nigeria) from which many slaves were captured and brought to the new world. A major influence in Afro-Cuban culture. Their descendants were founders of Santería or Regla de Ocha (the most predominant of Afro-Cuban religions), also referred to as Lukumi.

Orisha: deity, a god or goddess in the Yoruba religion from Cuba and West Africa.

Profile

Adrian Castro, Miami Beach. What seems like a whole bunch of years ago—*Miami Vice* time, probably—Paco de Onis, who ran a jazz festival in Cartagena, Colombia, took a lease out on the then very funky Cameo Theater on Washington Avenue in South Beach, what we old preservationists used to call the "historic district" but in point of fact was much more like the Black Hole of Calcutta. On weekends the Cameo would play host to punky groups with names like The Butthole Surfers, but on Wednesday nights Cessie de Onis would open the place—and a small bar—for Poetry Night. While that could mean quite anything, it meant for us that there was always someplace we had to be on Wednesdays. A coterie formed—Bob Gregory, young Jamaican Geoffrey Philp, Voudou jazz musician-poet Jan Sebon, Lower-East-Side Rose Lesniak, beatnik Glenn Gant, real-beatnik Lionel Goldbart who co-wrote "Dirty Old Man" for the Fugs, Ronn Silverstein, and this just-about-college-graduate, just-back-from-the-Naropa-Institute, Afro-Cuban experimenteur named Adrian Castro. In flowing gauze shirt and crocheted skullcap, Castro performed bilingual poems, often with drums behind him, in a language that spoke Miami.

We all grew up: the Cameo is now an ultra-chic venue featured on the covers of endless ultra-chic magazines; Cessie married ex-NPR/BBC correspondent Alan Tomlinson, had three kids, and moved to Philadelphia, via Brazil and Colombia; and Geoffrey, Adrian, and I do poetry in public places and in schools on our two-wheelers as "The Bicycle Poets."

—Jeffrey Knapp

Bio

Adrian Castro

Place of residence: Miami Beach.

Birthplace: Miami.

Day job: Building inspector for a private engineering firm.

Education: B.A. in psychology and English. Currently studying Chinese medicine.

Book: *Cantos to Blood & Honey,* from which the above essay is excerpted, forthcoming from Coffee House Press in 1997.

Anthologies: *Paper Dance: 55 Latino Poets. One Century of Cuban Writers in Florida. Little Havana Blues.*

Serial publications: *Forkroads. Bilingual Press Review. Conjunctions.*

Awards: NewForms Florida (sponsored by NEA). Florida Arts Council state grant.

Current project: Finishing another collection of poems, a collaborative performance piece with visual artists, entitled *Ogun: Iron, Conflict, and Creativity.* I will write the text and do the performance.

Favorite books: *Terra Nostra* by Carlos Fuentes, *Canto General* by Pablo Neruda, *Memory of Fire* by Eduardo Galeano, and many others.

Beliefs: Well, I'm an initiated Yoruba priest. I'm what you may call an animist. Belief is too complex to get into in a couple of sentences. See most of my poetry for what I truly believe!

Cravings: To be in constant communication with the essential energies that surround me and to summon them at will. To be able to go back in time to the decade before the turn of the 20th century. To be a plank of wood on a slave ship.

Donna Clovis

The New Jersey Devil

It seems to appear in the crispness of autumn
when the cool winds whisper through the swamps on moonless nights
and when visitors have gone and the Pine Barrens, most quiet—
something still lurks there as I speak tonight.

When I was a child, living in a small town in Easthampton, New Jersey, my mother used to tell me stories. The one that I remember most is the tale of the New Jersey Devil.

In 1735, there was a small, tattered cottage that belonged to Mother and Father Leeds and their twelve children. The cottage sat at the edge of a swamp near the Mullica River. This was the deepest and darkest part of the Pine Barrens region of New Jersey where green ferns grew in abundance in the sandy soil. There was a quaint village nearby. Tall pine trees surrounded the village for miles and miles.

Some villagers thought the Leeds were strange and whispered to others to stay away. Only a few spoke to Mother and Father Leeds on their infrequent visits to the village square. The Leeds family lived in isolation. Some say that Father Leeds was a farmer. Others believed him to be a hunter. No one really knew. And the darkness and quiet of the forest told no secrets.

Cooking and cleaning for twelve children day after day took its toll on Mother Leeds. Then she discovered she was going to have another child—

the thirteenth. "I don't want another child!" she shrieked. "Let this baby be a devil!"

Months later, on a cold winter's night in February, Mother Leeds, with the help of a midwife, gave birth to her thirteenth child. It was a beautiful baby boy with chubby cheeks and blue eyes. When he was only a few minutes old, however, he began to change. In place of the chubby little face grew the head of a horse with two great horns. His blue eyes became fiery red coals. Bat-like leather wings grew out of his back, and his legs and feet turned to those of a goat. But most frightening were his hands which grew into powerful, bony claws. As hours past, the baby lost the frail wailing of a newborn infant and began to make guttural animal sounds.

The day dawned cold and gray. By mid-morning the child was ten hours old and had become a creature with the strength of two men. That evening, the creature gave a bloodcurdling scream. His mother shrieked and his father lunged. But the creature quickly escaped through the chimney into the darkness of the Pine Barrens.

Though the creature was a devil, it also was the son of Mother Leeds. It lived in the shadows of the forest and never harmed the Leeds or their children, but preyed on forest creatures and sheep that strayed from the village. In time, Mother and Father Leeds died and their children passed away, but the creature lived on. The villagers hated the creature, and he took revenge by killing their livestock. Sometimes he even attacked travelers passing through the region. The New Jersey Devil continues to haunt the inhabitants of the pine woods. He has been sighted on desolate country roads and isolated campsites. Some have heard his bloodcurdling screams echo in the darkness.

If you ever come to the Pine Barrens, if you venture into a dense forest or swamp, or a long stretch of isolated beach on a moonless night, take care. When you hear the whisper of the wind through the trees—when branches crackle and break behind you—you may indeed have a visitor. Beware!

Profile

I must admit that I've known Donna Clovis for a long time. She started writing at the age of nine, yet I always expected her to be a doctor. How I arrived at this thought is difficult to say. Maybe it was the science courses she took and the Future Physicians Club in high school. But to my mind, it wasn't her theatrics and writing that took precedence. I guess I created my own expectations.

Eventually, we come full circle and do what we are meant to do. I attended one of Donna's first public readings in the crowded Borders book shop in East Brunswick. Donna read from a collection of her poetry which had won state awards. The audience was ecstatic, and I realized Donna is where she should be. She is my beloved daughter—the writer, the author, the teller of stories.

—Annye Brown

Bio

Donna Clovis
Place of residence: Princeton, New Jersey.
Day jobs: Educator. Consultant.
Education: B.A. in education. M.A. in linguistics.
Books: *Metamorphis*—poetry.
Awards: New Jersey Education Award (1995). Nominated for National Education Hall of Fame (1996).
Current project: A poetry anthology for kids.
Favorite book: *Alice in Wonderland* by Lewis Carroll.

Elizabeth Woodroof Cogar

Coming Out

Our family has lived in Richmond, Virginia for years and years—since the 1920s and 1930s. My parents' parents settled in Richmond's West End, a part of town where some of the families who built this town at the turn of the century have always lived. Traditions run deep here, and Richmond society tends to cling to the way things have always been done. One of its treasured rituals is the debutante season. As a college freshman in the 1970s, I found the idea of being "presented to society" to be archaic and nearly ludicrous. But I also found myself caught between my mother's generation, wherein being a debutante was considered socially correct, and my own desire to make my own way without having to wear white and curtsy on my father's arm. Reconciling my independence and my loyalty to family became the central issue in my mind. Ultimately, I came to realize that being a debutante was less of a statement and more of a ceremonial tradition embedded in Southern culture.

As a little girl I spent sunny spring mornings in musty garages with my mother, watching her paint. She was a volunteer on the Junior Board of the Sheltering Arms Hospital in Richmond, Virginia, and she was an artist whose skills were tapped to paint scenery for the hospital's annual fund raiser, the fancy debutante Bal du Bois. Though my mother quit her job teaching art in a nursery school when I was born, she never stopped giving her time. Volunteering, to her, was an imperative.

As with many other Richmond women, the question for my mother was not "if" but "what." She followed generations of privileged Southern women who were not part of the labor force at large but felt compelled to contribute. During those years she made puppets for the Children's Theater and painted murals at the Cerebral Palsy Center. But the cause to which she seemed most devoted was Sheltering Arms. "They've never sent a bill," she used to say, explaining the importance of the fundraiser, started in 1957. Somehow the event survived the tumultuous 1960s, never lacking for debutantes or patrons, and continued to raise twenty thousand dollars annually in the 1970s.

For years I knew Richmond's answer to New York and Philadelphia's charity balls simply as "the Bal." All spring was spent at meetings and working on the decorations that would be set up around the terrace of the exclusive Country Club of Virginia on the first Tuesday night in June. There was always a theme: Egypt, Greece, Russia, Persia, or some other exotic locale. On the morning of the big night, I would join the other volunteer offspring by helping to carry flowers and mop the dance floor. The year that my mother was chairman, the details were the topic of her every phone conversation. Who would do the music, the flowers, the programs? And, of course, "the girls"—who would be making their debut? And who would receive the honor of leading the figure (a choreographed presentation of the girls)?

And that's where things got complicated—at least for me. As 1972, the appointed year, approached, I began to cringe. Making my debut, for heaven's sake, was not my style. Granted, I had all the symptoms: I'd grown up in Richmond's West End, gone to a private school, had a mother who'd been on Sheltering Arms' Junior Board. But the very thought of donning white dress and gloves and curtsying before God and the hundred patrons of the hospital made me want to run fast to parts unknown.

At eighteen, I was not a conformist. I'd chosen a little known out-of-state college, not the University of Virginia or Hollins. I had a double-pierced ear and a boyfriend who read Nabokov and smoked unfiltered Camels.

To "do it," as signing on as a deb was called, seemed phony. Would I not be betraying my real self by playing the role of unsullied young deb? On the other hand, the guilt of not doing it was more than I could bear. After all, my mother had devoted years to the cause. Surely, she'd feel humiliated if her own daughter snubbed the Bal.

So I agreed. I'd keep the Bal at arm's length, but I'd do it. I'd show up at Thanksgiving, Christmas, and summer to do the party circuit. As was tradition, I'd have a party myself, but I'd do it with another reluctant deb. Together we'd snicker and smirk. Having made the decision, I thought I could put the whole ordeal out of my mind until the season was upon me.

Then one fall day, I plucked a letter from my little mailbox in the student union. I read with horror that I, along with another girl, had been chosen to lead the figure at the Bal. Other debs would have been honored. My first thought was, "How can I get out of this?" I dashed down to the pay phone, called my mother. "Had anyone ever refused?" I wanted to know. "Not that I know of," she said. She was excited and couldn't take my grievance seriously. Not only was I going to "make my debut," but I was going to have to do it front and center, walking a figure on my father's arm and curtsying on a summer night in June. How absurd! I trusted only my closest buddies with the tragic news. I'd be coming out—spending four nights out of seven making small talk over crab dip at deb parties, escorted by arranged dates.

The next June the process of coming out began. The tide turned at one of the very first parties, a dance held at Sherwood Forest plantation. I was placed with a boy who was to become my soul mate, my salvation, in this crazy episode. He understood my eye-rolling attitude, yet he underscored the duty I was performing and the fun that could be had along the way. Indeed, the music was always topnotch, from Peter Duchin to Lester Lanin, and the food exquisite. With my new friend, gone was the pretense of chit-chat, the worry of fitting into a crowd with which I had little in common.

The tradition gave my neo-1960s psyche a jolt, but it wasn't fatal. I returned to college in the fall unscathed by my deb experience, Indian tapestry skirts and clogs intact. Though I'll go to my grave denying that I was ever a real debutante, I'll boldly state that putting on the dress and gloves helped raise money for a hospital that never sent a bill. And, I confess, I had some fun.

Profile

I met Elizabeth Woodroof Cogar in 1994. She was editing and writing for *STYLE Weekly,* a newsy, high-toned tabloid that combines cultural happenings plus hot topic reporting. *STYLE* offices are located in the Fan, a district named for its spreading street alignment, a place with block after block of Victorian brick townhouses, gingerbreads, and granite dwellings that give way to Virginia Commonwealth University with its modern brick buildings, sub shops, pizza parlors, and corner markets.

I was doing freelance writing for *STYLE* and Elizabeth was my editor. She was affable, even-tempered, unruffled by pressing deadlines. Initially, her desk was in the news room and, later, it moved to a corner cubbyhole which was a study in creative organization, standard for a journalist. Magazines were strewn everywhere, stacks of books dared to topple over, and Post-Its stuck on every surface not already covered. How to leave messages for her? Where to put computer disks with the articles I was submitting? I stuck notes firmly to Elizabeth's computer screen. And I propped computer disks on her keyboard. How to find the disks later? Elizabeth had decided that her small desk drawer was the place to dump all freelance writers' disks. Looking for mine was like rummaging through boxes of cassette tapes at a backyard sale.

Elizabeth favored the spontaneous natural look: loose-fitting cotton jumpers, white Tees, wooden clogs, and long, casually styled hair. She's a good writer, a good editor, a great ideas person, a woman who balances family and career. She comes of a fairly old Richmond family, it turns out, and, in another life, was a debutante. Most debutantes I've known are polished, dressed-for-success socialites or businesswomen, and fit the image of Virginia gentry. But Elizabeth? She's definitely her own person.

—Lynne B. Robertson

Bio

Elizabeth Woodroof Cogar
Place of residence: Richmond, Virginia.
Birthplace: Richmond.
Children: James, 8, and Liza, 7.
Family pets: Our dogs are named Annie and Myrtle, our cats are Spot and Boats, and our turtle is Frank.
Day job: Arts and entertainment editor and editor of monthly home section at *STYLE Weekly:* In addition I edit another paper: *Family STYLE.*

Education: B.A. in English, University of Vermont.
Book: *Richmond: America's Renaissance City* (1996).
Favorite cause: Richmond CASA (Court Appointed Special Advocates). Our volunteers help city children through the juvenile court process.
Current project: Making mosaic stepping stones for my garden.
Favorite book: *The French Lieutenant's Woman* by John Fowles.
Favorite regional eats: Mrs. Fearnow's Brunswick Stew, Madame Eva candy, Pierce's Pitt Bar-B-Que.
An outdoor adventure: Sometimes we drive deep into the heart of Goochland County for a walk and scavenging expedition at an abandoned farm. My family used to own the place and, since the owner lives far, far away, we pretend we still own it.
A picnic spot: Hollywood Cemetery.
Favorite scenic drive: Route 5, down along the plantations on the mighty James River.
Belief: I worship great houses.
Craving: S'mores, Moon pies.

Doris Colmes

Escaping the Third Reich

Today is the fiftieth anniversary of the liberation of Auschwitz, and I can't bear it. In 1938, fleeing from the Nazis, my family and I got across the border thanks to Mother's American passport and Papa's Jewish cash. And now, fifty-seven years later, I find myself sobbing. Is this survivor's guilt?

January 26, 1995. The sky is weeping on Portland, Oregon, and I am plodding through the routine that starts every work day, brushing teeth and combing hair. Suddenly I am thrown back to September 1938.

It is the middle of the night. At a grim little station on the Belgian border, two border guards and an SS lieutenant have just taken Papa off the train. Mother sits quietly, looking at her lap. My sisters and I are in nightgowns with jewelry pinned to the hems for safekeeping. We watch, kneeling on the seats under the windows, shivering in the dark, our breath steaming the glass. We see Papa and other passengers who have been taken off the train standing with the border police. They are looking at his papers. Papa's hands make gestures while his face alternates between smiles and frowns. Does he want to fight or flee? Neither is an option. His eyes watch the guards' every movement. The train makes a sudden grunting noise, jerks slightly forward, then stops again. Papa is now out of sight. I hold my breath. Then we see him walking quickly toward the train, his head held forward rigidly, as if heading into a strong wind. He seems to be making every effort not to look back. I hear myself exhale. He appears in our compartment, breathing heavily, just as the train begins to move. The train picks up speed, and I watch the less fortunate travelers recede. "Why," I wonder, "am I worth more to God than they?" Then, with a giant belching lurch the train takes us over the border into Belgium.

Portland, Oregon. I am driving through the early morning streets of my North Portland neighborhood, and the car radio announcer has just introduced a survivor of the Auschwitz liberation. I start to cry again. I wonder if this was one of the people I left on the border platform so many years ago. I am headed to the supermarket. I drive and weep. At the store, I buy more food than usual. My tears drip onto a package of bagels. I take the food for which I imagine a child in Auschwitz might yearn: oranges and milk, sweets and butter.

I grieve for us all. For what we lost. Not just the poets, the healers, the visionaries. But for the others, too. The ones who would have grown up to light candles, hit their children, fail in business, have extramarital affairs, and pass gas in synagogue. Six million beings, officially designated as vermin who—by their absence—undoubtedly altered the course of humanity. Where would we be had any of them survived? I like to fantasize that one of them would have discovered the laws of anti-gravity, and we might all be floating.

The years have mellowed me, taught me the inevitability of genocide. But I still try to figure out the efficiency of this particular phenomenon. Death without passion. How did death become a gross national product with production schedules, assembly line annihilation with awards for exceeding stipulated quotas? This dispassionate efficiency continues to mystify me and contributes to my sorrow. I wish I had access to a real survivor. Someone who didn't get to Belgium. Somebody like Elie Wiesel who could explain, make sense of it, give me comfort.

But I am on my own: A counselor, expected to advise disturbed adolescents and their families. I smile through the tears, picturing myself attentively listening to a family disaster—a child not coming home by curfew—while I grieve for the ghosts of futures past, martyrs who died for Adolf Hitler's whim of iron.

I return home, unpack the unneeded groceries, blow my nose and get back in the car, heading for work. I need to stop at the shoe repair shop on the way, but I am afraid. Auschwitz was in Poland. When box cars full of Jews pulled to their destination, Poles stood by the railroad tracks, drew extended fingers across their throats, and laughed. Their children jumped up and down and threw stones. I am sure that Yakov, the shoe repair proprietor is a Pole. He has that accent. Can I face his well-fed middle age? Was he one of those guilty, stone-throwing children?

When he hands me change I look into his eyes and ask, "Where are you from, Yakov?" He hesitates. (Is there something in my gaze that disturbs him?)

"Russia," he says softly.

"*Spaziba*," I say—thank you—and smile.

"Thank you," he replies. He smiles, too.

Profile

I met Doris Colmes in 1993 through Janus Youth Programs, a small non-profit agency in Portland, Oregon that serves adolescents and their families. The agency occupies a tiny, unpretentious building in a marginal Northeast neighborhood which houses a plethora of dedicated, underpaid, sometimes inept, sometimes brilliant staff. Here, Doris worked for fifteen years. Her job? Preparing clients to contend with the world. A curious career for one who spent childhood being chauffeured around pre-World War II Berlin. For one who—after the war—married a jazz musician cum business man with family money in Brookline, Massachusetts.

When the 1960s hit, Doris left her elegant closets and drove west with a poet who was also her son's best friend. She produced light shows for this entertaining bard, became an overage flower child living the psychedelic hippie life in an anonymous Oregon commune run by a nameless shaman, slept in the bare San Francisco bedrooms of junkies, became a combination Tugboat Annie/Siddhartha as one of the first female bridge-tenders in Oregon.

Later, in the Portland business community, she was chased around administrative desks, ever the desired female, her face opening doors and her foot kicking them back shut. Doris completed her Masters in Social Work at Portland State University this spring, at age sixty-seven. School taught her that she wants to write: yet another curious career that she will render like her life—age, position, and gender just another challenge to meet and devour.

—Candace Crossley

Bio

Doris Colmes
Place of residence: Portland, Oregon.
Birthplace: Meiningen, Germany.
Grew up in: Germany, New York City and Brookline, Massachusetts.
Day job: Program Director, Willowlane Shelter, Janus Youth Programs.
Education: M.S.W., Portland State University.
Awards: National Ski Patrol, outstanding service (1963).
Current projects: Keeping sanity while working full time, finishing graduate school, writing.
Favorite book: *One Hundred Years of Solitude* by Gabriel Garcia Marquez.
Belief: Jewish/New Age.
Cravings: Fame and fortune.

Kathy Connor

Baby Blues

Ours was a small town in Iowa where people listened to country music, watched weather reports, bowled on teams, and gossiped at the local cafe. There was just one traffic light. The only traffic: dusty Chevys, Ford pickups, and rattling tractors driven by farmers or their sunburnt children. After chores, farm wives made quilts and pies for church bazaars while their husbands drank cold Budweiser at the local tavern along with bright-eyed youth and ill-reputed women—women like old Schafer's wife.

Schafer's Union 76 was on the corner of the first intersection of town, coming in past the fairgrounds and air strip. The station had two gas pumps with room enough for only one car to park between the pumps and the tiny office. Behind the office, the Schafers lived in an equally tiny house. Every time my dad and I pulled in, Schafer's wife would emerge looking tired, her big, droopy blue eyes made up with thick black eyeliner that seeped into her crow's feet. She wore hot pants in summer and parkas in winter. Her bleached hair wound around fat rollers the size of juice cans.

Schafer's wife spent all day pumping gas with those giant curlers tucked under a dark bandanna tied like a scarf. Her bulging breasts flattened up against the window as she reached across to clean it, the squeegee an extension of her arm. As her cleavage pressed on and off the glass, I'd stare straight ahead knowing my father was doing the same, each pretending we didn't notice.

I wondered why her hair was always in rollers. What was the point? Three-fourths of the town saw her that way and only that way, rain or shine, heat or snow.

Spending all day with her hair wound up meant she never laid her head down once between sunrise and sunset.

There were a few brief years when she stayed home at night. A child bride at fifteen, she played with her babies like they were dolls. She would fix their hair and paint their faces with her Mary Kay makeup. But babies get big and gasoline gets old. Schafer's wife began finding her peace at the bar downtown. And when her daughters started painting their own faces, her barstool search for solace grew desperate.

One warm summer night Schafer's wife ran off with the bank president's son, a college boy, back in town to celebrate his graduation. The local phone wires buzzed with the news: "Local bar fly whisks away banker's son, twelve years younger than she, thirty years younger than her husband, and of a different breeding."

At first I had a lot of sympathy for old Schafer who was left with three teenagers at home and a business to run. After his wife was gone Schafer himself emerged whenever a car pulled into the single space. Where had he been all those years when his wife was the one pumping gas in her big curlers, facing every kind of weather? All that time going through the motions, taking her hair down only at night, making it lie just right so maybe, in the few hours between work and sleep, she might catch a look from someone across the tavern. I realized that her big breasts slapping up against our windshield were a plea: "Look at me. Can you see me?"

While the rest of the town still shook from the scandal, I saved a smile for old Schafer's wife. Half her life spent wrapped around those rollers paid off in one night when her blonde curls hung just right and the smoke of the tavern softened those tired eyes into dreamy baby blues.

Profile

Kathy Connor is my youngest sister. The other day a girlfriend from our hometown, Waukon, Iowa, called and asked how Kathy was doing. "She isn't practicing law much lately. My husband and I just flew to Hollywood to see her perform the lead role in *Celebrity,* a new play at the Actors' Gang."

My friend was impressed, but not really surprised. Kathy seems able to do anything she sets her mind to.

I've often wondered why Kathy chooses to live in a place like Los Angeles, but she's always marched to the beat of a different drummer. Kathy skipped her last two years of high school to attend college, then moved to Malibu at nineteen on scholarship to law school. She spent her twenty-first birthday in Italy, roaming the streets of Venice with a friend and bottle of Chianti.

I remember when our little town was our world. We performed skits in our neighbor's garage and charged a nickel a show. Kathy also kept a diary. I remember her calling from her bedroom, "What did I do last Saturday night?" We all had to stop to help her complete an entry. Kathy figured her diary would be famous someday, like Anne Frank's.

Kathy's successes are bittersweet to me. It's exciting to see her on television or to help her edit a play. But the excitement fades when I remember she and her daughter Mara are not available to do everyday things with our other sister and myself—like taking our kids out for ice cream or choosing a shampoo together at Wal-Mart. There are memories for tomorrow that we should be making today. Talking on the telephone just isn't the same.

—Kealy Connor Lonning

Bio

Kathy Connor
Place of residence: Los Angeles.
Day jobs: Attorney. Acting teacher.
Education: B.A., University of Iowa. J.D., Pepperdine University.
Serial publications: *Los Angeles View. The Daily Breeze. Waukon Standard.*
Awards: University of Iowa Honor Society Essay Scholarship Award. Winner of London Moot Court Competition. Softball champion.
Current project: Acting.
Favorite book: *To Kill a Mockingbird* by Harper Lee.
Belief: Irish Catholic Democrat.
Favorite person: A little brown-eyed girl named Mara.
Hero: Miep Gies.

M. Cassandra Cossitt

Selections from "The Food Diary"

Swedish meatballs.
Whenever I think of Swedish meatballs I think of the day my father died. Mrs. Foley from down the street brought them. When Mother was diagnosed with cancer, Mrs. Foley brought them again. No tragedy was official until she was standing on the porch with a foil-covered platter and a grief-stricken look on her face. It will not be a good dream when I open one of the hundred dream doors in that endless corridor and find her there with her Swedish meatballs. That will not be a good dream at all.

Pizza.
Although he made a sublime spaghetti sauce, Daddy's specialty was pizza. He would start in the afternoon, making a simple flour, water, and yeast dough, let it rise, punch it down, and let it rise again. By dark he would have collected his army of young helpers. He'd pass out a dozen or so cookie sheets rubbed with olive oil and give us each a handful of dough. I remember not even washing my hands, and pressing grimy fingerprints into soft and fleshy folds. When the pies came out of the oven, he would slice them and we would sit around the picnic table in the kitchen eating directly from the pans. Once, when he came back from Italy, Daddy looked for a thing called goat cheese but found none. He looked for a thing called buffalo mozzarella but found none. And we were relieved.

Omelet.
The morning I was scheduled to have an abortion Frank made me an omelet. The egg was overcooked and the cheese was leathery and the vegetables were dry and raw. I thought I was going to throw up. I had never lost my temper with him in the year we'd been dating, but that morning I told him that what he made was disgusting. I pushed the plate away and walked into the living room and sat on the couch and watched the clock, waiting for it to tell me it was time to go. He wanted to go with me but I said, "Why don't you just do something else today?" I was angry. I was pretty sure I never wanted to see him again. Frank must have known. He sat down, all tender, beside me on the couch and said, "Are you sure you want to do this?" I answered with one word. Sometimes one word will change your whole life.

Take-out.
I took care of the baby without much help. I lugged the laundry three blocks up the street with the baby in a carrier on my chest. We ate a lot of take-out. We had sex a lot but he thought I was unfaithful. He was jealous of anyone I looked at and anyone who looked at me. And I wasn't the best housekeeper. I didn't vacuum enough and I never rinsed out the sponge. That was a problem. The day I left him I scoured the bathtub and mopped the floors and put clean sheets on the bed, crying the whole time. I swept the porch and washed the windows. I vacuumed. I rinsed out the sponge. Then I went back to Mother's.

Chicken and artichoke casserole.
Mother had been fighting so hard for so long. I made a huge batch of chicken and artichoke casserole and divided it up into little Tupperware bowls and put them in the freezer. I copied it from a caterer she used to use. When she was healthy she would take a bite of theirs and tip back her head and roll her eyes. "This is what I want you to make," she'd say, assigning me the task of replicating. I'd take a bite and try to identify the this and the that on my tongue. When she was sick, the celery seed and the sherry and the coarse ground pepper were off limits. It didn't taste as good, I know, but I would bump the spoon to her mouth and she would take a bite and say, "Mmmm, yes. This is delicious. This is just the way it's supposed to be."

Corn on the cob.
My mother's family handed Bluemont down for five generations. It was, always will be, my favorite place. Even though we have lost it now. It was a huge stone house with a porch wrapped halfway around on a mountain overlooking the Shenandoah Valley. Sometimes Grandma would stop at the roadside stand for corn and pass a steaming platter of it around the great long table in that gold-lit dining room with all the windows open and a breeze blowing the sheers into the room. When Grandma ate corn, we thought of a typewriter.

Club sandwiches.
When I say I am responsible for my own happiness, what I mean is that I cannot expect to go outside my own center to find fulfillment. My mother told me this when I was nineteen over club sandwiches at the diner near my apartment.

David was a socialist. He hated anybody rich and thought the world owed him a living. He said I was shallow and coddled. Once I took him up to Bluemont, and he sat in the dining room berating the upper classes with their summer retreats, numb to all the poor left back in the city, sweating and dying of tuberculosis. I took it upon myself to be his angel of mercy, the deliverer of his happiness. I decided he was right—that I was shallow and coddled and selfish, that I had nothing worthwhile to say. But then I ate club sandwiches with my mother, and she suggested I consider life beyond David. She said, "You can't be responsible for someone else's happiness." She also told me it was unwise to put someone else in the center of your life. Because if you have made him the center of your life then you will be lost in his absence. She said your center belongs inside your self. So when lovers leave or parents die or children grow up and move away, you still have your balance. I broke up with David. I took an efficiency on Franklin Street with a fireplace and a balcony and a view of Monroe Park and a bed with just room enough for one. And I found my center. This was a period I named The New Independence.

Popcorn.
Daddy made popcorn for the Saturday Night Dance Party—the oldies pro-

gram on WRFK. We'd dress for it. In a trunk upstairs we kept a huge pink crinoline and a black sequined vest and bright kimonos and hats and boas. My brother wore stiletto heels and an old silk chemise over his underpants. My sister became a middle-class housewife we named Madge, or a bull-fighter, depending on her mood. I remember a long, beaded evening gown and its heavy hem, dripping down the steps on my way to the living room.

Grilled cheese sandwiches.
My daughter remembers the first time she saw me cry. The divorce was finally final, and I felt the death of a family the way one might feel the death of an old friend. I came home from the courthouse and opened a bottle of champagne as if I were celebrating, but I started to cry. Mary, just three, stood in front of me and wrapped her arms around my thighs and pressed her face into my hips and held me tight. Then we made grilled cheese sandwiches.

Tongue.
My sister and I traveled to Greece on a freighter. Two weeks at sea, with no telephone or newspapers. Every night Costas made us something different for dinner. The day we crossed into the Mediterranean my eyes turned blue. That night I surrendered to the urge to kiss the ship's carpenter. He was dark and sweet and poorly shaven. The next night Costas made beef tongue and served it with mustard. The passengers commented on the rash on my face. I think Costas knew how I got it. I got it from necking on the bow of the ship, cozied in the arms of Gregorius, with a full moon, a cool breeze, and a glittering sea.

Profile
M. Cassandra Cossitt.

   I'm standing on the sidelines of the beer-slicked dance floor at a Halloween concert in the Mosque ballroom in Richmond, Virginia, in 1981. There is only one dancer worth watching: She is wrapped in gold lamé and sports a stiff, spiky mohawk spray-painted gold. Her legs are encased in sparkly gold tights and even her face seems to shimmer with gold dust. She flings her arms upward with reckless abandon, her long, gold scissor legs flash as she spins, and she does something with her shoulders and hips that turns men slack-jawed with simple lust.

A friend joins me, and his eyes are naturally drawn to the gold tornado. He should recognize her, he's known her for years. Instead, he whispers, awestruck, "Look at the moves on that gold chick."

"That's Cassandra, you idiot," I tell him. In truth, I sympathize. I feel the same way every time my sister lets me read something she's written.

—Macaria Cossitt Scott

Bio

M. Cassandra Cossitt
Place of residence: Richmond, Virginia.
Birthplace: Richmond.
Day job: Freelance writer, editor.
Education: Three years at Virginia Commonwealth University.
Serial publications: Local periodicals.
Cravings: Food, shelter, and a good merlot.

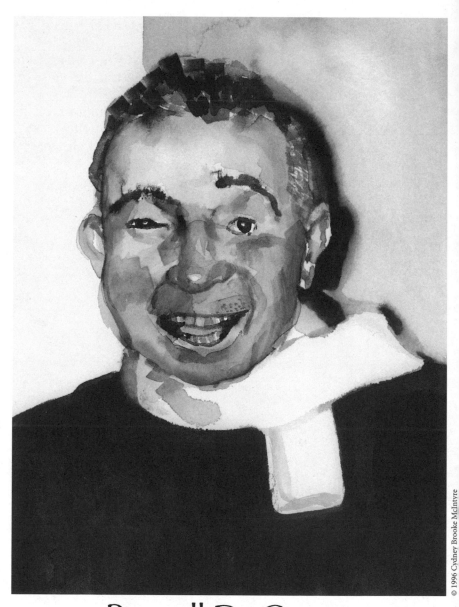

Russell DeGroat

Operation Flying Chicken

In 1954, during the Cold War, the people of communist Albania were starving, and the CIA, to win them over, decided to airdrop food. To test the idea, the agency selected a drop zone on a tiny Greek island in the Gulf of Corinth.

The drone from the twin engines of the Douglas C-47 quieted as I slowed the aircraft to ninety mph. The copilot's voice came over the intercom: "We're at 500 feet. Red light on. One minute to drop zone. Jump on the green light."

The big ship shuddered from the sudden blast of air when the jump door opened. Then the hellacious sound of squawking, screeching, and flapping of terror-stricken chickens filled the cabin. Sweating men cursed, tugged, pulled, and threw the reluctant jumpers out the door.

Smokey Kalbfan, our one-eyed jumpmaster, peered out through a wind-whipped, teary eye then hurried forward to report. "Damn, captain, the slipstream ripped the chicken's feathers off and filled the sky with little white fuzzy things."

"Did the chickens hit the target?"

"Yes sir! They hit dead center. But I'm afraid this was their first and last jump."

Below, the ground observers panicked and dove for cover as seventy-five naked chickens ricocheted off olive trees and ancient stone ruins, splattering across the landscape.

Undaunted, our superiors ordered seventy-five more chickens tied in heavy paper bags for the airdrop. They reasoned that the aircraft's slipstream would tear the bags off, leaving the chickens in full dress and able to glide down to a graceful landing.

Over the drop zone again, our men hurled the brown-bagged chickens out the door. Smokey Kalbfan came forward to report. "Holy cow, captain! The slipstream's wind stripped the bags and feathers off those chickens like banana peels. The last thing I saw was the whole bunch of nude chickens plunging down through a cloud of feathers and shredded brown paper."

Next, orders came through to rig seventy-five chickens with parachutes attached to static lines and secure the birds in sturdier paper bags. The CIA had clever cold war strategists plotting moves and countermoves against the Soviets. They figured the bags would survive the slipstream blast long enough for the static lines to automatically open the chutes. Thus, our free world chickens would retain their feathers and float majestically down into the arms of the joyous Albanians. The Albanians would be so grateful they would rise and throw off the yoke of their communist oppressors.

I visualized seventy-five frantic chickens sitting on both sides of the ship, nervously checking their parachute harnesses and static lines. Perspiring profusely in their bags, they would wait for the green light and final slap on the back and the shove out the door.

When I told Smokey, he blew up. "The agency wants chickens in parachutes? What will those crazy bastards dream up next? I've rigged chutes for the 101st Airborne in France, smoke jumpers in Montana, and communication teams here in Greece, but I never thought I'd be rigging parachutes for chickens."

Smokey did a masterful job fitting chutes on those chickens. When we arrived over the island, Smokey and his crew threw each chicken out of the jump door, leaving behind only a fading squawk and a static line.

Smokey ran to the cockpit, "That was the damnedest thing I ever saw, captain! The slipstream ripped the bags and all their feathers off, just like I thought. The static lines yanked the chutes open, but those chickens were too slippery—they popped out of their harnesses like they were greased. The sky is full of feathers and tiny white parachutes. And about now seventy-five chickens are hitting the drop zone."

When we landed in Athens three men wearing dark shades and suits met our plane. They were agency staff from the Albanian desk, anxious to know the test results. Our long faces gave them their first clue, and the seventy-five tattered static lines dangling from the jump door told the rest of the story.

The Company finally gave up. They had to admit that the starving Albanians were not going to get any relief from "flying chickens."

Profile

On walks around the Umpqua Community College campus, I often notice a beautiful grove of trees named after Russell DeGroat. I was surprised when I realized the sign honored a living person who was in my writing class; an unassuming, quiet man who always has a twinkle in his eye.

Russ is retired and spends his time writing stories "for his family." He also takes classes—everything from foreign languages to wood carving. He also continues to earn "psychic income" by doing volunteer work, like being a docent at Wildlife Safari. Russ defines "docent" as an ancient Swahili word meaning "do it for free."

Russ has worked as fire fighter and park guide. He has flown over the Burma Hump, worked for the CIA, and taught forestry at Umpqua Community College. These jobs took him all over the world, and he continues to travel. He and his wife are avid Elderhostelers. On his last trip to Germany, Russ was so thoroughly at home in his lederhosen that both tourists and locals assumed *Der Kapitan* was a guide. The tourists asked lots of questions and kept pressing money into his hands.

—Sybilla A. Cook

Bio

Russell DeGroat
Place of residence: Roseburg, Oregon.
Birthplace: Sussex, New Jersey.
Day job: Air Force pilot (retired).
Education: B.A., University of Montana. M.A., University of Pittsburgh.
Awards: Distinguished Flying Cross. Air Medal with three oak-leaf clusters.
Favorite book: *Zemindar* by Valerie Fitzgerald.

Mari Lynch Dehmler

Why Live Simply?

Our home is a place where the time-honored practice of conversation thrives. We choose to live free of TV, video games, and the Internet. Talking and closeness come easily. Tonight, for example, our twenty-four-year-old neighbor, Renée, dropped in for a visit. She is a spirited gymnastics instructor who swaps errands, skills, food, and affection with our family. Renée, my husband, and I sat around our table and indulged in ideas and laughter.

When we opened the door to say good-night, the frogs' chorus rising from our garden was louder than the cars down on the highway. None of our neighbors have pole lights, and all the porch lights were out. The moon was full, and the field in front of us was blanketed with soft light.

In our house there's no need for virtual reality. Hours after the evening's conversation, the voice of a red-tailed hawk called me from my reading chair, letting me glimpse a superb reality. I watched as the hawk, illuminated by the moon at midnight, flew from the old oak beside our house to the tall cypress behind us, then to a pine farther away. It returned to perch atop the cypress again. I was awed by its size and the intensity of its cry.

Here we have all we need, though our house is small and lacks some amenities. When I bathe, I hang sheets on the adjoining clothesline so neighbors won't see me *au naturel*, because our only bathtub is an old porcelain tub outside. After our daughter was born, we converted our home office to a third bedroom. I created a new office in our former dining nook, with an eastern view of Mt. Toro and a southern view of the fridge. We moved the dining table to the living room. When I first suggested it, my husband howled: "Eat in the living room?" But the unfamiliar arrangement sufficed.

It's easy to forget the plight of farm workers, hotel and restaurant workers, and other poor here in Monterey County. The Carmel-Pebble Beach-Monterey stretch of California's central coast is affluent. On peninsula roads, we see Porsches and Jaguars for mile after mile. One's perspective can be lost.

Someday we may move from the Monterey Peninsula to an area where real estate prices are lower and reflect the functional value of a house. There we could have a larger place. Still, while living here, we've learned that less can mean more.

Instead of buying apples from Argentina or blueberries from New Zealand, we buy local fruit in season. Rather than purchase a shiny car fresh off the assembly line, we repaint our 1976 vehicle. And we mend and dye a bathrobe for longer wear before buying another one. Are we deprived? No. I step outside the hot kitchen at night and swing the lettuce dry in a worn pillowcase as I look at the stars, never regretting that I have not purchased a plastic salad spinner. We are expanding our personal freedom while conserving resources and helping to create a future where everyone can live well.

As a seventeen-year-old leaving Mt. Pulaski, Illinois, for university life, I was introduced by a great aunt to New Thought Christianity's prosperity principles—ideas which made me aware of the bounty of this world. Twenty-five years later, these ideas and those from other traditions often seem to be confused and twisted into "You can have it all." Are material possessions so significant? And must people with fewer material goods be looked upon as having "poverty consciousness"?

Gaia, our Mother Earth, sustains over five billion people, including more than two billion children who require nourishment, shelter, and health care. Will those of us in the United States, Japan, and other first-world nations pluck the abundance of this planet to decorate dreams for our own children while other children starve? Will we persist in defining national success by gross national product (GNP) and per capita consumption? Or will another way of thinking—*less means more*—replace the consumer mentality and ease the way toward a wiser, more just use of resources?

Periodically, I reconsider my personal and household practices. Can my teenagers take the bus, or must I drive them in the car? Does my little one need a colorful plastic playground set, or will a rope swing tied to a tree and sand in an old tractor tire be as much fun?

Choosing a simpler life doesn't mean living in poverty or deprivation. Simplicity merely calls us to address our genuine needs, and to discern what is most valuable.

In July of 1990, when my father died, people formed a long line extending from the door of our small-town funeral parlor. Many stood for hours in heat and humidity, waiting to pay their respects. Their presence attested to my father's true wealth and achievements. At the time of his death he was a retired maintenance worker, and, to judge by his bank account, he was never a rich man. He would consider his greatest wealth and achievement loving and being loved by his wife, children, and friends. He had long found fulfillment in people, not things.

There are myriad styles of living. Lavish images of "the good life" are widely broadcast. But such a life is beyond the means of most people, is often devoid of satisfaction for others, and incurs heavy social and environmental costs.

Why not measure personal and national success in harmonious relationships, freedom to enjoy a relaxed pace, healthy wildlife, smog-free vistas, and a common experience of joy? The GNP could be replaced by the OSP—Optimism, Sustainability, Peace.

In the morning I awaken to my daughter's soft voice as she reads from a favorite book. Songs of the finch, warbler, and mockingbird cheer me from sunup to sunset. If we use prevailing methods for calculating prosperity, such blessings are left out of the calculation. But we are a self-determining people. We can apply our own standards and assess for ourselves what has greatest worth in our lives. And we can choose and cherish the gifts of living simply.

Profile

The drums and singing have stopped and within the tepee—part of Mari Lynch Dehmler's home near Jacks Peak—women friends who have gathered are reluctant to leave. As with past seasonal celebrations which Mari has hosted, this Spring Equinox has been marked with an evening of blended voices and shared thoughts.

From the center of this gathering, Mari Dehmler offers to each of us a kind word, a small gift, a humorous story. Her spirit dances. It brings people together with tenderness and compassion.

Outside the tepee in more common surroundings, she conducts the daily ceremonies of her life with love and simplicity. Many friends follow her quiet footsteps.

—Sandi Griffiths O'Neil

Bio

Mari Lynch Dehmler

Place of residence: Monterey, California.

Birthplace: Lincoln, Illinois.

Grew up in: Mt. Pulaski, Illinois (a small town where Abe Lincoln practiced law) and on nearby farms.

Day jobs: Freelance writer and editor. Waldorf-inspired homeschooling parent.

Education: Southern Illinois University, President's scholar.

Serial publications: *Your Health. Well-Being. Santa Cruz Sentinel.*

Professional contributions: National Writers Union journalism contract trainer. Delegate to NWU national assembly.

Awards: Honored with the privilege of mothering three souls—Nathan, Paul Noah, Sierra Grace.

Current project: Children's picture book.

Favorite book: *Family Matters: Why Homeschooling Makes Sense* by David Guterson.

Beliefs: "Truth is one, paths are many." Lutheran heritage.

Hope: That all children be cherished and nurtured in a manner recognizing their wholeness.

Cravings: High mountains. Making music. Visits with faraway loved ones.

❁

Grace Druyor

The Marriage Counselors

My daughter Michele was married in St. Petersburg, Florida, in June 1984. She has two brothers and an older sister. Richard, her groom, has four brothers and three sisters. Most of these siblings were already married at the time and were free with their advice. Michele and Richard listened politely, but their expressions, I noticed, were bewildered.

Aunt Margaret said, "Never go to bed angry—make up; apologize. If you learn to say, 'I'm sorry,' you will always be happy together."

Best friend Sue Gerhardt said, "Hey, listen to me and don't have too many children. In fact, one is enough. It sounds great to have a large family, but it puts a strain on your marriage. Other couples are always taking trips, and you are tied to the home."

Her older sister said, "I know you'd like to change him a little, but don't try. He won't improve, he'll actually get worse in those little faults. You cannot make a man over. Figure out a way to cope with his flaws, and you will get along."

Father of the bride said, "You two had better save up for a down payment on a house right away. Mortgage rates are going up, and you must try to get something before they go any higher. Just a small cottage is all right. I can help you with the plumbing repairs, and Sid would redo the wiring. The sooner you make an investment, the sooner you have a goal and can save for something meaningful."

Her mother warned: "Try to be broad-minded. I hope you will be more tolerant of this sweet boy than you ever were of your brothers. Count to ten before you snap his head off."

Grandmother said, "Don't think you have to have everything at once. We made do with a dishpan in the sink and a scrubbing board instead of a washer. You can, too. Half of these modern appliances are breaking all the time, anyway. If you stick to the old-time methods, you get things cleaner."

The preacher said, "Base your love in God. When the going gets rough, you will have more patience with each other if you trust in God."

Groom's grandfather said, "The thing to do is pay cash for everything. Don't let her have all these charge accounts. If she has only five dollars in her pocketbook, it will be easier to decide to buy chicken instead of that new dress!"

His mother said, "Be generous of your time, and listen to each other. Don't assume you know what she is thinking and act on that assumption. Ask a lot of questions."

His father said, "Let one be the boss of the children and the other be boss of the money. Mama always had the expenses figured out, and that kept us from quarreling."

Older brother said, "Don't argue about trivia. If you are going to fight, make it a big fight, and then you can have a lot of fun making up."

His younger brother said, "Are we still going fishing on Saturdays? I have a feeling that life will never be the same again."

Older sister said, "Make it an equal partnership. I give in all the time, and then I am bitter about it. My marriage has become too one-sided."

The bride and groom listened a bit absently to all the advice. Then they smiled at each other and said, "What are they talking about?"

Profile

Grace Druyor and I met at a gathering of the education committee of the League of Women Voters. We had both been teachers, and we joined efforts to write a column for the *St. Petersburg Evening Independent*.

For our column, "Two Schools of Thought," we took opposite sides of issues in education, often choosing stands arbitrarily, since our shared liberal mindset usually had us in agreement. We put off one particularly hot issue in our community at the time: busing to achieve integration. Finally, I said I'd write the "con," and took it as a challenge.

But the greater challenge went to Grace, when she was invited to speak to a group of black women—neither of us enjoyed public speaking! They loved her, however, and she was thrilled to share her feelings about school integration with an enthusiastic audience. Still, she was mighty glad to get back to her keyboard.

—Mary Ann Marger

Bio

Grace Druyor
Place of residence: St. Petersburg.
Birthplace: Richmond, Virginia.
Day job: School teacher (retired).
Education: B.A., University of North Carolina.
Serial publications: *The American Salesman. American Girl.*
Award: Best Essay of Clearwater, Florida. PEN Women (1994).
Current project: Family history.
Favorite books: Biographies of Thomas Jefferson, Abigail Adams, and Dolly Madison.
Belief: "Do unto others as you would have them do unto you."
Craving: That publishers were more open to new writers.

Hanna Eady

On the Back of a Donkey

My grandfather and I shared the same name. Grandmother called me "Little Hanna." Grandfather was "Big Hanna." The year was 1964, I was eight, and I lived in a flat-roofed house of limestone blocks chinked with mud and plastered with mud inside and out. This was in Buqayah, or what the Israelis called "ancient Peqiin," a remote northern village of Palestinian Christians, Druze, Muslims, and Jews in the Upper Galilee Mountains. Our two churches were small stone buildings: one was an Eastern Orthodox church down by the water mill, and the other a Catholic church on top of the mountain. The Druze worshipped in private, the Muslims did not have a mosque (they were mostly refugees from 1948), and the Jews worshipped in an old temple not far from our house.

It was August, and the night was cold. My grandmother came to my bed and woke me, and I sat up and tried hard not to fall asleep once again. The previous evening I had volunteered, begged my grandfather to take me with him to the small orchard where we grew olives. Some of our trees were very old, hundreds of years old, and some were young and needed a lot of care. I got my wish. "I am up. I am up," I kept saying. I finally opened my eyes and saw nothing but the weak, flickering light of an oil lamp. It was dark and everything was still. Nothing moved except the faint shadow of my grandfather, packing. Everyone else in the house slept. All the children in the village slept, and I thought that all the children in the world slept as well. I was in a different time, *nuss lile,* the midnight hour that the big people talked about. I had never known it before.

In a few minutes I was dressed in worn jeans and a cotton shirt and stood outside the doorway in the dark. I held a knapsack and a large canteen wrapped in cloth soaked in cold water. Our village seemed strange. It was dark and quiet, and the air was still. The village had lost its beat, as if it were dead. My grandfather brought out the donkey, no one in Buqayah had a car, and, in those years, cars came up the narrow road once or twice a day, at most. Donkeys, however, were everywhere. Every family had at least one. Ours was *himar kisrawi,* a donkey from Kisra, a nearby Druze village where donkeys were well-bred, well-fed, and respected. With a weaker donkey, my grandfather would have walked and let me ride, but with a strong healthy *kisrawi* we both rode. My grandfather was a lean, small man, wore a thin shirt, and covered his head with a white *kaffiah.* I wrapped my arms around his waist and rested my face against his back to keep warm. It was two o'clock in the morning.

We left the village behind and soon were passing other donkeys carrying farmers like us, but none with a child. My grandfather recognized these men from a distance. There were few farmers from our village who traveled to the groves so early, and those who did admired one another. "That's Abu Shariff Muhanna over there, and Abu Issa Raddi clearing under his trees, and look at Abu Yosef Abbass's grove. You can tell he tends it every day." We reached a higher point. Grandfather looked up to the constellations in the sky and named a few. "This is Thuraya," he said, the Pleiades, "and over there is the Mizan and al-Aqrab," Libra and Scorpio, "and that, all that," he motioned across the sky, "is Darb al-Tabanat, the women who carry bales of hay on their heads leaving trails behind them," the Milky Way.

We reached the top of the mountain on a dirt track that forked to the west, and I looked down and saw New Peqiin, an Israeli town with bright lights that cut through the darkness. A strange sight. The town looked like it was on fire, or like a star had fallen on it. Light but no smoke. It was like the burning bush of Moses: it burned but was not consumed. "Don't let the settlement fool you with its lights," my grandfather explained, "nobody is awake. They leave their electric lights on to keep their chickens awake so they'll eat and lay a second egg." We turned east to our grove and started working.

My grandfather was a humble man, a good boss. He never rushed me. We worked till eight and then sat down to eat our breakfast of *khubiz ra-qiqs*—very thin bread dipped in olive oil, with goat cheese and black olives. In a few minutes he got up and went back to work still chewing his food. "Take your time," he said, "and when you're done with your meal join me to finish the upper section. We'll come back for the lower one tomorrow." I looked at my watch, "What!" I thought, "No way we can do it. I thought we were working until nine o'clock today, or maybe he just doesn't know that it's almost nine. I should tell him."

"Grandfather!" I shouted, "it's half past eight." I hoped he would pack and head home, but instead he began working faster than ever. "I know, I know," he said. "It was eight when we pulled out that big white rock just before breakfast." Grandfather never had a watch and told time by looking at the length of his shadow on the ground. The next thirty minutes would be very hot: on top of the mountain we were first to see the sun rise, but we were also first to burn. If he had been alone, Grandfather would have worked into the heat. Today, however, he had mercy. "All right, all right," he said. "Go find the donkey."

As grandfather prepared to go home, I rode the donkey alone for the first time. I knew it was a donkey not a horse, but I could pretend. Instead of saying, "*Haa, haa*," to him, (the order for a donkey to go), I treated him like a horse: "*Diah, diah*," I said. I did not poke him with a stick on his neck (like you do to a donkey) but kicked with my heels to make him go faster. I knew that my grandfather was not in a hurry, so I rode a few times around the field before handing my "horse" over to him. Even then, my grandfather motioned me onward. He preferred to walk. About halfway home, grandfather spotted a large rock which he used to mount the donkey. He rode in front of me until we got back to the village.

By that time the other kids were awake, and, in daylight, our village was a familiar place once again: the low, flat-roofed stone houses, the gushing spring water running by the church, and the smell of fresh baked bread. On this day nothing was changed except me. I had returned to the village with the soil of our land between my fingers. Now I was a young man. I spent the rest of the day in the shadow of my grandfather, did not play with the rest of the kids. My grandmother no longer called me "Little Hanna." Now grandfather and I were both big.

Many years later, I remember the night I rode to our orchard with grandfather. I look back and think of what I learned. Grandfather taught me to name the stars, to work the land before breakfast, to ride the donkey by myself.

Profile

Hanna Eady and I sat in the sparse, tidy living room of an apartment in Seattle's Magnolia neighborhood, listening to stories. We had listened for hours as various family members spoke of the recent past. The listening was arduous: the aunts, husbands, cousins, and children were Bosnian refugees speaking in Serbo-Croatian, and the stories, carefully repeated by our translator, Peter Lippman, were their horrifying memories of war. As I dutifully recorded the tales I later would weave into a play for Hanna's New Image Theatre, I also measured my capacity—and an audience's capacity—to grasp the lost world behind these stories.

Suddenly Hanna asked about life in Bosnia. Before the war. What did they do—the husbands and wives, sisters and brothers—on holidays? What were the customs of a traditional wedding celebration? For the first time all night a few people smiled. They took turns describing an old fashioned wedding, ending with an elaborate tale of ill-advised romance and elopement. As the middle-aged uncle regaled the rest of the family with old and new details to enliven the story, Hanna laughed along with them. This story was beautiful and hilarious.

By asking, "What about life?" Hanna had broken the language barrier, and helped evoke a world achingly real and funny, glimpsed darkly between the fragments of war.

—S.P. Miskowski

Bio

Hanna Eady
Place of residence: Bainbridge Island, Washington.
Birthplace: Buqayah, Israel.

Day job: Executive Artistic Director at New Image Theatre.

Education: B.A. in social work, University of Haifa. B.F.A. in theatre, University of Wisconsin. M.F.A. in drama and directing, University of Washington.

Dramatic productions: Several scripts produced by New Image Theatre including *Abraham's Land* (1992), which was staged with Jewish and Arab actors playing opposite parts. *Seeing Double* (1991).

Current projects: *Sahmatah,* a docudrama and theatre production on tour. A book. A CD of Middle Eastern music and Palestinian poetry.

Favorite book: *The Inner Reaches of Outer Space* by Joseph Campbell.

Beliefs: Baptized Eastern Greek Orthodox, practicing none. I believe in a good actor.

Instruments: Oud, Arabic keyboard, tabla (small drum used in Indian and Arabic music).

Linda H. Elegant

Good-bye Virgil

In 1958, in the conservative Western railroad town where we grew up, Virgil Acuña died while working at the local newspaper.

Virgil, you were small for a high school kid even though you were 15 or 16. You had large ears, dark olive skin with big freckles, and red curly hair that stood up so you were visible even in a big school like ours. You had a wily, playful way of horsing around and calling attention to yourself. You worked in the evenings at the town's newspaper as part of a crew that included other high school kids. I knew one of them, a boy named David.

On the night you died you were, as the newspaper said, the "object of a prank." The other fellows grabbed you and inserted an air jet from one of the big presses up your rectum. The blast of air ruptured your intestines and stomach. I never knew how soon you went into shock, how quickly you lost consciousness, how much you suffered. They told us little. The police arrived, there was an investigation, an autopsy, a funeral, news stories. But this whole event was hushed up. Afterwards the kids at school said, "Virgil got goosed." When kids talked about your death, they wondered if the boys involved would "get in any trouble." I never heard an adult speak about what happened: not my teachers, not my parents.

After the investigation, the newspaper reported that the boys who had pulled this prank would not be charged with any crime. Their actions had been "foolish" but not "malicious."

I remember you now, and for the first time, I know that the crime those boys did was rape. The real reason the boys were not charged was because they were white and you were Mexican, a "spic" as kids in our high school commonly put it. The newspaper led the campaign to make light of this whole affair because they wished to excuse themselves from legal responsibility. Your parents might have sued. The people of our town accepted the newspaper's characterization without question.

I never knew your family. No Mexican family lived in the white, middle-class neighborhood where I grew up. Only in church on Sunday could we have come in contact, but we didn't. In our high school of 2,000 students, there were many Mexicans, yet even at school I could never really have known you. You would have been one more student who responded to his name when the roll was called. And of course you weren't in senior English or drama or creative writing or chemistry or trigonometry or Latin. Instead you were in auto shop, ROTC, gym.

So you died. Your death was made to seem an unfortunate stroke of bad luck. Your name appeared on the final page of the yearbook imposed on a photograph of clouds. The memorial page. Poor Virgil died and went to cloud land.

Virgil, now I know that you died as a result of a crime. And I know the town, the newspaper, and the high school all conspired to cover up this crime. As far as I know, your family or neighbors or priest never protested. It would have seemed impossible. They would have been treated as trouble-makers. Your death tells a lot about our town and the people who lived here. It tells a lot about me.

Profile

Linda H. Elegant's voice has Utah in it, and her last name suggests beauty polished into distinction. And Linda's work has both of these qualities—earth and refinement.

I met her in the fall of 1995 in Portland at the Pacific Northwest College of Arts where The Oregon Writer's Workshop shares a space on the third floor with the print shop. The fan was blowing the kerosene fumes out into the rain. She wore the seasoned Oregonian attire: rain gear, plaid sneakers, and a loose white shirt over jeans. Bejeweled. Elegant.

She spoke with authority and conviction of her family of women raised in Utah and the intersection of the human and the natural. Much of her writing tends to myth. In a family photo her father holds, with some help, a 250 pound cat fish. In another, snow all but buries her family, posed in the aftermath of a blizzard.

Elegant, and eloquent, is what I'd call her work, and there's a commitment and a discernment that characterizes the best writing.

—Bruce Smith

Bio

Linda H. Elegant
Place of residence: Portland, Oregon.
Birthplace: Junction City, Kansas.
Grew up in: Ogden, Utah.
Day job: Community college writing teacher.
Education: M.A. in English.
Serial publications: *Friends Journal*—poetry. *The Oregonian, Island Park Bugle*—essays.
Awards: Second prize, Clark Poetry Contest (1996). Excellence Award for teaching, U.S. Bank and Portland Community College (1996). Belva Seaberry Award (1994).
Current project: Developing a neighborhood history center to serve the African-American community in Portland.
Favorite book: *Desert Solitaire: A Season in the Wilderness* by Edward Abbey.
Belief: I am a Quaker continuing to learn meditation and prayer.
Cravings: More time, more good food, more success in writing.

John Felstiner

Looking for Kafka

I'm looking for Kafka—I mean, for books by him, possibly even a first edition, as you might say to a friend or a dealer, "I've been looking for Kafka lately, anything published during his lifetime." And I'm looking for Franz Kafka himself, the writer behind and inside every story, sentence, and phrase, such as this from his notebooks: "Writing as a form of prayer."

We lack, we've lost, the past, and because old books, rare or not, inhabit that past, benchmark it, we feel we can redeem the past, literally buy it back: At least *these* forty or fifty cubic inches of paper and cloth haven't utterly fallen away!

A first edition (that magical term!) matters because it was hoped for, overseen, proofed, and welcomed by the author. It bespeaks authenticity, purity, originality, and brings you flush up to its creator. Perhaps *this* copy Kafka himself saw in Prague, and maybe even touched—remember his meager print runs (one or two thousand) and limited distribution. And if a first edition bears Kafka's own inscription, then you (with your second mortgage) pass into the inmost circle.

Kafka cared acutely about the visual, tangible quality of his publications, though they might not meet the almost religious standard he set for his art. "All I ask for is the largest possible typeface," he wrote to the publisher of his first collection, and a month later: "The sample page you so kindly sent me is altogether exquisite." On another occasion he rejected a binding: "One can hardly look at it except with disgust." After a manuscript had been wrested from him and had overcome various obstacles to appear in print, the generous type and format of a "fine book," Max Brod tells us, could give Franz "genuine pleasure"—a pleasure, I like to think, not immeasurably distant or different from my own.

Kafka was even more fastidious about correcting proofs. In a letter to his publisher Kurt Wolff, who vigorously and faithfully served him from 1913 on, Kafka rejoices at the chance to see a second set of proofs for his story "The Judgment," because he catches a "terrible typo: 'bride' [*Braut*] instead of 'breast' [*Brust*]."

Reading those proofs, a few months later, Kafka recalled how "the story came out of me like a regular birth, covered with filth and slime." Writing, for Kafka a form of parturition no less than of prayer, displaced whatever else life had to offer him.

We do Franz Kafka an injustice, we compound the injustice his art already registers, to regard him as unrelievedly mournful and macabre. His friends record frequent episodes of sweetness and lighthearted humor. Kafka once wrote to Max Brod about his job, a fairly high position in the Workers' Accident Insurance Institute of Bohemia: "I've got so much to do! In my four district headquarters . . . people fall as if drunk off scaffolds and into machines, the planks all tip, there are landslides everywhere, the ladders all slip, what people put up falls down, what they put down they fall over themselves. I've got headaches from all these girls in china factories incessantly hurling themselves down stairs with piles of crockery."

The clarity and concreteness of Kafka's sometimes Chaplinesque vision underlie another comic moment, a great moment in Western civilization. In 1914, shortly after war broke out, Kafka read aloud the first chapter of *The Trial*. Now keep in mind what happens there: Joseph K. awakens one fine morning to find himself rudely arrested under dubious authority for an unspecified crime. So Kafka sat and read. "We friends of his," Brod says, "laughed quite uncontrollably when he let us hear the first chapter of *The Trial*. And he himself laughed so much that at moments he couldn't go on reading." The scene is akin to Lewis Carroll reading his young friends the Knave of Hearts' trial, where hilarity jostles with horror as in Kafka's tale. Opening my copy of *The Trial*, I try to conjure up Franz Kafka in 1914, laughing so hard he had to stop reading, and it almost softens the pain of imagining him ten years later, dying voiceless from tuberculosis of the larynx.

Kafka's scruples over his books went deeper than typeface and format. Take *The Metamorphosis* (another hard gem to find): "As Gregor Samsa awoke one fine morning from uneasy dreams, he found himself transformed in his bed into a monstrous insect." Because Kafka deliberately refrained from specifying the kind of insect—dung beetle, cockroach or whatever— he was alarmed that his publisher might use an illustration of it. "Not that, please not that!" Kafka said. "The insect itself cannot be depicted. It can't even be shown from a distance." The point is, this story's matter-of-fact absurdity and ambiguity must take shape only sentence by sentence, for the ear and for the mind's eye.

Even more than *The Metamorphosis*, where a human being is rendered subhuman, Kafka's other major novella, *In the Penal Colony*, is regularly seen as a presentiment of Nazi totalitarianism. In that story an ardently detached officer demonstrates the capacities of an ingenious apparatus, whose steel-toothed harrow inscribes a sentence—the very words of legal judgment—on the back of a guiltless prisoner. While it may extend the appeal of these works to see them as prophetic, really they probe inward into Kafka's own world and self. Alongside its vision of dehumanization and unjustifiable justice, *In the Penal Colony* makes writing itself into torture or punishment. And when the officer perishes in his own machine, that may make Kafka's severest judgment on his writerly vocation.

He withheld *In the Penal Colony* from publication for five years. Finally, in 1918, Kurt Wolff promised him a "fine edition" of "this composition, which I love quite inordinately, though my love is mixed with a certain horror at the terrible intensity of its frightful material." Kafka agreed, and (in a letter written on Armistice Day) made a very specific request about the officer's death at the story's climax. After the words "through his forehead went the point of the great iron spike," Kafka wanted—and got—"an extra-large free space between paragraphs," as he put it. Critics have since wondered why. Perhaps that free space would leave time for the story's point to sink in?

Despite acute wartime shortages, *In the Penal Colony* was printed on fine handmade paper with a two-color title page and sharply etched print. A small portion of the one thousand copies, including the one I now have, came in a bibliophile edition with half leather binding. Every once in a while, when no one's in my study, I take my copy down and stroke the leather a little and check to make sure that after "the great iron spike" there is still Kafka's "free space."

"I believe," the twenty-year-old Kafka wrote a dear friend, "one should read only those books that bite and sting . . . a book must be the axe for the frozen sea inside us." And a decade later: "My whole existence is directed toward literature, I've held fast to this direction till my thirtieth year; if once I forsake it, I simply will not live anymore." But as if responding to such drastic demands, Kafka's own body forsook him. Desperately ill, he still entered into earnest and impossible liaisons with women, continued Hebrew study for a year with Puah Ben-Tovim, and began writing *The Castle*.

At a Jewish children's camp in 1923, suffering from TB, Kafka met the only woman with whom he was able to have a close, harmonious relationship. Dora Dymant, half his age and from a spiritually strong Polish-Jewish family, lived with Kafka and cared for him throughout his last year. They had the notion of emigrating to Palestine, and Kafka wrote to a kibbutz asking if he might serve as its accountant. They even thought of starting a restaurant in Tel Aviv, with Dora in the kitchen and Franz waiting on tables—a fantasy that seemed to Kafka not much more improbable than surviving the winter cold, inflation, and scarcity of 1923 Berlin.

He did survive that winter, but just barely. Staring out from his last photograph, under thick dark hair, is a face with deep-set eyes, mouth very faintly smiling, ears jutting above sunken cheeks. With the help of Dora and a young physician friend, Robert Klopstock, Kafka lived just long enough to correct his last set of proofs. He entitled this collection *A Hunger Artist*, after his story about a sideshow entertainer whose great achievement consists in fasting publicly. The artist reveals in his dying words that he has starved only by necessity, "because I couldn't find the food I liked." This story smacks of Kafka's own frustrated yearning as an artist, which makes it all the more ironic that he could hardly eat or talk during his last weeks. He used conversation slips, one of which actually refers to the proof copy for *A Hunger Artist*: "I want to read it now. Perhaps it will excite me too much, but I have to experience it afresh."

Although the book appeared shortly after his death, scholars are reluctant to call it a posthumous publication—he saw it through to the end. I try not to let a kind of Kafkalatry, a reverence for the pathos here, inflate my attitude toward the (lamentably frayed) copy of *A Hunger Artist* I came by last fall. But I don't always succeed.

Books have their fate, and the fate of Kafka's seems symptomatic. Ten years after *In the Penal Colony* appeared, its one thousand copies were not sold out. And in 1935, the president of the Reich's Literature Chamber ordered the Berlin Gestapo to "seize and confiscate" Kafka's complete works as "harmful and undesirable"—Kafka, who once wrote: "What have I in common with Jews? I have scarcely anything in common with myself . . . ." Later it was this alienation, as much as his Jewishness, that made Kafka suspect in the Soviet bloc. The question came up: Is he the mouthpiece or critic or victim of decadent bourgeois imperialism? All of these, we would say, which is why ten thousand copies of *The Trial* were snapped up the day it was reissued in Prague in 1958. And his lucid mysteries keep their freshness, keep making their demand, which is why the manuscript of *The Trial* recently sold for close to a million dollars.

Franz Kafka's stories speak, however enigmatically, for human freedom and for spiritual presence. When photos of the crowds celebrating in Prague's Wenceslas Square came out several years ago, I found myself scanning the faces, looking for those familiar dark staring eyes and those capacious ears . . . looking—for Kafka.

Profile

I met John Felstiner in the fall of 1968 at Stanford. He was an assistant prof in the English Department, had just moved from Harvard with his wife, Mary Lowenthal Felstiner. Several times a week, the two of them came for dinner at Grove House where I lived. Grove was an experiment in coed living and in-house seminars designed to thwart the "barbarism of our age," an intellectual mecca on a campus with its share of fraternity beer parties. Except that now, by the time John and Mary arrived, even the frat boys had been radicalized by the Vietnam war and spent their evenings chasing the Santa Clara County cops back and forth across campus, tossing tear gas canisters against lines of men with batons.

John and Mary were an island of calm in the political storm. They were warm and sympathetic—pure intellectuals who talked ideas the way other people talk sports. To an undergrad like me they seemed very old, nearly thirty, and cloaked in authority. John and Mary spent hours listening and offering encouragement. John read my poetry and, in his office on the quad, gave comment. "In a poem," John said, "what comes after must have something to do with what comes before." A simple statement, yet one that I've been thinking about every week for the past twenty-five years. And then there was John's way of reading my longer poems. He would speak for five or six minutes about each word in the first line, one at a time, until I felt like begging for mercy. Words belong to families, John taught me, words have character, words pick up associations from the contexts in which they are used.

The following spring John and Mary came to dinner less frequently. Mary was pregnant, and in June she gave birth to a girl, Sarah. I remember talking to John in his office. "A difficult birth," he said. John had put his feelings into a poem. I talked to Mary on the phone: she was hurting. We spoke of God's love.

Mary was completing a degree in history, was the mother of a young child, and academic jobs in the Bay Area were like snow in Saudi Arabia. I had placed her in my hero class and wanted her to write a big, complicated book—to show what it was possible for me to accomplish. But it looked as though Mary was down for the count, so that left John. As a scholar, John was a writer, which gave me hope. In the spring of 1970, he completed the manuscript of his first book, a careful scholarly study on Max Beerbohm. "What's next?" I asked. John was tired. He had spent months rewriting his manuscript and sending off letters for permissions. He was not thrilled with the idea that, as my hero, he needed to speed up his literary output. "No thanks," he said. "I'll never write another." John was discouraged and so was I. John Felstiner was a thoughtful man. He had something to give to the world. But his wit and warmth and depth hadn't come through in his initial effort.

After school I ended up in Seattle. Every few years I wrote to John Felstiner. His wife had somehow managed to juggle motherhood and a career. She'd completed her degree and was teaching at San Francisco State. And she'd given birth to a boy, Alek. John was translating from Spanish and German, writing articles, and he wrote a book on Pablo Neruda. He began a study of Paul Celan, a Jew and a poet from Bukovina (Romania) who survived World War II and made it to Paris where he lived and married and wrote. And where, in April 1970, he threw himself off a bridge into the Seine.

Several years ago, John gave a talk at the University of Washington. My wife and I sat in. It was a raffish, high-spirited affair, a dozen comparative literature teachers speaking to one another in four or five different languages. This was academics, and John was in his element. He spoke with great enthusiasm on scholarly approaches to Celan.

John's daughter Sarah is grown up now, and recently moved to Wallingford, a Seattle neighborhood not far from mine, to be with a kite maker from Yale who set up shop near Seattle's Lake Union. John's son Alek is still living at home. He's a music buff, everything from Mozart to Nirvana. Last fall, John and Mary came to Seattle to visit. Mary told me about her book *To Paint Her Life*, the story of the artist Charlotte Salomon, a Jew who came very, very close to escaping the Holocaust. On Saturday evening, John read from his new book at Elliott Bay Bookstore in Pioneer Square—a basement room, exposed brick, clanking glasses from the bistro on the other side. The scene at Elliott Bay was familiar to me, very low key, nothing intimidating like twelve Ph.D.s speaking in tongues. But John seemed nervous and, as he waited to speak, I realized that he was outside his world, facing a live, nonscholarly audience. As John waited, more and more people walked in. Now I was nervous. John's talk would have to be from the heart. Risky. A rebuff by this crowd, and there'd be nothing left but a wet spot on the white, tile floor.

John told about writing *Paul Celan: Poet, Survivor, Jew*. For fifteen years, John had lived in the mind of the brilliant, quirky poet. John went to France. He met Celan's widow, worked in Celan's libraries in Paris and Normandy. He wrote this book a little at a time. John quoted letters from readers. One man put John's book on the same shelf as the Bible. A woman was deeply moved. Here it was, I realized, the book I'd waited 25 years to read.

The audience at Elliott Bay applauded. John autographed, then he and I and Mary and Sarah retreated to the other side for lattes.

—Scott C. Davis

Bio

John Felstiner
Place of residence: Stanford, California.
Birthplace: New York.
Grew up in: New York and New England.
Day job: Teacher.
Education: B.A. and Ph.D., Harvard University.
Books: *Translating Neruda: The Way to Macchu Picchu* (1980). *Paul Celan: Poet, Survivor, Jew,* (Yale, 1995).
Awards: Commonwealth Club Gold Medal *(Translating Neruda)*. British Comparative Literature Association, First and Second Prize in Translation. Council for the Advancement and Support of Education, Gold Medal (*Kafka*).
Current project: Translating Paul Celan.
Favorite book: *Tesserae: Memories and Suppositions* by Denise Levertov.
Belief: Jewish.

Horton Foote

On Writing and Risk

Keeping an unpublished manuscript in a drawer and not sharing it with an audience, even if it is a small audience of friends and acquaintances, is a mistake.

When I think of the writers that I admire like Flannery O'Connor or Katherine Anne Porter or William Carlos Williams or Marianne Moore—they all lived through literary magazines and made hardly a living out of it but it certainly was a place for them to be read and to be seen. And finally they gathered an audience and perfected a style. Whereas if you kept it in a drawer and waited for a Knopf to pick it up you would never develop as a writer. I think of Elizabeth Bishop, Randall Jarrell—all the poets that I know of—they finally found publishers. But in the meantime they kept using small magazines and publishing and reading each other and disciplining each other and discussing their work.

Poets have always seemed to accommodate themselves to just pursuing their craft and not worrying about the commercial aspects of it. A lot of them had to teach, and some people think that's not a good thing. It's very hard to evaluate. All I feel is that if you want to write you take your risks and you look around. For instance I've just had four plays done at the Signature Theatre Off Off Broadway. I'm the fourth playwright they've done, after Romulus Linney, Lee Blessing, and Edward Albey. I didn't get rich from this, but I got rich in many intangible ways. It was an extraordinary experience. Many people found their way down to see our plays and compare them to the others. It's the project of two young men and one in particular, Jim Houghton, who has envisioned this theatre. It's not always easy. He has to use a ninety-nine seat house and has to be very careful with his budget. He's attracted extraordinarily talented people, directors and actors. Each year he has a playwright who is willing to turn over four of his plays to him.

You need to listen for ideas. When Jim first got the idea he knew there would be many obstacles. He persisted and not only did it work—the first season was in 1991—each year it's grown.

It is always very difficult in theatre. It always meant a lot to me to know that people like Pound and Eliot and a lot of the other writers who I consider our base really were in love with the process of writing, and they had high standards. You might not always agree with them. But they made great sacrifices for their work and the integrity of their work. In the case of Eliot he had *Criterion* magazine, which had a very low readership. But the influence of the magazine was profound. It touched many people and influenced many people.

We have to be careful that we don't equate success with how much money we make. I know that we all have to find a way to support ourselves. Certainly we want our work seen and read. But I have always been more comfortable with the goals of someone like Eliot who seemed to be interested in the work itself. And finding a way to bring out the highest sense of it he can.

The way I got started? When I wrote my first play I was still an actor. I got a job (this was in New York) and saved my money, and I went back home to Texas and wrote the play. The first play was reviewed and had a wonderful reception but it was produced in an Off Off Broadway venue and made no money. I had to think what to do so I could write. Then I got a job running an elevator on Park Avenue. It was long hours, and the pay was not very large. But the good part of the job was that most people were home in bed by ten o'clock. I started at six and didn't end until six the next morning—a lot of that time was just silence. So I could spend the night writing. I wrote *Only the Heart* there. That was 1943. The play was produced in Provincetown in 1944 and on Broadway in 1945. It had a wonderful reception off Broadway but when it got to Broadway it wasn't well received and made no money, so I again had to figure out what to do to support myself. I worked in a bookstore, but that didn't leave me any time for writing, so I began to teach, and ended up taking a series of teaching jobs.

In the meantime I got married, and my wife and I and some friends went to Washington, D.C., where we started a theatre school and theatre. After that I came back to New York and did some teaching. But I always allowed time for writing. Everything was organized around that. My work began to sell. And so my career developed.

The main thing is that you find a way to live modestly. The great problem, particularly for theatre writers and screen writers, is that they get involved in an expensive lifestyle that they feel they have to support. That's a real trap. I've had a very blessed marriage. And my wife felt that an extravagant lifestyle was a thing to be avoided—both for me and for our children. So we found a way to live modestly. And whenever I made some money, I'd take time off and write.

I've spent a great part of my life in New York, and I love it. But it never occurs to me to write about this place. My plays are set in the fictional town of Harrison, Texas. I didn't decide on this location. It chose me.

Critics write about "regional" and "local" writing in a disparaging way. I don't think you should pay any attention to it. Some of our most distinguished writers have a great sense of place. Elizabeth Bishop, Flannery O'Connor, Reynolds Price, Eudora Welty. It doesn't mean their writing is parochial, and it doesn't mean it's quaint. That's to be avoided. What you try to find is the universal in the particular. That's the search.

Profile

I met Horton Foote in Seattle in August 1993. He had come to town to do a benefit for the Belltown Theatre Center. The event included a screening of his film *Convicts* with Robert Duvall and James Earl Jones, a reception after, and talks with small groups. Also, the following day, the theatre group performed Horton's one-act play, *The Oil Well*.

My wife and I arrived at the Neptune Theatre in the University District at eight. I'd never been into the Neptune before—it was known in town as the place to go, at midnight, to see the *Rocky Horror Picture Show*. And I was surprised to see a crowd of 300 that had come, at twenty-five dollars per head, to do honor to a good playwright and a good man.

Horton Foote is known for the insight and substance of his dramas and screenplays. His play and movie *A Trip to Bountiful* tell the story of an elderly woman fleeing a city apartment for her old home place in the low farmland on the Texas coast. His screenplay *Tender Mercies* (starring Robert Duvall) is the story of a musician who travels from city to city until his life disintegrates and he finds himself living in a nondescript roadside motel—a place where he begins to anchor himself, reestablish his links to humanity, to discover, once again, his own soul. Foote's work is deceptively simple. It is deep. And there is a lot of it. His screenplays *To Kill a Mockingbird* and *Tender Mercies* have won Oscars, he won a Pulitzer in 1995, and he is featured every year or so in the arts pages of *The New York Times* and *The Christian Science Monitor.* Yet comparatively few people recognize his name.

After *Convicts,* my wife and I drove downtown to the Belltown Theatre Center where we ate delicacies, tried out the new small theatre seating, and schmoozed with the theatre crowd. Before long Horton Foote arrived. He stood in the corner, white hair, gentle smile, and sat to autograph his published plays. I introduced myself and gave him a copy of my first book. He thanked me. I mumbled a few words. What I took away was an impression of his sincerity.

Horton Foote is not even slightly interested in the glitz and money we associate with Hollywood. He lives and writes to express meaning—no car chases, naked dancers, or machine gun battles in his work. And Horton Foote doesn't hesitate to donate his time to support a pioneering theatre project. I was buoyed by the man, and even more by the audience. Three hundred people doing honor to a writer and his quiet, perceptive work? There truly is an audience for thoughtful writing: this truth is a life-ring for scriveners like me who have ideas but slight notion of how to make them pay.

—Scott C. Davis

Bio

Horton Foote
Place of residence: Wharton, Texas.
Birthplace: Wharton, Texas.
Family: Horton's father was a shopkeeper in Wharton.

Education: Wharton High School. Pasadena Playhouse Theatre (1933–35). Tamara Darkarhovna Theatre School (1937–39).

Awards: Nineteen major awards. Pulitzer in drama (1995). Oscars for the screenplays *To Kill A Mockingbird* (1962) and *Tender Mercies* (1983). Theatre Hall of Fame (1996).

Plays/film scripts/television dramas/books: More than forty, including the original play and filmscript *A Trip to Bountiful* and the film script *Tender Mercies* (starring Robert Duvall).

Undiscovered stars: *The Chase* (1966) was a movie with a screenplay by Lillian Hellman based on Horton's original play. It starred Marlon Brando and featured "unknown" actors Robert Redford, Jane Fonda, Angie Dickinson, and Robert Duvall.

Favorite fictional locale: The town of Harrison, Texas, an old-time, rural community near the Texas coast which is the setting for all Horton's original plays including *The Traveling Lady* (1954, adapted in 1964 for the screen as *Baby, the Rain Must Fall* starring Steve McQueen and Lee Remick).

Historical note: In the 1950s Horton wrote for the prestigious "Playhouse 90" and the "Philco-Goodyear Playhouse" among other shows—serious television work from the early years of that medium. Horton has had a long association with the actor Robert Duvall—as one Hollywood insider puts it, "Horton Foote got Duvall his first job." Robert Duvall's first film was *To Kill a Mockingbird* (1962), and the two worked together on *Tomorrow* (1972), Horton's film adaptation of a Faulkner short story.

Recent screenplay: *The Man of the House* (1994). To be produced by Eddy Murphy Productions.

Current project: A new play.

Favorite book: *The Autobiography of William Butler Yeats* (currently published as *Yeats* by William Butler Yeats).

Favorite food: Fried chicken.

Catherine Foster

Salad Days

Short skirts are back and I for one am glad. In my salad days, I wore them in ever-shortened versions (to the rising dismay of my mother). After I got back from a trip to Europe while in college, I chopped off my hair and adopted a more refined look. My knees have been hidden ever since.

Oddly enough, it's the *innocence* of wearing short skirts that appeals to me; I feel as if a sculptor has carved away the marble, freeing up a French schoolgirl.

I'm sure others will feel they've been put *in* bondage; you can't take as long strides in these short ones, and anyone with a scrap of modesty will agree that adjustments have to be made in how one sits and picks up things. But long skirts are no picnic, either; you have to lift them up every time you climb stairs. Not so fun when you're carrying a briefcase.

Yet the true reason I'm glad short skirts are back is that I can start sewing again. For the past few years, when styles were long and wool expensive, it was a whole lot easier and cheaper just to buy skirts. Especially the ankle-length kind with all those tiny pleats.

In junior high and high school, short on cash, I sewed all the time—everything from smocked aprons for my mother to pants and straight skirts. Skirts took a yard of material, a zipper, a couple of seams, and an hour of time. Now that I'll be adding such grown-up touches as a kick pleat, lining, and a hand-sewn zipper, it'll probably take me three hours. But what a wonderful thing to be able to buy a wad of material and a few hours later walk out wearing it.

I've missed sewing. Missed the hours spent mentally polishing the dream until I could see the garment, the color and weight of the material, and what I would look like in it. Missed the twenty-minute walk to Maxim's, my hometown fabric store, with hundreds of bolts of material stacked this way and that on dusty shelves. Missed pawing through demure cotton prints, fuzzy pink bathrobe material, slinky satins, and crisp linen until I saw the fabric that matched the vision in my head.

Then came the scary moment of telling the clerk how much I wanted and hoping I had calculated correctly. Unlike shopping in an ordinary store, where you can return an item you've bought, once the material is cut, you are stuck with it. Committed.

When I'd gotten back home, I'd wash and iron the material, fold it in half, and line up the selvages (finished edges of the fabric). One of the big thrills was first opening up a new pattern and laying out the thin, crinkly beige sheets on the material.

Next came cutting the material. That, too, was a point of no return. If you put the front piece on the selvage and not the fold, forget it! No skirt. So I always spent a long time chewing my lip, checking and rechecking, before taking that first, irreversible cut.

Compared to the decisions, the sewing itself was almost a breeze. Darts. Back center seam. Zipper. Side seams. Waistband—sewn on the outside of the skirt, flipped over, and hand-stitched down. The final step involved my mother. I'd stand on a chair while she'd measure the hem with a yardstick ("Middle of the knee, dear?" "No! One inch above!")

Slipstitch the hem. Press. *Voila! une* skirt!

It's too bad that sewing is not mandatory in school anymore. It teaches some great things. Practical things, like making decisions and living with them. Doing it right the first time: When I got too cocky and roared off without reading the directions, that was when I spent a lot of time ripping out seams and starting over. Creative things: imagining and then creating a piece of clothing that expresses exactly how you feel about yourself.

The time sewing worked best was when I dreamed up the idea of making a bright yellow linen dress—sleeveless, empire-style, with a white collar and a black ribbon tie. I was able to find a pattern and just the right materials, and the dress came out fine. It had an extraordinary impact on the ninth grade boys. Their eyes told me that the wallflower was, all of a sudden, somebody to be reckoned with. Heady stuff for a fourteen-year-old. And all from a needle and thread.

Profile

Catherine Foster. Starry sky, mid-autumn, and a cold snap that sends the Indian summer of 1984 into memory. A group of friends are camped at the base of Mt. Chocura, in New Hampshire. Toward midnight, when the temperature plunges into the teens and even the trees are still, conserving warmth, I hear a firm voice suddenly speak: "This isn't working."

Someone chuckles.

"Go on," says the indignant one, "laugh at the neophyte sleeping nude in a down bag in the cold—just like you told her to! Dammit, you guys, I'm *freezing*!

More sleepy laughter. The next morning, the first of her camping life, Foster climbs the peak, energized by her battle with the cold and the steep slopes. She delights in the world.

Her fifteen years' work for *The Christian Science Monitor* reflects Foster's perspective—the long, inclusive view and the telling detail. Along the way, she's interviewed people as diverse as John Updike, Nora Ephron, Peter Jennings, a Poet Laureate, a Chinese theatre director, and aborigines in Australia's outback.

—Diane R. Hanover

Bio

Catherine Foster
Place of residence: Cambridge, Massachusetts.
Day job: Assistant Foreign Editor, *The Boston Globe.*
Education: B.A. in English, University of California at Santa Barbara.
Serial publications: *New York Times. Saturday Evening Post. Reader's Digest.*
Favorite book: *Angle of Repose* by Wallace Stegner.
Secret desires: Be the next Jane Austen. Sing back-up in a rock 'n' roll band.

Jamal Gabobe

Termites and Clans

In February 1993, I returned to Somaliland for the first time since I left with my parents when I was five years old. This time I was there for five weeks, most of which I spent in Somaliland's capital city, Hargeisa. One clear morning at ten o'clock, I began scouting the Shaab area, which is in the western part of Hargeisa, looking for termite mounds.

Two days earlier, I had seen one of these mounds and instantly became curious about its odd shape, the prodigious amount of labor that went into its construction, and the fact that it was made of simple materials: sand mixed with termite saliva. It is difficult to see termites at work, but one can tell the result of their most recent efforts by the wet appearance of the new deposit compared with the rest of the mound.

After twenty minutes of searching, I spotted the reddish top of a termite mound behind some bushes. I waded through the bushes to find a five-foot high structure that looked like a female fertility figure, the kind I had seen in books.

I got my camera out, angled for a good shot, and was just about to press the button when I heard a man's voice declare in Somali, "You better not do that."

I turned around and saw a short, light-skinned man, wearing corduroy pants and smoking a cigarette.

"Are you talking to me?" I asked, also in Somali.

"Yes," he replied.

"Are these termite mounds yours?" I inquired.

"No, they aren't mine," he answered, "but there's a story behind what you're doing."

"What could this story be?"

The short guy puffed his cigarette a couple of times, moved a step closer to me, then asked, "Do you really want to hear it?"

"Yes."

He looked both ways, then said, "You may not believe what I'm about to tell you, but it did happen. There was this guy who was originally from here, but who lived in Saudi Arabia for many years. Two years ago he came back here and, like you, took many pictures of these termite mounds. When he returned to Saudi Arabia, he showed the pictures to the Saudi government. He told them that most Somalis were pagans who worshipped those mounds, and that he was engaged in a project to convert Somalis to Islam, and needed help."

"And what did the Saudis do?" I asked.

"They believed him and gave him a lot of money to carry out his project. He took the money, came back here, bought a lot of real estate, trucks, and cars and kept the rest of the money for himself. He's a rich man today thanks to the Saudis."

"But the Saudis know that Somalis are almost one hundred percent Muslim," I said.

"They must not know it," he answered, "otherwise they wouldn't have given him the money."

I was speechless. A complete stranger was accusing me of planning to cash in on the people of Hargeisa by misrepresenting them to the outside world, and this stranger hadn't made the slightest effort to get to know me first. A snap judgment. I was angry. Why had I listened to him in the first place?

Later that afternoon I went to the Bar Hargeisa to have dinner with two of my acquaintances. Bar Hargeisa occupies a low brick building with a courtyard, and, despite its name, does not serve alcohol—the same way that Somali coffee shops do not serve coffee but tea, although Somalis call them "coffee shops." My acquaintances Hassan and Osman were already there, sitting in the courtyard. Hassan was a grade school teacher with thick glasses and a penchant for explaining things. Osman worked at a clothing store.

I ordered lamb shanks and a side of rice. We ate and talked about the news. Hassan updated us on his marriage plans. Although it was hot, a steady breeze made it more tolerable. There were only a handful of men in the restaurant, since it was already past lunch hour.

Then I told them about my encounter with the short man and the elaborate con game he'd described. Hassan and Osman listened attentively. But as soon as I revealed the name of the alleged con artist, Hassan became angry. "He is a good man. He would never do such a thing," Hassan said.

"Yes, he did do it," replied Osman.

"How do you know he did it?" asked Hassan.

"I've heard it from several people," answered Osman.

"Come on, this whole story was made up by his enemies," said Hassan.

This went on for a while with Hassan insisting that it never happened, and Osman equally adamant that it had. After listening to their assertions and counter assertions, it gradually became clear to me that neither had any proof. Everything they said was based on hearsay. Also, since the one defending the alleged con man was from his sub-clan, while the one condemning him was not, and since there was no other connection between the con artist and either of them, I came to the conclusion that this was just another case of Somali clan rivalry in action. Neither Osman nor Hassan was interested in finding the truth, only in defending members of their clan and attacking those who were not.

I had seen similar arguments between Somalis abroad, but there was a major difference. If you argued or quarreled with another Somali in London or New York, and decided, as a result, not to see him or have anything to do with him, you stood a good chance of doing just that. But here in the land of Somalis, everyone belongs to a clan. Consequently, even if you succeed in avoiding your antagonist, you cannot escape other members of his clan who may number in the thousands. And clan memories last for generations.

Whenever I think of the Somali tragedy I think of the short guy who accused me of fraud without any evidence. I also imagine how easily the debate between Osman and Hassan could have turned violent. In both cases, one person was unwilling to give the other the benefit of the doubt. It is such an attitude of blind loyalty to one's group and visceral hostility towards everyone else that is at the root of the Somali catastrophe.

Profile

The first time I met Jamal Gabobe was on bus number forty-eight leaving the University of Washington on its way to south Seattle. As we talked and I got to know him better, I was amazed at his international background. He was born in Somaliland to a Muslim family. When he was five years old, however, he immigrated with his parents to Aden where he was educated in a Catholic school. This means that he was taught in English, spoke Somali at home, and spoke Arabic in the streets and bazaars of this ancient city.

Jamal is a regular at Cafe Roma, a hangout on the Ave, the U District's busiest street. Roma looks like a warehouse with a glass wall on one side. On the opposite wall a local artist displays his or her work each month. Roma also has a balcony where people ranging from students to street kids sip coffee, chat, read, and watch the local U District hipsters, deadheads, jocks, geeks, chi chi gals, and preppy kids walking past. The place is menacing and disorganized, but this doesn't seem to bother Jamal. If anything, it reminds him of cafes in Aden where the high and the low mix freely. Roma's main attraction for him, however, is that people leave him alone to do his writing.

Jamal is primarily a poet, but he has also written short stories, a novel, and a play. His book of poems *Love & Memory* chronicles the twists and turns of his life. He is doing graduate work in comparative literature at the University of Washington, and works at Suzzallo library.

"All roads lead to Roma," Jamal says. Roads and journeys are things he knows a lot about.

—La'Chris Jordan

Bio

Jamal Gabobe
Place of residence: Seattle's Central District.
Birthplace: Hargeisa, Somaliland.
Grew up in: Aden, Yemen.
Day job: Staff member of Suzzallo Library.

Education: Pre-med studies at Central State University in Wilberforce, Ohio. B.A. in comparative literature at the University of Washington. Currently completing a Master's in comparative literature at the University of Washington.

Awards: Finalist in multicultural theatre group in Seattle.

Book: Recently published *Love & Memory*, a volume of personal and political poems (Cune Press. Call 800-789-7055. $15.95.)

Current project: A book on Somalia and Somaliland based on Jamal's family memory and recent travels in East Africa. Working title *The Somalis: A Personal Account.*

Favorite literary movement: "The Internationals," a Seattle underground literary project which grew out of readings and discussions that Jamal and fellow expatriates have held for many years in Seattle's University District, at Leroy's restaurant, and later at The College Inn.

Favorite book: *Madame Bovary* by Gustave Flaubert.

Belief: The unity of being.

Craving: Chocolate-chip ice cream.

Kathryn Flynn Galán

This Room and Everything In It

We built the bedroom together. "With our hands," you promised me. I loved your hands, olive and square, that held me tight when you proposed that we marry. I loved how they traced that balsawood model of the room you envisaged. I knew then that they could build this place for us. You chose a curving pine-barrel roof. I added cupboards, a shy window, and planters for columbine.

You held the throbbing concrete hose to pour the floor. On hands and knees I spread sealer on the slab, then buffed it to a liquid shine. You came to me with a rust splinter in your eye from sanding the steel beams. I kissed the lid and found you a doctor. I worked on ten-foot ladders to sand and coat and sand the doors and window frames like a boatswain tending his beloved teak hull.

We moved in before the work was done and slept those first nights on the floor. Glass windows stretched up from our feet to let in starlight and a draft of jasmine. We heard the ocean. And we were awakened each morning by Spanish stucco masons who peered in at us as we lay naked on our mattress. We hoped that some day soon they would all be through.

The week our room was finally finished, we married in the courtyard right outside. Guests piled gifts and hats on the bed. Friends stood in the French doors and watched us say our vows. The party flowed under the barrel and beams, around perfect block pillars and warm wood. You drew me to you, beautiful hands on my bare back, and we danced close on the concrete floor. A magician lofted a playing card twenty feet to the ceiling where it stuck. And then you slept. "A year," you said. You needed a year to recover from building that room.

"No," I tried to say, but never found words that you believed. "It's not just glass and steel and concrete, this room. It's where we began our public life together. It's where our marriage dwells." To me, it was a garden that needed to be watered and trussed and fed. It was not a project completed, but something just begun.

You insisted that what you needed was to rest from your labors, after all the weekends of building and the stress of construction. But nevertheless, something did begin to grow. Not just Fairy Lantern lilies on the patio or the primrose-pink peach tree along the block wall. Something else grew—a local lichen, fuzzy and dark. It dusted the soles of our shoes and invaded the ash cupboards you had built. It tickled the books on our nailless shelves. We became congested, too stuffy to kiss. The dogs fought. And still you slept.

I wanted your help but you offered no ideas. I tried an air purifier from Switzerland. A dehumidifier from Sears. I did a Lysol wash every week. Finally the architect proposed a cure: a heat lamp perhaps would kill the lichen.

So I left on an infrared bulb, night and day, to dry the bedroom's concrete pores. I thought it was helping. I dry-cleaned the mildew smell from the clothes. But then one day the lamp conspired with dust mites, and maybe the errant corner of a sheet. The room burned down. The room that we had built and everything in it.

The fire burned the bed and the books, the inky Orientals and the butter leather chair. The big Sony television melted like a Dali clock. The barrel ceiling blistered twenty feet up. The playing card finally fell onto the flames.

Our friend Dara came over that night, after she heard the bad news, and brought the architect Mark. They studied the room's black bones and made us Stoli martinis. Dara noticed that my altar of Tibetan bells and I Ching coins, sacred sage and abalone shells was unscathed in the embers. Mark shut the door and assured us that the room would be built back completely by insurance contractors. Maybe better. Certainly faster.

And they were right. Soon the floor was clean again and more highly polished. The bookshelves were wider. The ceiling was varnished like new.

You and I bought a new bed and plush cotton mattress. My sister embroidered our wedding date into a sampler for the fresh white wall. My mother trekked to Laddak to replace the rug. A Picasso drawing from Mark fit into a nook in the bookcases. Dara sent a wheeled stand so the new TV would be easier to move.

But on the first night back in our room, we didn't lie under starlight and count waves. We weren't naked on the cotton mattress. We were just back.

Our life resumed. You rose early. I worked late. The peach tree stretched. The lichen stayed away. The roof didn't leak much anymore. But we spent very little time in our room.

I was sent out of town for five months on business. You wanted to consider it a separation. I came back once to talk to you but the room was no longer mine. You had stored away our wedding album and my antique porcelain dolls. The icons from my altar were hidden out of sight, along with all of my clothes and the raw rubies that you gave me one Christmas for love.

The bed, the lamps, the books   they were there. The Rug. The Picasso. The Sony. But no hint of you. No diary. Nothing in your hand. None of my letters. Maybe a strand of her hair.

I found a new house for myself. When I moved out and left the room to you and your new lover, you begged me to leave the bed. And a sheet. And two feather pillows.

I left just that. As well as the wave sounds at night. And my wedding ring, buried under the peach tree against the block wall of our room.

Profile

I met Kathryn Flynn Galán in a writing workshop I taught at a private home in Brentwood with Zen poet Peter Levitt. Later, Kathryn and I met for tea at the Peninsula Hotel in Beverly Hills. The sitting area is a sumptuous antique green, gold, and white. Here we sat among international businesspeople, movie stars like John Travolta and Uma Thurman, wealthy suburbanites, and sybarites of all professions. Over watercress and tomato sandwiches, Darjeeling tea, dry champagne, and ripe strawberries, we talked about writing and our lives.

I discovered that Kathryn had been a child prodigy with a genius IQ who became a concert pianist and a professional violinist at fourteen. She has trekked in the Himalayas, speaks fluent French and Spanish (she is of Spanish descent), and is also a first-rate cook.

She had a high-powered job as a film producer (e.g., *French Kiss* with Meg Ryan). On location in Nova Scotia shooting a movie for Disney called *Squanto*, she still managed to FedEx thirty-page stories to our workshop every week. Kathryn's father worked for NASA. I think she's powered by rocket fuel.

—Cathy A. Colman

Bio

Kathryn Flynn Galán
Place of residence: Los Angeles.
Birthplace: Ann Arbor, Michigan.
Day job: Movie producer.
Education: Amherst College. University of California at Los Angeles.
Anthology: *Sexual Secrets.*
Serial publications: *Alaska Quarterly.*
Current project: Movie on the life of Art Pepper.
Favorite book: *Postcards* by E. Annie Proulx.
Beliefs: Buddhism, the Dali Lama.
Craving: To go everywhere at least once.

Peter Galperin

The Language of Trains

Emerging from darkness, the train heads north along the Hudson River. I remove my shoes, take out some magazines, and settle in for the two-hour ride.

After the initial excitement of motion, the passengers around me are soon lulled by the rhythmic clacking of wheels on track, only to be roused by the conductor's announcement as the train approaches each stop. It's still daylight, and I feel a guilty pleasure at having escaped the city so early. The air-conditioned car will soon be too cold, but for now it's a welcome relief from the oppressive heat in the station we've just left behind. To avoid sitting with a stranger, I sit on the landward side of the train. The more popular river side is full, and I always like to have two seats to myself.

For the first time I notice the ponds and waterways that are cut off from the river by the train tracks. Scattered fields of corn sway within an arm's reach of the rail. Perched randomly on the hillsides are what appear to be great castles and estates. They seem too large to be private homes, although they most certainly once were. Maybe now some of them are schools or institutions. Maybe some are empty.

For many miles a grass or weed has spread along the bank, turning much of the river green. The opposite shore is hazy. At times I see four or five distant ridges rising one after another. The last one so faint it might be my imagination.

My grandfather worked for the railroad. Not this one but another one, many years ago in Canada. Riding back and forth over hundreds of miles in a manually powered pushcart, he maintained a stretch of track in northern Saskatchewan. His job was to keep the line open for the grain and cattle trains that crossed the prairies.

"Poughkeepsie!" yells the conductor. He walks up the aisle, his change purse jangling. The whistle blows several times, short, long, then short again, and our train slows to stop.

More passengers board: a young girl in a summer dress and a backpack, an older woman rolling her luggage behind her. A man on the platform sits and stares, oblivious to the train's noisy intrusion. Soon we're moving again. Whistles sound: I imagine each one to be a coded message. The language of trains.

Grandpa's dream was to own land and be a farmer, but the only work he could find was for the Canadian National Railroad. Even the hard life of a farmer would have been easier than working for the railroad on the harsh Canadian prairie.

"Rhinecliff!" calls the conductor. Well-dressed people line up in the aisle, anxious to begin their weekends.

There was little difference between weekends and weekdays for my grandfather. My grandparents had fled revolutionary Russia, sailed across the North Atlantic from Riga, Latvia, to St. Johns, Newfoundland, where they were met by the railroad. The Canadian government was sending immigrants out west to settle in the prairie provinces. Everyone else from the ship was greeted by friends or relatives, but my grandparents and their three small children were alone. They didn't speak English. On the platform an official was calling out destinations and pointing to different trains. When "Saskatchewan" was called, Grandpa chose it because he liked the sound of it.

"Hudson in twenty minutes!" the conductor calls out, pointing toward the door at the far end of the car.

My grandfather bought his first farmland in Alberta, sight unseen. It flooded out before he could harvest it, a complete loss. My grandparents weren't able to try farming again until their children were grown. Well into their fifties, they purchased a small raspberry farm in British Columbia and labored there for the next thirty years. It was a meager living, but they were content. One side of the farm bordered a railroad track. At night, inside their small farmhouse, they could hear the trains rolling through the valley. Maybe that's why Grandpa bought that particular piece of land. He still liked the sound of the trains. He knew what the whistles meant.

Hearing rain, I look up and see droplets racing across the glass. The conductor sings out, "Beautiful, downtown, rainy Hudson!" End of my ride. Slowly rounding a long bend, the whistles blow, the train stops. Darkness has swallowed the river. In a misty, blue haze, I pack up my unread magazines and search the platform for a familiar face.

Profile

Peter Galperin is a graphic designer. Last fall he invited me to join him and his wife for a weekend at their house in the Berkshires. The morning after I arrived, I was sipping coffee on the deck with a view of a valley and a pond. Peter brought out his laptop computer and let me in on a little secret. He'd been writing stories.

This admission came as something of a surprise. Especially because I'd been his hired writing hand for all these years at his design firm in New York. He proceeded to read a few of the stories to me. They were economical, to the point—like Peter, direct and honest. What I saw in Peter that day is the kind of private glee writers get from the act of writing itself.

—Beck Lee

Bio

Peter Galperin
Place of residence: New York.
Grew up in: Everett, Washington.
Day job: Graphic designer.
Education: B.F.A., University of Washington.
Awards: Three-legged sack race championship team (1967).
Current project: Advertising campaign for a large Brazilian bank.
Favorite book: *Water Music* by T. Coraghessan Boyle.
Cravings: Simplicity, solitude, and cashews (unsalted).

Arun Gandhi

We Are the Problem

Growing violence in the United States and in the world must concern all of us. Little children shooting each other intentionally or accidentally. Little girls becoming mothers when they should be learning to play hopscotch. At thirteen and fourteen young people are becoming drug addicts or drug couriers. By fifteen they are planning their funerals. By eighteen many young people have accomplished more evil than many of us do in eighty years of our lives. Why?

Are young people irresponsible? Are they born evil? The fault is not entirely that of children. We adults have lost sight of our responsibilities. Fifty-one percent of our marriages break up—many are divorced several times. We are more concerned with our careers and our freedom than with love and respect for each other. Sex has become the most important ingredient in marriage and in life. There was a time when marriages were made to raise a family of whom parents would be proud. Parents not only gave birth to children but nurtured them and gave them a foundation on which to build their lives. Children were loved and family life was centered around their needs, their hopes, and their aspirations.

Marriages now appear to be centered on sexual compatibility. The issue of prime importance: How can we get the most enjoyable sexual experience? In the event sexual drive slows down, love dies. Seeking sex outside the marriage is no longer considered moral turpitude. For the most part children are regarded as unwelcome by-products of sex that have to be tolerated because they are living beings. We are now told by experts that we need be concerned about just two important issues in life: seeking physical pleasure and climbing material heights. Both must be achieved by any means possible.

When my generation of the 1930s and 1940s was growing up on Phoenix Farm, eighteen miles north of the city of Durban in South Africa, our parents focused our minds on constructive outdoor activities. For instance, our parents seldom bought us toys. My two sisters and I, and also our friends, had to make our own toys with what was available. There was a rivulet abutting our farm with black clay in the bed. My friends and I would dig for the clay under the supervision of my mother. We learned to make cars, bullock carts, horse carriages, and human forms. Sometimes we made miniature homes and farmhouses. When we wanted a change we would break up these models and make new ones.

When we grew up we made bigger toys. We would hunt the countryside for discarded wheelbarrows and salvage the wheels. When we had four of them we would find broken limbs of trees to fashion strong axles and a frame for our automobile. We would get discarded wooden planks to build the body and have great fun dragging the contraption up the hill and roaring back down.

Later still, my friends and I got interested in playing tennis. Our parents said we would have to build our own tennis courts. They would get us whatever we needed but we would have to provide the labor. We built three tennis courts at the homes of three friends. We did everything manually from leveling the ground, to digging holes for the posts, to laying the special clay under the supervision of an expert so that the top was smooth and level. We had to water the court and pull the heavy roller over it until the court was ready for use. And then we had to water and roll the court every Saturday so that we could play on Sunday. We even built our own little club house with bricks and mortar—everything from digging the foundation to nailing the roof. It was hard work but educational and entertaining at the same time.

We did have girlfriends and played with them too, but we were taught to respect them as human beings and not treat them as sex symbols. Besides, all the physical activity left us with little energy for any mischief. Young girls in those days did not become pregnant at today's rate. The thought of sexual intercourse, even if lurking in one's mind, was rarely implemented. Such a healthy respect for the opposite sex now seems like a Utopian dream.

Sexual activity today begins early, and girls are becoming mothers at twelve and thirteen. At a workshop on "Nonviolent Parenting," which my wife and I organized through the M.K. Gandhi Institute for Nonviolence in Memphis, there were more than 160 participants, a third of them teenagers. Several had given birth to two or three children before eighteen years of age. Most of them confessed that they had begun sexual activity at the age of eleven or twelve—soon after reaching puberty.

In modern times sex has become an obsession and the message from parents and from publicity is that there is no difference between a desire for sex and the desire for food. Both must be satiated immediately. There are fewer and fewer scruples attached to premarital sex. It is natural, it is physical, and—like animals in heat—humans must find an outlet for this urge. Consequently, children become parents before they learn what parenting is.

Teen sex is just one aspect of the violence we practice against each other. In 1946–47, when my parents traveled from South Africa to visit the family in India, I was twelve and spent most of my time with Grandfather, Mohandas K. Gandhi. I learned from him that violence in the human heart is multifaceted and is often practiced unknowingly. It is not just "physical" violence that should distress us but also "passive," or non-physical violence. Our suffering has many causes: the way we bring up our children; the things we do or don't do for them; the hate, prejudice, intolerance, anger, abuse; the suppression, the oppression, and the countless other ways in which "passive" violence has become a part of human nature. All of these aspects of our negligence add to the corrosion of our morals and ethics.

"Materialism," Grandfather said, "has an inverse relationship with morality. When one increases the other decreases." It is obvious that materialism today is in the ascendancy while morality has been consigned to the waste bin. Capitalism, materialism, market economy, the pursuit of one's goals, and the right to democratic privileges are wonderful goals but decidedly harmful when overindulged. For any society to be cohesive, rather than corrosive, we have all got to come together to knit a strong fabric. We are almost obsessively concerned about our rights in a democracy, but not all of us are willing to share the responsibility of making democracy healthy and viable. Grandfather taught me what he called the "Seven Sins of the World." They are: Wealth without Work, Pleasure without Conscience, Knowledge without Character, Commerce without Morality, Science without Humanity, Worship without Sacrifice, and Politics without Principles. Recently, I added the eighth "sin"—Rights without Responsibilities.

Understanding the extent of "passive" violence in our lives is the only way we can find solutions. It is not enough to know what ails us. We must also be aware of what caused the ailment if we are to find the right remedy. As part of my education under Grandfather, and later under my parents, I was required to draw a "family tree" of violence. On a large sheet of paper pinned on a wall at home I wrote down all the "physical" and "passive" acts of violence I experienced or practiced during the day. My sisters, Sita and Ela, and my parents would contribute their experiences too. This became an after-dinner, family exercise. Often, the family would debate our differing perceptions. The purpose of the "tree" was to educate us in all aspects of violence and its effects on human relationships at all levels from two friends to two nations. Whenever any of us had the time, we would study the tree to understand it better and discover for ourselves what is "right" and what is "wrong" in life.

In 1994, during the Renaissance Weekend in Hilton Head, North Carolina, I was amazed when a twenty-five-year-old university graduate confessed to me that she had stopped evaluating what is "right" and what is "wrong." Therefore, she explained, she could not determine what is "good" and what is "bad."

"Whose perception of right and wrong am I to follow?" she asked in all earnestness.

"What do you mean?" I asked. "It has to be your own perception."

Like several generations before and after her, she was confused because "right" and "wrong," "good" and "bad" have been linked to religion. Consequently, when one dominant religion tries to impose its interpretations upon others the tendency is to ignore morality altogether. The choice most people make is not to believe in anything. Morals, ethics, peace, justice, nonviolence, and a host of other values are not a prerogative of any one faith or denomination. They are common to all religions. As long as all religions honestly pursue "truth" they are equal and must be respected as such. His inter-faith prayer meetings were held every morning and evening. At most of them Grandfather's sermons would emphasize one idea: different religions are only different highways leading to the same point. Why should it matter to anyone what highway one chooses to take, so long as the destination is the same?

Religion is the means to ultimate salvation, not an end in itself. Among other things, religion should teach us respect for one's self and for one another whatever our gender, color, race, beliefs, and understanding. Is respect for life itself lacking? Do various religions of the world play the better-than-thou game? If so, what we are sowing in the minds of people is not love but hate, not understanding but suspicion, not respect but contempt.

When the two most important elements of society, the yin and the yang, have a love-hate relationship, how can the children be expected to grow up with understanding and respect? From our sexual relationships to our spiritual quest, our attitudes lack the very fundamental understanding of what is right and what is wrong. We may go to temples, mosques, churches, synagogues, and other places of worship ten times a day, every day of our lives, but salvation will elude us because our hearts remain full of hate and disrespect. If existence is all that living means to us, then we can be self-centered and selfish in our attitudes without any concern for anybody or anything. That's because, ultimately, we all have to die, and death, we believe, will put an end to existence. However, if we accept that death is only a transformation of life from one level to the next, then we will appreciate that life must be more meaningful. Only then will we reach out to the basics—understanding, compassion, love, and respect—and make them a part of our search for salvation.

Profile

I met Arun Gandhi in January 1995 at Southern Oregon State College in Ashland, Oregon, where he had been invited as the principal speaker for events commemorating Martin Luther King, Jr. Day. I began a busy day with him by sitting in on a sociology class on social stratification, where Gandhi cogently drew together the caste system in India, apartheid in South Africa, and racism in the United States.

"Merely passing laws is not going to help," Gandhi said. "What we need to do is change the attitudes of people."

I interviewed him that day, followed along as he took part in a broadcast for the local public radio affiliate, then heard him address a packed auditorium at the college. My article on Gandhi appeared in *The Christian Science Monitor* in February 1995.

Arun Gandhi grew up in South Africa, where he learned about hatred and violence first-hand. As a teenager, he spent 18 months in India living with his grandfather, Mohandas K. Gandhi. This experience at the side of the man who personified nonviolent resistance to oppression has shaped the younger Mr. Gandhi's remarkable career.

Following twenty-eight years as a journalist and author, during which time he and his wife Sunanda founded India's Center for Social Change to help the lives of poor villagers, Gandhi moved to the United States. Here he and his wife established the M.K. Gandhi Institute for Nonviolence in Memphis, Tennessee. As part of his work, Gandhi conducts classes and workshops on nonviolent conflict resolution.

In his speeches and writing, Gandhi stresses the need to address passive violence—anger, hatred, and prejudice—as well as the importance of personal responsibility for one's thinking and action. Along with poet Maya Angelou, civil rights veteran Rosa Parks, and anti-war activist David Dellinger, Gandhi has received the "Courage of Conscience Award" from the Peace Abbey in Sherborn, Massachusetts.

—Brad Knickerbocker

Bio

Arun Gandhi
Places of residence: South Africa. India. England.
Memphis, Tennessee.
Birthplace: Durban, South Africa.
Family: Grandson of "Gandhi."
Day job: Lecturer on nonviolence.
Education: Experiential.
Awards: Humanitarian Award from Memphis City Council. Courage of Conscience Award from Peace Abbey .

Current project: *Kasturba*—a book about my grandmother.
Favorite book: *On War and Morality* by Robert Holmes.
Belief: Oneness of creation.
Craving: Chocolate cake.

Jerome Gold

Reflections on *War Against War!*

I was not wounded in Vietnam but after I came home. It was an accident, something I was holding in my hands exploded. My flesh opened but did not bleed, at least not immediately. I could see bone and tendon in their pristine whiteness. Miraculously, I was not blinded.

In the years since, I have not been able to explain to my own satisfaction what it was that seeing part of my skeleton meant to me. I know the bit about facing my mortality, I've heard it a thousand times. That isn't it. Shortly after beginning my tour in Southeast Asia, I recognized that I would not live through the year. While obviously I did, that kind of deep-penetrating fatalism has not left me. Death is the natural state, life the anomaly. I've not been able to uncover an argument to convince me otherwise.

So the issue is not one of mortality. Rather, it has to do with disfigurement. Not the stark fact of disfigurement, but with witnessing a thing that parodies life. In this case, what I saw was some of my internal works: the parody came from the knowledge that they were part of me. I was still alive but I had no control over this thing that was happening to my body.

All of this is by way of introducing *War Against War!* by Ernst Friedrich. The first time I saw this book was on a perusing trip to the University Book Store in Seattle. I had never heard of it, never seen a review of it. I think the illustration on the cover is what drew me. The drawing shows a soldier overcome by what I assume is remorse at having just killed another soldier, presumably his enemy. There is more to the illustration but the remorse is what attracted me. When I got blown up, one or two people accused me of having done it to myself, so guilty did I feel at having survived the war when most of my friends had not. Perhaps so, perhaps not. Memory is selective and there is such a thing as survivor's guilt. Still . . .

So I picked up the book and flipped through it, beginning at the rear. It is at the rear that the most horrible of the photographs are. I do not want to take away from their impact, should you see them, so I am not going to describe them in detail. I want to say, though, that the worst of them are of men who, at least physically, survived their wounds. That is, they were alive when the photos were taken following the end of World War I.

Since seeing these photographs for the first time I have thought much about the time I spent in an army hospital. I've written about parts of it in my novel, *The Negligence of Death,* but I don't think I captured the appreciation of the enduring damage that a wound can visit on the human body. Even the smallest of affronts leaves permanent effects. I suspect that because most of us Americans have been removed from the scenes of combat—I do not mean motion picture or television scenes, but those the movies or TV pretend to represent—for so long, war not having been fought on US soil for many generations, that we tend to believe that the professions of medicine and pharmacology can make everything better, that is, as it was before the injury.

In my own case, apart from the scarring, I lost most of the sense of touch in my left hand. A minor loss, really. A friend was shot in his right shoulder. He lost the use of the middle and ring fingers of his right hand. Probably not a major loss. One bullet did it. Another bullet took away the entire left arm of another man. Granted, it was a larger bullet, or maybe a ricochet, than the one that severed the nerves in the shoulder of the first man. In the movies I grew up on, these would be called "flesh wounds." When a character had a flesh wound, he winced, gritted his teeth, and continued fighting. Sometimes he limped for a few frames if he had a leg wound.

The photos in *War Against War!* show what can be done to the human face. Facial wounds are the worst to view because we see our own faces reflected in others. The idea of parody again comes into play here. The faces shown in these photographs are our faces as they might have been or may yet be. It is mostly luck, I believe, that determines who will lose his life or his arm or his eyes. Once we are committed to war, we as individuals have little to say about what befalls us.

War Against War! is propaganda. It does not pretend to be anything but propaganda. Originally published in 1924, it was a response to World War I, to Europe's making of itself an abattoir. The book was intended to help build an antiwar movement. It is anti-nationalist, anti-capitalist, and pro-socialist. In the light of all that we as a species have done to one another since the first world war, I have to consider the author naive. In the late twentieth century, it is apparent that the socialist countries are not less bloody-minded than the capitalist ones. Such a strong ideological statement as Friedrich presents in his introduction to the book will have the effect of reaffirming the common stance of those who already believe in socialism but, I suspect, will alienate those who do not.

War Against War! is much too important a book to be given over to ideological factionalism. The photographs speak honestly to all people regardless of class, nationality, or political prejudice. This book deserves the attention of every person who can think or feel.

Profile

I met Jerome Gold in October 1988. I had gotten a call from Stephanie (a woman who, several years later, would emerge as the dramatist S.P. Miskowski). Stephanie was editing an issue of Seattle's *Literary Center Quarterly* (later called *Upstream*) and wanted me to write a profile of Jerry Gold. What had Jerry done that was so special? Jerry was a novelist who had a pile of unpublished manuscripts, including a Vietnam war novel that he called *The Negligence of Death.* While the rest of us were flogging our manuscripts around New York and whining the whole time, Jerry had taken action: he founded Black Heron Press.

In 1984 Jerry had been broke and in graduate school and without any visible means of support. A good time to start a publishing company, Jerry decided. So he teamed up with Les Galloway, an older writer whose unpublished novel, *Forty Fathom Bank,* was a fantastic piece of writing. Jerry and Les scraped together a few shekels. But what of the technical complexities involved in book production? That's where Everett D. Greimann came in.

In 1969 Greimann had opened Bozotronics on North 36th in Fremont. Bozotronics specialized in the repair of amps, sound systems, electronic keyboards, and guitars. Its logo, painted ten-feet high in green on the side of the building, featured a big, shaggy, dog-pound dog panting out from beneath a tag that read: "Bozo." In 1979 Greimann bought an Itek quadratek photo typesetter—one of the first computerized typesetting machines—and set up Dataprose as a separate business upstairs from Bozotronics. Greimann supported himself with commercial work and then made his expertise available to local poets and novelists at cut rates. Fremont in those years was a haven for artists, slowly aging hippies, drugsters, and penniless poets who hung out at the Still Life in Fremont coffee house and at Yak's deli where you could get a pile of teriyaki chicken on rice for a dollar.

In 1984 Jerry did not have a desktop publishing system, but he had Everett. And Everett did more than typeset: he guided the young publisher through the shoals of book production, advised him on printers, paper, artwork. Contemporary desktop publishers, looking back, may regard this as a golden era. Now that desktop publishers all have Pagemaker, FreeHand, and Photoshop, paradise is lost. We can do it all—by ourselves, at home, at night. So we never get any sleep. And we have to keep pouring out thousands of dollars for upgrades each year. And we get edu-stress from forcing ourselves to learn printing presses, dot gain, screen angles, paper, ink, type, page design, film, Iris prints, press match proofs, comps, separations, and all other manner of interesting, exhausting arcana.

Four years later Jerry was working for the Census Bureau, counting houses and people. The other sixteen hours of his day were divied up minute by minute, each parcel of time devoted to a publishing task or reserved for those few, inescapable lost hours that human beings must devote to eating, sleeping, and commuting to work. Jerry's was an incredible regimen which he kept up week after week for years at a time. The results: in seven years Jerry published twelve books, including *Infra* by Seattle writer Ron Dakron and a historical novel about the English peasant revolt: *The Confession of Jack Straw* by Simone Zelitch.

In March 1994 I got back in touch with Jerry. I had questions, he had answers: Cune Press was the result. By now Black Heron Press had achieved one "bestseller": *When Bobby Kennedy Was a Moving Man* by Robert Gordon.

Jerry was doing final edits on *Publishing Lives*—interviews with Northwest publishers, a hymnal for grassroots publishing. Jerry was working with children in an institution for juvenile felons. More satisfying work than his earlier gig, but one which left him exhausted. Hence the contradiction that is Jerry Gold: he'll talk to you for hours, giving all kinds of helpful advice, an Everett Griemann for our times. On another day Jerry will be clipped, inaccessible, rude: parceling out his time, facing hours of work with only minutes at his command, worried, probably a little panicked, definitely unavailable.

Since 1994 our nation's major presses have collapsed. By that I mean they largely have lost their ability to discern good writing that will appeal to the public and to edit it into shape—they have degenerated into distribution and marketing machines. Now large presses cruise regional bookfairs looking for self-published titles to snatch up. The grassroots publishing movement is exploding. And Jerome Gold is looking more and more like a man who was ahead of his time.

—Scott C. Davis

Bio

Jerome Gold
Place of residence: Seattle.
Birthplace: Chicago.
Grew up in: Attended highschool in Southern California.
Day job: Juvenile rehabilitation counselor.
Education: B.A. in history, M.A. in anthropology, University of Montana. Ph.D. in anthropology, University of Washington.
Books: *Publishing Lives: Interviews with Independent Book Publishers in the Pacific Northwest and British Columbia. The Negligence of Death. The Prisoner's Son.*
Awards: For *Publishing Lives:* Bumbershoot Book Award (1996).
Current projects: Short stories, a novel, another nonfiction project. Editing two books for publication.
Favorite book: *A Farewell to Arms* by Ernest Hemingway.
Comment: I pity the human being who doesn't read.

Jan Haag

Manzanar

In 1944, Ansel Adams made one of his most famous scenic photographs—it's of Mt. Williamson, a neighboring peak of California's highest, Mt. Whitney, in the Sierra Nevada. Adams, still a young man but already making a reputation as a premier nature photographer, set up his tripod on his car's rooftop platform. From the floor of the Owens Valley, he shot west toward the mountains, but he also turned his camera east into the Manzanar War Relocation Camp.

A friend of camp director Ralph P. Merritt, Adams was one of the few outside photographers allowed to document the lives of the ten thousand ethnic Japanese kept behind barbed wire by government decree. As the United States battled Japan during World War II, many of Manzanar's residents lived for more than three years surrounded by eight armed-guard towers.

Adams was not allowed to photograph those guard towers or give any hint that the people there were, in fact, prisoners. His book documenting Manzanar, *Born Free and Equal,* made an eloquent statement against the imprisonment of innocent people. In that book, he also envisioned life after the war.

"When all the occupants of Manzanar have resumed their places in the stream of American life," Adams wrote, "these flimsy buildings will vanish, the greens and the flowers . . . will wither, the old orchards will grow older, remnants of paths, foundations, and terracing will gradually blend unto the stable texture of the desert."

I traveled to Manzanar, one of ten such relocation camps, fifty years after the camp closed. I was accompanied by a photographer who wanted to find the site of Adams' photos. I hoped to see what was left of those temporary residents who made the inhospitable land home for a time.

Here is what I saw:

Two stone sentry houses at the entrance, with names painted on the wooden frames over the doors and windows. One said: Haji Moto/Blk. 26-6-3/1-1-86—a former internee's barrack and the date he returned. Inside, more names were scratched into the rock walls: Tsukumura, Kitabayashi, T. Hazama, E. Segawa, Fukura, Hashimoto. . . .

Near the front of the camp, a round stone wall that perhaps once surrounded a tidy garden. Now partially covered by thistles, words neatly carved into concrete read: Built by Wada and Crew, June 10, 1943 A.D.

A well-kept cemetery with only a few marked graves and a white obelisk constructed by camp residents in 1943 that reaches twenty feet into the sky. Black *kanji* (Japanese characters) declare: Memorial to the Dead.

The photographer and I drove past the cemetery, past the camp's barbed wire, and toward Mt. Williamson. Where did Ansel Adams place his tripod to catch the mountain under winter storm clouds? Now summer clouds, high and fluffy white, showed no signs of rain. We kept our eyes to the west, looking for the huge boulders in the foreground of Adams' picture.

Then, I spotted a gully running north. "Stop!" I yelled. I saw something in the hollow, something that gleamed bright white. I rolled down the window.

"Their dishes?" I asked the desert.

"Can't be," said my companion.

I ran from the car, turned over pieces of white and beige crockery, and found what I was looking for. TEPCO, read one piece: U.S.A. CHINA. I knew that name; the Tepco company made china for restaurants well into the 1960s. My mind flew to Sacramento, hundreds of miles away, where identical 1930s and 1940s dishes rested in my china cabinet. It was—it had to be—remains of their dishes.

We stepped carefully over the shards, picking up pieces and handling them like antiques. A piece read: USQMC, Jan. 6, 1936—from the Army Quartermaster's Corps. One fragment with a medical insignia proclaimed in red: United States Army Medical Department. One read, with quiet irony: Made in Japan.

"Who dumped the dishes?" we wondered aloud as we kept driving. Eventually we found the field of boulders where Adams made his famous photo.

The next day in Independence, a few miles from Manzanar, we visited the Eastern Sierra Museum and found other camp memorabilia—paintings and furniture made in camp, a reproduction of the camp sign, a record player. A cardboard box cradled a square-shaped piece of wood. A handwritten note identified the square as the pitcher's plate for Manzanar's baseball diamond: "found in 1985 by Hank Umemoto in its original place after forty-three years."

And encased in glass were white dishes—a cup and saucer and dinner plate. I peered through the case to look at the undersides. TEPCO, they said, all of them.

I fondled the small piece of crockery I'd saved from the pile, Adams' views of Mt. Williamson and the camp residents in my head. I could not leave without a piece of their dishes—my dishes—pieces of those lives alive in my hand.

Profile

I remember a brief trendy period in Jan Haag's life. She was the editor of *Sacramento Magazine*. Hair streaked blonde, she wore dark hose and pumps with her red wool suits and went networking.

Jan had all the flashy skills of a practicing journalist, editor, and writer, so why not try the look? And a great look it was. But it lasted less than a year. Before long the blonde streaks grew out. Her jeans and crepe-soled shoes came back. By then she was teaching—but still networking, raising funds for *Susurrus*, the literary magazine she'd started at Sacramento City College. She was writing *Louie, Louie,* her novel-in-progress. Last week we met for coffee at Greta's in midtown, a building painted blue on the outside, mustard yellow walls and dusty trees inside. The afternoon sun poured in on us, long after the lunch crowd had come and gone. In that hazy golden afterlight, I knew that the look might change again, but not the lady behind the look. She'll write the novel. She'll produce the magazine. The phrase for Jan Haag? She just does it.

—Constance Warloe

Bio

Jan Haag

Place of residence: Sacramento.

Birthplace: Long Beach, California.

Grew up in: Roseville, California.

Day job: Teaching journalism and writing at Sacramento City College.

Education: B.A. in journalism and creative writing; M.A. in English and journalism, California State University at Sacramento.

Serial publications: *Sacramento Magazine. Sacramento News and Review.*

Anthology: *I've Always Meant to Tell You: Letters to Our Mothers* (edited by Constance Warloe, Pocket Books).

Awards: Fellowship for Literary Artists in Arts Education, Sacramento Metropolitan Arts Council (1996). First Class Girl Scout (1975). Most Improved Percussionist, Oakmont High School, Roseville, California (1972).

Current projects: A novel, *Louie, Louie.* Raising funds for *Susurrus,* a literary journal at Sacramento City College.

Favorite book: *Psmith Journalist* by P.G. Wodehouse.

Craving: Mrs. Field's chocolate/macadamia nut cookies.

Within the image: "© JOSEPH BRANCHCOMBE 1996", "PORTRAIT OF JAMES E. HALL"

James Hall

I, Pterodactyl

I've worked at San Quentin prison for twelve years. I never really wanted to work here. Like most guards, I just needed the money.

The old timers used to say, "San Quentin never changes." What a lie. The history of San Quentin is nothing but change. At times, a day feels like a month. A month feels like a career. The tall yellow walls may still look the same. And the massive six-story housing units that look out over San Francisco Bay haven't changed too much. But the way the place is run—the feeling once you've gone through all five security gates and are inside the main walls—that's changed.

Some old guards saw it coming. I remember one sergeant saying, "We're all becoming a bunch of clerk-typists." Maybe he was right. Personally, I'd rather type than fight. Maybe that's why I'm still around. The prison guards are gone. We're all "correctional officers" now. Well-groomed, bright-eyed, and surprisingly literate professionals. This fact hit home, again, the last time I visited Donner Section.

Donner Section is one of four housing units that make up San Quentin's South Block. It's easy to find. After being admitted through the pedestrian sallyport gates, just walk across the plaza, take a left at the adjustment center, continue the full length of the upper yard, take a right to the South Block rotunda, turn left, and you're there.

Contrary to current etiquette, I banged my old, unpolished black boot hard against the steel door a couple of times. Habit. Used to be, you'd kick the door and wait. Eventually some brute of a prison guard with two days' growth would sneer at you through the scratched-up Plexiglas. His reason for peering out before opening the door was security, of course. But he was also checking to see if you were somebody important—somebody whose presence might be vital intelligence to the other apes in the unit.

That day I heard the jingling of keys almost immediately. A couple seconds later the lock clicked and the door slowly swung out. Before me stood a smiling, five foot two inch, 100 pound correctional officer. She was adorable. I knew the inmates thought so too. In the 1980s we shared an in-house joke that San Quentin recruited its guards outside liquor stores. Not this one. A modeling agency maybe. Or a pageant. But I suppressed my urge to gawk, managed a weak smile, and lumbered past. I felt young and nimble, like a triceratops.

Donner Section. My old proving ground. The place was immaculate. Quiet. Climate-controlled. And Broadway—the main floor of the building—was spotless. Only thing it lacked was some damn ferns.

The cute, young correctional officer walked up next to me and asked a question. But I continued to stare down the long, narrow housing unit: a cement shoe box set on one side. On the left, five stories of empty space rose above Broadway. The gunwalk jutted out from the wall and ran the length of the unit, slicing into the space at the third story. On the right, five tiers of fifty cages faced out, toward the void and the gunwalk.

I remembered standing there twelve years ago, gazing upon a preview of hell. The stench of gutters clogged with rotting food and standing water slowly replaced the fresh air in my lungs. Broadway was buried under six inches of trash—thrown from the tiers. The din of blaring radios, TVs, and grown men yelling to each other from inside their locked houses engulfed normal conversation. Waterfalls caused by convicts flooding their cells cascaded from the higher tiers down onto the lower tiers and eventually onto Broadway, soaking the trash. And the haze of smoke from small, smoldering fires blurred the entire scene, making it ghostly and strangely appealing.

The young woman next to me saw none of it, and probably felt none of my apprehension, no urge to look behind her. A few men in clean blue shirts and jeans pushed brooms and walked calmly in and out of their cells on the first tier.

In 1984, we had gangs on every tier. Whites on five, Mexican mafia on four, *Nuestra Familia* on three, and Crips on two. The inmates were supposedly locked up, but it didn't matter. They made knives, spears, zip guns, and match bombs. And if they ran out of weapons, they hurled piss or boiling water.

But the truth is, a lot of the time, it struck me as a giant party. I remember once, while sweeping the trash on Broadway, an inmate yelled, "Man, you like this shit, don't you?" It seemed ridiculous, but I did like it. I liked pushing a broom to Tower of Power. I liked feeding the white boys dinner to Led Zeppelin. I liked hearing every northern Mexican crank up his box for "96 Tears." And I liked laughing with the other long-haired scraggly guards about some off-the-wall thing that this inmate said or that officer did. This was "the hole." Conformity to the rules and the assumptions of the department stopped at that big steel door.

But then one of the gangs went too far. They speared a sergeant in the chest. Killed him. Just like a damn Tarzan movie. Overnight, things began to change. Money poured into the system. The gang bangers were split up and shipped out to modern prisons. The crazy old guards who couldn't conform were driven out. And the result was before us. Antiseptic. Orderly. Quiet. Everything in compliance to a rule. Every cop out of the same cookie cutter.

I looked again at the young woman. She was earnest, optimistic, eager to do the right thing. I wondered, "Did I look that way when I drove up to the big house?" And then I thought to myself, "Old man—just keep it inside."

Profile

I got to know James Hall at Dominican College, a venerable Catholic institution in San Rafael. He was the quiet type—or so I thought. It was the first night of our second semester and those of us in a business class had just been divided into groups of four for a project.

I was in Jim's group, along with my aunt and a beefy weight lifter. At the ten-minute break, Jim looked our way and said, "How about some coffee?"

"Sure," I said.

"In ten minutes?" My aunt was concerned, but followed us out to Jim's van—dark-tinted windows, black bumpers, gray carpet—more like Darth Vader burning up Hollywood and Vine, than Jim's persona in class.

Jim's driving reinforced the image. After he ran the first red light, my aunt turned her swivel chair so it faced backwards. I prayed she wouldn't have a heart attack. The weight lifter gripped the dash. We forgot about the project.

For me, I didn't mind—this escapade felt like we were back in high school cutting class. And Jim was more animated than I had ever seen him. When he screeched to a halt in front of the Royal Grounds—the local java hangout—he actually spoke. "Give me a Double Depth Charger," he said. I ordered herbal tea. The weight lifter went for a latte. My aunt asked for the bathroom.

Inside of ten minutes, we were sitting back in class. I glanced at Jim, and he looked as quiet and unobtrusive as ever. The only clue to the other side of his persona was that steaming Depth Charge on his desk.

—Sabrina Smith

Bio

James Hall
Place of residence: Forest Knolls, Marin County, California.
Birthplace: Portland, Maine.
Grew up in: Cape Elizabeth, Maine.
Day job: Correctional officer, San Quentin State Prison.
Education: B.S. in business administration, Dominican College.
Current project: Applying to graduate school in law or creative writing.
Favorite book: *Trinity* by Leon Uris.
Belief: In flux.
Cravings: Beer, recognition, laughter.
Interest: Great sots of the twentieth century.

Nathalie Handal

Boston Yellow Cabs

I feel most at home when I am sitting in a Boston Yellow Cab. The ride from Logan airport to my apartment in that yellow cab brings me peace. It calms even the echoes of my breathing.

Every time I travel, I am comforted knowing I will be welcomed in a yellow cab. My addresses change, the concierge changes, the furniture changes, the bed sheets change, and even I change, but the yellow cabs are still yellow. I open those heavy doors, sit on those bouncing back seats, and feel a sense of relief. It's like trying to convince myself that if one day I am lost, at least, I'll find a piece of myself in one of these cabs. . . .

I was sitting in a yellow cab going to the airport to fly to Iowa. Isn't there always a time for Iowa? *Maybe not.* Most people I spoke to asked me with their eyebrows rising, their foreheads wrinkling, "Why are you going there?" To begin with, I was invited by my friend Nastasia, who is Bulgarian and happened to be working in Iowa City. And why not Iowa?

Nastasia picked me up at the airport in Cedar Rapids. She had been in Iowa one month and had already gotten used to driving there, not that one needed any real time to know one's way around. Anyhow, after driving in Beirut or Paris, where she had lived, pretty much anything was possible. We had met at a Lebanese Cultural Gala two years before, in France. Since then the two of us kept in touch. We had gone to where I am originally from, Palestine. Then we went to Boston, and now we were in Nastasia's Jeep Cherokee driving in the pig state.

Before the sun departed, it gave us a majestic golden orange horizon with red waves in the middle of the skyline. We were driving through fields, and I felt like I was entering a yellow kingdom. I had never experienced such unity of earth and sky. As it grew darker, I also realized that I had never really been in the night. An absolute silence, a sense that all is resting or gone . . . when only stars and moon remain. It was so dark that I could hardly see the road. It was so quiet that I was afraid to listen to the whistling of the heater, afraid that my thoughts were too loud. Nights exist in Iowa.

At one point, I asked Nastasia where we were going. Iowa City was only thirty minutes from the airport, and we had been driving for an hour. She told me we were going somewhere else for the evening and that it was a surprise. I was impatiently waiting to see whether that somewhere had electricity or moonlight. She suddenly turned left into a slightly dusty, narrow road. We drove for about five minutes, and there, in the middle of emptiness, stood a house with lights. Nastasia parked in the front driveway, we walked to the house, she opened the door, and five people stood up. "Welcome, welcome," they all said at once. They spoke with a heavy midwestern accent. I was a bit confused but relieved to have finally arrived. "It sure is good to be here," I said.

In middle America, in a remote corner, surrounded by fields, I met a Palestinian family. There was Nessim, his wife, Marie, and their three children. Nessim was born in Palestine and immigrated to America in the 1950s. He first lived in Michigan where he met Marie, who was a student. They eventually moved to Marie's home state, Iowa. After their marriage, Nessim got accustomed to life in America and didn't want to go back to the instability in the Holy Land.

Marie and the children had slight knowledge of the Middle East—only what they saw in the news, what they read in the newspaper, and what Nessim had told them. But he had been away for forty years. Time and circumstances had created a large space between him and his family in Palestine. His parents had passed away, and he didn't know where his only brother was. What was left of their Arabic heritage could be summarized in one word—food. They surely knew how to cook Arabic food.

While we ate, we talked. I told them of a land far away, yet close in the way it could still breathe around them, a memory, but a memory still strong enough to survive. I played the Arabic cassette I had with me. They loved the rhythm of the music. The youngest daughter was particularly excited. As Nastasia and I danced, she naturally followed. I observed Nessim, he was crying. They were lost tears, tears put away for many years that had finally found a window. I felt saddened by his expression. Was it regret or melancholy? The evening ended with the final note of the last song on my cassette. It was difficult to leave. There where hugs and kisses and a crying laughter which I didn't want to hear.

When I got to Boston I sat in a yellow cab and closed the heavy door. Once again, I had changed a little. I felt a void. My moment in that cab, however, remained the same. The yellow cab filled the empty corners of my heart. By the time I got to my apartment, my yellow ride had already helped me return, return but not forget.

Profile

She's a riddle. Nathalie Handal officially lives in Boston but she calls from Paris, tells you about her last trip to Spain and her next trip to Jordan—like the impossible homeland, her address is unattainable. One is sure to receive her letters, mailed from here and there, anywhere, everywhere on a planet that occasionally accepts her feet to stand. Whether doing literary research, writing, or acting as public relations person, she is devoted to all she undertakes. And one can never forget the way she moves her hands, head, and body to explain something; one can never forget her zest for life.

We are doomed the moment we go beyond the surface of her words, for we become captives of a voice that creeps into us. East and West, *abayas* and jackets, *kaffiahs* and hats, a Palestine deeply rooted in civilization, and an unquiet, newly invented America.

I met her in Al-Kashkool Bookshop in London, *the never field* (that's the name of her long poem) and the whole field. Longing but content, calm but full of life, present but distant. Her opposite sides often come all at once—the contrast between her inner and outer self forms the portrait of a poetic character. Whenever you turn you will find her, or maybe not.

If you want to know her name just turn the page upside down.

—Lina Tibi

Bio

Nathalie Handal

Places of residence: Boston and Paris.

Grew up in: Boston, Europe, and the Caribbean.

Day job: Poet, essayist, and literary researcher.

Education: B.A. in international relations, M.A. in English and literature, Simmons College, Boston, Massachusetts.

Serial publications: *Graffiti Rag. Visions-International. Involution. En Plein Air.* Poetry.

Current projects: Editing *Modern Arabic Women Poets* (an anthology). Editing *Arab-American Literature* (an anthology). Giving lectures and/or presenting papers on Arab-American poetry in Paris, Jordan, California, Rhode Island, and Malaysia.

Forthcoming book: My poetic sequence *the never field* will be published by The Post-Apollo Press in 1997.

Favorite books: *Memory for Forgetfulness: August, Beirut, 1982* by Mahmoud Darwish and *The Double Flame* by Octavio Paz.

Languages: I speak French, Spanish, and Arabic.

Cravings: Dark chocolate and definitely coffee, coffee, and more coffee.

Pastimes: Traveling, reading, listening to opera, and going to good restaurants.

Favorite thing to do: Stare out into space and let my mind wander.

Beliefs: Peace, equality, and lots of freedom.

❖

Václav Havel

The Quiver of a Shrub in California

In my country forests are dying, rivers resemble open sewers, people are sometimes advised not to open their windows, and television advertises gas masks for children to wear on their way to and from school. Mine is a small country in the middle of Europe where the borders between fields have been destroyed, the land is eroding, the soil is disintegrating and poisoned by chemical fertilizers that in turn contaminate the groundwater, where birds that used to live in the fields have lost their nesting places and are dying out, while agronomists are forced to combat pests with more chemicals. My country supplies the whole of Europe with a strange export: sulfur dioxide.

For years I was one of those who criticized all this; now, I am one of those who are criticized for it.

When I think about what has brought about this terrible state of affairs and encounter on a daily basis obstacles that keep us from taking quick action to change it, I cannot help concluding that its root causes are less technical or economic in nature than philosophical. For what I see in Marxist ideology and the communist pattern of rule is an extreme and cautionary instance of the arrogance of modern man, who styles himself the master of nature and the world, the only one who understands them, the one everything must serve, the one for whom our planet exists. Intoxicated by the achievements of his mind, by modern science and technology, he forgets that his knowledge has limits and that beyond these limits lies a great mystery, something higher and infinitely more sophisticated than his own intellect.

I am increasingly inclined to believe that even the term "environment," which is inscribed on the banners of many commendable civic movements, is in its own way misguided, because it is unwittingly the product of the very anthropocentrism that has caused extensive devastation of our earth. The word "environment" tacitly implies that whatever is not human merely envelops us and is therefore inferior to us, something we need care for only if it is in our interest to do so. I do not believe this to be the case. The world is not divided into two types of being, one superior and the other merely surrounding it. Being, nature, the universe—they are all one infinitely complex and mysterious metaorganism of which we are but a part, though a unique one.

Everyone of us is a crossroads of thousands of relations, links, influences, and communications—physical, chemical, biological, and others of which we know nothing. While without humans there would have been no *Challenger* space shuttle, there would have been no humans without air, water, earth, without thousands of fortitudes that cannot be fortuitous and thanks to which there can be a planet on which there can be life. And while each of us is a very special and complex network of space, time, matter, and energy, we are nothing more than their network; we are unthinkable without them, and without the order of the universe, whose dimensions they are.

None of us knows how the quiver of a shrub in California affects the mental state of a coal miner in North Bohemia or how his mental state affects the quivering of the shrub. I believe that we have little chance of averting an environmental catastrophe unless we recognize that we are not the masters of Being, but only a part of Being, and it makes little difference that we are the only part of Being known so far that is not only conscious of its own being but is even conscious of the fact that it will one day come to an end.

Profile

How can a playwright succeed as president? Václav Havel, president of the Czech Republic, has done just fine. Why? The secret is this: playwrights and presidents must do the same two things—listen to many voices and synthesize those voices.

Václav Havel was a political dissident, prisoner, and playwright before becoming president of Czechoslovakia in 1989. He has devoted his life to fighting against the Communist regime and defending human rights. His 1965 play, *The Memorandum,* satirizes the dehumanizing effects of bureaucratic language. In the play a memorandum proposes a more efficient language in which words are as dissimilar from each other as possible. The result is a breakdown in communication, complete gibberish. Was this play a send up of Soviet bureaucracy and the quisling regime in Czechoslovakia? Apparently the regime thought so. Three years later all of Havel's plays were banned.

In the 1970s, Havel was arrested and jailed for his human rights activism. He continued to write plays that he couldn't sell or produce, and survived by stacking barrels in a brewery. He sent his writing abroad, and in 1977 the regime charged him with "subversion of the public." During his years of protest, Havel never sought political power. In *Summer Meditations* (1992) he wrote, "With no embarrassment, no stage fright, no hesitation, I did everything I had to do."

As president, Havel has reduced his country's dependence on its arms industry and has worked to protect human rights. Among his more serendipitous ties to the West: he appointed musician Frank Zappa to the Ministry of Culture for a brief time, causing outrage in the conservative community.

I always thought a playwright would make a good president.

—Krista Koontz

Bio

Václav Havel
Place of residence: Prague, Czech Republic.
Birthplace: Prague, Czechoslovakia.
Day job: President.
Family: The son of a building contractor and restauranteur. In 1964 he married Olga Splíchalová. Olga was active in dissident activities during the Communist era. She passed away in January 1996. Václav has one brother, Ivan, who is a specialist in artificial intelligence.

House: A four-story art nouveau brownstone apartment building constructed by Václav's father on the east bank of the Vltava River in Prague.

Education: Due to his "bourgeoise" background, Václav's options for higher education were limited. He attended the Czech Technical University in Prague (1955–57). After completing his compulsory military service, he worked as a stagehand at the ABC Theatre in Prague. From 1962 to 1966 Václav studied dramaturgy at the Academy of Performing Arts in Prague.

Plays: More than twenty. *The Garden Party* (1963). *The Increased Difficulty of Concentration* (1968). *Temptation* (1985).

Books: Monograph on painter Joseph Capek (1963). *Slum Clearance* (1987).

Awards: More than ten major awards. The President's Award, PEN Center USA West (1990). Honorary degree, Columbia University (1990).

Beliefs: Postmodern science that fosters self-transcendence, as in the Gaia hypotheses (first stated in 1972 by English thinker James Lovelock). Also in the anthropic cosmological principle, originally enunciated by English physicist Brandon Carter in 1974.

Most historic season: The Prague Spring. Václav was active in Prague political and cultural life during the era of reforms which ended with the Warsaw Pact invasion in August 1968.

Most important signature: Charter 77, a human rights manifesto, signed by Václav and 273 other Czechoslovakian revolutionaries in 1977. The manifesto charged the Czech regime with violations of the Helsinki Accords. Václav was one of three spokesmen for the Charter 77 movement and served as a member of the Committee for the Defense of the Unjustly Prosecuted, founded by a group of Charter 77 signatories.

Best writing while under house arrest: In 1978 Václav wrote "The Power of the Powerless," one of his most influential essays.

Underground publisher: As part of his resistance to the regime, Václav was active in the Czechoslovak samizdat press. While Václav was in prison his wife Olga produced and disseminated samizdat materials.

The fall: In November 1989, Václav became one of the leaders of the Civic Forum opposition movement which helped bring about the end of Communist rule.

Two elections: On December 29, 1989, Václav was elected President of Czechoslovakia. On January 26, 1993, he was elected the President of the Czech Republic.

Favorite 1960s American rock bands: Andy Warhol's Velvet Underground. Frank Zappa's Mothers of Invention.

Kurt Hoelting

Dreaming of Salmon

I grew up by the shores of Puget Sound, dreaming of salmon. My childhood summers were spent on Liberty Bay, in a cabin near Poulsbo. It's where my strongest memories were wrought. Winters were passed somewhere in the confusion of the city. But with school's ending each spring, we made a bee-line for the cabin, and life began again. From earliest memory the waters of the sound pulled me to them as inexorably as the tide.

There was magic in those waters, and nothing held more power in my imagination than the elusive salmon. My father worked in the city right through the summer and had no interest in fishing, so I did the best I could, drop line in hand, working my way up the ladder from bullheads to sea perch to dogfish—always dreaming, dreaming of salmon. I read books about salmon, drew pictures of them in fine detail, plotted endlessly and fruitlessly to lure one onto my hook. My brother was almost always with me when we went in search of salmon. Yet only once, in all those youthful summers, did we actually approach our quarry. Trolling a spinner behind our rowboat, with dusk coming on, my brother hooked what could only have been a salmon. His pole nearly jumped from the boat, line singing off the reel. In one majestic run, the fish stripped the reel, snapped the line, and was gone.

To this day, the memory haunts me. It's part of the enduring lore of our family.

We never did catch a salmon in Puget Sound. Nor did we suspect how many had already been lost. No one told us about the Elwha River kings that commonly reached 100 pounds, or the Quinault River sockeye that were coveted by Indian tribes in trade up and down the coast, all gone. We didn't hear tales of Graywolf pinks, Soleduck summer coho, Satsop steelhead, Skokomish chums. No one was there to tell us.

We knew little, and understood less, about the true stature of salmon in the ecological and cultural heritage of our region. But we knew our own yearnings. And the tenacity of our efforts to catch a salmon for ourselves, however futile, was testimony to the power of this astonishing creature. Our lives were shaped in part by the strength of the encounter, even if this encounter occurred only in our imaginations. Years later, as a college student working on a salmon seiner in southeast Alaska, I finally caught salmon myself. I also witnessed the spectacle of wild salmon returning to their streams in huge numbers. In a place far to the north, I caught a glimpse of the lost legacy of my native Puget Sound. Year after year, through college and graduate school, I left the sound to head north for the salmon-rich waters of Alaska during the summer, "just one more time."

Somewhere along the way I figured out that this annual migration was my life, not merely a prelude to a "real" job in the city.

This summer will be my twenty-fifth season fishing in Alaska. The passing years have done little to diminish my enthusiasm for catching salmon or for being present at the return of the world's last great wild runs. But I am more reflective now, more aware of the tragic ironies that pit one region against another, healthy runs against threatened runs, wild salmon against their genetic step-cousins from the pen. These ironies offer themselves now as a metaphor for our times, a poignant case study in our efforts to rethink the place of human beings in the natural world. For me, the contrasts are jarring. The last two seasons in Bristol Bay, for example, have each seen returns of over forty million sockeye salmon, making them the first and third largest runs on record. When the Bristol Bay fishery dies down in late July, I travel to the southeast Alaskan panhandle to purse seine for pink salmon. With returns of over fifty million pinks the last two seasons, these numbers are breaking century-old records at just the time when once-great runs to the south are sliding toward extinction, and coastwide closures are being ordered in a desperate attempt to save them.

My own life is divided between two worlds, one to the north, one to the south, one of plenty, one of want. I am framed by the contrasts, unsettled by the collision of opposites. For years I have taken for granted the necessity of traveling long distances away from home to find what was once the heart and soul of my own region. I have become intimate with the waters of Bristol Bay and southeast Alaska, while remaining a stranger to Puget Sound itself, even though more of my time is spent here than in Alaska. With the eclipse of salmon in the Northwest, the region slides toward economic irrelevance. Never mind that Microsoft is busy producing millionaires, and Boeing is filling the earth's skies with ever larger jets. The salmon are gone, and with them goes the biological and cultural bedrock that has held the region together since the retreat of the last ice sheet.

The cultural historian Thomas Berry has observed that our sense of the divine is linked inextricably to the diversity and splendor of the natural world. Nature provides the raw materials, the primordial context out of which all imagination grows. As the exterior world shrinks and decays, so goes the seed stock of natural inspiration. Perhaps it is our capacity for wonder that is the final victim of an unbridled devotion to progress. What does it mean to our collective imagination to gaze out on waters emptied of wild salmon? What does it mean to have scattered the cloud of witnesses— bear, wolf, orca, eagle, seal—who gathered so faithfully each year through the centuries to celebrate the salmon's return. To my mind, nothing can ever replace salmon in the religious imagination of the Pacific Northwest.

The poet Gary Snyder is on the right track. He has suggested that we prepare a 10,000 Year Plan for the management of our national forests. I propose a 10,000 Year Plan for the Restoration of Wild Salmon Runs in Puget Sound. It is a reasonable proposal, precisely because it offers a time frame that wild salmon understand. I'll believe we have a chance when such a plan is proposed not by poets and philosophers, but by engineers and politicians. We will have reason for hope when, as a people, we understand that our endowment of the future extends far beyond the pittance of time that is granted ourselves and our immediate offspring. That endowment must include wild salmon, if we want it also to include children who dream.

Profile

For more than twenty-five summers now, Kurt Hoelting has worked as a seine fisherman in southeast Alaska. For ten of those years, he lived in Petersburg. Now he lives on Whidbey Island in Puget Sound in a house he built himself on the rise above Maxwelton Valley.

One day, Kurt and I took a low-tide walk across the wet sand below the bluffs of Maxwelton Beach. Our conversation ranged from his recent fishing trips in Alaska to the Inside Passages Project of "contemplative pilgrimage" that he directs. We wound up talking at length about the Internet and the World Wide Web. "I admit I have a certain distrust of this technology," Hoelting said. He worried that it created a network of connectedness at the same time it was isolating people from their immediate environment. We had to cut our walk short that morning. This wiry forty-six-year-old poet of the spirit and the wild was, ironically, off to do some carpentry work for the nearby Whidbey Institute's new Cybercafe in the town of Clinton. It reminded me of some inherent clarity created by contradiction.

—Drew Kampion

Bio

Kurt Hoelting
Place of residence: Whidbey Island, Washington.
Grew up in: Puget Sound region.
Day jobs: Commercial fisherman. Founder/director of Inside Passages Project, which takes small groups on week-long kayak meditation journeys through the Inside Passage of southeast Alaska. (Contact: 3677 Woodland Hall Lane, Clinton, WA 98236, 360- 579-1498.)
Education: Harvard Divinity School.
Anthology: *Earth and Spirit: The Spiritual Dimension of the Environmental Crisis,* Continuum Press (1990)—essay.
Favorite book: *The River Why* by David James Duncan.
Beliefs: A former Congregational minister and practitioner of Zen Buddhist meditation.

Frederic Hunter

Fathers and Sons

We climb onto the Van Nuys Flyaway bus and take the seats directly behind the driver. Across the aisle from us sit a man and his teenage son. The man is in his forties, burly and gravel-voiced. He wears glasses, an anorak, and one of those brimmed caps with the plastic snap-band in the back.

The son wears sweat pants. His hair is very short. He sets his brimmed cap on the knee he has cocked against the partition that delineates the entry area; the word "Navy" is embroidered on its front. At first glance, I estimate that he is eighteen. I wonder if he is in college, and I do that because my own son is in college. In fact, my wife, Donanne, and I have just flown into Los Angeles from Albuquerque, New Mexico, after seeing him. We visited Anasazi Indian sites with Paul and his friend Abe during their final week-long spring vacation in college.

As we pull away from the airport, moving toward the freeway and the parking lot in Van Nuys where we've left the car, the man across the aisle makes desultory conversation with his son. Overhearing his words, I smile. He is trying to connect with his kid. And the kid is replying in the barely audible monosyllables that make fathers feel like the most superfluous creatures on earth. I revise my estimate. Maybe the man's son is only sixteen.

The next time I look over we are on the freeway, and the kid is asleep, his head pillowed on his dad's shoulder. The man is holding his son's knee—not because it is necessary to do so, but because he loves his son. He wants this small bit of contact with the boy while he sleeps.

In my mind I say to the man: "If you are wise, you will memorize the feel of your son's head on your shoulder, the feel of his knee grasped by your hand. Your son is almost a man, and he won't be sleeping with his head on your shoulder much longer."

In directing these mental words to the man across the aisle, I am, of course, talking to myself. That's because my son, almost twenty-two, two months away from being a college graduate, slept with his head on my lap this morning. And as Abe drove us through the rain that became snow, moving out of Chinle, Arizona, at the mouth of Canyon de Chelly into New Mexico, I wondered if Paul would ever sleep with his head on my lap again.

Probably not.

Perhaps before we know it—you seem only to look away for a second and these things have happened—Paul will have married and have a child of his own sleeping on his lap.

As a kind of confirmation of his pulling away, a funny thing often happens when he is with Donanne and me. "Why don't you get out of Santa Barbara?" he asks us. "It's so stodgy."

"Why don't you move to Santa Fe?" This he suggested during our recent trip. He was holding a real estate brochure—he always finds them somewhere—and was touting a place that would be just right for us up on the road toward Taos.

Thank you, but we like California. In fact, my only real estate thoughts focus on paying off our mortgage. The truth is: I don't want to move to a house Paul has not lived in. I like living in a home that has a "Paulie's room." I like his being with us—even when he's far away.

Musing about houses, I remember walking my son around the neighborhood of the first house we ever owned. I would come home from my job where things were not going all that well, and we would take walks. Paul was two. With his tiny hand held in mine, we would trudge along a lane behind the houses, a place where no cars came. We would make a daily inspection of the neighborhood, note seasonal changes, and say hello to pets.

Sometimes walking with your two-year-old is less than fascinating. But I do recall telling myself: "Be here now. Don't think about other things: tomorrow's work, this job that isn't going well. Be here right now—with your child. Let your thoughts be in the hand holding his. And then later you will know what that hand felt like as you held it."

Once again, I notice the man across the aisle. His hand pats his son's knee. And in my mind I say to him: "Remember what that feels like." And I'm glad that I can remember what it felt like to have a two-year-old hand in mine on late afternoon walks.

And I think of my dad. I wish I had known him better. The 1950s were a time when men did not expect to express their feelings. Perhaps I remember the feel of my father's handshake. I think I do. But we didn't hug each other—and I am privileged in this less-uptight time to hug my son—and I don't remember his arm around my shoulder.

But he certainly loved us. When my brother and I wrote a musical show in college (we were in the Midwest), we turned to Dad. "You're in LA Can you find us an arranger?" And somehow he made time from his architectural practice to locate a man in Hollywood who taught people to play piano by ear. That man scored our songs—quickly and nicely—for a five-piece band.

Dad also enrolled my brother and me in a very expensive college and my sister in boarding school—all at the same time. My mother told me later that sometimes at night he paced the floor. I did not know that then. I suppose my brother and sister and I just thought that Dad was doing what every father did. But as I reach the finish line on college payments, I know how much love that represented.

The 1950s, when I was Paul's age, now seem an innocent and idyllic era. (With the cold war and nuclear threats, they did not seem that way then.) Even so, I'm glad that we live now in a more expressive time. We are better able to hug, better able to talk about who we are.

As a last whole-family activity, my parents took all five of us to Europe. It was 1957. During that trip, my dad notified us that he'd been nominated to become a Fellow of the American Institute of Architects (AIA). I remember our stopping the trip for a day or two while he organized data to support the nomination.

As it turned out, he was not elected. Some time after we returned from the trip, our mother broke the news to my brother and me. We said: "Oh," and "Gee, I'm sorry." And nothing more was ever discussed. Not: "How come?" Not: "Gee, Dad, how does that feel?" Not even: "Can you be nominated again?"

(In fact, he was nominated again and elected. Later he served as chairman of the jury that selected AIA Fellows, the Institute's highest non-elective post.)

In the 1950s, young people had no idea—and little concern, I admit—about what people experienced in their middle years. In movies that appeared just before the emergence of TV, people got married and the movie ended. Everyone lived happily ever after.

In this more expressive era, I've tried to share my life with my son. To enjoy the flush times and fill them with laughter. And not to deny the lean times—when laughter is maybe more important as we bite our fingernails and tighten our belts.

I've tried to express to Paul how it felt to get fired from that job that was not going well when he was two. And how getting through that experience led to opportunities I'd never dreamed would come my way.

The bus moves off the freeway at Sherman Way. The man across the aisle nudges his son awake. The boy sits up and looks around. Glancing at him, I think maybe he is only about fourteen. After a moment he snuggles back against his father's shoulder.

When the bus parks at the Flyaway station, the kid stands, still half asleep. His brimmed cap drops into the aisle. I pick it up and hand it to the father. "Thanks," he says.

I scramble out of the bus and hurry off to fetch the car. It's parked in the far reaches of the lot. By the time I bring it back to the baggage-loading area and help Donanne with the bags, the man who sat across the aisle is moving off to get his car. The kid, still stuporous with sleep, sits nestled among the family baggage. In my mind I say to him: "Remember this moment, kid. Your dad loves you. I hope you know it."

Donanne and I shove our bags into the trunk of the zippy little red Honda. ("Why did you get that car?" Paul asked when we told him we'd replaced the Cadillac.) We are already thinking of home, of the house in Santa Barbara where Paul is present even when he's not there. We get into the Honda and flyaway home.

Profile

Creative writing has always been second nature to Frederic Hunter: a column for his college newspaper in Illinois; essays while in the army in Alaska; corporate public relations materials for the two companies of the old Bell System in New York and San Francisco; letters (seven pages long, single-spaced) from his US Information Service post in the Congolese jungle. And plays, there were always plays.

In 1965 when Fred and I met, he wrote to me, even though we were both living near UCLA. He wrote by telegram, on a sheet of Saranwrap spread across the windshield of my car, on a page wrapped around a milk bottle on my doorstep, on a tidy curl of paper inserted ever so carefully into an emptied walnut shell. Then, after a while, he went traveling—and intriguingly, didn't write. On his return he didn't ask me to type the manuscript of his African novel. A perspicacious man. And so we were married.

Fred has made his living by writing all our married life. Now—many news dispatches and plays later, many essays and teleplay assignments completed—he sends me faxes when I am across town at work. A creative writer.

—D. R. H.

Bio

Frederic Hunter
Place of residence: Santa Barbara.
Birthplace: Los Angeles.
Grew up in: Los Angeles, boarding school in St. Louis.
Day job: Writer.
Education: Principia College, Elsah, Illinois. UCLA.
Current project: Revisions to a spec TV movie script sold to a cable network.
Favorite book: Maybe Mark Twain's *Huckleberry Finn*. I notice I've quoted from it in two recent scripts.
Craving: To see *An Ear to the Ground* in print!

Cy Keener

El Capitan

Day one.

El Capitan's sheer granite walls soar skyward for over three thousand feet. Its base, more than a mile wide, rises out of a forested boulder field. Halfway up, white granite is split by a horizontal gray band. Then the headwall—looming steep and featureless above. We have driven twenty-four hours to get to Yosemite. We have come to climb El Cap. Twenty-five years ago, just making it to the top was worthy of media attention, but now dozens of parties can be seen ascending different routes across the face on a sunny summer day. Still, an ascent of El Cap is the mark of a serious rock climber—climbers come from all over the world to make the attempt, and many arrive back in their homelands with stories of defeat.

Matt Simons, Chris Carithers, and I are a couple of years out of high school. Matt is strong—he never gets tired and doesn't complain. Chris, who recently completed a stint as a bike messenger, has all-day-long endurance. I'm the most experienced, but I was just discharged from four weeks of physical therapy due to a climbing accident in which my ankle was smashed. Also, I needed seventeen stitches to sew up my chin. We think we are ready. Still, the climb is twice as long as anything we've previously done, and we've yet to climb as a threesome.

We pack and hike to the base. I lead the first pitch (rope-length) of free-climbing. We are starting up the Muir route. It feels great to sink my hands into clean granite cracks, but near the top of the pitch I find myself thirty feet above my last piece of protection. I am wriggling up a section where the crack flares to five inches, and remember how intimidating Yosemite can be. After I finish the pitch, Matt and Chris follow and then work slowly up the next two pitches of aid-climbing while I watch and relax. They finish at dusk.

Day two.
Clouds swirl above us all morning, and by early afternoon they enter the valley below as though someone has broken a dam in San Francisco. We are soaked in thirty minutes of rain. Dark streaks on the wall soon become trickles and then waterfalls. We retreat, and I am frustrated with our progress. "We're supposed to climb eight pitches a day?" Chris asks in disbelief. I blame the rain. Our pace today is far too slow for us to make it to the top with the amount of food and water we have.

Day four.
We waited on the valley floor for two days, and now the weather clears enough for us to resume climbing. Today our goal is Mammoth Ledges. We jumar up our ropes to the top of pitch six and begin climbing again. Hauling the 150 pounds of food, water, and gear is a chore, but by four in the afternoon we are only a hundred feet short of our goal. As Matt is leading the last pitch it starts to rain. His smooth-soled free-climbing shoes and gymnast's chalk are useless against the slick surface of polished wet rock. He is in a race and makes it to the anchors just as the rock becomes impossible to climb.

The weather is bad, I am angry, and it's taking us forever to set up a place to sleep. Chris is frustrated too, but Matt seems imperturbable, calmly organizing gear while Chris and I eat canned chili and pudding. "Let's get this gear ready for tomorrow," Matt says, "before it's dark." We are a third of the way up the wall and equipped to wait a while, though the weather is not promising. We only have so much food, and by eating now we risk going hungry later.

Day five.
More clouds. We are really up here now. The slabs run out below us for over

a thousand feet. Climbers at the base of the route are so small I can hardly tell what they are doing. The second pitch requires that Chris climb down fifteen feet to a ledge and then traverse thirty feet to another crack before climbing up. Due to rope drag, Chris cannot protect this section. When he is twenty feet above the ledge, Matt yells over, "Hey Chris, ya got any pro in?" Chris replies, "Just putting some in now."

Chris has no backup, if he falls he will hit the ledge. We are over a thousand feet up, and you'd think a roped fall would be safe, but hitting the large ledge would be just as bad as hitting the ground. Chris wiggles an eighth-inch-wide wedge of brass that is soldered to thin wire into a constriction in the crack. As Chris climbs higher, the crack flares, becoming more difficult. He inserts a camming device to support his weight. He is only five feet from easier climbing. Suddenly, the cam pulls out, and Chris hurtles down thirty feet. Finally the rope catches him just above the ledge. He is saved by the small wire, which is only supposed to hold 700 pounds, and that under ideal conditions. From my position, all I see is Matt flying sideways across the rock like a prop in a special effects studio.

"Are you all right?" Matt yells.

"Yeah," Chris says.

I take a deep breath, and tell my heart to stop beating so fast. We are OK. Matt's hip is bruised from catching the fall, and I have the feeling that something really serious happened. Chris complains that we don't have the right equipment, and I begin to doubt whether we will make it to the top.

We continue cautiously upward. The day ends at the Gray Ledges, part of the horizontal gray band. We are now halfway up El Cap and through the most technically difficult pitches. Still, the overhanging headwall—the steepest and most exposed part, the mental crux—looms above.

Day six.

The first few pitches traverse across the wall in a series of pendulums that connect vertical crack systems. Slow going. We finish the traverse by one thirty and begin climbing on the Nose, the most prominent feature of El Cap. The cracks are beautiful, overhanging, and we move quickly—hand jambs, short sections of aid, frequently yarding down on fixed gear. I start leading just after four and continue by headlamp until ten o'clock. I am exhausted from the sixteen-hour day. It takes forever to set up our portable ledges before we can eat. The night is clear, the moon bright, clouds disappearing along with our fears of being trapped by a storm. Descending through overhangs from this high on El Cap isn't an option anyway.

Day seven.
We are ten pitches from the top. During the last two days we have climbed ten pitches total, but we need to top out today. The first pitch is fixed from the night before, so we each will have to lead three pitches. Chris leads the first few pitches, I clean, and Matt belays. We move like clockwork. Our system is finally working.

Matt takes over just after noon. He fires up the first pitch, but moves slowly on the second. While I am waiting at the hanging belay I cannot help but notice the three thousand feet of exposure beneath me. We are completely disconnected from the world below. I try to avoid looking down.

Matt is the fastest climber of our group but he takes forever to finish his pitch. Something is wrong. I ascend to the belay. "Are you doing OK?" I ask. "I'm not sure what's wrong with me," he replies. "It's just like I'm going to drop everything I touch." His eyes are glassy and tired, yet he does better on the next pitch, and by five thirty in the evening we are only three rope lengths from the top. It's my turn to lead.

"Seems like I work the night shift," I joke. I had been tired all day, and the exposure is making me slow and overcautious. Once I'm in lead, though, I find that I am alert and energetic. I climb as fast as I can, and Matt and Chris come up behind me. The final pitch is a bolt ladder straight though dark overhanging roofs. I climb almost to the end, before I'm stopped by lack of light.

The sky above is black. Closer to the horizon the sky is shades of blue illuminated by a full moon. The horizon itself has a crisp, red edge. I can hear the other two cheerfully talking at the belay below. I haul my headlamp up a free rope. They are confident now but I'm worried. I will have to free climb in the dark. At the end of the bolt ladder the route eases back. I slip into my free-climbing shoes and scramble the last fifty feet, returning to a horizontal world. The night is still and peaceful. A few minutes later Chris and Matt join me on top.

Profile

I met Cy Keener in May 1993 when he was still a student at Lakeside, Bill Gates' alma mater. I ran into Cy in a pizza parlor in Spokane. Five of us had come to town to participate in a rock climbing competition on the fearsome Minehaha Rocks—you've heard of the Eiger Nordwand? Well, the Spokane equivalent is Minehaha Rocks, totally horrific cliffs, some of them towering seventy feet in the air. I'm joking, of course. Minehaha may sound terrifying, but it's rock climbing—much safer than the alpine ice climbing on the Eiger where climbers are bombarded by falling ice and rock.

I rented a van and decked out our climbing club in Team Davis T-shirts. (This whole Italian-bicycle-racing-team-applied-to-climbing concept was inspired by Charlie Buell, another Seattle building contractor/climber who gave his construction crew Team Buell T-shirts.) We climbed hard, had fun, and, through a series of accidents, ended up placing in beginner, intermediate, and expert categories. The awards ceremony was on the other side of town, which is how we got around to adopting Cy Keener. He was young, lanky, and lucky: during the ceremony his name was pulled from a jar—he won a nine millimeter perlon climbing rope. I didn't have a rope, he was from Seattle, and it seemed only courteous to introduce myself.

Two months later I borrowed Cy's rope to climb a waterfall on Mt. Rainier. Hundreds of chunks of ice and rock fell down the waterfall while I was climbing, but not one landed on Cy's rope. How do I know? Well, the next summer I talked Cy into climbing the Nisqually Icefall on the other side of Rainier. Cy, of course, brought his rope along. Part way up, a heavy, grinding ice avalanche fell over us and caught Cy's partner, Matt Simons, sweeping him down the mountain to his death. And then the rope came tight, pulling Cy off his stance, snapping a Black Diamond carabiner like it was yesterday's toothpick, flinging Cy forty feet through the air, and placing him down beside my brother. So I know that Cy's rope was still good—otherwise it would have broken. Cy's partner? He lay in the ice debris at the bottom of the slope, totally destroyed, his hard hat compressed by the collision. In a few minutes, however, Matt Simons came to and has lived and climbed ever since—although, these days, both Cy and Matt pretty much stay away from ice. "Rock climbing is a lot safer," said Cy.

—Scott C. Davis

Bio

Cy Keener
Place of residence: Seattle.
Birthplace: Tacoma, Washington.
Day jobs: Student. Occasional construction work. Climbing gear sales.
Education: Colorado College. Currently studying at Oxford.
First concrete pour: A hillside foundation in Seattle's Magnolia neighborhood with the Scott Davis Company in July 1994.
Coolest vacation: Rock-climbing with my dad in Spain.
Preferred hangout: The Vertical Club in Seattle.
First literary reading: August 15, 1996. Read the above essay to a packed house on Capitol Hill in Seattle.
Current project: Learning ancient Greek.
Favorite book: *Narcissus and Goldmund* by Herman Hesse.
Craving: To climb alpine big walls in South America.

Brad Knickerbocker

Boys and Guitars

In the other room, I hear the boy loosening up with some old Peter, Paul, and Mary tunes. "Five Hundred Miles." "A 'Soalin'." Fatherly pride sets in as he jumps a generation to Led Zeppelin's "Stairway to Heaven." Then he's back to folk-picking "House of the Rising Sun."

I love hearing these old songs, these earnest songs, which I imagine is how my father would feel if I started noodling Hoagy Carmichael.

Finally, the boy settles down to the serious scales and chord progressions his guitar teacher will want to hear tomorrow—with a break for Neil Young's "Needle and the Damage Done."

I suddenly wonder why this thirteen-year-old picks out the dark tunes, but then decide not to worry about it. He had new braces installed today—the heavy metal bands of adolescent life—and the music helps soothe the discomfort. Who says a kid can't be a blues man?

Thirty years ago, I sat in a room like that . . . sorting though dreams and memories with music. Sometimes I still do.

Profile

My father, Brad Knickerbocker, works with wood—or so I thought in 1982. I was only six years old when we lived in Vienna, Virginia. Once farmland, our modest cul-de-sac served as home for commuters. Every morning my father hopped into his orange '76 Volkswagen van and buzzed into Washington like a dedicated worker ant, along with thousands of other office workers whose homes orbited the city. Every evening he returned home just as the table was set for dinner. My world, however, consisted of the creek and a tangled clutch of woods that rolled into farmland behind our brick house. The distant office, the mysterious necktie, the skyscraped city itself were all linked to my father's weekday world, a world largely myth to me.

One of my teachers at grade school asked me what my father did, and I answered with innocent logic, "He works with wood," for that is what I saw. On weekends he stayed home, and I saw him "at work"—out by the woodpile, hefting his battered maul and bringing it down on upright hunks of hickory. Later we fed the wood to the old cast iron stove that stood like a grandfather dwarf, snapping, popping, mumbling warmth into the living room. My father's weekend chopping was an immediate, tangible "job" that made sense to me. Feeding the stove meant warmth for the family room, the center of our household.

Later I deduced that my father was known in the city world as a journalist for *The Christian Science Monitor*, not a handler of mauls. He was a man who worked with words. My father's name printed at the top of his articles became more impressive than the calluses he earned by gripping the wooden maul handle. I saw him go to work every day to write, like a coal miner rising before dawn to chip away at the earth, picking out the important parts and leaving the dross. This gave words importance—writing was serious stuff. Sustenance came not only from the wood we burned in the stove but, more important, from the writer's paycheck.

In 1989 we moved to Ashland, Oregon, a place near giant trees older than our nation. My father no longer commutes to the city. In fact, his tie rack is graced with a healthy layer of dust. He writes at home now, when he's not out scouring the West, rubbing elbows with sagebrush rebels and eco-warriors. Now I have the opportunity to see the writer at work. Or I can lure him away from his computer screen to go play *in* the environment: to hike up Wagner Butte or Mt. McLoughlin in the surrounding Siskiyou and Cascade mountains, to paddle the wetlands of Rocky Point. We no longer have a cast iron stove, and when I think of my dad's work the sound of a maul swishing the air is replaced by the chatter of a keyboard. My father no longer works with wood—now he writes *in* the woods.

—Scott Knickerbocker

Bio

Brad Knickerbocker
Place of residence: Ashland, Oregon.
Birthplace: Muskegon, Michigan.
Grew up in: Delmar, New York.
Day job: Staff writer for *The Christian Science Monitor.*
Education: B.A. in English, Hobart College, Geneva, New York (1964). Master's degree in how to land single-seat jets on aircraft carriers (1966). Doctorate in how to do that at night after being shot at over the Ho Chi Minh trail (1968–69). Postdoctoral studies with Vietnam Veterans against the War (1970–71).
Current project: Cover the West for the *Monitor,* with a special emphasis on environmental issues.
Favorite book: An impossible question, but with bamboo slivers under my fingernails I would say *A Sand County Almanac: And Sketches Here and There* by Aldo Leopold—then immediately regret it and say *The Practice of the Wild* by Gary Snyder, or *Fools Crow* by James Welch, or *The Complete Works of William Shakespeare,* or *You Must Revise Your Life* by William Stafford, or *Dakota: A Spiritual Geography* by Kathleen Norris, or the Bible, or *The Songlines* by Bruce Chatwin, or *Almanac of the Dead* by Leslie Marmon Silko, or. . . .
Belief: "I like to think that art has something to do with the achievement of stillness in the midst of chaos." (Saul Bellow.) "Love is the fulfilling of the law." (*The Epistle of Paul to the Romans.*)
Cravings: Hike the Pacific Crest Trail from Mexico to Canada with son Scott, then learn how to play clawhammer banjo as well as Bob Carlin or Cathy Fink.

Krista Koontz

What to Do with a Lawn?

Weston, Massachusetts. Town dump. 1975.
My dad and I hurl trash bags over the ledge. I get a pleasant, dizzy sensation watching the bags spin all the way to the ground. I consider jumping over the cliff and landing in the soft mass of plastic bags and lawn clippings below. We are a family of four and we produce a lot of junk. Paper plates at every meal. "It saves dishes," explains my mother. When we go to McDonald's, my parents grab twenty napkins and fifteen ketchups. "Make it twenty-five napkins," my father jokes to my mother, "These kids are messy."

My dad looks forward to our Saturday dump trips. It's partly a break from my babbling mother and partly the beauty of our dump. Hundreds of seagulls chose this place as their home. How could they be wrong? I launch the last bag and wait to see it hit bottom. We slap the dirt off our hands and leave like bandits. A cloud of dust follows our car. The next Saturday morning project is mowing the lawn. Unlike going to the dump, mowing the lawn is something my father hates.

Woods Hole, Massachusetts. New Alchemy Institute. 1981.
It's a field trip, so everyone is giggling and poking each other. Our science teacher, Mr. Jordan, is undaunted by our antics and leads us into a geodesic dome. He describes how the plants, the sunlight, and the fish pond interact in a perfectly balanced, symbiotic system. We don't remember exactly what

he says, but my friend Helen and I vow to return here someday for an internship. New Alchemy is a vision of the future. No trash is produced and all the food comes directly from gardens and greenhouses.

Outside, in the main garden, vegetables and flowers are thriving on rich soil. Helen flicks a fava bean at me. It's bigger than any bean I've ever seen. I threaten her with a cherry tomato. We're supposed to be listening. "Helen and Krista," Mr. Jordan says firmly. He thinks we're a lost cause.

Elsah, Illinois. Principia College cafeteria. 1987.

Students line up for lunch as we try to pull them aside and hand them flyers. "Save Our Soil!" we chant. The twelve of us have gathered under a giant banner that reads: SOS. Some people don't want to hear about topsoil or earthworms before lunch. Others gather around.

"The college is handling their land in a way that's illegal, immoral, and makes no financial sense," I tell them. "The soil is eroding at an incredible thirty-three tons per acre per year. They are farming 360 acres of their land as if there were no tomorrow. They've got a local farmer who plows the fields every year and plants a monoculture of either soybeans or corn. We want the administration to change the way they are farming or convert the farmed acres into native prairie grass. We're asking you to join us in skipping lunch today. Help us raise awareness about how soil erosion affects people around the world."

"How does it affect them?" a student in a tennis skirt asks me.

"It starves them."

Cottage Grove, Oregon. Aprovecho Institute. 1988.

We sit on tree stumps and eat stew. We are people from large and small countries all over the world. Each of us has a different project under way. *Aprovecho* means "I make the best use of" in Spanish. Behind me is an earthen cookstove, developed by Ianto, one of the founders of this place. Its design and materials are simple, chosen especially with third world conditions in mind. Anyone anywhere can build this stove.

The stew is difficult. Craig, today's cook, does not believe in cutting vegetables. "It tears their souls." He looks Neanderthal as an entire onion hangs from his mouth. "What about chewing? Doesn't that tear their souls anyway?" Craig doesn't answer me. I've already wearied him with questions during this morning's gardening. I finish my stew and dip into the steaming side dish of fava beans. The beans, and everything else we eat, have come from the garden.

Brookline, Massachusetts. Efficiency apartment. 1989.

I'm already married at twenty years old. Our first apartment is the size of some people's closets. We are in love and space isn't an issue. Harry makes breakfast for me. I bite into a piece of toast and then stop eating it abruptly.

"Harry," I ask. "Did you make this in the mouse toaster?" He beams with delight. On trash day, Harry found this toaster on the curb, and it had a dead mouse in it. He cleaned the toaster thoroughly, he insists, with bleach and a toothbrush. Besides, it's a curvaceous, chrome toaster, too much of a classic to let slip away.

"It's recycling," Harry defends.

"We've stooped to a new low," I say. I finish my toast.

Portland, Oregon. Our new house. 1995.

Our house sits on a half-acre lot. Harry and I hate mowing the lawn. The permaculture group straggles in and puts homegrown potluck dishes on our kitchen table. I look forward to their salads, which are topped with dandelions and other edible flowers. Harry distributes a map of our yard. I greet people at the door. The group is fondly known as p-pig, Portland Permaculture Implementation Group. Appropriate to our acronym, these are people who are not slaves of hygiene. Deodorant is a dirty word.

At our design party, people hover over a white board and map out our yard. We discuss wind direction, slope, rainfall, and native plants. We decide to make a corner of the front yard into a flood plain, just as an experiment. We'll absorb the runoff from the road and water some bushes and dwarf bamboo with it.

Half of the group goes to the back garden and prepares the soil for planting fava beans. I hand out gloves and shovels to the outdoor crew. Seth Greenley, a permaculture instructor, comes to the backyard bearing gifts: Five barrels of wood shavings for making walkways in the garden. A bucket of rich compost, complete with earthworms and the ashes of a dead friend of his. And a couple of branches of Oregon grape. "Just stick these in the soil," he says. "They will grow."

In a few years, fruit trees, vegetables, herbs, chickens, and maybe a goat will fill up the yard. We will mulch and plant, a gradual process, and the lawn will lose ground, piece by piece, until it is gone. Anyone who comes over to play croquet will be sorely disappointed.

Profile

I met Krista Koontz at Principia, a small liberal arts college on the bluffs above the Mississippi River, where students spent hazy autumn days strolling along tree-lined back roads, playing Frisbee on the common, engaging in philosophical debates. Principia, however, was not cloistered. It's the place where I first encountered militant feminism and "deep ecology." It's the place where I first encountered Krista Koontz.

Krista and I had nothing in common in 1990. I noted this quickly as we filed into our first feminist literature class. Where I had bright pink fingernails, Krista had natural, tennis-playing hands. Where I had tightly permed and coifed hair, hers was short and without pretense. And where I'd painstakingly applied various shades of pink and brown to my face, Krista's remained defiantly plain. (I remember keeping my pink nails curled tightly into my palms so Krista wouldn't notice them during class discussions.) My conservative, Republican upbringing was to receive its first and fatal blow in this class. Worse yet, I was convinced I was the only person in the group who didn't study Gandhi and listen to alternative music. My studied success in polite society marked me for social failure among this group of my peers. And Krista comprised my imagined judge.

By a peculiar turn of events, I now live with Krista, our husbands, three cats, and a vegetable garden in Portland, Oregon. Firm in her conviction that the number of cars on the road should be decreased, Krista rides her bike in all kinds of weather, rain or rain. She works in a group home for developmentally disabled adults and writes plays in her off time. She also teaches basic writing and English as a second language in local community colleges, tutors a Vietnamese family in English, and attends the regular meetings of the WBS (Who Brought Something) Writers Group which she founded a couple of years ago. Her interests include permaculture, organic gardening, and energy-efficient living.

—Julie Finnin Day

Bio

Krista Koontz
Place of residence: Portland, Oregon.
Grew up in: Massachusetts.
Day job: Social work.
Education: B.A., Principia College, Elsah, Illinois. M.A. in English, University of Rhode Island.
Dramatic productions: *Don't Be a Stranger*—produced at the Rexall Rose Idiot Room Theater, Portland (April 1996).
Serial publication: *The Oregonian.*
Current projects: Building a straw-bale house for Julie and Ryan in our backyard. Swiss chard, blue potatoes, purple cabbage, Walla Walla onions, mustard, bok choy, tomatoes, strawberries, kale, chives, lettuce, peas, green beans, and fava beans.
Favorite book: *A Confederacy of Dunces* by John Kennedy Toole.
Belief: Christian Science.
Craving: Lobster, but I'm a vegetarian.

Zoë Landale

Power and Transparency

"I'm interested in working with power," I say to my father.

He shifts on the high-backed green couch across from me. The lamp on the wall behind him throws his face into shadow. "Don't say that to anyone but me," he says vehemently. "You might be misunderstood."

"Well, I am."

We are talking about spiritual power, the upwelling of sweetness and strength that, once felt, can never be forgotten.

"Why do you think," I ask, "that so many people have left the conventional churches? It's because they found their prayers didn't do anything. They didn't work. I can understand that. But I've found something that does work."

"For you," Dad says.

The tip of his cigarette is orange. Shadows beat at us from corners of the room. Everyone else is asleep. We are sleepy but the need to talk is stronger than tiredness. Every three years we see one another, or so it seems; a long, expensive plane trip across the country separates us. We are in a cottage a hundred miles north of Ottawa. Everything in the cottage clashes: the curtains with the rug, the two couches with the curtains and each other. It's a wild blend of stark polyester turquoises, olive greens, worn autumn-colored prints, and sizzling blue carpet. The blue's so artificial it hurts.

There is something curiously freeing about the jumble. We are here for two weeks. Most of our time is spent at the beach. It is only occasionally, like now, at midnight, that the colors poke long spikes of unease at me. The effect is like the fast food restaurants (Denny's is one) who decorate so the customer will not feel too comfortable and will move on in a short time. Deliberate dissonance. It's very effective in restaurants. "One more cigarette," Dad keeps saying tonight. "Just one more and we'll go to bed."

"So why shouldn't I say that about working with power?" I ask.

"It just isn't a good thing to talk about," Dad says. He hunches his shoulders.

The extraordinary thing about spiritual power is that it doesn't belong to us. I have felt it rising up in waves around me, thick and strong, the sense of rightness becoming so solid I could let myself be carried along as if in the grasp of a benign tsunami. And yet it was not mine. It came from nothing I had called up; it was the undiluted reality of being, which, just for a moment, I could glimpse. When I pray or meditate, or study with the intent of healing, I spend my time trying to reach through the mystification of the senses, to get back to what is primordially true. I try to become translucent, to admit light through my interstices.

It is perfectly clear to me why Jesus, the greatest healer in recorded history, said, "I can of mine own self do nothing."

I remember my ex-in-laws, a few years back, concerned because a neighbor's house had been broken into and vandalized. My relatives are elderly. They live in the country, down a long driveway and behind a scrub of pine, hollies, chestnuts, and lilacs. They felt vulnerable. I had just finished a course on healing, as it happened, and I thought for one grand moment: *I will protect you. I will know what is true for you with such astonishing clarity it will hang in the ether like glowing runes of protection. You will never be troubled. It is not right that you or anyone should have to accept this unjust notion of victimization.*

Then I came to my senses. Just who did I think I was? A wizard in a child's story book, taking out my staff and setting to work? Magic stories are appealing because they contain the notion of acquired power, of making ourselves greater and greater, shellacking on layers of knowledge. Study hard and you too can grow out of being the apprentice and become the sorcerer.

There was nothing wrong with my idea of trying to protect my in-laws. But I was not the representative of a cosmic security service. Nor could I, if I really wanted to bring peace to the situation, afford to look at my relatives as if they were in danger. In order to bring them that sense of safety I wanted for them, I had to allow my jumbled thought to be soothed by that spiritual force Dad was so reluctant to have me name.

How do I use power? I give up the notion of myself as separated from good; open myself to the slow pulse of the world beneath. I have spent whole nights, not awake really, but waking with every other breath while I uncurl the clenched fist of self and reach through circumstances—the problem—to hold onto good. And I ask the intelligence behind the beauty of spiral galaxies, the great whirling arms of rose and blue and white, to show me what is true. I am willing to leave old ideas and accept new ones. Gratefully.

I met a man last week who is a witch, probably the most public one in Canada. He is a good witch, a white witch, but still, to me he was scary. We met at a small party. I've seen the witch before at public gatherings and avoided him. Long white hair, a rumpled white beard, a very tall man dressed in black with rings on each finger, including thumbs; I didn't feel I could deal with him. What could I say? What could we possibly have in common?

Across the room I listened to him talk about nursing his mother-in-law, who is ninety-one and has just had a stroke. She needs round-the-clock attention. This witch and his wife look after her mother at home. They are in their seventies. Both were suffering from lack of sleep. What could we have in common?

Well, tenderness, perhaps. A few minutes later he and I talked about a mutual friend who had feuded, nastily, with someone. The witch leaned forward in his chair. "We tried to stop it," he said sadly to me. "Oh my yes, we did. All of us who cared about them did."

I met his soft brown eyes and knew I had made a mistake. I had allowed all the talk about "occult" to frighten me, but this witch and I were on the same side. What side? Healing.

We are always choosing who or what we will serve. In each tiny conflict with a family member, what side do we come down on? It's so easy to go for being right, for the quick incisive remark to prove it—but will that bring healing to the situation? Will it make us feel secure, loved, respected? Can we extend that to others?

Last weekend my almost-nine-year-old daughter was scolding me: "You had to have that permission slip back to the teacher right away. Now I won't be able to go on any walks or outings and it's all your fault. I told you to get it in." And I was exhausted after a week of deadlines, protested feebly I had filled it out, sent it back the very next day in fact. It would be OK; I'd write a note to the teacher. Still my daughter would not be mollified, waved the white paper in my face—I was lying down, I had been reading—"See?"

I feel I spend my whole life trying to be a good mom. The paper in my face was too much. The one I had sent back to school had been blue, I remembered cutting it on the dotted line with the kitchen scissors, their handles spattered with red paint. I leapt to my feet, grabbed the beaded Indian moccasins from my feet and hurled them to the floor. Even in my rage I was glad I was not tempted to spank my daughter. "Get out," I yelled. "Out."

She left my room, crying.

Guilt seized and shook me. I knew better. I had bitten hard, hard on that hook of irritation.

I fell asleep even though it was morning, and I never nap then. I could hear my child being comforted by her father. In half an hour I would get up and apologize.

So where was the power then when I needed it? Right where it's always been. It's the central fact of the universe, it doesn't go anywhere. But I forgot to check in. I allowed anger to make me opaque.

The woman who owns the cottages where my father and I talked bought them years ago. She furnishes them from the thrift store. The resort does not exist to make money, it's for the benefit of her son, who has Down's syndrome. Many people with Down's syndrome die young. This woman didn't want this fate for her son, she wanted him to grow up strong. So, during the summer, her son brings wood for the cottages, wheels away garbage, rakes the sand and gravel beach, goes swimming. She has done, my father says, a marvelous job. Those who stay at the resort are expected to behave lovingly, acceptingly toward the young man, now in his mid-twenties.

Rather than acquiring power, I view my role in life as more of becoming something. Someone, really, the person I was meant to be. Am, in an absolute sense. A zebra is always a zebra. It may grow up thinking itself a horse, the same as a wolf cub can be raised as a dog. But the animal's essential nature is zebra, is wolf. That is where they will operate at their area of greatest strength. My essential nature is spiritual. Until I grow into that, accept it, acknowledge it, I haven't a hope of being able to understand and to use what's out there for us all, the underlying goodness.

The next day I invited the witch and his wife to come home and have a meal with us. I could feel that repeated coming down on the side of good in him. These things leave their marks. His way is not my way—but I will honor the clasp of our eyes across the room, the recognition I felt then. We have not talked about the shadow play of the universe, the flick-flicker of images and allurements past our eyes, but it stands there, potent in the background of things unsaid.

I wonder if it wasn't fear that was behind my father's reluctance to talk that night. Fear on behalf of all the women throughout the centuries who were burned as witches. The wisewomen, the healers. Identification with church didn't save them. "I have observed countless men and women in AA develop extraordinary relationship with the gods," my father said, "as they understand them, absolutely sure every move, every new insight, every benefit received is the direct result of divine intervention into the world of their mundane existence. It's a chimera, of course. Some make it back, others don't."

I see again my father bending forward, the lamp behind him against the paneled wall of the cottage. His face is dark from where I sit on the opposite couch, but I see the skin around his eyes crinkle when he smiles anxiously, lovingly. "You might be misunderstood."

Those of us who take spirituality seriously put ourselves in the camp of holy fools. The usual notions of layer-by-layer acquisition—education, material possessions, prestigious jobs—not only don't apply anymore, they become irrelevant. They don't transmit light.

The Father in me, he doeth the works.

The Mother in me, she doeth the works. How clearly abdication of a personal sense of power radiates through those words.

I read once that we are most ourselves when we are least self-conscious. Much as I like having friends, I dread the process of making new ones. I dislike watching myself laugh, drink tea, be conscious of trying to act as I always do. I always know when a friend has finally become one, because I am suddenly at ease. No longer aware of my feeling of separation from that person, I can enjoy her company and, as my sister says, "Feel comfortable in my own skin."

Equally we are most ourselves, most potent and individual, when we stop being conscious of ourselves as separated from the infinite sustaining power that created—is creating—the universe. I am not a zebra pretending to be a horse, nor a wolf trying desperately to fit into the tame, constrained world of dog. I am a spiritual dab of light. I may forget this, I may deny it for a time, but when I do I will be less than I really am, will believe I am dull and powerless. I don't want to accept this. For one thing, I don't believe it; for another, what a boring, reduced world it is when all a person looks at is materiality. When all I see, for instance, is the moon face and slurred diction of Down's syndrome instead of a spiritual idea worthy of respect.

I want to acknowledge the illumination of a much greater reality shining through others and through me. I want to do my laundry, bake chocolate chip cookies for my daughter's party at school in the knowledge that here, too, I can let the great actuality of the spiritual—the Mother, the Father—glow through. I want to side with joy, weigh in on the side of healing, of transparency, however domestic, however small.

Profile

I met Zoë Landale on a blustery March evening in Bellingham, the old part of town, on a hillside above the blue-black sea. I found Zoë in the cafe of Village Books, this town's most widely known bookstore. She had come with her husband to read from her new volume of poetry, *Burning Stone*. If the book had been mine, I'd have called it *Hot Rock*—which is one reason that Landale is one of Canada's finest writers, whereas I have chosen to retire from versifying altogether. Those death threats I kept receiving had something to do with it too.

Landale's husband is a building contractor—I can sympathize—and as I fitted my mouth around a mass of bean sprouts, he talked about construction work on their side of the border. Landale and her husband are designing and building their own house on Vancouver Island, and are raising a daughter. Zoë is hard at work on a new book of essays which she says involve "family and place."

—Scott C. Davis

Bio

Zoë Landale
Place of residence: Courtenay, B.C., Canada.
Birthplace: Toronto, Canada.
Day jobs: Partner in construction company. Parent. Freelance writer.
Education: M.F.A., University of British Columbia.
Books: *Burning Stone,* Ronsdale Press (1995). *Colour of Winter Air,* Sono Nis Press (1991). *Harvest of Salmon,* Hancock House (1976).
Awards: *National Magazine* Gold (1994). Stony Brook University Short Fiction Competition (1993). *Event Magazine* Creative Nonfiction Award (1992).
Current project: Book of star poems.
Belief: Christian Science.
Craving: More time in my garden.

Anson Laytner

Compassion and AIDS

I direct an organization that provides subsidized housing for people living with AIDS. We work out of an old brick church on Capitol Hill in Seattle. What do we accomplish? We draw together people of good will from many faiths. We help other people in need of love and care.

AIDS is only a disease. It is erratic—some individuals get infected, others do not. But more judgment is passed on people with AIDS than on victims of any other disease. Many of us still unleash upon victims of AIDS all the loathing once reserved for those afflicted by leprosy. I have seen: condemnation when love and compassion were called for; good, decent human beings rejected by family and friends; clergy walking past the open doors of hospital rooms where AIDS patients lay longing for comfort. This makes our work all the more important. For many of our clients, we become surrogate families.

Having a terminal disease does not transform people into saints any more than it turns them into sinners. People with AIDS are just ordinary people. But in the course of helping many of these "ordinary people," I have learned some great lessons and sensed the presence of the divine. My work with people who live with AIDS has changed me, making me more aware of life's immediacy and preciousness.

One thing I have learned from firsthand experience: life is tragic. Life is tragic because we live life individually, separately, and alone. Life is tragic because from the moment of birth until the day of death, life is made up of innumerable minor losses and a number of great ones, each with its own special grief. Then there's death itself—the ultimate separation. Although life is tragic, I have learned one need not despair.

Life's experiences can be either a mill stone or a stepping stone, depending on what one chooses to make of them. Contracting AIDS brings some people low, yet it also raises some people up. I think of J., a thirty-nine-year-old man, already emaciated when he came to live at our Rainier Valley House, but still brimming with vitality. Since his teens, J. had lived on the streets, wandering from city to city, a heroin addict, always looking for his next fix. Once infected with AIDS, he was forced to confront the consequences of his actions. The awareness of his impending death made him value the time that remained to him. It gave his life new meaning. He kicked his drug habit and sought to warn young people about the dangers of drug use and unsafe sex. His crusade gave his life purpose. It helped keep him physically and spiritually alive. Not only that, his dedication and courage inspired those who knew him.

Others have shown me that maintaining a sense of humor and an appreciation of the little joys of daily life are effective antidotes to despair. "What design pattern do people with AIDS prefer?" asked a man whose face was spotted with Kaposi sarcoma. The answer to his riddle: "Polka dots."

What have I learned from people living with AIDS? I've learned to cherish the people I love, to live in the present, to never give up hope, and to laugh when facing adversity.

But now comes the dilemma. Shall those of us who base our faith on the Bible condemn the many people with AIDS who are homosexuals because the Bible, in the book of Leviticus, is unambiguously hostile to male homosexuality? Judaism, Christianity, Islam, and Baha'i all traditionally view homosexuality as a grave sin. But through my work with people living with AIDS, I have come to know many gays and lesbians. They are good, decent people—not sinners.

How can I reconcile my experience with the traditional prohibition against homosexual behavior? Some traditional Jews and Christians I know suggest that we should "hate the sin, love the sinner," but I can't separate a person from his or her sexual identity, and besides, I'm not sure homosexuality really is a sin. A Muslim acquaintance suggested that, even if homosexuality is a sin, it should be weighed in the context of a person's entire life. However, I don't believe God operates like a divine scorekeeper. Some Jews and Christians would interpret the Biblical prohibitions in their ancient historical and cultural contexts as a way of abrogating the force of these laws. But I can't do that either, because I do not know why my ancestors—or as traditionally believed, God—made the law in the first place. Nor can I, as a Jew, simply ignore a prohibition that has been in place for some three thousand years.

I can only resolve the dilemma by considering how God might respond. In the book of Exodus in the Torah, the first part of the Jewish Bible (also called the Pentateuch or the Five Books of Moses), God is self-described as "a God compassionate and gracious, slow to anger, abounding in lovingkindness and faithfulness, extending lovingkindness to the thousandth generation, forgiving iniquity, transgression and sin." Commanded to emulate God, we are also enjoined: "Love your neighbor as yourself," or, as more correctly translated: "Love your neighbor; he is like you."

In the Jewish tradition, the word for this sort of behavior is called *hesed*. The word means lovingkindness, faithfulness, righteousness, and more. Every religion has its own terminology for *hesed*, but the behavior described is identical and universal. Love means standing together, living together, building together, and caring for one another. Love is the only thing that binds us to one another. We must learn how to love and to love well.

Ultimately, I must confess to being an agnostic about homosexuality. I don't know why the anti-homosexual commandments in Leviticus (or similar sentiments in the New Testament) are there. I don't know for sure if homosexuality is a genetic predisposition or something freely chosen. I don't know if it is a sin or not. I only know that I don't know how I can judge people who are homosexual. Let God pass judgment, if we think judgment is needed. In the meantime, let us love our fellow human beings. It is no sin for us to err on the side of compassion.

Profile

I would say that Anson Laytner is the funkiest rabbi that I've ever met, except that I'm a Quaker from the Midwest and haven't hung out with many rabbis.

On the surface he appears to be a mild-mannered dude from Canada. But I know that Anson likes blues and the Stones and was a hippie in his twenties—or close to it. Is Anson a rebel, an adventurer? Or does he just promote those images to offset pre-judgments about what a rabbi should be?

Anson has compassion and also courage. He is not afraid to address difficult subjects like anger at God. What should we do when things don't go as we planned? Misfortune can toss everything in life to the floor. Anson beseeches us to realize that misfortune and suffering do happen, sometimes in horribly unjust ways—but that it is our goal to somehow loft a kite of hope in the sky, and not lose hold of the string.

—Beth Balderston

Bio

Anson Laytner
Place of residence: Seattle.
Birthplace: Toronto, Canada.
Grew up in: Toronto, with formative years in Beijing and Jerusalem.
Day job: Executive Director of the Multifaith AIDS Project.
Education: B.A., York University. Rabbinical Degree, Hebrew Union College. M.A., Seattle University.
Books: *Arguing with God: A Jewish Tradition,* Jason Aronson (1990).
Current project: An adaptation of the medieval Hebrew/Arabic environmental tale, *The Letter of the Animals.*
Favorite book: *Letters from the Earth* by Mark Twain.
Belief: Iconoclastic Jewish.
Cravings: The basics—food, sex, love, confrontations with God.
Comment: I bake challah bread as a spiritual practice.

❀

William I. Lengeman III

On Freedom, Headless Pigeons, and the Captain of the Yuengling Juggling Team

Jim Vance looks like someone you'd expect to see rappelling out of a pickup truck with really, really big tires. He's a solidly built guy. The words "stocky" and "beefy" come to mind. In his olive green T-shirt he reminded me of a miniature tank rolling along the grounds of the community park in Hegins, Pennsylvania.

When I first saw Jim he was arguing, something he does well. He was balancing two twelve-ounce Yuenglings, the local beer, and a crushed empty in one hand. He used the other to smoke a cigarette and angrily gesticulate, adding emphasis to his arguments. It looked effortless. It was like being in the presence of a master, a Marcel Marceau of drunken soapbox oratory.

Jim was battling with an animal rights activist, a member of the Maryland-based Fund for Animals. They were duking it out, debating the merits and demerits of shooting pigeons for fun and sport. A crowd had gathered to watch. Like Vance, most of them were wearing battered baseball caps emblazoned with the names of heavy equipment manufacturers.

The animal rights people bristle when anyone refers to pigeon shooting as a "sport." But live bird-shoots have always been a part of American life. During the late 1800s John James Audubon and Alexander Wilson reported flocks of passenger pigeons containing more than two billion birds—flocks so vast that they took hours to pass one spot and darkened the skies. By 1914, the passenger pigeon was extinct, largely as a result of merciless hunting.

The practice of shooting pigeons for recreation reached a pinnacle of popularity in Schuylkill County, where Hegins is located. Local historians have written of the bootleggers, gamblers, and pigeon shooters who ruled the roost in this once thriving hotbed of coal mining. They recount the enthusiasm for "the sport that is unique to the anthracite region of Pennsylvania." Although anthracite coal mining fizzled out after reaching a peak in 1917, the pigeon shooters remain.

The Fred Coleman Memorial Shoot has been a fixture in Hegins every Labor Day since 1934. The shoot is named for a legendary pigeon shooter who flourished at the turn of the century. The Hegins event is the world's largest live bird-shoot, and in 1985, animal rights activists began to set their sights on Hegins, turning it into a rallying point, something of a Wounded Knee for their burgeoning movement.

Hegins is a fairly typical slice of pro-gun, pro-hunting rural America. It's the kind of place where you'll see bumper stickers warning "They can have my gun when they pry it from my cold, dead fingers" or T-shirts exhorting you to "Kill 'em all, let God sort 'em out." One wit, speaking of Hegins, cracked wise about the unique difficulties of dealing with the kind of people who have major appliances on their front porches.

It's easy to write Hegins off as just another hick backwater, replete with albino banjo pickers and bootleg stills. But the reality's more complicated. Though somewhat insular, people who attend the shoots are generally rather friendly. A carnival atmosphere prevails, complete with cotton candy, fried chicken, and live entertainment. Many spectators don't seem to care what's happening on the shooting fields.

Pigeon shooting is a deep-rooted tradition here. It has been since Civil War times. Shoot supporters aren't about to give up their fun, or the fundraising dollars the event brings in for community projects. They view animal rights protesters as meddling outsiders with a suspiciously liberal bent. It all smacks of a threat to their liberty, as evidenced by the most popular pro-shoot T-shirt, which reads "It's not about pigeons, it's about freedom."

I came to Hegins as a journalist, not a defiler of freedoms. But this distinction didn't seem to matter to Jim Vance. Later in the day, at the other end of the park, I came upon a mob. The same protester who'd squabbled with Vance was giving a statement to a Hegins Township police officer. Someone had torn the head off of a wounded pigeon. This type of incident is not uncommon at Hegins. A small faction of shoot supporters take great pleasure in spiting activists with such acts of cruelty. Other torments include setting birds on fire or squeezing them until blood oozes out.

Standing in this rabble, I spotted Vance, who appeared to have put away quite a few more Yuenglings. He and his drunken entourage were loudly boasting, "We killed that one, and we'll kill any more we get our hands on." More police arrived. The mob was dispersed.

A few minutes later I saw Vance standing by a shooting field, trying to convince a shoot staffer to retrieve a wounded bird and turn it over to him. The field was off limits to anyone but shooters. Vance knew if he stepped onto it he'd be arrested.

A clump of animal rights activists stood by watching. Vance launched into a vile tirade, spewing forth obscenities that would bring a flush to the cheeks of even the crustiest miner. Then Vance saw the protesters, who were using video and still cameras to document as much of the day's action as they could. He shifted his screed into high gear. I should have sensed danger when he bellowed, "I don't want my picture pasted all over anti-socialist America!"

I stood about fifty feet away, furiously scribbling. Before I knew it Vance had invaded my personal space. If he'd gotten any closer I wouldn't have respected myself the next morning. Vance's posse was hot on his stumbling heels.

"What are you writing?" he smirked. The alcohol fumes were making me dizzy.

"I'm just making some notes."

"Notes about what?" He leered, wavering to and fro.

"I'm just writing about what's going on out here. I'm a journalist."

"Is there anything about me in there?" Vance reached for the notebook. I flipped it shut and gripped it tightly, assuming that once he had it I'd never see it again. I looked around. Another crowd had formed, mostly pro-shoot people. There were several activists, mostly diminutive women, and no police in sight. I was on my own.

"You people come up here and write stories about us and you don't even know what we're doing here. This shoot raises money for the local community. Do you write about that? People come out here to have a good time. So what if they're shooting pigeons? They're just rats with wings. They shit all over the place, and they spread disease. I was in the Marines. I served my country. What have any of you people done for your country? Do you know how much pigeon shit they have to clean off the Vietnam Memorial down in Washington?"

Vance paused to glare at me.

"Where are you from?"

"Hummelstown . . . down near Harrisburg."

He pondered this for a moment.

"Yeah, I got some friends down there . . . If I don't like what you write I might be gettin' in touch with them."

A reel of *Deliverance* was unspooling in my head. Discretion seemed the better part of valor. Vance was the town loudmouth, all bark and no bite. But I wanted some information in case anything happened.

"I'll tell you what. When I finish the article, I'll send you a copy. You can check it out for yourself. See what you think of it."

Vance took a swig of beer.

"Fair enough."

"Give me your address." I flipped open the notebook.

He did.

"I'll tell you what. Give me your phone number too, and then I can give you a call and talk when you're sober."

Vance juggled his three cans of beer. Finding a full one, he drank from it, spilling half down the front of his shirt.

"I'm not drunk," he said, swaying back and forth. He gave me his number. We shook hands, and he and his boys lurched off into the sunset.

The crisis was over. I never saw Jim Vance again. Nor did I follow through on my promise to call him, though I'm still thinking of sending him a copy of this article. It's the least I could do.

Profile

My first encounter with William I. Lengeman III was by chance. I happened to be passing by his house one day. Despondent over the ream of rejection slips that he'd accumulated over the years, he was poised on the ledge outside his office, threatening to jump. Since it was a basement office this posed no real threat to his well-being. But his pitiful whining was disturbing the neighbors, so I stopped and "talked him down."

Today Bill seems to have more or less adjusted to the emotional rigors of the freelance writer's life. His home and office are located at a point midway between Middletown and Hershey, Pennsylvania. On a good day, if the wind is right, you can walk to the end of the block and see the steam from the cooling towers of Three Mile Island and smell the sickly sweet smell of brewing Hershey's chocolate. Perhaps it's this threat of impending nuclear doom combined with a contact chocolate high that lends a strange warp to the stories in his collection-in-progress, *Death by Sneezing.*

—Wendy Deeley

Bio

William I. Lengeman III
Place of residence: Hummelstown, Pennsylvania.
Birthplace: New Cumberland, Pennsylvania.
Grew up in: A state of bewilderment.
Day jobs: Journalist. Fiction writer.
Education: High school.
Serial publications: Contributor to various magazines.
Current projects: A novel and collection of short stories.
Craving: All-natural peanut butter.

Gary Lilley

Hard Shoes:
Reflections on Childhood in Washington, D.C.

I was a school kid in New York and ran with a group of neighborhood boys crazy into our teenage years. We were rebellious, we forced music, clothes, and thinking to change. We had rivals from different neighborhoods and warred with them continually. We were ballplayers of the serious type and would crush you on our court. Any disagreement that couldn't be settled with a game could be resolved in a fair fist fight. We were irreverent in our young-boy arrogance, but we were safe in the neighborhood's tolerance. As long as we understood that we were automatically under the discipline of every adult in the neighborhood and knew the exact line not to cross, we were tolerated. Being young was very simple. Now, I'm over forty. I live in Washington, D.C., and nothing is simple anymore.

The end of the '96 shutdown. The government is back at work, and New York Avenue is a bumper commute. The last few mornings have seen three lanes of winter-nasty cars heading downtown. The city has a shortage of public works equipment, and O Street, a snow-choked apocalypse, is in the line of sight of the commuters. Stranded cars are buried windshield-deep, and homeless men kick through snow toward the kitchen.

The east end of O Street has been bulldozed to a stop at the cross of North Capitol. It is now a makeshift basketball court where I find bullets when the weather is good. Bullets—not the Washington professional basketball players—but shell casings and live rounds. The houses at the east end are dying. There are no trees.

The west end looks on the back of Paul Laurence Dunbar High School. In the middle of the block there is a drug house in the apartments that also carry the poet's name. A chainlink fence separates the school from the street. The amount of federal funding and/or privatization of the D.C. public school system is still in debate. There are no art programs. Artists literally have to walk into the schools. And they do. Some teachers find the children's drawings and poems frightening.

On the corner there is a candy store owned by an Ethiopian family. Behind bulletproof glass they sell cigarettes one at a time and are as courteous as you will allow. Outside the store, the young crack dealers known as The First 'n' O Street Crew work the corner. They operate as a collective and push their product by just waiting. They are polite to the Ethiopians and don't allow any trouble. The young men have marked the alley wall as a boundary, their spot. They have spray painted warnings along its length. Around ominous drawings are scattered names.

The majority of these young men hit the street for the same reason: to take care of the family. They have brothers, sisters, babies, and mothers in desperate lack, and they need to help. And they can't do that on minimum wage. While some are pulled in by the "gangsta" lifestyle, mystified and commercialized through various media, most of this crew consist of reluctant hustlers. If a forty-hour week on the present minimum wage could pay the rent and buy food, many of them would push burgers.

Everything is political here, especially money to live with. This is O Street, D.C., where there are American citizens with no congressional vote surviving hand-to-mouth. Congress is cutting funds for education and building more prisons. Already chain gangs do the road work in several southern states, and in the Oregon Penitentiary they manufacture a line of blue jeans. I can see the next move coming: prison as a profit-making industry. I see it as plain as a fresh-pressed D.C. license plate. I can also see this crew, under the three-strike law, setting themselves up to become free labor, if not more immediate casualties.

All of the crew wear hard shoes, rough outdoor shoes for urban terrain, workboots, Timberlands. They have microscoped me, looking for addictions. They trust almost no one, especially an "older" black man. Most of the youth here have lived as children in a home without a father. Men have walked in and out of their lives. In their eyes I lack the proof that I haven't abandoned anyone.

Once the crew came upon me in the alley reading the names on their wall.

"What's up, man?" the first one asked me.

"I'm reading your wall," I replied.

"Yeah, but why?"

"I want the spirits to guide and protect." They looked into each other and shouldered closer toward me. I knew some of them were armed.

"What are you, some kinda holy man or something?" he asked. "All these names on this wall still live people!"

"Then you should thank the ancestors," I said.

They got silent. At that moment they knew that I was crazy. They didn't know what to do. The tall one in the back of the group studied my face.

"Rasta, go 'head and bless that wall anyway," he said.

Since then I have lit candles, left offerings to the spirits, and poured libations. I have talked with these young men. I see them as unguided warriors lacking rites of passage. I worry for them.

One night late, I stepped out while the crew were making plans. They were gathered in their big jackets beside a drift of snow. They checked me out and then continued with their discussion.

"I say we come up through the alley behind them," one was saying.

"Naw! They got someone watchin'," said another. "I say we just roll down on 'em!"

"All right," said the tall one, "y'all get ready." I slowed down as I neared them. "What the hell is going on now?" I thought. There had already been several shootings in the city since the blizzard. I could see tit-for-tat being played out right around my door. I didn't want any of them knocked down in front of me.

Everything inside of me slowed except the fatal scenarios framing in my mind. In D.C., young blacks in Timberlands are considered dangerous. And dangerous is considered deadly. Elementary school children develop a survival stoicism about death and violence. Junior high schools have metal detectors. Yellow police tape has become a metaphor for inner city blues. In my mind I was seeing medical teams, cops, and wailing mothers.

Each hesitant step closer to the crew brought me a different response, each one inadequate. I knew I would have to say something, but I didn't know what. What words do you say to teenage boys in their hard life, who shoot their guns just to see if they still work? I stood before them, and as I began to speak I noticed that they were making snowballs. A snowball fight. I laughed. They ignored me. I remembered the snowball fights of my youth on winter nights in New York, block versus block. That was long ago when I was a child. Now I'm grown, the First 'n' O Crew are the children, and nothing is simple.

On July 2, 1996, Dennis was shot and killed by unknown assailants while he was sitting near the wall alone. He was no angel, but he was no hoodlum either. He was sixteen and hustling just to make it. Everyone on O Street has been changed by his death. We remember the night of cordite, flashing lights, and unabashed weeping. He leaves to mourn: his parents, his woman, his child, his neighbors, and his crew.

Profile

The first time I invited Gary Lilley to my small O Street studio in Washington, D.C., was November of 1993, on an extremely cold evening. So cold in fact, that I was wearing a zillion sweaters, and Gary never removed his heavy army coat. As I showed him around we discussed my art and his poetry. He recognized the legendary bluesman Robert Johnson in a picture I had placed high up on a shelf.

"You know," he said, "I used to perform some of my poetry in a pinstripe suit and a hat just like that."

It was then that I knew I had found another one of the blues people, a fellow parishioner of the church of the unconverted.

Continuing in the tradition of the blues, Gary uses his poetry as a means to bear witness and convey truths for the community he is a part of. And just like the music that inspires him, he always manages to find life-affirming humor even in the most painful situations.

—Renée Stout

Bio

Gary Lilley

Place of residence: Washington, D.C.

Birthplace: Hobbsville, North Carolina.

Day job: Washington, D.C. Writers Corps.

Education: University of North Carolina, Greensboro.

Poetry: *African American Review. Greensboro Review. WPFW Anthology.*

Award: Recipient of Washington, D.C. Commission of the Arts Fellowship for Poetry (1996).

Current projects: Creating a collection of blues-based stories. Recording project with the band Franko Jazz.

Favorite book: *Cane* by Jean Toomer.

Craving: Homemade ice cream.

Lisa Suhair Majaj

Tata Olga's Hands

My grandmother's hands were brown as the eggs she boiled in onion skins for Easter, rough like the bark of the jasmine vine that twined its way up the back wall of her chipped-stone house. She ladled *maftoul* in steaming portions, chick peas and onions like islands in the gold brown sauce, hands firm as she hefted the bowl from stove to table. Tomato in one hand, knife in the other, rivulets ran to her wrists. The bread was paper thin and tore in long strips, dusting her hands with flour. Afterwards she poured tea over mint leaves, stirred a spoon round and round till the sugar dissolved, offered the steaming glass.

When my uncle died, *Tata* Olga washed his body with a stained white rag, wrung the cloth out fiercely in clear cool water. In the kitchen, bitter coffee boiled in a huge pot over an open flame. Her knuckles were white on the ladle. She carried the tray without wavering, offered tiny cups that mourners tilted between thumb and forefinger. Cigarette smoke hung on the air. All evening she held out her palms: has God willed this?

Profile

Lisa Suhair Majaj was one of the first, and remains of the most insightful, scholars to explore Arab-American literature. At the same time, she has been patiently and unpretentiously writing her own very moving poetry and prose.

Born to an American mother and Palestinian father, and married to a

Greek Cypriot, Lisa knows a lot about crossing borders with integrity. In a world where too many people see only what they are prepared to see, her work urges us to realize much more.

Lisa lived briefly here in Worcester, Massachusetts. During the Gulf War, I used to see her at the peace vigil in Lincoln Square. This square is actually a large circle with a flagpole and World War I memorial. It is bounded by a convergence of streets that could be charitably described as a historical accident.

During rush hour, backed-up drivers rolled down their windows to punctuate the vigil's prayers and witness with honking, hoarse obscenities, and cries of "Traitors!" When the war ended, Lisa and others tied black ribbons to the skinny trees in memory of the dead.

She still keeps faith, speaks out, does good. One recent example: a Jewish peace activist, writing in response to terrorist attacks, quoted Lisa's poetry for its clear vision, sense of justice, and anguished humanity.

—David Williams

Bio

Lisa Suhair Majaj
Place of residence: Cambridge, Massachusetts.
Birthplace: Hawarden, Iowa.
Grew up in: Amman, Jordan.
Day job: Adjunct college lecturer.
Education: B.A. in English literature from American University of Beirut. M.A., A.B.D. in English literature and American culture from University of Michigan.
Serial publication: *Forkroads: A Journal of Ethnic American Literature.*
Anthologies: *Unsettling America: An Anthology of Contemporary Multicultural Poetry,* Penguin Books (1994). *Memory and Cultural Politics: New Approaches to American Ethnic Literatures,* Northeastern University Press (1996). *Food for Our Grandmothers: Writings by Arab-American and Arab-Canadian Feminists,* South End Press (1994).
Awards: New England Poetry Club—best published poem (1995). Worcester County Poetry Association—fourth prize (1989).
Current projects: Dissertation on Arab-American literature. Coediting a

collection of essays on third world women writers.
Favorite book: *Woman Warrior* by Maxine Hong Kingston.
Belief: Respect for all peoples and cultures.
Cravings: Peace in the Middle East. A Palestinian state. Chocolate.
Favorite memory: Reading books in the crook of the cherry tree in the backyard.

Bruce Duane Martin

Fury

The twins arrived prematurely in the June heat of 1963. "Feeding eleven mouths already," my father said. "Guess two more won't make us any poorer." Then the summer rains stopped. In the fall, crops failed, beef prices fell, and farmers began dumping their milk in the fields.

In November, a neighbor gave my father a sick, emaciated dog. "Can we keep her?" my brothers and I pleaded. "If we get her healthy, can we keep her?" My father relented. "But remember," he said, "the dog stays in the barn, not in the house. And she better learn to work the cattle." My brothers and I named the dog Goldie. We loved her, cared for her, nursed her back to health.

One cold December Sunday, I trudged to the barn to do the evening chores. Goldie bounded across the yard, yapping and running circles around me and licking my hand. My eyes watered as I stepped into the shadowy interior of the barn. I cleaned the stalls, spread clean sawdust, threw hay down from the mow, and slopped the hogs.

Then I slouched across the unlit yard, watching the clouds swirling around the barn, scudding across the corn field into the forested darkness beyond. Lightning flashed, yellowing the entire eastern horizon. Thunder stumbled and mumbled drunkenly across the sky, and the cold night began to howl. I turned and raced for the house with Goldie nipping my heels.

Goldie whimpered and lunged for the door and safety of the farmhouse foyer. Catching her long shaggy coat, I stroked her head and guided her to safety under the broken-down porch just as the deluge broke. In seconds, the unseeded lawn became a muddy torrent, deepening pools in the cattle yard near the barn.

In the mud-room, my brothers and I began removing our clothing. Suddenly the door burst open—driving wind and rain—and my father charged in, sputtering, drenched to the bone. Seeing her last chance, Goldie bolted through the open door, nearly knocking him off his feet. She sat trembling behind the mud-room door.

Grim-faced and muttering, my father reached for the cowering dog, groped for the collar buried beneath her matted coat, and jerked her, choking, from behind the door. Reaching just as quickly, fluidly, with the other hand for the cast-iron bootjack, he brought it down with crushing force on Goldie's head. Screaming in silence, I watched helplessly as he struck her blow after blow. Finally, he released her and she fell, crumpled, to the floor, her last life gathering in a thick red pool around her head. Extending her paws toward me, she shuddered, stiffened, and was still.

Standing motionless in his manure-covered, blood-splattered coveralls, my father stared, detached, at his callused hands, his breathing heavy and ragged. Finally, taking hold of Goldie's leg, he dragged her through the foyer, opened the door, and dumped her body over the side of the porch into the mud and water below. Following the swath of blood across the grimy linoleum floor, I winced when Goldie's head bounced over the threshold and disappeared. My eyes watering, ears pounding, and lungs surging into my throat, I swallowed and turned my back to finish removing my chore clothes.

"What're you bawlin' about?" my father asked.

The storm subsided, its fury spent, and I readied myself for Sunday evening services. When the tiny Main Creek congregation began to sing, my father sat rigid, slumped forward in the pew with his face in his hands. His lips trembled and fists clenched. During the second hymn—"Marvelous Grace of Our Loving Lord"—tears slid down between his fingers, leaving little dark stains that glistened on the hard pine floor.

Profile

Above his pale sheaf of chopped hair, Princeton's Latin diploma declares Bruce Duane Martin a Master of Divinity. At his back, the half-acre of books on theology and psychology announce his profession as university chaplain.

But Bruce talks about his writing: personal narratives garnered from boyhood years on a Wisconsin farm and an Ojibwa Indian Reservation. Places harsh and cruel; without books or the leisure to read them. No culture at Angle Inlet—on the border of Manitoba, Ontario, and Minnesota—to nudge a boy towards writing. That would come later. After the sermons: first in his youth with a tent evangelist who later robbed a bank and went to prison; then the polished Presbyterian homily to a Mennonite congregation in Maine; and now a university pulpit. Always, a weaver of tales—oral vignettes, he calls them—for sermon illustrations and his three children's bedtime rituals. His audiences forgot his fine exegeses, but remembered the stories, many as dark as the emotional landscape of his youth.

So, now Bruce writes stories. "Hard work," he declares of the task—writing at midnight, pen to paper for the first draft, wrestling with language and memory. Bruce says, "I want life's experiences to have mattered—must get them down." But there is nothing nostalgic here. A driven man, sometimes angry, he forges language that is as sinewy as his body. Without whining, without whimpering, without bitterness, without cynicism, his stories portray the redemptive capacity of personal suffering.

—Omar Eby

Bio

Bruce Duane Martin
Place of residence: Harrisonburg, Virginia.
Birthplace: Ladysmith, Wisconsin.
Grew up in: Ladysmith, Wisconsin, on a poor dairy farm, and Angle Inlet, Minnesota.
Day job: Chaplain and instructor in Bible and Religion Department, Eastern Mennonite University.
Education: B.A., Philosophy and Psychology, University of Wisconsin, Eau Claire. Master of Divinity, Princeton Theological Seminary. Currently a doctoral student at Princeton Theological Seminary.
Serial publications: *Gospel Herald. Weather Vane. Festival Quarterly.*
Accomplishments: Gave a speech at the Ladysmith County Court in fifth

grade on soil conservation. Expelled from high school four times.

Award: A full academic scholarship to Princeton Theological while legally blind.

Family: Married to Jewel who, like me, is a minister in the Mennonite Church. We have three children, Jonathan, Sarah, and Arielle.

Current projects: Completing doctoral studies. Working on three longer pieces, an essay, and several short stories.

Favorite books: *Snows Falling on Cedars* by David Guterson, *Saving Grace* and *Family Linen* by Lee Smith.

Religious heritage: When the Civil War divided Virginia, Mennonites refused to bear arms for either side. Having fled from persecution in their homelands, Mennonites sought to abolish slavery and secure freedom for all people through nonviolent means. Today the largest concentration of Mennonites in the eastern United States is found in the Shenandoah Valley.

Favorite New Testament parable: Mark 5:24.

Beliefs: Shaped by orthodox Christian faith in general and by the Anabaptist/Mennonite traditions of community, service, and peacemaking in particular. Having grown up with Ojibwa people, I have a deep appreciation for other cultures and for the American Indian community in particular.

Cravings: Solitude. Time to read and write without interruption, and time with my wife, Jewel, and our three children.

Exercise: I run from five to nine miles most days.

Grew up with: Wally, a baby Woodchuck dropped by his mother on the highway. My mother nursed Wally from a bottle until he could eat pancakes from the kitchen table. Wally grew up without a clue about what it meant to be a woodchuck. He cleaned up scraps around the table, clicked his teeth at strangers, slept in my bed, and sat in the front seat of our 1960 Ford for the trip to town.

Favorite quote on writing: "Storytellers should be aware that they are dealing with dangerous materials. Life and death flow to us through stories. Words have almost unlimited power to destroy and to heal. . . . More lives have been destroyed by words than by bullets and more lives redeemed and made whole." *The Healing Power of Stories* by Daniel Taylor (Doubleday, 1996).

Doug Nathan

Bus Ridden

After traveling throughout Guatemala by bus for six weeks, I am unaccustomed to riding buses in Seattle. I long to hail another Blue Bird school bus for an over-crowded ride. Seats designed for two American children hold three and sometimes four adult Guatemalans with more people squeezing in the center isle. When there appears no room left between shoulders and butts half on and half off the seat, that's when thirty more people push and smoosh their way on, and the ones not quick or aggressive enough are left behind. Then the *audante*, the ticket taker, collects fares. It's an art learned over many sweaty, bumpy miles. Bus riders lean heads and rotate hips and learn to ignore elbow jabs. If it's really crowded, the *audante* walks on top of the chair backs balancing himself on body parts beneath him as the bus slams into potholes.

   Out of city limits away from police supervision, the *audante* lets people climb the rear ladder to the cargo roof rack. Roof riders help load and unload 100 pound bags of coffee beans and unwieldy *canastas* of live chickens. Roof riders duck tree branches and electrical wires and gaze at patchwork vistas of mountains tilled into cornfields. Roof riders sing and nobody stares. God is alive on buses in Guatemala. Wooden crucifixes swing from rearview mirrors. Windshield decals proclaim in Spanish: "I am The Way: Christ" and "God Bless this Bus and All Aboard." For more wayward souls, there are Tweety Bird and Speedy Gonzalez decals to contemplate. Some bus signs speak metaphorically to travelers far from home: "Not Responsible for Forgotten Objects." Or my favorite sign: "Do Not Litter," which refers to the American-made bus. Do not litter the bus. Plastic bags, straws, corn husks and papers red, blue, green, white fly out bus windows to adorn the countryside. Guatemalans seem ignorant of all that litter, the same way we ignore our own isolation.

I have not climbed any bus roofs since returning to Seattle, but I can't stop riding buses. I crave reminders that I am not alone: the mustiness of wet wool, the rustle of folding umbrellas, and the sickly sweet smell of discarded chewing gum as a man unsticks his coat from the seat. I like the way we tailor our buses for physically challenged riders, the way the bus drivers actually wait and strap in the wheelchairs. I'm glad we don't throw our litter out the windows to keep the inside of the bus clean.

I met an elderly woman who started riding the bus after her husband died. She's too uncertain about steering herself alone through town. She, like other people new to bus riding in the United States, is easy to spot, eager to talk. She hasn't closed down within the anonymity of the bus ride. She doesn't notice the silence of people sitting next to each other who stare straight ahead as if their attention is needed to keep the bus moving forward. New bus riders appreciate this novel society on wheels: the hurried pace and congestion of traffic outside; inside is room for sitting next to strangers, talking and creating experiences. Like the little girl and her mother who sat behind me last week. The little girl kept asking questions: "Who is the bus driver? Is the bus driver a man or a woman? Who's driving the bus? Who is the bus driver? Who's driving the bus?"—a playful song which for several minutes amused her and, OK, her song was sort of annoying, but cute, and made my ride worth more than the bus fare.

Profile

After sailing on the Golden Hinde and climbing the glacial slopes of Mt. Rainier, after teaching English in Japan and then working hard and fast as a freelance journalist, Doug Nathan accepted a technical writing contract at Microsoft in 1992. Once he settled in, he sought out fellow refugees from the natural world, teaching, and the arts. We had lunch in one of the large, raucous cafeterias at Microsoft's Redmond campus. Ever since, we've been talking about poetry, politics, translation and transformation, and the writing life. The discipline of writing has been a major topic, and we've had fun speculating about the forces that fuel the spirit which drives these "greeny" things.

In the time I've known Doug, I've come to admire most of all the integrity of his relationship to his work. Not much concerned with prizes or celebrity, he sees poetry as a cultural and social catalyst to clear-headed, clear-hearted action. He not only contributes his poetry and prose to our cultural life, but has taken direct action to help sustain the arts and his fellow artists in our market-driven economy. If this seems like high praise, well, the guy has earned it. Look for his work, look for him.

—William O'Daly

Bio

Doug Nathan
Place of residence: Bainbridge Island, Washington.
Birthplace: Syracuse, New York.
Grew up in: Eleven cities before high school graduation.
Day job: Owner/president of Beyond Words.
Education: B.A. in English literature, University of California at Los Angeles.
Serial publications: *U.S. News & World Report. Los Angeles Times. On the Bus.*
Award: Gift certificate for double kayak rental, Olympia Outdoor Center.
Current project: Bringing back the wild.
Favorite book: *The Song of the Dodo* by David Quammen.
Beliefs: Baptized Catholic, confirmed Episcopalian, awakened by Buddhism.
Cravings: Many.

Reba Owen

Body Surfing

I am a middle-aged mom and a surfer. In November 1995, for the first time, I tried cold-weather surfing. We were at Falcon Cove on Oregon's north coast. I had lost enough weight so my new wet suit didn't make me look like a baby pilot whale.

A three-day gale and 9.1 tide made the surf abnormally high. Gray sky and sea seemed as one. Waves exploded. Driftwood logs jumped in the air. Incoming waves hit rips going out, causing huge fans of water and spray. It seemed wise to wait for the tide to turn.

An hour later, when the logs and debris were on dry sand, we pushed out into the surf, and struggled to get to deeper water. Even with the receding tide, the ocean was still spectacular. Waves came sideways. Double and triple waves overtook one another, sending us like watery toboggans hooked to a freight train.

That morning we had a wide choice of waves. I lay flat on my short board, body-surfing style. I pushed hard to start each surcharged ride to the beach, and leaned right or left to steer and accelerate. Several waves peaked and prolonged, before cascading. I caught one of these curls and slipped along the wave's face. When it crashed, the power sent me airborne, a brief flight free of earth and ocean.

At noon a fog formed, causing an eerie loss of visibility. The waves still rolled in long combers toward shore. We floated and waited for rideable swells. A strange quiet encapsulated us. Something was wrong. I looked for any abnormal disturbance in the smooth, rolling water outside the break.

Winter surfing requires a certain mental edge. For winter is white shark migration time. At Falcon Cove there have been no recorded shark attacks, just one at Cannon Beach to the north, and one at Short Sands to the south. A couple hundred stitches closed the north wound. The south merely lost his board.

We continued drifting and waiting for the right wave. Nearby a gray harbor seal popped up, as did my pulse rate. A school of candle fish appeared as something dark, just under the surface, undulating closer and closer.

The bait fish sank from sight. Suddenly the right wave was there. It loomed so high that it blocked out the horizon. I felt an unseen force take control and send me down a steep glacier of surface tension. I lost peripheral vision in the silver oxygen and foam. My mind jettisoned all superfluous cargo. In front of this massive wall of water, I yelled all the way to the shallows. Terror and pleasure melded as if I were on a roller coaster; a long, bumpy ride almost to dry sand. I recovered, rose, and had turned to go back out when a sneaker wave hit me in ankle-deep water. My board flew skyward, and I went down without a sound.

My companions, who had duck-dived under the enormous breaker, looked for me to surface from the turbulence. I never surfaced, having beached on dry sand like a porpoise with bad sonar. As the younger trade call it, "a wipe out." I lay there. The warm comfort of my wet suit belied the forty-eight degree water temperature. The fog was thickening now, erasing the spruce and hemlock on Cape Falcon, and bringing along an excuse to quit for the day.

Profile
Reba Owen.

My family owns a small, handmade cabin perched so close to the edge of the Pacific that on a clear day you imagine seeing Hawaii. Huge waves spawned by wicked storms far to the west pummel sand and rock in an unrelenting quest to claim the quaint shelter. While the rest of us fret over the diminishing distance between the front window and the world's largest ocean, my sister Reba dons a slick black wet suit and paddles a "boogie board" into the frothing, monster waves. She consorts with the enemy. She revels in it. She's fifty-five years old. Is she wacko? She has traveled to the other side of this ocean. Why? I think she wanted to see if the waves traveling in reverse direction are somehow different. Yes, it is hard to accept, but my lovely sister might well be wacko.

—Dudley W. Nelson

Bio

Reba Owen

Place of residence: Wheeler, Oregon.

Birthplace: Portland.

Grew up in: Milwaukie, Oregon.

Day job: Supervisor for Services to Children and Families in Oregon.

Education: B.S. in recreation, Oregon State University.

Chap book: *Green Highways.*

Anthology: *Library of Congress Anthology*—poetry.

Current projects: *Aegis,* a book about my experiences in child protective services. A biography called *Fishermen.*

Favorite book: *Blue Highways* by William Least Heat Moon.

Belief: Good will outweigh evil, eventually.

Craving: Good surf.

Pastime: I try to save and cure wounded and sick animals.

Joan Piper

Worry Seeds

Okay, so I'm a worried mother. Can't help it. People who've lived in our bodies for nine months—we've marked them with our scent and track them wherever they go. So maybe it's not a good idea for me to listen to the news.

The other day I heard Noam Chomsky on the radio, reciting the gap between rich and poor. Poverty, he says, is lapping at our shores.

The poor are coming, and some of them are turning into us, and some of us are turning into them. They turn out to be real people hidden in a costume of soot and grime, people who just don't have time to write a resumé or start a business. They're too busy being sick or can't get a bus from Zanzibar to Nordstrom. They creep in and infect our edges, blur the line, tire the eyes with their endless wars and debris. Tidy they are not.

Last night I laid awake, shouting prayers inside my skull to drown away the fear that this poverty is catching, that my children, too, could slip into the ranks of the poor. I saw the image of my son, turned 30, struggling to find a moment to read a book; he and his wife struggling to find a moment to breathe between long, spinning runs down the freeway to workplaces and paychecks; then long runs back up the freeway to home. They are trying to make the same home for their baby they had as kids in the 1960s, when average Americans were the richest people in history. When it took only one nine-to-five paycheck to buy a three-bedroom house with a lawn and two cars.

My son moonlights on weekends, usually, so he and his wife had only one weekend to put in a lawn: create soil, rototill it in the sun, rake it, roll it all by hand. At the end of the blistering day she drove off to work her usual graveyard shift. Even though it's graveyard, her job requires a college degree. She came back in the morning to take over from my son, who then went to his weekday job.

While my son's away, she takes on the non-work of mothers, the twenty-four hour work that doesn't register in the economic indicators: changing diapers, feeding the babe, washing clothes, cleaning house, and trying to find out what the hell is wrong with that child that he won't stop crying—when she needs so desperately to sleep an hour or two. Please. Just a couple of hours before the night job looms up again, as soon as dinner is done.

So where will my son and grandson go? Will they be fly fishermen, botanists? Or will they be landfill raiders? Entrepreneurship, of course, is the American way. You used to hear that 90% of small businesses fail in the first year. Now you hear we should all be entrepreneurs or "independent contractors"—gleaning crumbs of business like downsized mice, under the table at the stockholders' feast. Should I worry? Or turn off the news?

Profile

Joan Piper
A.D. 2020, Seattle.

I'm rummaging through the storage room of my book shop, and I find an unusual book, one the Thought Police haven't confiscated. A collection of heartfelt sentiments, outside approved commercial formulae. This book is an artifact. Unlike nearly all other thoughtful writing from the late twentieth century, this book has not been turned to ash.

My eye scans the table of contents, and I recognize an author's name. Joan Piper and I once spent an afternoon at her home on Bainbridge Island in the mid-1990s sharing our artistic efforts with a group of writers, musicians, visual artists, and actors. As we watched ferries gliding into Eagle Harbor beyond blackberries and apple trees, I shared my "Trips Though Minefields" series of paintings, and she read from her current potboiler about a beautiful, red-headed alcoholic spy. Her book teemed with characters seeking to express themselves. Local author Mike Pryor sang cabaret tunes from the play "Seattle: Land of the Long Yellow Crayon," and Joyce Keller read her poems of Seattle street life—from ballerina girls on the bus to the bag lady with visions of leopards and oranges. Jay Piper amused and shocked us with tales of a sailor's slave-like existence during Vietnam.

Events such as these were a normal part of life back in the mid-1990s. Ten or twenty of us would gather in homes around Puget Sound for Share-a-Thons, where we ate food and gave praise: we accepted one another's art works as the gifts they were—leaving it to the world to supply judgment and rejection. In those days it was a challenge to live a creative life in a hostile, mass-market money culture—yet such a life still was possible. It seems long ago.

In the year 2000, The Events began. Now free expression is a rumor from the past. This book is one of the few that survived the Great Fires of 2010. I read this collection three times. I will not tell another soul. Even so, I know that the Monitors have detected me. My time is limited. I will re-read this book until the Thought Police come to my door.

—D.A. Murray

Bio

Joan Piper
Place of residence: Bainbridge Island, Washington.
Birthplace: Chicago.
Grew up in: San Francisco Bay Area.
Day job: Director of exhibits and programs in a museum.
Education: B.A. in English, San Diego State University. M.A. in Educational Technology.
Books: Poetry chapbooks.
Serial Publications: Professional journals.
Awards: Education Award for African Rock Kopic Exhibit in San Diego Zoo. Bank of America Achievement Award.
Current projects: *Liar Liar Pants on Fire,* a novel about a beautiful alcoholic spy named Poppy. Painting fish patterns on silk—Fishey Raiments.
Favorite book: *Joy Luck Club* by Amy Tan.
Belief: Yes!
Cravings: Travel. Reading my poetry to a group. Lying under a tree.

Laura L. Post

Race, Chocolate, and Dogs

People don't tell the truth, and the world is a poorer place because of it. I could introduce myself by saying that I am a white person, and I do check the box marked "white" on standardized forms, yet that would be a lie. The truth is that white people are tan, not white, and black people are brown, not black. Everyone else is a related earthtone. I am called "white" in a social system which polarizes us "whiteys" from everyone else.

Another set of lies relates to size. I am thin (5'10", 152 pounds), used to be skinny (130 pounds), but no one told me to my face that I was skinny, for fear of hurting me. My partner Judith is fat (5'7", 280 pounds), but she is referred to as "big-boned," or "big," or "hefty"—sometimes *zoftig,* a Yiddish term which alludes to large breasts, a misnomer here. Her personal favorite is "queen-sized." She tells me that she is past "pleasingly plump" and "a good eater," though these terms are still occasionally applied by people who are baffled, uncomfortable, or have limited vision or vocabularies.

People will tell me that my added weight looks good on me, but the only comments that Judith hears about her size have to do with the difficulty of finding nice clothes that fit (from other fat women) or condolences on failed diets (from thin women). Invisibility can be more painful that facing difficult things about ourselves.

Humans are capable of assessing and naming objects as they are. We don't need euphemisms and polarities. We are capable of telling it like it is.

Think of how we refer to animals. People don't say: "Look at that pleasingly plump dog." Instead, they say, "Look at that old dog. Her teats drag on the ground. Isn't she cute? Here, girl!"

People also don't say: "See that dog of color? He's got dark spots." Rather, they say, "Check out that tan dog with the black and brown patches." Dog colors come out of the Crayola box. Human colors come out of an imaginary box devised for white superiority (black is evil, white good) and maintained out of fear of other people and anxiety about change. I don't mean to transform well-intentioned euphemisms born of respect into bigoted, pithy epithets or vice versa. Nor am I aiming at bringing private honesty into the public forum before society is ready. (If you called my lover "a fatty with saggy tits," she probably would be offended; though, with reconsideration and in the face of sincere attitude, she might appreciate the refreshing honesty.) I'm hoping that we all can nourish the ability to accurately perceive. Though I'm thin and white and speaking for myself and other folks who might be like me, these phenomena extend to everyone. Apply these analogies to height, disability, Jewishness, gender, gayness or any other "difference" from the North American-white-Christian-right-handed-heterosexual-male gold standard, and you'll see what I mean.

I don't pretend to have a solution to the world's economic and political conflicts. I believe that, if we humans express what we perceive without the distortions dictated by custom, then humankind and the world will be better off.

How about starting with "race by chocolate"? Here's what I mean. Chocolate is a common denominator. Most people can relate to it without prejudice. For example: One of my black friends has skin which is the color of milk chocolate; another is more bittersweet. My own skin color is a mix of white chocolate (which really *is* white!) and milk chocolate, because my ancestry is Eastern European Jew which happens, in me, to be darker than a person whose heritage is Western European, and lighter than a person whose heritage is African.

My theory is that telling the truth gives us a head start on doing what we actually want in the world. If we begin by naming what is around us the way children do: fat, thin, sort of thin (kids don't use polarities much) or taupe, red clay, caramel, mocha, then perhaps we'll end up by being able to identify true things within us. And then we may find that we connect better with other people.

Profile

I first heard Laura L. Post speak almost ten years ago—eight o'clock on Tuesday, April 7, 1987, to be exact. An early spring evening at the Tralfamadore Café in Buffalo, New York. Laura, then a third-year medical student, had just won $250 for being the best in psychiatry. She invested the money in a production of women's music for Erie County.

Though busy with her hospital rotations, Laura not only made all the phone calls necessary to set up the gig for the singer-songwriter Tret Fure, she also interviewed the artist for the local feminist newspaper, the now-defunct *Common Ground*. Unwittingly, Laura's actions in producing the concert also pulled together the disparate factions in the small town, who were all present; her speech had to address each group's concern without seeming to make too much effort in doing so. She did it with humor, sagacity, and presence.

Her current writing brings me back to that smoky club in upstate New York where Laura and I lived in independent unhappiness. That first concert-related interview showed Laura a niche—women's music production. The writing she has done since has made her something of a celebrity in women's music. After moving to California, still in love with words and questions, she splits her time between writing about the arts, sports, cultural events, and working with mentally ill addicts in Oakland.

—Judith Avery

Bio

Laura L. Post
Place of residence: Oakland.
Birthplace: New York City.
Grew up in: Manhattan and Los Angeles.
Day jobs: Psychiatrist. Educator.
Education: B.A., Harvard University. M.A., Université de Paris IV. M.D., State University of New York, Buffalo.
Serial publications: *Ms. Out. Deneuve. Advocate. Outlines. Washington Blade.*

B-Side. Spirit/Southwest Airlines, and over 150 other publications—fiction, poetry, features, columns, and reviews.

How I describe myself: A left-handed, Jewish writer of mixed-class heritage.

Awards: First Class Girl Scout. First prize, 1995 Arizona Authors Contest for an essay on lesbian battering. Best Journalist, *Hot Wire: The Journal of Music and Culture* (1992).

Current projects: Collection of feminist interviews with women musicians, forthcoming from New Victoria Press (1997). Lady Phoenix Productions—educational seminars.

Favorite book: *Stone City* by Mitchell Smith.

Beliefs: I am a person in recovery, and I try to be present and mindful.

Arthur Quinn

The Miracle Harvest

The last time I was in Plymouth, I found myself eavesdropping on a tour group. These modern pilgrims were, not surprisingly, disappointed by the famous rock. Looming like a Gibraltar in our national mythology, Plymouth Rock was in fact a sad little boulder under a Victorian awning. Then a question was asked about Thanksgiving, the Pilgrims' other claim to fame: "What kind of a farmer has a harvest festival in late November?" Answer: "A bad one."

I had to bite my tongue. The first Thanksgiving dinner was actually held in October—October 1621. Plenty early for a harvest festival. Perhaps I should have told the tourists that the November date was Lincoln's doing, in 1863. But that might have required a disquieting explanation, for what we often forget is that we as a nation get Thanksgiving not from the Pilgrims but from the Civil War.

The Thanksgiving tradition was still alive and well in the Northeast (with locally fluctuating dates) when Abraham Lincoln became President. But it had not caught on nationally. In declaring Thanksgiving a national holiday, Lincoln gave it so late a date he detached it from its agricultural origins. This was fitting, since he intended to use the holiday for political purposes.

In that autumn of 1863, the Civil War had taken a bad turn for the North. After the victory at Gettysburg in July, Major General George C. Meade had allowed Robert E. Lee's army to slip away, to live to fight another day. The

Union was then defeated at Chickamauga—and the Union command was left, in Lincoln's words, "confused and stunned like a duck hit on the head." The country, Lincoln knew, was itself becoming increasingly confused and stunned by the sheer magnitude of the carnage. The casualties at Chickamauga alone were being estimated at more than 35,000.

So Lincoln was, quite understandably, worried about the coming election, particularly about the American people's willingness to gather in this vast harvest of death. The Thanksgiving proclamation can thus be read as a first salvo in his re-election campaign. This proclamation did concede that the Civil War was "of unequaled magnitude and severity." But it asked the nation to view the losses from a broader vantage.

"Needful diversions of wealth and of strength from the fields of peaceful industry to the national defense have not arrested the plow or the shuttle, or the ship; the ax has enlarged the borders of our settlements, and the mines, as well of iron and coal as of the precious metals, have yielded even more abundantly than heretofore."

This continued prosperous growth of the Republic, the proclamation added, was truly miraculous. It gave proof, for those who still needed it, of America's providential destiny. We should, therefore, expect this same "Almighty Hand to heal the wounds of the nation" and to restore peace and tranquillity and union "as soon as may be consistent with Divine Purpose."

One Lincoln admirer caught the religious spirit of the proclamation when he exclaimed in response, "No ruler of millions, since King David the Psalmist, has clothed great thoughts in sublimer language."

Well, perhaps. But I cannot help wondering about the original Pilgrims. What would they have thought of Lincoln's use of their modest harvest feast?

They would not have objected to a Thanksgiving feast in the face of horrific death. Their own feast had been just that. They had arrived in Plymouth in the winter, a group of about 100, inadequately supplied and weakened by the anxious months of preparation and the arduous voyage. As a result, during the ordeal of that first winter, approximately half the colonists died, including the governor. Women routinely sacrificed themselves for their families—whether the mothers gave up their own food or just worked themselves into exhaustion in caring for the sick, thirteen of the eighteen wives died, but only three of the twenty children.

Moreover, the Pilgrims had survived their ordeal, if barely, only because a previous people had not. The colonists had found Plymouth deserted but with many signs of previous inhabitants. They found large corn caches, without which they almost certainly would have starved. They also found human bones scattered around—not just the occasional skeleton but piles of them, as if this had been a battlefield where corpses had been left to rot. The Pilgrims subsequently learned that the Pawtuxet Indians who lived there had recently been wiped out by an epidemic, a catastrophe that would become all too familiar to the indigenous peoples of eastern North America.

Squanto, the lone Pawtuxet who survived because he had been kidnapped by European sailors before the epidemic, adopted this strange new people occupying his ancestral lands. And at their first Thanksgiving dinner in 1621, the Pilgrims acknowledged that they had a harvest to celebrate largely because of the advice of their new friend. As for the numerous dead innocents, the Pilgrims did not need to remind themselves that the works of Providence were usually inscrutable to human reason.

Nonetheless, a true Pilgrim would have been appalled at Lincoln's proclamation—not because of its general thanks amid innocent suffering but because of its politically cunning appeal to religion.

The Pilgrims were separatists, Protestants who had despaired of a true reformation of European society. Even to be part of such a corrupt society was to risk being polluted or entirely swallowed up. The only alternative was to seek a hallowed seclusion, to separate from the greedy, struggling, self-seeking world, to live in an artificial circle of exclusion from ordinary humanity.

They had first fled to the Netherlands. They were not persecuted there, but they did struggle incessantly against the insidious erosion of their community by Dutch prosperity and cosmopolitanism. So they heroically set out for the New World, and for a time they seemed to thrive in their own peculiar way. But then, as colonies became established around them (including a New Netherlands on the Hudson), the erosion began again, and this time their leaders had no heroic remedy to offer. Plymouth would eventually be absorbed into the far more ambitious and aggressive Massachusetts Bay Colony.

The Pilgrims' greatest governor, William Bradford, would look back on the early days of Plymouth with a perplexed sadness as he brooded over their failure. But he never lost his conviction that God speaks only through pilgrim peoples, separate and small and weak. As for the eventual appropriation of Thanksgiving by a great and prosperous nation, this was exactly the pollution of godly religion by worldly politics that he and his people had fled Europe to escape. But in the final analysis they failed. The world eventually despoils everything within it.

Nevertheless, we, if any reverence for the distant Pilgrims and their beliefs be in us, should at least remember on this day that our Thanksgiving, like our America, is not theirs. The holiday of Thanksgiving is properly of Lincoln and of our bloody crucible as a people, the Civil War.

Profile

Arthur Quinn is an impressive guy, an old-fashioned man of letters, a respected professor at a big university. Yet, like most writers, Art struggles to put his work into print. Once we were bookstore hopping in Cambridge, Massachusetts, and Art came upon an old Modern Library edition of *Moby Dick* with illustrations by Rockwell Kent. Foursquare in black boards, it was a brick of a book. It reminded us of Art's unpublished manuscript, *A New World*, a monster-sized work which had garnered nothing but rejection slips over the years, though Art had rewritten it many times. We laughed—I'm not sure why. Laughter was contagious that day. We both remembered that *Moby Dick* had bombed with the critics yet survived to become a classic.

Now *A New World* is in paperback. *New York Newsday* called it "a good, voluminous, gossipy read"—one of Art's favorite blurbs. Art has published *The Rivals*, another piece of his mosaic of America, has finished a third volume which he calls *Hell with the Fire Out*, and is now researching the revolutionary period. Of course word mavens still enjoy his brief, clever exposition *Figures of Speech* (a must for creative writers and anyone else who needs to know the difference between a zeugma and an enallage).

For a guy who once feared he would be a "posthumous author," Art is quite irrepressibly and irreverently alive and bent on telling the rest of the decentered, manichean story of America. Strenuous labor, but, like Melville, Art Quinn has a whale of a subject on his hands.

—A Friend

Bio

Arthur Quinn

Place of residence: Berkeley, California.

Birthplace: Ross, California.

Grew up in: Northern California.

Day job: Professor of Rhetoric at University of California, Berkeley.

Education: B.A., University of San Francisco. M.A., Ph.D., Princeton University.

Books: *The Confidence of British Philosophers. Broken Shore: the Marin Peninsula.*

Awards: Award of Merit, *Sports Illustrated*—baseball player. Life membership in Clare Hall at Princeton.

Current project: Historical writing about America.

Favorite book: *Montaigne: Essays* by Michel De Montaigne.

Belief: Roman Catholic.

Craving: Baseball.

Sara Nadia Rashad

Walking Like an Egyptian

I am from LA, but for the last three months I have dreamed of the pyramids. My greatest fantasy has always been to become Princess of the entire Arab world like I was when I played Princess Badr al-Budur in "Aladdin and the Magic Lamp." When I boarded a plane bound for Cairo I thought my fantasies would dissipate. I was wrong.

I slipped into an aisle seat. I was wearing a leopard print dress. My body felt like Cheez Whiz and my mind like Swiss. The man sitting beside me possessed a cow-like voice and his body was attached to the hairiest arms I had ever seen. He was wearing an egg-yolk yellow sports shirt and beige slacks, his pudgy face framed by thick, brown hair. He had a wide grin, and you could stick a quarter between his two front teeth. After a polite nod I stashed the sterilized pillow behind my head and attempted to rest. The pillow quickly became an Arabian Prince with whom I've mingled saliva time and again in my dreams.

Later, I was entertaining another fantasy: a school of sting rays attacked as I was scuba diving with my prince in Ras Mohammed at the Egypt-Israeli border. The stewardess broke my reverie with her lecture on the oxygen mask. I flipped through the pages of *Vogue*. Christi Turlington and Cindy Crawford on every other page. In swimsuits their breasts popped out like the two step-pyramids at Giza. Split Tooth leaned over my shoulder and stabbed the magazine with his finger. "This one very nice!" Christi in a cobalt blue leather miniskirt and jacket. I handed him the magazine, and he offered me his hand, "My name is Magdee."

"Magdil?"

"No. Mag*dee*! Mag*dee*! I show you." He unlocked his briefcase and grabbed his business card. He handed it to me.

"Mag*dee*?"

"Yes, that is correct. And your name?"

"Sara."

"Ah, Sara! Arabic name in Qur'an!" He pronounced my name correctly on the first attempt, unlike most Americans.

"You Arabic girl?"

"My father is Egyptian."

"You visit him?"

I explained to him that my father was the only one of his family who had emigrated to America. At twenty-one, I was going to Egypt to visit the rest of my family for the first time.

I didn't catch a wink due to Magdee's incessant chatter, and before I knew it we had landed in Cairo. In the airport lobby I strained to see past glass doors smudgy with cigarette smoke. On the other side I saw hundreds of faces with bovine eyes as brown as mine. These images were all too familiar—I had seen them in my dreams. Poking out of the crowd I spotted a slip of crumpled paper waving in the air. The man who was waving it bellowed my name, "Sara Nabil Rashad. Sara Nabil Rashad."

I squeezed through the crowd to find a bulbous mass of flesh accompanied by a head, two arms, and two legs. "Hello. I am Sara Nabil Rashad."

"You?"

"Yes."

He inspected the slip of paper, rubbed his prune-like forehead then continued to bellow my name. He sounded like an auctioneer.

The crowd dissipated, so I made another attempt at convincing him. "Hi! I am Sara Rashad. Nabil is my father. Who are you?"

"OK, Sara!" The auctioneer pushed me away, and a new influx of travelers—robust and pungent—flattened me against a wall. All I could see was the auctioneer's arm waving in the air and his shiny head.

Plowing my way through the frantic crowd, I tugged on the auctioneer's left sleeve until I received his complete attention. "Excuse me, sir! I am Sara Rashad!" I jabbed my fingers into my chest. "Were you sent to collect me?"

"You?" The last thing he was expecting was a woman draped in leopard print. "OK, Sara!" He traipsed his eyes through the airport lobby one last time. "Passport?" I hunted for it in my backpack. He smiled at me, a look of total disbelief. He had the raunchiest teeth I have ever seen.

In the passport control area, white plastic paddle fans sliced two-month-old air. The flies weren't even dizzy. Men lit up cigarettes at the rate of two per minute. The silver-green, gritty tile floor was a storehouse of ash, cigarette butts, and peasant women crouched down to rest. Saudis stood in long, white floor-length gowns—garments that resembled tailored bed sheets. Their wives in black body-bags sat hip-to-hip on the green and blue plastic chairs. They were covered by black muslin except for a tiny slit for eyes. Children bounced on their mothers' stomachs or grabbed at their heels. The medley of Arab dialects, cigarette smoke, and body odor became more powerful minute by minute. My head spun. The auctioneer grabbed my hand, yanking me through the crowd. I tightened my grasp and kept pace.

We arrived at a green-gray room. Another official—especially rude and unintelligent—was speaking on the phone in loud, guttural tones. The auctioneer escorted me to the plastic chairs against the wall. The auctioneer left, and this new, featherheaded official stared at me. I was obviously overdressed for the occasion. He continued to stare. The minutes passed like a snail crossing the street. "Did somebody call for me?"

"I no understand."

"Did Samir Rashad ask you to take care of me?"

"Yes, don't worry. You must sit. OK! No problems!"

"Who called for me?"

"Sami Nagira Mustafa called. Chief of Police." Oh great! Tomorrow's headlines: American woman wearing jungle clothes is arrested in Cairo airport. I asked a dozen more questions and received oblique answers. I was at the man's mercy. I was losing it.

I tried to modulate my breathing. Tears welled up in my eyes. At last, the auctioneer returned with my passport and tossed it on the desk.

"OK! Come with me, Sara!" He grabbed my hand and a few minutes later, in baggage claim, I watched the last of the bags pass on the conveyor belt.

"My bags! They're not here."

"No? They will come," said the attendant. If there were a flood the Egyptians would still be smiling. The conveyor belt already had made four complete cycles. The crew unloaded stray baggage. Still no sign of my maroon suitcases. I filled out paperwork.

The crocodile in my throat continued snapping at my vocal chords. I couldn't speak. I returned the paperwork, then sat in a row of plastic chairs.

"Miss . . . you need taxi?" asked an official. He disappeared into the back office. I stared at the stragglers from my plane and swallowed my tears. There was one man left. He offered me a cigarette. After smoking it, I swung my pack over my shoulder, pulled down my skirt, and recharged my demeanor.

I pushed open the steel double-doors and wandered into a crowd full of waves, smiles, cigarettes, and hand-drawn signs. Hundreds of faces that resembled my own stared back at me. Then I saw an apparition. My father? The man was holding a cardboard sign with my name on it. I pushed my way through the crowd and tossed my arms around the stranger—my father's brother. People lunged toward me from all directions! Somebody prodded my left shoulder. I turned my head to find a five-foot-tall woman supported by a cane, Nanny Zuba! I bent down to hug her. Children galloped toward me and pulled me down to offer their love. A boy close to my age grabbed my back pack and introduced himself as my cousin Basheer. He asked about the rest of my luggage.

"They lost it," I said. Basheer laughed. A security guard approached and informed us that my bags had been found in London and would arrive in two days. We left for home in several cars. The city of Cairo stretched out across the blackness of the sky.

When I finally fell asleep, it was the deepest sleep I had experienced in three months. In the morning I wandered downstairs. A robust woman rushed towards me with a cup of Turkish coffee. Her name was Hoda. She had lived with the family as house maid for over ten years. As I took the first sip, the doorbell rang. Cousins, aunts, uncles, and their children surrounded me, grabbed my cheeks, and showered me with kisses. We sat down on couches. Abdelbaie, one of my nine uncles, teaches about Islam in remote villages throughout Egypt. "Do you know the story of the Qur'an?" he said.

"No," I replied. Everyone else had heard the story many times before. As we spoke, the kids started playing and the women began their own conversations.

"It's your history! You must know it!" He proceeded to describe the creation of the world as it is depicted in the Qur'an.

I had never known the story of the Qur'an. My father has been a ghost throughout most of my life, passing in and out at his convenience, assisting me financially as a way to express his love. We never had a conversation about his past, his life in Egypt, and what brought him to America. That is why I had always dreamed of going to Egypt—to fill in some of these gaps. By being close to people who knew him as a child, who understood his ambitions, I hoped to feel closer to him as well.

During my time there I came to know my father through the men and women of his family—my family, through the crowded city, and through the Egyptian people themselves. The Egyptians I met possessed a vitality which has remained unconquered by famine or foe. In Egypt, you cannot survive without a tenacious sense of humor against the poverty, the corrupt government, the timewarp that makes everything happen tomorrow and tomorrow takes a week. Beneath each wizened face lay secrets never whispered. Every Egyptian man and woman was a vessel of a hundred tales that could not be spoken. Still, I learned what I could by documenting every conversation.

For the previous three months I had imagined what Egypt would be like. The reality, it turned out, was different. Egypt was painful, and yet, I now realize, it was my home.

Profile

I met Sara Nadia Rashad in Seattle in March 1994. Born of an Irish mother and an Egyptian father, Sara was raised in Hawaii and Alaska before settling in Seattle during college years. She lived on Capitol Hill, a "New York" neighborhood of artists, expatriates, intellectuals, and politicos who bedded down in eighty-year-old brick apartment buildings smelling of stale cooking-gas, and spent most of their free time in coffee houses like the B & O Espresso or bookstores like Red and Black Books.

In 1994 the war in the former Yugoslavia was raging, and a hundred

Bosnian refugees had made it as far as Seattle. They came from Serb concentration camps, their bodies marked by torture. Local theatre producer Hanna Eady decided to do a play for his New Image Theatre. He and playwright S.P. Miskowski interviewed the refugees and, two weeks later, S.P. had fashioned a script. Now all they needed was a group of actors, including a woman who could master many parts, quickly. Sara fit the bill.

Sara was young, beautiful, and full of energy. She had recently graduated from Cornish College of the Arts with a degree in acting, and she also displayed an instinct for the important issues of our time. She wanted to portray the Bosnian conflict on stage. And so it happened: Friday night in Chinatown, the Theater Off Jackson— exposed brick, wood floors. Bosnia opened with a chorus of "Bosno Moja" ("My Bosnia"), and a rousing peasant dance. The play, like the war, was a tangle. Sara portrayed a newspaper reporter for *Oblijenski,* a waitress, the anchor on Prague radio B94, a Red Cross relief worker, and the playwright herself. At play's end, the entire cast bowed to Bosnian refugees in the audience. No curtain call? The critics howled. Only Misha Berson of *The Seattle Times* understood: On the Bosnian war, she wrote, the curtain has not gone down.

Another thing about Sara: market savvy. In March when she first talked to me, Sara was well aware that *Bosnia,* the play, would flop unless someone developed an audience. So Sara transformed herself into a publicity machine. As a favor to Hanna, I had contacted six media outlets, the PR basics. Sara proceeded to contact thirty more. Who was assisting whom? This woman was total energy.

An audience? When we arrived at the Theatre Off Jackson, the place was packed. KUOW, the local NPR affiliate, had come through for us. *The Christian Science Monitor* ran a two-page spread, and—what was this? Cameras, movie lights, men in blue jeans shooting video: "McNeil/Lehrer" was here as well. "We've been around the country interviewing Bosnian refugees," the producer said. "We came to Seattle today to film one family, and this family happened to attend the play." A coincidence? Or had Sara come with a bonus—the favor of heaven?

Two months after the play, Sara followed by flying to Germany and traveling overland with a filmmaker to the Balkan War itself. Back in Seattle in July, she turned this adventure into reportage for *The Stranger,* a quirky, sometimes kinky alternative weekly which at the time carried interesting political and cultural coverage and was edited by S.P. Miskowski. That's Sara. One swipe is never enough. She's a woman of great energy who always is hungry for more.

—Scott C. Davis

Bio

Sara Nadia Rashad

Place of residence: Los Angeles.

Birthplace: Honolulu.

Grew up in: Hawaii and Alaska.

Education: B.F.A. in theatre from Cornish College of the Arts. Currently enrolled in M.F.A. program for film production at University of Southern California.

Serial publication: *The Stranger*—essay.

Current projects: A short 16 mm film dramatization on women in the Arab world. A screenplay.

Favorite book: *Haroun and the Sea of Stories* by Salman Rushdie.

Cravings: Chocolate and travel.

Interests: Digs anthropology and the study of other cultures through narrative form, whether in film or words.

Jerry Reid

The Manly Thing . . . Rivalries of Racing

Going into 1996, I had driven on virtually every road racing course east of the Mississippi in a twenty-six year career as a driver/owner. I had spent more money than I earned, alienated other drivers by being too aggressive for their tastes, and created a rocky road for a marriage that started in 1969—the same year I started racing. Racing is an addiction, no more and no less. "Win at all costs" takes over as soon as you suit up, and the adrenaline begins to flow. Believe this.

Racing is a society unto itself, and the rules are different. Cheating to gain advantage is rampant and creates hard feelings. "It ain't cheatin' unless you're caught" is the operative sentiment when the teams, crews, and drivers arrive at the track. Soaking tires with a witches' brew of chemicals to soften them up and make them bite better is one trick used to gain an edge. Laser-cutting holes in manifolds to get more air into an engine is another.

In racing, rivalries develop that can get downright nasty. Most of these confrontations are fueled, whether in road racing or on the short-track bullrings that make up stock car racing, by one basic, simple fact. In any accident, drivers invariably blame the other driver for what happened. There is a big difference between road racing and short-track oval racing. Road racers are under a microscope to prevent car-to-car contact. Oval track racers and officials accept what's known as "rubbin," or fender-to-fender contact. And the smart drivers know how to spin another car out in a heartbeat without getting caught. There's the real "rub." Tolerated or not, this contact causes temper flares that could light up a football stadium. There is, however, one major no-no: don't go after another driver with your car when he or she is on foot.

Capron, Virginia, site of Southampton Speedway, is a tidy dirt track with modern amenities and a history of ferocious rivalries that have, at times, spilled over into dangerous, white-hot anger. Some drivers have gone after others with tire irons or any other implement of destruction they could get their hands on. Speck Edwards, nicknamed "Hurricane" because of his fiery temperament and hyper personality, and Tony Edwards (no relation) worked each other over on the track all of 1995. The end result was car to flesh contact that resulted in some legal proceedings.

Speck could be the testosterone poster boy, and he's either hated or loved by the fans. But they buy tickets to come and see him do his thing. His speech is staccato. Every other word starts with "f" when he's riled. And maybe when he's not, for all I know. After one fender-banging night I interviewed him for a weekly racing publication. The only printable quote, and that was edited, came as he was holding court sitting on the hood of his car. "He got what was comin' to him," is the clean version.

Hero or villain, this driver and countless hundreds like him around the country swirl in and out of controversy and refuse to let the "good ol' days" die. In those days long ago, every dispute was settled with fists.

As a writer and a racer, I thought I would pull some strings and try short-track racing to see if I could play their game. I covered the track weekly and was connected with a female racer named Sunny Hobbs who was trying to move her career along. My stated purpose was to write from the inside.

That's a racer's lie. I will still drive just about anything that looks safe at any race track where I get a chance. Remember the word "addiction." This opportunity served all my purposes.

Southside Speedway in Chesterfield County, Virginia is called The Toughest Short-Track in the South. This one-third mile flat course ringed by boiler-plate walls has cowed many a driver, and sent some cars home looking like they'd visited a crusher at the local junkyard.

As things worked out, I qualified twelfth out of twenty-four in the Charger division, a class for limited modification Detroit iron. One row up, in tenth place, was Ms. Hobbs. My chances in the race ended early, like in the first turn after the green flag flew when a car tried to pass me by driving over my left front fender and hood. The result was a flat tire, a pit stop, and a front row seat to some boiling-over rivalries before I was mobile again and drove to the finish in back of the pack.

The clearest way to describe short track racing people is sweat-ringed blue collar to the core. Sunny Hobbs is the antithesis of this. She graduated from American University with a degree in International Relations, modeled in six European countries, and works in marketing with an architectural firm. Tall, leggy, and with a face the camera loves, she looks out of place at a weekend bullring. But she has driving talent, dedication, and gets lots of press attention. Her attributes, to put it plainly, piss off male drivers because she knows how to play the gender card. In 1995 as a second year driver and the only member of the Ovarian Set in her division who competed on a regular basis, she was hit, bumped, and ground up all year long by the mostly chauvinist male drivers. And on this night, she fought back.

She had been spun out three or four times during the race and so, afterwards, she picked out a perpetrator and rammed him in the rear bumper twice going down the back stretch. He didn't like that and dropped his car into reverse and locked bumpers with her with tires boiling smoke while trying to back over her hood. The confrontation ended there, but she had sent a clear message that she wouldn't be pushed around.

I drove around Sunny and her antagonist as I was heading to the pits, parked my car, and took a minute or two to think about the experience. One thing a racer told me came to mind—at the time I thought he was joking. "I'd put my Mother into the wall to win a race," he said. "But I would come back around and see if she was OK."

I don't believe this guy was joking. After my experience, I don't believe anyone could race on a short-track twenty-six weekends in a row without thinking, "I'll get that sumbitch back. I'll put him (or her) in the cheap seats."

Profile

I met Jerry Reid in 1994. I was in the pits at Southside Speedway in Chesterfield County (near Richmond, Virginia) on a Friday afternoon. I'd just qualified for the Friday night stock car race, and I saw him loping by, the way he does. "Anyone want to drive a sports car," I heard him say. I stuck my hand up in the air and looked around—no one else responded because they were stock car racers. But for me, sports cars is what I originally wanted to do but it was too expensive. That's why I was driving stocks.

Jerry came over and we started talking. "I don't drive my sports car anymore," he said, "so I need a driver. You want to learn how?"

"Yeah," I said. Jerry wanted to pass on his twenty years of experience to a young driver. In those days he had this Mazda RX-2, a great car which died just last year in the twenty-second hour of a twenty-four hour race in Moroso, Florida.

We went to Summit Point raceway, a two-mile, ten-turn course in Winchester, Virginia. And I got in the car and did a four-hour night endurance race my first night out—totally dark, no lights at all. We kicked butt. I won the sprint race and came in second in the night endurance race. Jerry's coaching? One of the differences between his sports car and my stock car: your braking zones. You've got to pitch the car in the corner (throw the nose in there and then drive out) because it's got a push condition (when you're turning the wheel the car's not turning at the same radius, the wheels can't respond). So you just have to approach your corners differently.

The big thing about Jerry, he never let me hesitate or doubt myself. "I can't do that," I said. "Sure you can," he said, "I've seen you race. I know you can. It's the same as what you've done, just a few things different." And then I'd go out and do it—things that I thought were impossible for me. I learned that sometimes you can't do something until someone says you can.

On another subject, that altercation at Southside Speedway that Jerry mentions in his essay. During the race, with one lap to go, I was driving down the straight-away when some guy rammed me and spun me out. He had been way back in the field, and had been making up ground recklessly, like a kamikaze, hitting people left and right. So, instead of racing me, he took me out. After the checkered flag I caught up and rammed him pretty good, then he dropped it into reverse and lit up his tires, trying to run over me. But I lit up my tires too—kind of a shoving match with a lot of noise and smoke and burnt rubber. He didn't actually run up on my hood but he wanted to, and his pit guys were mad and wanted to fight, and mine were making an equal amount of noise, and then I just wanted to get out of there. After that the driver in question wouldn't talk to me for a long time, but now we're pretty good friends.

—Sunny Hobbs

Bio

Jerry Reid

Place of residence: Richmond, Virginia.

Birthplace: Clifton Forge, Virginia.

Grew up in: Tightly wrapped poverty with wonderful extended family.

Day job: Public relations and sales for Southern National Speedway in Kenly, North Carolina.

Education: One year of college.

Previous publication: *Inside Motorsports* (news editor and columnist).

Awards: "Most column inches" as sports editor for high school newspaper. Sixteen race wins. First and second place color ad awards, Virginia Press Association.

Current project: Building ninth race car, a Mazda RX-7.

Favorite book: *The Unfair Advantage* by Mark Donohue and Pete van Valkenburgh.

Belief: Greater power called God, patriarchal and caring, lets you stumble and picks you up.

Craving: Platonic relationships with a variety of women. I love them.

Scott Richmond

Clackamas

I haven't been arrested yet, but I'm sure some day soon there'll be a county sheriff waiting for me at the Carver boat ramp. He'll tell me to put my big rod down—"real slow now"—cuff my hands behind my back, and push me into his patrol car.

It's the guys in jet boats, the ones who fish the Clackamas in winter. They want me off their river. They've probably already told their legislator to draft a new felony law: "fishing from an inferior watercraft."

The Clackamas runs through Portland's east metro area. Although the salmon and steelhead runs have declined, there's no shortage of moneyed fishermen. Since it's hard to impress anyone with your catch, some anglers buy fancy boats instead. There used to be a lot of McKenzie-style drift boats on the river, but these days nobody fishes it without a motor—except me.

I don't have anything against jet boats. Some decent folks own them, including one of my best friends. But the Clack attracts the worst of the bunch, real power anglers who think nothing of paying $25,000 for a boat with a brand name like "Predator" or "Intruder." They roar up and down the river wearing sunglasses, hard grins, and camouflage jackets. Camouflage—what a joke. The only place they could blend in would be a drag strip.

Then there's me, a recalcitrant reactionary in patched waders and a Barbour sweater making quiet one-way drifts in my McKenzie boat and doggedly arranging shuttles for my car and trailer. You still see a few drift boats on the Clackamas, but mine seems to be the only one without an eight-horse outboard on the transom. I once met a guy who claims to fish the river from a twelve-foot cataraft, a small, twin-tubed affair, but I've never seen him there. I think he fishes the Sandy now, on a section where jet boats are banned.

And there's the matter of my tackle: I fish for winter steelhead with a fly rod. Steelheading is tough enough, even pulling plugs behind a jet boat, but fly fishing for them in winter is a low-percentage game. I've never seen anyone else do it on the Clackamas.

To top it, I use an English-style spey rod, a fifteen foot, two-handed stick with a big Hardy reel. This makes me an oddity among eccentrics, a dangerous nut case according to the jet boat crowd.

One day last March I was searching for new runs to fish. The river was a bit high, but it was dropping and had that rich emerald color favored by steelheaders. Bright green buds dotted the willow stems, and flocks of Canada geese flew past. Geese honk a lot when they fly. They're like the jet boat guys: they can't go anywhere without making noise. I like the geese better.

I stopped at one spot, parking my boat along the bank upstream from the run. I walked down and checked it out. It looked too fast, but I figured that if the river dropped a foot it would be fishable. I waded in and took a few casts anyway, just to feel what the current was like.

I was into my fourth cast when a big jet boat came around the bend like thunder across the prairie. The guy throttled back as he went by me. He looked at my rod and smiled (he'd already passed my boat). Then he pointed at the water and said, "Ya think that's going to hold the big one today?" He had that tone of voice people use when they describe their neighbor's religion.

After he passed me, he revved up the engine—a few rpm more than necessary, I thought—and accelerated around the next bend. The noise faded until all I could hear was the river hissing against my legs. I knew what that jet boater was saying to himself: "Har, har, har. Couldn't afford a *real* boat."

Two runs later I was alone and fishing a good stretch of water. My fly hung up in mid-river. Rock or fish? I swung the rod toward shore and felt a throbbing resistance. In the river, I saw a broad flash of silver. Ten minutes later I had the steelhead on the bank, a wild hen of about seven pounds. Not big, as winter fish go, but respectable. And caught *my* way.

Before releasing the fish, my ears sifted the sounds of the river. They found nothing but wind and an occasional goose. I strained for what I longed to hear. The fish will be OK; she's in the water, resting, and if I held her up for a few seconds to show her off, it wouldn't hurt. But the air was empty of unnatural sounds.

There's never a jet boat around when you want one.

Profile

Scott Richmond stood in the casting stanchions of my drift boat, settling a bass bug to the water against the bank as gently as a well-chosen word lands in the bed of its sentence. We were half-way through the first day of a long float down Oregon's desert John Day River. The weather shifted from sunshine to pelting rain. The water shifted from quiescent to nearly violent. Rowing became taxing. My cranky shoulder went out and I had to coax Scott down off his platform to take over the oars.

There is something at once reassuring and unsettling about turning over the oars of your drift boat to someone who then handles it more gracefully, shepherds it through rapids more safely than you're able to do yourself.

Scott traded success in the computer business for the doubtful renown of an outdoor writer. He and I often share rivers and the enjoyment of quiet along them.

—David Hughes

Bio

Scott Richmond
Place of residence: Oregon.
Education: B.S.E.E., University of Washington. M.S.E.E., Stanford .
Books: *The Pocket Gillie. Fishing in Oregon's Deschutes River. Fishing in Oregon's Endless Season.*
Award: First in fourth grade class to memorize multiplication tables.
Current project: *River Journal: Rogue River*—collection of short fiction.
Favorite book: *Love Medicine* by Louise Erdrich.
Favorite flies: Size 10 Olive Woolly Bugger. Size 14 Tan Elk Hair Caddis.

Ronnie Ritts

The Taxi Life

When you hear the words "Taxi Driver," what vision comes to mind? Perhaps the image of a disturbed Robert de Niro asking a mirror, "Are you talking to me?" Or more likely you see a strange-sounding immigrant with an aggressive driving style and an attitude to match. While both of these types exist among the for-hire chauffeurs, they are in no way the sum total of their ranks.

Cabbies represent the entire spectrum of human experience. In my twenty years of driving taxis on the streets of Miami, I've known an ex-junkie working on her master's degree and an ex-CEO who was usually working on a bottle. Lots of lovers and losers, boozers and users, all mixed in with college students and family men between jobs or just down on their luck.

Loners by nature and alone by rule, the cabby exists in a nether world closed and veiled to the uninitiated. You see cabbies nightly cruising the great white way: near the trendiest cafe or the hottest new club, outside the track or after the big game, waiting by the hour for arriving trains, boats, and planes. Summoned at all hours, the cabby responds to the unknown voice on the line. What will the next call bring? One moment you're in the company of tourists, calmly driving them to a fine restaurant. The next, with a nervous and sweating junkie in search of his supplier. An hour later, the unwilling party to a volatile and dangerous domestic dispute. After midnight, drunks are the norm; they come in both sexes and in all kinds of moods.

We cabbies get to do all the things your mother told you never to do. Not only do we talk to strangers, we let them sit in the seat behind us as we drive them to places your mother would never allow you to go. All the while the cabby hopes that at the end of the trip money will change hands, and it will be in his favor. The street is no place for a faint heart or a slow wit. To steal a slogan from the Navy, "It's not just a job, it's an adventure."

It's this very element of danger and uncertainty that some of the old-timers say is part of the allure of the streets. I often think that the word "chronic" rather than "career" better describes the full-time cab driver. The novice, if he survives the dangers and temptations of the street, will not only develop a sixth sense—so-called street smarts—but will experience a marked personality change and never see the world quite the same again.

Cab drivers speak a language of their own—this job is no place to bring your sensitivities. They refer to each other as "Camel-Jockeys" or "Towel-heads," "Ruskies" and "Rednecks." Nothing personal, you understand. There are "Wacky Packies" and "Hyper Heebs." A Latino driver is just another "Ricky Retardo."

The jargon of cabbies is brutal, nothing is sacred. A gay bar is a "Fruit Stand" and a funeral home the "Body Shop." Most drivers can swear fluently in three languages. Street names abound. Cabbies answer to such titles as "Pepe La Pew," or "El Boniato" (sweet potato), and "The Happy Haitian." You have been "scooped" when another driver has stolen your fare. "Rabbit" is the guy who ran out without paying. "Double Doored" is what you are getting when your fare says, "I have to go up and get the money, I'll be right back." Cabbies have a slang term for everything, none of which you will hear in a Sunday school class.

In the drama that is human life, cabbies, while always present, are never essential to what is happening. They're like props on a stage, faceless and nameless, a shadow-like presence. This same anonymity can have an unusual effect on people, particularly on those suffering some type of emotional stress.

In one twenty-minute encounter, cabbies may hear the most intimate revelations, things most people would not tell their priest, lawyer, spouse, or therapist. Sometimes these words of confession spew out like lava from an erupting volcano—all strung together in a confused babbling. At other times the words of such fares come slowly in a painful monotone. These people don't want you to reply, nor are they interested in your opinion. It's as if they feel compelled to speak only their innermost secrets in the presence of another human being. When they have finished, they will avert their eyes as they press cash into your hand. Then, as if they had never been there at all, they are gone.

Sitting alone now, mouth open as he stares out his windshield, the cabby can only wonder, "What did I just hear and why?" True, he's not really involved, yet he's never untouched. The streets will leave their mark on the cabby. We call it the "New York Attitude." I think of it as a "Conditioned Condition," a temperament not uncommon to police officers and, in a more subtle way, essential to the full-time cab driver.

The cynical eyeball, the cabby's ability to quickly sense danger, is the only trait he has in common with the police. Their actual relationship is one of antipathy. The police view the cabby as a much too free spirit—a kind of freelance, freewheeling satyr of the late night, a vagabond predator who roams the street ever ready to take advantage, a necessary evil, and one to be watched. Now, while this may sometimes be true, it is the exception rather than the rule. It's the cabby's high visibility in the streets, the domain of the police, that is cause for friction. The cabby can legally loiter. Licensed to drive a for-hire vehicle and expected to be available at all hours of the night, a cab cruising slowly through your neighborhood at three in the morning is not cause for suspicion. Occasionally, law enforcement agencies have taken advantage of the taxis' immunity from suspicion and painted their own surveillance vehicles in taxi colors.

The police, in their role as buffer between citizens and criminals, see the cabby as one who moves freely between the two. To the police, the cabby is not quite righteous, not quite evil. Police are unable to protect the cabby because of the nature of these movements and think of him as a "probationary citizen" who deserves protection, but only after scrutiny. Meanwhile, the cabby toils in a solitary world where he may at any time become the victim of a citizen, a criminal, or the police themselves.

While the TV series "Taxi" was an accurate portrayal of the cabby life, Miami adds its own special flavor with its Casablanca-like atmosphere. Haitian boat people, Cuban refugees, moneyed South Americans—Miami is a crossroads filled with strange and mysterious people in an epic migration, the good and evil alike, all in search of their own place in the sun. The windshield of my taxi has provided me with a front row seat from which to witness this adventure. The close of this century is filled with movement and change. It makes me think of my immigrant grandparents at the beginning of this century, of the pioneer spirit, of a blending thread that weaves through all of us and makes us American.

I have come to know and count as friends a rainbow of faces—other taxi drivers as well as fares from exotic locations. I have been in their homes, tasted their foods, and, as we shared our stories of the streets, experienced their cultures in ways that cannot be gleaned from any textbook. I have learned about people in a way made possible by living The Taxi Life.

Profile

I first met Ronnie Ritts in a banquet room of the Rusty Pelican Restaurant on Key Biscayne when he received an award from the South Florida Writers Association for his essay "The Taxi Life." The room was filled with expectant writers and local celebrities like Pulitzer Prize winner Edna Buchanan, ex-crime reporter and author of *The Corpse Has a Familiar Face*. Ritts stood out with his rough beard and sharp eyes that seemed to size us up as if we were uncertain fares. I was intrigued by his looks.

Miami is Ron Ritts' territory. He's a fifty-four-year-old native, a widower with three sons. He spent twenty-two years here as a union journeyman ironworker. When work slowed, he tended bar, worked as a cook—anything to the feed the family. The tourist boom led him to taxi driving.

Stories? Ron says there are hundreds of them, another one begins with each new fare. He is currently at work on a novel set in Miami featuring an Irish-Cuban detective, just like a guy who once rode in his back seat.

—Barbara Weston

Bio

Ronnie Ritts
Place of residence: North Miami.
Birthplace: Miami.
Day job: Owner and operator of taxis. Before that I was an ironworker.

Worst day as an ironworker: I once fell off a warehouse and landed about 40 feet below. Fortunately I was dragging welding leads across the joists, and I kept ahold of them and they slowed my fall. I broke both ankles.

Favorite writers group: South Florida Chapter of the National Writers Assn.

Most creative pitch to a literary agent: When the American Booksellers Convention was in Miami I gave rides to a lot of literary agents. You get an agent in a cab and start telling her about your novel. "Ah yes, send me anything you write," she says. What's she gonna do? A captive audience.

How we get taxis: Ever wonder how taxis get to smelling like taxis? We buy recycled police cars.

Favorite part of town: South Beach, across Biscayne Bay. It's a squirrel cage. All the kids on roller blades and everybody selling T-shirts and sunglasses and all these weird people. It's very trendy, very "in" right now.

Best place to see fashion models: The Booking Table in South Beach, which everyone calls the "Strike-a-Pose Cafe." That's where all the young women go to be noticed by fashion photographers.

Favorite dive: The Cloverleaf in the north end. You'd think you'd just walked into a PLO cell meeting. Everyone in there is a Palestinian, shooting pool and drinking Budweiser. They all run mom and pop stores and come in after midnight, after closing down.

One of my best friends: Murphy, a customer at the Cloverleaf. He's not Irish but Palestinian. His real name is Musa. He and his family run a small grocery.

My dangerous job: I was robbed once near Robbie stadium. I didn't follow the first of the cab drivers' ten commandments: never let two tough-looking young men into your cab at once.

A more dangerous job: Running a mom and pop store. The Palestinians at the Cloverleaf emigrated to America to become Americans. They are seeking the new Promised Land. And some have paid the ultimate price.

Post Cold War: Since the Cold War is winding down, we have decided to single out Palestinians and other Arabs to be the bad guys.

Current project: *Inalienable Right*—novel.

Favorite author: John D. McDonald.

House pet: A ferret named Hemorrhoid.

Hillary Rollins

The Juiceman Cometh

I woke up this morning determined to start eating nothing but liquid food. Raw vegetable juice, elixir of life—uncooked celery and parsley and spinach and lettuce—anything that's green, green, green. . . .

The Juiceman has his own TV show. (Actually, it's an "infomercial," but I'm sure the Juiceman's mother would like to think it's his own show, and who am I to disabuse her?) On this show, the Juiceman said that all life on this planet comes from stuff that is green. Then he held up a bunch o' parsley and ran it through a huge extraction machine that looked suspiciously similar to one of those old butt-reducing exercisers from the 1950s. I watched, transfixed, as lumpy green liquid came out of the wide plastic spout and—glub-glub—filled a cut-glass tumbler to the brim. It did not exactly make me want to belly up to the bar.

But then the Juiceman explained that this parsley extract had to be mixed with carrot juice, at a ratio of one to three. And only moments before he'd pulverized twenty-five innocent bystander carrots, reducing them to two ounces of unjustly victimized carrot juice. Now I don't *love* carrot juice, but in a fit of self-improvement pique I can sort of imagine getting to *like* carrot juice. It is, after all, orange—an acceptable color for a potable substance. But that green stuff . . . I mean, I like parsley, but mostly when it's served up as a garnish next to a double bacon cheeseburger with raw onions. "If You Eat A Sprig of Parsley, You Needn't Eat Your Onions Sparsely." I read that once on a sign in Burger Heaven. But apparently the Juiceman has never dined at that particular establishment, because he insists that the proper way to ingest parsley is in liquid form, mixed one to three with carrot juice, shaken not stirred. Do you know what happens when you mix one part dark green with three parts bright orange? Your cup runneth over with thick, pulpy, murky, muddy, polluted-looking brown.

What is really more disturbing than the grotesqueness of the Juiceman's potion is my own sudden need to extract. Because for me, any radical commitment to lumpy brown parsley/carrot juice means I'm feeling out of control and frightened. When I'm feeling OK—when my emotional, psychological, and spiritual energies are relaxed and sane and accepting—I know it doesn't make a damned bit of difference if I eat barbecued spare ribs and chocolate mousse because we're all going to die anyway so we might as well live *now*. But when I am running scared—afraid of every shadow in my future, panicked by every scar from my past—when I'm spiraling down into that psychic pit (at whose bottom, incidentally, bubbles an evil, steaming brew resembling one part parsley and three parts carrot juice), then I'm desperate enough to try and make that bargain with God, with Mother Nature, with the Juiceman. Because then I feel, taste, smell, and especially *hear* Time passing, as if somebody put tiny little microphones on my gasping molecules. And let's be honest: my face is falling, my joints are creaking, and each scarlet pimple seems a suspicious, malignant lump. I still don't have a husband who loves me—hell, I don't even have what I *used* to have, a boyfriend who loathes me—and any potential suitors are either married, crazy, or resemble suspicious, malignant lumps. Then, speaking of lumps, there's my career . . . well, what's the point, right? We're all out of control. We're just going to die anyway, so we might as well kill ourselves *now*.

But wait! Cometh the Juiceman and his promise of eternal youth. If only I'm willing to give up flesh-eating, spirit-imbibing, dairy-suckling, and the ingestion of *anything* warmer than room temperature. ("Eat it raw!" he intones. Same to you, Juiceman.) Still, he's got me. I've got to live. Forever. Right now. I've got to control my life; it's all out of whack, going crazy, slipping down the eternal river in a leaky inner tube. But if I eat nothing but live foods pounded to a watery pulp, I know I can beat the house at its own game.

So I woke up this morning determined to start eating nothing but raw vegetable juice, elixir of life—uncooked celery and parsley and spinach and lettuce dutifully liquefied in my new butt-reducer/juicer. I ordered it from the infomercial, using the convenient 800 number, and I remembered to have my credit card handy because operators were standing by. (Of course, I know they really get to sit down at those comfy little Formica cubicles.) I'm going to live forever, and my juicer only cost two hundred forty-two dollars and ninety-five cents. Plus shipping and handling. The Juiceman was right: All life on this planet comes from stuff that's green.

Profile

The first thing about Hillary Rollins is the hair: a waterfall of pre-Raphaelite auburn curls cascading to her knees. In addition to its nineteenth century allure, her hair is also a good metaphor for Hillary herself: beautiful, grand, full of life, and, above all, dramatic.

The next thing is the laugh—big and generous. We first met at Columbia University, where we were both candidates for our MFAS, and I recall an evening when a gaggle of first year students convened at the local hangout. Hillary was holding forth, surrounded by new friends and all that glorious hair, looking intelligent and glamorous (not an easy trick). She had us in thrall, delivering one hilarious joke after another in the most authentic old-lady Yiddish accent this side of Minsk. That's Hillary.

—Jill Bossert

Bio

Hillary Rollins
Place of residence: New York.
Day job: Freelance writer.
Education: B.A., SUNY, Empire State College. M.F.A., Columbia University.
Credits: Television—numerous shows for Nickelodeon, The Disney Channel, and others. Special projects for ABC, Nick-At-Nite, USA Network.
Current projects: Playwright in the Summer Shorts Festival at City Theater, Miami. Participation in the HBO New Writers/Performers series at Melrose Theatre, Los Angeles. A full-length play, *Love & Work*. Promotional campaign for ABC Daytime. A book-length memoir about growing up in Manhattan.

Vada Russell

Mr. Garibaldi's Cabin

I fled Los Angeles in 1961. I was a flower child wanting simplicity and a quiet place where I could flourish and be queen. I bought a house and two acres of land in the foothills of the Sierra Nevada from Alberto Garibaldi.

Mr. Garibaldi's aged face was brown under a khaki hat centered squarely on his head. He wore a khaki shirt and trousers, with brown boots stained red by the soil.

The house was a squat, unpainted rectangle with a large front window facing east. The interior had unfinished plywood floors and plasterboard walls. Mr. Garibaldi had furnished the kitchen with a 1920s black-iron wood-burning cookstove with sturdy bowed legs and white porcelain oven door and warming shelf.

My two acres sat smack in the middle of his two hundred. Black oak, black walnut, and yellow pine grew on my land, which was shaped like a kite, the tail angling straight down to the creek. Manzanita was so thick in places that if I went for a walk I ended up crawling on hands and knees through tunneling deer paths. I drank water out of the kitchen faucet until the day I saw a dead deer floating in the utility ditch that supplied the house.

One week after closing escrow, Mr. Garibaldi coasted up in his brown Toyota pickup truck. He'd decided to develop his remaining acres.

Every day thereafter he strode up and down the hills squarely waving work-gloved hands, directing a bulldozer to cut roads. The roar of the bull-dozer reminded me of the LA freeways I'd so recently fled.

One day Mr. Garibaldi came to my door and asked if he could use the iron stove to fix his breakfast. I agreed. He extracted a flat loaf of sourdough bread from his knapsack, followed by a long knife, a grapefruit, and a spoon serrated on the leading edge. He made himself at home in his former home.

Breakfast time became routine: the thick slice of sourdough bread tossed upon the stove's hot surface, the sooty bread thickly spread with ricotta cheese, washed down with swallows of spring water, a whole grapefruit dug out with the serrated spoon, and then Mr. Garibaldi would depart to wake up the bulldozer.

Two acres had seemed huge in Los Angeles.

Mr. Garibaldi began to build a cabin down the hill from the house.

"Um, Mr. Garibaldi," I said, "it looks like maybe you might, um, be build-ing inside my property line. Like, um, maybe in my front yard."

"Maybe just a little bit," he said. He took a swig of spring water from a plastic jug, his gaze on the tips of the yellow pines, and told me a story in his accented English. "I was raised on polenta and tomatoes in Roma," he said. I'd heard it before. Every breakfast, Mr. Garibaldi told a story about his childhood.

"My poor mama. She had twelve children. I stole fruit and vegetables out of gardens. I stole firewood. When I come to San Francisco, I was nineteen. I work hard. I start a restaurant. I never am hungry again."

The cabin walls rose. I heard the bulldozer in the morning, and hammer, saw, and "Santa Lucia" in the afternoon. The weekend after roofing his cabin, he brought his six-year-old grandson Alberto III. In the morning, I could hear him calling, "Alberto. Alberto. Wake up, Alberto." I wondered how many grandchildren he had, and would they all come to visit? Did he carry their photos?

One September Saturday, the Toyota didn't arrive. I prepared an extrav-agant breakfast and ate it with Thoreau. I took a leisurely walk past a slum-bering bulldozer. I sunbathed nude until vultures began to circle overhead.

Sunday I washed the breakfast dishes and sat on the front porch. The air was warm and scented with pine. The cabin below was in shadow. I waited for Mr. Garibaldi to see the rising sun, to come up and make toast. But there was no Toyota, no Mr. Garibaldi.

A month went by. One morning the Toyota roared up the road. It was driven by Mr. Garibaldi's son. His passenger was a blonde and thickly lip-sticked woman: his wife, Mr. Garibaldi's daughter-in-law. Alberto II looked triumphant and sly.

"Gee, it's great up here." The daughter-in-law laughed. "It's nice to come up and get out of that San Francisco rat race." She sounded like a scrub jay.

"Um, where—I mean, I haven't seen Mr. Garibaldi."

"Oh, he died, honey. His heart. He was seventy-six," she continued. "His time, I guess." She joined Alberto II. They surveyed their kingdom.

I slept little that night. I felt pain in my chest and, surprised, identified it as grief.

In the morning, I marched down the hill.

"He built this cabin on my property."

"He was an old man. He made a mistake."

"It's inside *my* property line. You are in *my* front yard."

Alberto II cursed me. They climbed into the Toyota and roared away.

I drove into Sacramento for supplies. When I came home that evening the cabin was gone, torn down and hauled away. A circle of trash tangled in the Manzanita marked the site.

People left alone won't survive more than eight months, I've read. For me, it was less. I did not flourish as queen. I rented my house and returned to the city.

My tenant's young son, left alone, attempted to rekindle the stove with gasoline. He survived the explosion with a broken arm and burns. My house burned down. What was left? The rectangular cement foundation, and the ruined 1920s wood-burning cookstove.

Profile

I met Vada Russell in a white clapboard bungalow, a temporary classroom, in the parking lot of Sacramento City College one Tuesday evening in 1992. Five of us maneuvered classroom desks in a circle and one by one read our nonfiction out loud. Russell recounted her life on a piece of shared open land—its dwellings, characters, and flora. I sheepishly pushed aside my urban preoccupation with speed and greed and stepped through a pastoral doorway.

—Janne Graham

Bio
Vada Russell

Place of residence: Sacramento.

Birthplace: Fort Sill, Oklahoma.

Grew up in: Oklahoma, Washington, and California.

Day job: Secretary.

Education: B.A. in theatre, California State University at Sacramento.

Awards: Ellie awards for acting and directing.

Current project: Directing the premiere production of *Hurry Up Please Its Time* by Joyce Lander.

Admiration for Václav Havel: I played Flasta in *The Increased Difficulty of Concentration* by Václav Havel at The Actor's Theatre of St. Paul in Minnesota in the 1980s.

Apaches: I was born in the town of Fort Sill, Oklahoma, where the Apache Geronimo died. At the time of his death he was a Christian. On the bulletin board by my computer there is a picture postcard of Geronimo holding a rifle and looking fierce. Next to that is a postcard of part-Cherokee Will "I never met a man I didn't like" Rogers, who is smiling. I like the juxtaposition.

A strange time: I toured five states in the Midwest with The Dakota Theatre Caravan, fondly known as "Car and Van," since that's how we traveled. We played in high school gymnasiums, 1930s movie houses, and churches. I wrote country songs and crocheted afghans to while away the miles. I also became a professional spoons player.

Where I live: My neighborhood in Sacramento is called Midtown. The blocks are filled with Victorian, Queen Anne, and Craftsman homes, interrupted with concrete and brick apartment and office buildings. There are a dozen coffee houses within a half-mile radius, each with its particular clientele. There are bikers here and chess players there; political, theatrical, sexual preference coffee houses where minds brew.

For fun: Once a month I don a yellow hard-hat and an orange, reflective vest and pick up litter along Highway 50. As I work, Mack trucks are speeding 70 miles per hour six feet away from me. My co-pickers once found a cheerleader's pompom, a quarter-mile later another pompom, farther along a cheerleader's short skirt, then a shirt, and finally the boots. They did not, however, find the cheerleader.

Family: I am mother to Kendall, twins Shelley and Shannon, Jason and Larri, and grandmother to Noelani, Christopher, and Nora Belle. These are the most important people in my life. I hope to be an example for them—an example of what my mother used to tell me: "*Can't* never did a thing."

Carol Schirmer

Switched Over to Cruise Control

"This ferry's runnin' late. No way are we going to make it to the dock in time," mused my brother Richard. We stood inside the enclosed observation deck.

"Yeah." Enormous goose-feather snowflakes illuminated a dark dawn sky. "If they hadn't forced the ferry terminal to move to Auke Bay for those blasted cruise ships . . . floating plastic cities . . . ." I stopped. I knew Richard would assert his opinion that a town needs a solid economic base, and for Juneau to be the capital of Alaska was not enough. Yet I felt our city leaders had sold out, allowed the town to be trashed and overrun by the cruise ship industry.

There was no point in arguing. We were both tired. Heavy snow and low visibility had prevented our return flight from landing in Juneau, a southeast Alaska town only accessible by airplane or boat. The plane diverted to Sitka, a few hundred miles away, and scores of us had scrambled to catch the twice weekly ferry back.

David, our brother and a captain on a fishing tender, had planned a brief January call into Juneau to take on more fuel. Our rendezvous was stymied by our flight cancellation, and now our ferry would arrive at one harbor as David's boat departed from another. I silently prayed to see him before his risky passage across the Gulf of Alaska to Chignik. The waters south of the Aleutian Islands conjure up fishermen's winter death nightmares of howling gales, sub-zero temperatures, and unforgiving ice. Crabbers and fishing boats capsize every year.

Mountains completely encircle Juneau, save for a narrow water passageway—Gastineau Channel. The state ferries had always had first rights to dock at Juneau's town harbor. Increased tourism in the 1980s, however, created ship overcrowding. Cruise ship demands for more time at the docks had delayed ferry schedules, inconvenienced regional businessmen, and angered local residents.

Juneau, a borough of 29,000, stood to gain over $100 million every summer in tonnage fee collections from sixteen separate cruise lines. The city elected to rebuild an expensive dock, whitewash buildings, relocate the drunk and disorderly of wino's alley, and move all ferry traffic to Auke Bay fifteen miles north of town.

"Cruise ships?" A bearded schoolteacher dressed in a gray halibut jacket overheard me. "Did you hear? Lyle's Hardware and the Imperial Cafe are closing."

"What? No way." I bought my first bread bowl at Lyle's twenty years ago. I duplicated my cabin-in-the-woods key there when I thought I should start locking my door. Local shop owners couldn't compete with resort gift-store chains originating in the Virgin Islands, snaking through the Mexican gulf, and infiltrating Alaska coastal towns. Commercial rents had skyrocketed.

Several ferry riders edged in closer.

"Yep. We'll be seeing more Little Switzerland shops and Columbia Emerald boo-tweaks this summer." A few laughed, which only encouraged him to continue. "Jeez, where do you buy a light bulb, nails, work boots? I can't caulk with moose shit jewelry . . . though maybe we should try it on the City Assembly walls!"

Richard piped up. "That doesn't bother me. They can have all the false-front stores in town they want. I quit driving to town in the summer, years ago." Everyone nodded in agreement.

"But try and get away from all the helicopter flightseeing and floatplane noise," I said. "You can't hike out by the glacier anymore without running into twenty tour buses. You can't have a peaceful trek up Salmon Creek Trail without feeling like a militia of helicopters will strafe you every twenty minutes." I was shaking. "There's a plan to create thirty more landing sites in the Tongass Forest."

No one said anything. Snowflakes were thinning out. Our faces reflected in the ferry window. Summer solitude on a mossy rainforest trail was becoming rare. I hoped that the camaraderie of the townspeople would rekindle each winter.

The previous summer, a friend and I observed mass bewilderment as cruise ship passengers disembarked the *Legend of the Seas,* the *Sun Princess,* and other mega-ships. Many were elderly gentlefolks who at last were realizing a dream, The Alaska Experience. They were shuttled to cruise-line buses by the hundreds, slammed into floatplanes for a rapid flightsee, and hustled by Tijuana hawkers on the dock.

"Auke Bay," the loudspeaker announced. I glanced at my watch—one o'clock in the morning. The few taxis waiting at the ferry terminal would be overwhelmed by the extra passengers. Richard and I would try to reach town before David's boat pulled out, but it wasn't looking good for anyone.

Profile

Carol Schirmer is an oxymoron in the flesh. She is a rebel in conservative skin . . . soft-spoken and resolute. She is not the kind of girl you would imagine being suspended for breaking high school dress codes or choosing to live with a man in a tepee in Juneau, Alaska. She is full of wonderful surprises and an interesting juxtaposition of a Nordstrom wardrobe packing through the southern tip of Thailand. I am never sure where the other end of the line is on any phone call—I am sure she is calling to jog my now domesticated travel bug . . . looking for a playmate.

Carol has acquired her education in a series of short stints. Some of these in my company. She sort of jolted her way through those college years and then decided that taking all her money and moving to Anchorage would be a sound decision.

Carol has had her life tempered in a certain amount of pain. A marriage come and gone, other loves won and lost along the way. And in the same juxtaposition, a real vulnerability mixed with grit.

—Chris Cocklin Ray

Bio

Carol Schirmer
Place of residence: Juneau, Alaska.
Birthplace: Anchorage, Alaska.
Grew up in: Seattle area.
Day job: Airline ticket agent.
Education: University of Alaska and University of Washington.
Serial publications: *Explorations. Inside Passages.* Short stories, poetry.
Award: A. Shields Award (University of Fairbanks) for "Unjust Desserts," a short story.
Current projects: *One of Us Probably Shouldn't Be Here*—a novel. Also a collection of short stories. Both are set in southeast Alaska .
Favorite book: *Child of the Dark: The Diary of Carolina Maria de Jesus* by Carolina de Jesus.
Cravings: Mangoes and raspberries, my own chocolate-espresso brownies, and Droste chocolate oranges (I used to own a dessert catering business).
Pastime: Learning Portuguese.

Steven Schlesser

Saving the *Titanic*

I'm a moulding salesman and spend much of my time driving across the Pacific Northwest on sales calls. As I drive, I find myself thinking about events in history and one event in particular—the moment when, in my estimation, the twentieth century awoke.

Sunday, April 14, 1912.
The North Atlantic. Latitude: 41°46´ north. Longitude: 50°14´ west.

The *Titanic* brushed an iceberg at 11:40 PM. Passengers noted a faint grinding noise emanating from below and lasting less than thirty seconds. Captain Edward Smith, a white-bearded veteran of the White Star Line, rushed to the bridge and began cracking off orders. Reports from his engineers below indicated serious trouble. Smith summoned Thomas Andrews, managing director of Harland & Wolff Shipyard, the *Titanic's* builder. Andrews understood the *Titanic* better than anyone, and the captain requested he sound the ship.

Andrews descended the crew's stairway to attract less attention and inspected first the mail room and the nearby squash court (water lapped against the foul line on the backboard), and then boiler rooms five and six. He then ascended through the A deck foyer, where a group of passengers studied his face to detect the gravity of the problem.

Just outside the bridge, the ship's builder and her captain conferred beneath a star-filled sky. Smith stared hard at Andrews. In a quiet voice, Andrews explained. The gash made from the iceberg was over two hundred feet long. The first five watertight compartments were flooding. A sixth was damaged. The bulkheads between each compartment did not create a complete seal. In fact, the bulkhead between the fifth and sixth compartments went only as high as E deck. The *Titanic* could float if any two or three of these compartments were flooded. It could even float with four compartments flooded. If the first five compartments flooded, however, the pull of the water would force the bow of the ship to start sinking. Once that happened, water in the fifth compartment would flow over the bulkhead into the sixth and then, as the bow continued down, water in the sixth compartment would flow into the seventh and so on. Andrews knew. The *Titanic's* doom was a mathematical certainty. As if to underscore his explanation, the ship began to list slightly, almost imperceptibly, towards the bow.

Captain Smith raised his eyes heavenward. He was fifty-nine years old and had planned to retire after this trip. In fact, he would have retired sooner, but he traditionally took the White Star ships on their maiden voyages. It was his greatest boast to be alive and active in a time when shipbuilding had reached its zenith. Earlier he had said: "I cannot imagine any condition which would cause a ship to founder. I cannot conceive of any vital disaster happening to this vessel. Modern shipbuilding has gone beyond that."

Now, it was clear to both men that the ship would sink, and they would not live to see the morning. I imagine the two of them lingering for a few seconds, as if, by parting, they would trigger the events which would cause more than 1,500 men, women, and children to drown in an indifferent sea.

Profile

Steven Schlesser.

"A wise and trusted consular," thus does the dictionary define a mentor—that figure which writers, especially beginning writers, dearly need and seek and so rarely find. Writing workshops, seminars, classes, all those programs designed to satisfy that need are in fact seldom one-on-one enough to do the trick. For implicit in the notion of mentor is the casual intimacy of two people, not a class and teacher at a certain scheduled time. In contrast, a mentor is a person who is pretty much always there, to help with a special writing problem, even to read a whole manuscript and to give time and thought to it, or someone just to chat with about books and writers and the craft in general. But most important, a writer's mentor must be a person who has read widely with discrimination and whose judgment the writer can fully trust. For any writer such a mentor is a prize.

Steven Schlesser found that prize in Celia Stoddard Ralston. Mrs. Ralston, born in the first decade of the century, grew up in Baker City and in a time when small-town Oregon life was more cultivated than is the case today. One of her high school teachers was a summa cum laude from Wellesley, another a Reed College graduate. When the traveling opera company came to town, she never missed a performance. And it was in Baker's Carnegie Library that she first read Proust.

The young woman, who then went on to the University of Oregon, was hardly a hick. She majored in English, with a minor in Greek, and in time became a teaching assistant in both fields. She was the favorite pupil (and perhaps more) of Dr. Lesch, the University's legendary professor of English literature. One of her unacademic pleasures was skinny-dipping in the mill-race—this some forty years before the "way out" 1960s.

After a rather Bohemian life in San Francisco and a marriage that didn't work, Mrs. Ralston came to settle permanently in Portland, and here she married again, this time most happily. Employed as a social worker, she retired early—which not only gave her time to read even more voraciously but also to travel extensively. It was on the last of her journeys, descending a Greek mountain on a less than sure-footed donkey, that she received an injury which left her crippled for life and thereby with still more time to read.

By the time Schlesser first began calling on Mrs. Ralston with his work and questions, she had been reading for some seventy years—poetry, fiction, essays, drama, biography, a whole range of literature, ancient and modern—and, what is more, reading with that essential asset, discrimination. But what was most important for Schlesser, she was ready to read his work and pronounce her judgment, with utter truthfulness, of what he had done.

And so the sessions began, there in the old room with its heavy mahogany, the fading Persian carpets, the wall of books. Or out on the summer loggia, the city below, she with her glass of ouzo, Steve with his beer, questioning, criticizing, praising, there with his mentor, a true prize indeed.

—Terry O'Donnell

Bio

Steven Schlesser

Place of residence: Portland, Oregon.

Birthplace: Portland.

Day job: Manager/owner of a moulding company.

Education: B.A., Claremont McKenna College. J.D., Vermont Law School.

Serial publications: *The Schlesser Review, Schlesser Times*—monthly newsletters. *Cune Magazine*—online. (For newsletters 800-445-8032. For *Cune Magazine* http://www.cunepress.com/cune.)

Favorite books: *The Guns of August* by Barbara Tuchman. *James Joyce* by Richard Ellmann.

Favorite novelist: Anthony Trollope. I admire Trollope not for what he wrote but for his discipline. Seven days a week he rose at 5:00 AM, drank a cup of black coffee (tea came later), ate bread with butter, and wrote 2,500 words by 8:30 AM, after which (Sundays aside) he left for his job at the post office.

Work-in-progress: *A Study in Failure.* I am obsessed by the course of the twentieth century, and I'm working on a short book composed of three essays. Each is devoted to an event in recent Western history which has helped shape this century: Custer, The Titanic, and the opening of World War I.

Former work-in-progress: *The Red Staircase.* I spent twelve years writing a literary novel which was accepted for representation by the William Morris Agency, shown to twenty New York publishing houses, and received a medley of editorial comments.

Favorite rejection letter: On *The Red Staircase.* An editor at Dell wrote: "On the positive side, it reminds me of some of Christopher Isherwood's earlier writings; on the negative, it conjures up a bunch of confusing metaphysical foreign films I have tried to like over the years."

Beliefs: Conservative Episcopalian. I focus, still, on the means to enrich and improve our lives on this earth, although I do feel that a higher power is, ultimately, cradling our shared existence.
Craving: Stronger communities.

Cheryl L. Schuck

High Heels and a Yellow Pickup Truck

I am a licensed private investigator who specializes in criminal defense law. From alleged murderers to litterers, my job is to answer the question: "Did he do it, or didn't he?" A simple question. Many times, however, the answer is complex.

One case involved a forty-three-year-old man and a twenty-six-year-old woman. The woman reported that the man picked her up at a bar, drove her to a gas station, parked between two garbage bins, and raped her. The physical findings were consistent with rape. They showed that she'd had sexual relations within the previous twenty-four hours.

The police investigation included the statement of the victim, an interview with the gas station attendant, and an interview with the man. The victim said: "All I did was ask him for a ride home." The attendant said: "I was here that night, but I don't remember seeing or hearing anything out of the ordinary." The man said: "I was with her, but I didn't rape her. What we did was consensual."

I didn't have much to work with. How do you prove consensual sex wasn't a rape? The physical findings in consensual sex (unless there's evidence of beating, abrasions, rips, or tears) are the same as rape. There is no distinction that physicians can make between a legal sexual entry and an illegal one.

My job was to find evidence that would show that the entry was legal.

The address the victim gave to the police was an empty apartment in an area frequented by prostitutes. My hunch was that the woman wasn't picked up at any bar. So with high heels and a red miniskirt on, I walked the streets near the gas station. I was looking for anyone who may have seen the woman hanging around before the rape. Sure enough, two gas station customers remembered her. "That's the lady that hangs out in front of the liquor store," said one, "over there next to the telephones."

I showed the photograph of the woman to the liquor store owner. "She's a prostitute," he said. "Haven't seen her in a few weeks, but I think she lives with another one, right down the street." I showed him a picture of the man and asked if he had ever seen him. "Oh yeah," he said, "he was here about two weeks ago." He remembered the man because the man was wearing a tailored suit and drove a new BMW, which he thought was odd for the area. "He met the woman right outside the store," he said. "I guess they worked out a deal because the woman got into the man's car, and they parked right over there behind the gas station."

With the information the owner gave me about the roommate, I set up for a long wait. I parked my big bright lemon-yellow Chevy truck, which looks like a work truck (especially with the equipment rental service name inscribed on the side) at the gas station. After two weeks of gas station fare—coffee, stale donuts, rubber hot dogs, and cheese puffs—the roommate appeared.

I watched her for thirty minutes. I was hoping that the victim would show up. Then I made my move. I flashed a picture of the victim. "I don't know her," the roommate said. "Never seen her before."

"That can't be true," I said, "because I know she lived with you. You can either tell me where she is, or I'll follow you until I find her."

After she had me pull down the straps of my coveralls and lift up my shirt (she thought I was a wired cop), she said: "OK. I'll tell you. The lady is in Florida. She left because she was afraid of being arrested for filing a false police report. She told the cops that some rich guy raped her, but he didn't. He refused to pay her so she turned him in on a rape."

So, why didn't the man tell me that he was with a prostitute? "Because my wife," he said, "could deal with me having a one-night fling, but not with a prostitute. That would have ruined my marriage."

I turned my findings over to the defense attorney. Rape charges were dismissed and the man walked. I thought I had done a good job. Every detail I investigated pointed to the man's innocence. But later I talked to the lady in Florida.

"He refused to pay me," she said. "I tried to get out of the car, and he raped me . . . who would ever have believed me?"

Consensual sex? No. It was rape.

Profile

When Cheryl L. Schuck isn't haunting The Bookman in Orange County, writing poetry, essays, or short stories, she's haunting criminals. Since opening her detective agency in Los Angeles in 1987, Cheryl has been hard at work presenting her case stories in court. Her work as a private investigator often takes her to the harsher side of society—experiences that she has turned into fine writing.

Cheryl's love affair with words extends far beyond putting her own words on paper. As a tutor, she helps others learn to read and write. She buys books and delivers them to shut-ins. As she says, "There's a lot more than words that go into writing a story."

An old-fashioned person, Cheryl prefers handwriting to email, fax, or telephone. And as a reminder of the art of writing, she gives away unsharpened pencils—a unique trademark.

Cheryl is currently working on her first nonfiction book, *Dear Writer: Postscript, Paper Relics.*

—Colleen Adair Fliedner

Bio

Cheryl L. Schuck
Place of residence: Bellflower, California.
Serial publications: *Cappers. The San Gabriel Valley Magazine. Lucidity.*
Current project: *Dear Writer: Postscript, Paper Relics.*
Favorite books: *84 Charing Cross Road* by Helene Hanff. *Martin Eden* by Jack London.
Clubs: Lead Pencil Club. Los Angeles County Volunteer Corps.

Jody Seay

Lunar Love

Do you ever feel as if the moon belongs to you? I do. Maybe not to me, personally, but more like to all of us. Yeah, the moon belongs to all of us, especially when it's doing something snazzy like an eclipse or slashing a smile at us across the night sky.

On warm summer nights in Texas when I was a kid, the sky was so big and clear we could see the stardust. My mom would spread quilts in the backyard, and we'd lie on our backs, Mother and her pajama-clad crew, staring up at the stars, making up stories about the moon. We'd ask a million questions.

"Why is it called the Milky Way?"

"What makes the stars?"

"Are there people lying in their backyards on the stars looking at us?"

And Mother would answer each question the best she could. When I asked her, "What is the moon?" she replied, "A reflection of the sun."

In my child's mind, a reflection was an illusion, like a spot on the wall reflected off the mirror in Mother's compact, not a real thing or place to go. When President Kennedy announced that one of our goals as a nation was to land a man on the moon, I thought, "Boy, are those guys gonna be surprised! They're gonna fly right through it!"

There is lots to know about the moon involving craters and moon dust and lunar modules and such, but that's never struck a chord with me. What's important to me has more to do with how we *feel* in our hearts when we look up in the sky and see it there, shimmering, almost close enough to touch.

At least one night each month the moon gives us its very best shot. No longer is it 238,857 miles away but just *right . . . out . . . there*—stunning us all, taking our breath away. We scramble into our homes, a look of half-crazed joy on our faces, screaming to our loved ones, "Have you seen the mooooooon???" and we drag them outside to ooohh and aaahh with us and sit on the porch and admire it some more and maybe say thank you to God or the universe or whatever power thought the whole thing up in the first place. The native Americans call the moon Grandmother, and that's always been a sweet thought to me—something beautiful and glowing, steady and dependable, something you can count on. Yeah, Grandmother Moon.

But it's more than that. Squinting into a telescope at a full moon a few weeks ago, I remembered how I felt as a kid. Lying in our backyard on a quilt that always smelled vaguely like my Aunt Roxie, it occurred to me then (and I still believe now), that mine couldn't be the only family lying in its backyard admiring the moon. And if there was only one moon for us all to enjoy and we all did, then somehow we were all connected and maybe not nearly so different as we tend to think. If the moon affects the tides and our moods and how rapidly our blood flows, then it is easier to understand how gazing up at it can make you kiss a stranger and fall in love. I find this thought most comforting—to know I'm not the only one who looks at the full moon and wants to yell, "Yahoo!" and jump off the garage.

The moon is our touchstone, a luminescent reminder that we are all in this together. We sing songs about it, write poems about it, and plant crops by it. We watch for it, stare at it, and respect its power. So I had this idea, you see, one not too far-fetched for a person who spends a lot of time staring, moony-eyed, up at the sky.

Although not perfect, our world is changing. People everywhere are standing up for freedom, demanding their voices be heard, and all of this seems to have happened simply because it is *time.* So, since we are now pals with Russia and it looks like we won't be needing that squillion dollar defense budget after all, whaddya say we cash in a big old bomber and put that money to better use? Yep, just drag that baby over to the recycling center and plunk it down. Then we can take that money and buy quilts for the world. Yeah, quilts would be good. In the fall and winter we can all cover up. In the spring we can go on picnics. And on those velvety, lukewarm summer nights, we can spread our quilts out on the earth, our communal backyard, and lie on our backs gazing up at the sky, feeling at one with the world, and the moon. Thank you, Grandmother.

Profile

Jody Seay.

Portland's winter of 1995–96 was one for the history books. Record floods, rain, cold. In the midst of natural catastrophe, I was giving author reading/signings at local bookstores. As it turned out, on every night that I was scheduled, the newscasters warned the public to stay indoors "or else." Just what every author wants to hear.

On one such night of high natural disaster in mid-December, I was to give a two-hour forum on my book *Animals as Teachers and Healers* for New Renaissance Bookstore, a lovely shop in downtown Portland that I refer to as the incense capital of the Northwest. That night I met Jody Seay. I had invited her to read a story of hers, "Holy Cow," that appears in my book. I feared that she and I would be the only souls brave enough or stupid enough to face the weather. I was wrong. We filled the house that night— every last seat. New Renaissance was stunned and suddenly delighted that the weather was so bad. "We'd never have been able to accommodate the crowd," they said.

Perhaps it was the electricity of the storm raging outside, or maybe the collective enthusiasm of a death-defying, animal-loving audience. Simply put, the evening became magical when Jody took the floor. All Texas drawl and desert-dry wit, Jody is a woman who could make a bunion belly-laugh or a stone weep. I suspect the audience was disappointed when she sat down, and I came back onstage. I know I was. I thought maybe I'd ask her if she'd be willing to impersonate me at future readings.

Jody has completed her first novel, *The Second Coming of Curly Red*. A book of her own essays is also in the works. And she rolfs my husband once a week.

—Susan Chernak McElroy

Bio

Jody Seay
Place of residence: Milwaukie, Oregon.
Birthplace: Dallas, Texas.
Day job: Certifed rolfer.
Education: English major.
Serial publications: *Dallas Life. Massage. The Justin Wheeler.*
Award: Junior Bowler. Ten-Year Record for High-Point Game, 1963.
Current project: *Gentle Tales from a Ragged Life*—a collection of essays.
Favorite book: *Animals as Teachers and Healers* by Susan Chernak McElroy (Ballantine; originally New Sage Press).
Fantasy: Compete in dangerous sports.
A past life: I once won a drinking, spitting, and cussing contest in Central City, Colorado—back when I drank, a long time ago. The contest was spontaneous, a bunch of drunk people in an alley between two bars.
Advice for film-lovers: Next time you are at the movies, get a couple of Milk Duds going pretty good and then stuff a handful of popcorn in there— it's so good it will make your tongue jump up and slap your brains, as we used to say in Texas.
Meat: One of my grandfathers was a cattle rancher in Nocona, Texas. We grew up on red meat, but when I became an adult I couldn't always afford it. And then I became a thinking person and didn't want it. Still, sometimes I miss the homestead.
A secret: Broke and hungry? You can take a baked potato and run it through some steak sauce and fool yourself into thinking you've just had a T-bone.
Life membership: The thing about being a Texan, wherever you go you'll still always be one—it's stamped on your DNA. Even if your parents just broke out of Huntsville State Prison (that's down south of Houston) and they stole a car and headed east, and your mama gave birth to you just before the state line at Texarkana, and they kept on going—you'd still be a Texan.

✹

Claire Simons

The Greatest

I met Muhammad Ali on the street the other day. I saw him as the Fifty-Seventh Street bus inched its way across Manhattan. He was signing autographs for a small crowd of passersby in front of the Meridian Hotel. A swarm of cab drivers, double-parked, was blocking traffic so they could shake his hand. He looked jovial as he sparred with men half his size and listened to their stories. They reached up to pat him on the back before they sauntered to their cabs, proudly waving their autographed copies of the *Daily News*.

Seeing him jarred a cherished memory, a reminder of strength and youth. Ali was my father's hero. He was my link with greatness and love. "I too must touch the legend," I thought.

"Getting out!" I demanded of the bus driver. The doors opened, and I jumped to the curb, narrowly missing a speeding bicycle courier. "Ali. Ali. Ali." I had to tell him that my father said he was the greatest fighter that had ever lived. My dad cried the day the boxing commission took Ali's title away. I was too young to understand. Still, my father cried and his crying frightened me. "The man is a champion," Daddy said. "They cut him down. The fight game isn't what it used to be."

I had to tell Ali that my father was a heavyweight champion, the "Buckeye Bomber." Dad fought the pro circuit: Chicago, Detroit, Cleveland—tough-guy towns—once on the same fight card as Joe Lewis. He won the Cleveland

Golden Gloves and retired victorious. Dad got out of the fight game because he "didn't want to get hit no more."

I New-Yorkered my way through the crowd, elbowing and pushing with finesse, now arm's length from the greatest fighter that had ever lived. His face was pudgy, eyes sunken. He was no longer a killer. "Ali! Ali! Ali!" Daddy said it was all in the footwork, "Mark your spot, stay low." The crowd was multiplying behind me, but I held my ground.

When I was twelve Dad taught me to shoot craps, pick horses, count cards, and throw a punch. "You gotta stay in training," he said.

He warmed up by jumping rope, magically twisting and weaving it into precise patterns. The rope made hissing and shooshing sounds as it cut through the air—my dad jumping an inch, his leather shoes gently tapping the concrete. We worked out on the body bag in the basement. He bandaged my hands in yards of white gauze to protect my fingers from being bent or smashed. When they were safely cushioned, he brought down his boxing gloves from the shelf. He put them on me, making sure that they were well-laced and that my hands would not shift or twist inside them. I felt powerful. "Hit clean! Cover! Cover! The punch starts from your foot. Spring off your heel, let it go through you." The speed bag took more time. He told me to find my rhythm, "Let the bag come back to you. Wait for the punch. Don't think about it so much. Breath."

Dad was a southpaw. I knew that I should have been too, but the nuns in boarding school insisted that writing left-handed was unladylike. They confused me. Dad said my timing was wrong, that I had forgotten my natural inclinations. His teachings were simple, a legacy to his only child, life lessons for a blossoming daughter. "Don't be afraid to get hit. You have to believe that you can win. Don't take no bullshit! Fight clean!" Mom ignored us. She refused to let Dad sit in the living room after he put his smelly liniment on. Her home would not become a locker room.

Ali was getting tired. The crowd had trapped him in their frantic circle.

He was alone in the ring and going down. He looked for his handlers. His brow furrowed, his vacant eyes begging to find a friend. I could see his staff standing in the hotel lobby door, flirting with an ebony woman in a white fur coat. Ali started to sway. He needed me. I had to reach him so that he could lean on me. The crowd pressed hard against my back. I pushed back. "Ali! Ali! Ali! They all must fall in the round I call."

When Dad was dying, the nurses bound his hands so he couldn't pull out the life supports. I stood by his hospital bed staring at the white gloves; pristine bandages protected him from himself. His hands were crossed, the right one defending his face, the left hand ready to punch. The boxer's hands were no longer lethal weapons. The final round was over. He lay on the white canvas sheets, an ashen hero, down for the count. No crowds cheered him on. The only sounds were the beeping machines and my sobs.

"I must touch Ali, he is my talisman," I thought. I teetered on my three-inch heels, caught myself, and adjusted my designer coat and bag. I crouched low and jammed my stiletto heel into the foot of the man behind me. I could feel my spike penetrating leather. The man bellowed in pain, stumbled, and fell back into the crowd. People behind him screamed. I could feel the crowd going down around me, like dominos in a row.

I sprang forward, leading with my left, and I hooked my arm under Ali's. I looked into the eyes of The Greatest but could not speak. I studied his hands and knew the stories they told. His crooked fingers, huge knuckles, stone wrists, had fought the pro-circuit tough-guy towns, dried a sweaty brow, held trophies, and greeted fans. The man's life was in those hands. I kissed his crooked fingers and looked squarely into his eyes. Raising my manicured, bejeweled hand, Ali studied it. "Southpaw," he said. "Sometimes," I murmured. "Hits clean," he said. In a moment Ali was gone.

Three huge men appeared at Ali's side, dwarfing him by their presence. "Thank you all for comin'," they said. "Ali loves New York!" The sidewalk erupted into applause and cheers. Encircled by his bodyguards, Ali was ushered safely inside the posh hotel.

"Hey lady, I was standin' here." I turned to face my challenger from Brooklyn. He stood eye-level to my chest, wearing an old navy pea coat. He hobbled on one foot, looking like a lame elf. "I do apologize. I hope I didn't hurt you. It's just that I lost my balance and—"

"Youse got to touch the greatest fighter that ever lived," he said. "The man was a champion, they cut him down. I cried the day they took away his title." He spoke my father's words. We cherished the same memory, our link with The Greatest.

"I remember that day," I said. "It *was* very sad. The fight game isn't what it used to be, is it?"

He snorted through his broken nose and peered at me from sunken eyes. He turned and crossed the street against the light, defying the traffic. The taxis screeched to a halt to avoid hitting him.

I walked to Fifth Avenue and ducked into Bergdorf's in time for my hair appointment. My timing was right; my natural inclinations were keen. I too had fought the pro-circuit, tough-guy towns. I believed that I could win, didn't take no bullshit, hit clean, cover, cover.

Profile

Ocean Beach (OB), California—Claire Simons and I are crunching down lobster tacos at the Ocean Beach Pier Café, five miles south of La Jolla. The town is still trapped in the 1960s. Local activists have defied gentrification, and the preferred mode of travel is 1970s VWs, bumper stickers proclaiming "US out of OB" I love it. I was born here. But Claire moved here from New York and is the soul of sophistication. What's she doing in Ocean Beach?

"It reminds me of a remote Greek fishing village where I once lived." Sure. I choke on my taco. Across the pier, an Asian woman in multi-layered flannel hauls in a striped bass. A guitar-toting guy in a serape is talking intensely with a navel-ringed girl in black shorts. They do a quick two-step to avoid being hit in the face with a fish.

"It's also a lot like New York City." Oh, right. I'm tempted to heave my salsa at Claire, even though she's the best writer I know. She's calling Californians a bunch of mall-driven, casual-chic strivers, desiring only to merge into the sun culture. "But I love Ocean Beach," she says, just in time. "Like New York, people here are tolerant of diversity. And you can walk to the grocery store, do your errands, and get to know your eclectic neighbors." OK. It fits. May she finish her book of short stories, her TV scripts, and live happily forever in OB.

—Carol Bowers

Bio

Claire Simons
Place of residence: San Diego.
Birthplace: Harrisburg, Pennsylvania.
Day jobs: Public relations. Freelance writer. Office and closet organizer.

Education: B.A., Penn State University.
Dramatic production: Television series.
Current projects: Book of short stories. PR Chair, League of Women Voters.
Favorite book: *The Good Earth* by Pearl S. Buck.
Belief: The Wheel of Fortune Philosophy of Life: if you stay in the game long enough, your number will come up.
Cravings: The love of my life. An Emmy Award. Peonies.

Sande Smith

France:
Feeding the African-American Artist

I'm in love with France—a country that I snubbed for years. I once thought, "What can France offer me that will feed my soul—African-American woman, writer-dancer-wanderer?" Then I learned that France had offered solace and the sanctuary to write, paint, and study to a stream of African-Americans during the nineteenth and twentieth centuries. Some African-Americans, like novelist Richard Wright and artist Henry Ossawa Tanner, never returned to the United States. Others, like writer James Baldwin, went back and forth. Still others, such as pianist Hazel Scott, or artists Meta Vaux Fuller and Romare Bearden, spent a few years in Paris before returning to the States.

I went to Paris for the first time in November 1995 to visit a friend and see what made Paris such a haven for African-Americans. While there, I felt relieved of the invisible borders between white people and black people that exist in the States—the evil legacy of slavery biting at our heels. The barriers that were clearly drawn until the 1960s are now gone, yet many still fear to say "Hello," or to look a person of a different race in the eye.

I learned that Richard Wright had been sickened by the acid racism of the United States in the 1940s. The "little" things built up: His daughter not being allowed to use the bathroom in Bergdorf Goodman. Greenwich Village neighbors complaining when he, a "black man," moved in. Not being allowed to ride the hotel elevator to go to Sinclair Lewis's room. So, in 1947, he moved to Paris. In France, he could live where he pleased and could spend long hours in cafes, conversing with people such as Jean Paul Sartre, exploring parallels between Sartre's existentialism and Wright's own novels. Yet, he also saw France's struggles with former colonies Algeria, Senegal, and Morocco—which were playing out in France as well as Africa—demonstrate another form of racism.

In Paris, seeking the African-American past, I joined Julia Browne Figuereo's "Walking the Spirit Tours." Julia was an Afro-Canadian filmmaker who had lived in Paris for six years. She led me through the narrow cobbled streets of the Latin Quarter, pointing out hotels and apartments where African-American talent flourished. In a romantic tale that captured something of the city's magic, Julia explained that Paris saved bebop pianist Bud Powell. Given a year to live by the doctors in the United States, he moved to Paris . Here his health improved so much that he performed for many more years. Across from the Hotel Louisiane, where he lived, is the famous Buci market—it smells of roasting chickens and salted cheese. The huge Comice pear that Julia picked for me was juicy, satiny sweet, and so ripe that I could almost believe that the Parisian food alone cured Powell.

Sadly, there are few markers of the African-American expatriates. For this reason, I am moved by the memorials of Richard Wright's life: the plaque at 14 Rue Monsieur le Prince where he lived from 1949–1959, the black marble square at Pere Lachaise cemetery which marks his resting place. I followed the Seine, seeking out cafes where Baldwin came to escape his cold apartment and craft his books, where Wright gathered with his friends. I marveled at this country that seemed to value its past as much as its present: row after row of sixteenth-century buildings standing next to modern apartments. Even as a woman alone, I found the streets safe at night.

In April, I returned to Paris. Hungry to learn about present-day African-American musicians in Paris, I attended a gospel brunch at Chesterfield Café on Rue de la Boétie. African-American women in the audience (who now make France their home) responded to the soulful music with tears in their eyes. "Yes," they murmured, and "Oh, Lord," while softly waving their hands. Even some of the French people in the restaurant joined in.

The next day—over a lunch of fried chicken, spaghetti, and Spanish red wine—Tori, one of the gospel singers who performs at Chesterfield, told me that although Paris is still a wonderful place to live, Paris is not loyal. Tori explained that she was reluctant to teach her music for fear that once the French could perform it, she would not be hired. She echoed Julia Browne's claim that French musicians are hired more readily than African-Americans with the same musical repertoire. French nationalism is strong.

Yet the French love of art and creativity is equally strong. It is that appreciation—together with a curiosity, rather than disdain, for the African-American artist—that continues to cultivate the talent and careers of those of us who sojourn to France.

Profile

I met Sande Smith dancing—that's how we developed our sistah friendship. We went to the Third World Lounge at Forty-Ninth and Baltimore in West Philadelphia. It's a nightclub. We didn't do any square dancing! This was African dancing, world African, the dancing and music of the African Diaspora. So we danced *merengue* and *souka* to African and Calypso music. Dancing, that's so much of who Sande is.

There was a DJ sitting in a booth, who I can't remember—this was seven years ago, in 1989—but today most DJs at the club are in their mid-thirties and definitely into pleasing the crowd. Sande was wearing something bright and form-fitting, as always. Sande is a striking woman, fairly tall. Her cheeks have a strong bone structure. Her eyes are intense, and when she is dancing she looks you in the eye and pulls you in.

This club caters to West Indians and West Africans. Of course there are also Ethiopians and Kenyans and other East Africans. Also, about a quarter of the dancers are African-American. When I take my African friends there, they say, "*Wow!* This place is just like home." The food at the club has aromas of the African Diaspora—fried plantains, rice and peas, and *digag iyo baris* (chicken with rice and cabbage and vegetables and spices). This part of Philadelphia is a predominantly African-American community, nothing unusual. When you walk into the club, suddenly you are in the West Indies or somewhere on the continent. The room is drab, lights are dim. On the walls are posters from Jamaica and Ethiopia, posters of Bob Marley. And the place is jumping. People are dancing, eating, and conversing. It's vibrant and full of life. Sande and I danced until closing, 2:00 AM.

Our birthdays are three days apart, and Sande and I are kindred spirits, sistahs in the Diaspora. Sande is a serious writer who is definitely going places. Her creative energy inspires and challenges me as an artist. So does her commitment to documenting the lives of people of African descent. She pulled me into the National Writers Union and also has supported me in my own film and video career. We meet occasionally at Borders Book Shop at 18th and Walnut and drink iced coffee and iced tea to catch up on our lives.

So, if you want to know one thing about Sande, it's dancing. Dancing is her life—not like a career, not like making money. But something she does for herself. For Sande, dancing is the whole African Diaspora: Brazilian, West African, Caribbean, African-American. Dancing is a way that Sande recognizes herself as a citizen of world African culture.

—Aishah Shahidah Simmons

Bio
Sande Smith
Place of residence: Philadelphia.
Birthplace: Philadelphia.
Day job: Marketing writer for the Free Library of Philadelphia.
Education: B.A. in Portuguese and Brazilian Studies, Brown University.
Books: *The Life and Times of Malcolm X* (Chartwell Press). *Martin Luther King, Jr.: A Man With a Dream* (SmithMark Press). *Who's Who of Women in the Twentieth Century* (Crescent Books)—contributing author.
Current project: Picture book on lives of African-Americans in France.
Favorite book: *Beloved* by Toni Morrison.
Craving: Late night dancing until the sun rises . . . in whatever city I find myself.

Shauna Somers

All for Love

I walk Los Angeles, where the laying of pavement is an art form. I walk out of necessity: I've survived nine car accidents, received eighty-six parking tickets, blown out eight tires hitting curbs, locked my keys inside the car five times—once with the motor running.

I saunter in and out of produce stands on streets inhabited by old Jews who smell like overripe bananas. I walk to see the paprika-tainted roasted chickens, hung by the neck in the window of Haim's poultry. To hear language: sausage-thick Russian spoken from the appliance repair shop, rolled-up-white-shirt Spanish, vying for work in front of Standard Brands Paint. For the city's smells: morning scents of pancakes on griddles, eggs frying, toast burning. Evenings of boiling sweet peppered sauces seeped in marjoram, bay leaves, and vermilion-hued wines. I witness other feet: the woman wearing imitation patent leather loafers, dressed in a scratchy chicory-striped suit, snapping twenty-proof stained fingers, skipping to avoid cracks. The sugar-cane thin man with knees like street lamps, exiting the Post Office, chanting, "Why deny you are in a dictatorship when you know you are?"

I walk for community: the liquor store owner who sells me my daily libations—strong cup of breakfast tea, breads with thin crusts, sap-thick jams. "Still walking?" he asks. For the girls who paint nails, pray at short altars, mimic my shifting arms, and giggle in ripples as I pass. The hunched brown-vested man heaping newspaper clippings into his fire-hazard-filled garage—X9134L, the Holocaust forever imprinted on his wrist. The pony-tailed men drinking lattes curbside at Revival Cafe, reflecting each other in amber jeans, charred T-shirts, hi-tops untied.

I walk to avenge the death of my great-grandfather, Samuel Katz, who fed pigeons each Saturday while walking to Sinai Temple. He was run down by a freshly painted peony-blue Packard. I stalk in outrage: for my grand-mother, Lilyan, shattered by a marshmallow-white untuned Toyota. Her canary crinoline dress was ripped at the waist, discolored by blood. "My nails were wet," the gum-chewing driver said.

I demonstrate signs of the old woman I'll become as I whip my arms in circles, scream at drivers who rev engines as I cross the street. I climb ridges that outline the city, as I rebuke tarnished air-kisses from the rough lips of gardeners in trucks missing mufflers, plumbers behind schedule, men driv-ing Porsches.

I walk in August to inhale pineapple-sweet sweat from flesh. To see wa-terfall-smooth men as they shoot hoops in schoolyards. To see melted words of love on sidewalks: *Tito y Pena . . . Por Vida.* I walk in September for *Rosh Hashana*, the Jewish day of redemption. I claim my sins when I hear the ashen-teared sounds from the *Shofar*, the ram's antler being blown like a French horn.

I walk Los Angeles for lost love, memories cemented over, and prayer. This city is my point of reference, my ground, my home.

Profile

Shauna Somers, ever punctual, meets me at King's Road Café. It's a Beverly Boulevard coffee house that straddles, in every sense, the line between Hol-lywood and its hipper neighbor, West Hollywood. The place is trendy, crowd-ed with the surgically augmented, the tattooed, and the beautiful—but it was my choice.

Shauna's dressed in black except for a snappy-looking pair of lavender Hushpuppies. Sunglasses, white teeth, trim and toned figure, a hint of a tan—she's still all LA. She doesn't, however, pause even once to admire her-self in the mirrors that line the cafe walls, and she's not carrying film script. Odd behavior for these parts. She calmly sips her herbal tea while the rest of us latte drinkers gawk at the three-car pile-up—BMW, Cherokee, and Datsun B210 (we can't tell who's at fault)—on the street outside.

Shauna is an original—poet, novelist, writer of short stories and screenplays. She's also a performance artist and has an M.A. from the USC film school. Traveler, adventuress, feminist foot-soldier, she's a Valley girl turned LA woman who lives healthy and looks you in the eye when you speak. She has more friends than anyone I know. Her best friend is a septuagenarian. Shauna is just thirty. She is the busiest person I know, and the coolest.

—Wooten Lee

Bio

Shauna Somers
Place of residence: Los Angeles and Santa Barbara.
Birthplace: Los Angeles.
Grew up in: Encino.
Day job: Writer.
Education: B.S., University of Southern California. M.A., USC School of Cinema and Television.
Serial publications: *Hair. Poetry Revival.*
Awards: Millay Colony for the Arts Fellowship. Writer-in-Residence, Vermont Studio Center. Finalist, Adult Screenplay, Austin Film Festival.
Current project: A novel.
Favorite book: Whatever I'm reading.
Belief: Life is vibrant. Take the risks. Live your dreams.
Cravings: Life! Wandering!

Cynthia J. Starks

A *Piccolo Paese*

In the summer of 1979, my husband Giorgio and I spent two months in Pizzo, a *piccolo paese*—his poor, provincial hometown on the coast of Calabria in Southern Italy. I hated almost every minute of it. Seventeen years later, I know why. And I know what I missed.

I had met Giorgio in Bermuda while on vacation in the fall of 1976. He was a crew member on the SS *Doric*, in port for a few days. After a night of slow dancing and soulful looks, he asked me to marry him.

I said, "No," and instead began a long-distance courtship, undaunted by Giorgio's tentative English and my meager Italian. I studied Italian, and we exchanged letters and phone calls. Each Saturday I took the train from New Haven to meet his ship when it docked in New York harbor.

We married on July 8, 1978. Giorgio had difficulty with English, couldn't find a job, and had a hard time settling into life in New Haven. Each evening when I finished work, he wanted to go out. He had no American license, so I'd drive us around town, stopping at the ice cream parlor in the summer and at the movies when the weather grew cold.

I took it upon myself to find work for Giorgio, taking him to an interview for a dishwasher's job at a restaurant owned by a friend. He walked out in a huff. "Are you trying to humiliate me?" he asked. Another friend got him a factory job in Waterbury. Six weeks later, his boss made a remark that offended him. Giorgio walked off the job.

Giorgio went to night school to learn English, but dropped out after one class. "I don't have to learn English," he told friends, "my wife has learned Italian." But my Italian was rudimentary, so our conversations lacked grace, depth, or beauty.

Giorgio wanted to move to Italy, and we decided to try it for the summer of 1979. I took a leave of absence from my job, sublet our apartment, and off we went.

We arrived in Pizzo on a steamy July day. We carried heavy valises down narrow alleys and up crumbling steps to Giorgio's house. His sister Maria wouldn't let us in. Giorgio cajoled her through the heavy black door. When she finally opened it, Giorgio introduced me as his wife. Maria refused to believe him, relenting only after we showed her the wedding album we hastily pulled from our suitcase.

The flat itself was just two rooms, a kitchen and bedroom separated by a faded red curtain. Maria slept on a bed in the kitchen. The bathroom was a closet with a toilet.

We flushed the toilet with pails of water and bathed in a large, round bucket in what privacy we could fashion in a corner of the kitchen.

Maria never left the house. She dressed daily in a black sweater and skirt. Sitting on her narrow kitchen bed, she was by turns silent and talkative. She spoke to the sparrows that sometimes flew around the flat, and to herself, but never to me. Each morning before we arose, Maria combed her hair and dried her hands on a towel she'd take from our dresser. She repeated this ritual four or five times. Then she'd scream for Giorgio to get up and make her cappuccino.

When I complained, Giorgio dismissed me with a wave of his hand. "*Dai, dai,*" he said in his Calabrian dialect. "Go on, go on, leave." I felt as if I'd been struck.

My dislike of Maria and my surroundings masked a more troubling conviction. I didn't love my husband. Would our marriage survive the summer?

For many years, my memories of Giorgio colored my memories of Pizzo. Only recently have I begun to remember other moments—moments of humanity and sweetness.

I remember Zia Filomena. Each afternoon Aunt Filomena walked across town with a covered dish of homemade pasta or chicken for Maria's dinner.

(Maria was suspicious about what she ate and usually refused anything Giorgio or I fixed.) Maria never thanked her and Filomena never expected it.

Maria's perversity disgusted me in those days. But I failed to note that Filomena's loving impulse enabled her not only to tolerate Maria, but to serve her as well.

I remember Paolo and his dog, Benno. A striking widower in his eighties, Paolo zipped around town on a vintage German motorcycle, Benno in the sidecar next to him.

One hot afternoon, Benno eagerly consumed a large bowl of ice cream and promptly keeled over. A grieving Paolo posted death notices throughout Pizzo. Friends contributed to a funeral service. And the next day, wearing black armbands, we followed a tiny coffin to a hillside grave. Paolo prayed and cried and handed out, as mementos, pictures of Benno sitting obediently in the sidecar.

Back then, I mocked Paolo's sentimentality and the town's silliness. Today, the event seems an example of compassion on all sides.

I remember a little bakery on the outskirts of town where we'd buy fragrant bread fresh from the oven at two o'clock in the morning, take it home, slice it, spread it with oily tuna, and devour it. And a roadside fruit stand where we'd wake the sleeping proprietor in the wee hours for watermelon, and then sit, laughing, at sticky tables under the stars, melon juice dripping down our chins.

On cool nights in the piazza, it seemed all nine thousand Pizzo residents strolled purposefully up and down, up and down, arms linked in a friendly mating dance. Giorgio and I licked cool *gelato* and sipped inky espresso as we judged the outfits and attributes of our neighbors. Sometimes we'd get up from our table and join in the dance.

Giorgio and I returned to New Haven that September and continued our clumsy dance. He was unable to embrace life here. I was unable to span the cultural divide. When I filed for divorce the following September, he asked, "Who do you think you are, Marilyn Monroe?" Giorgio moved back to Pizzo.

Fourteen years later I remarried, and my thoughts of Giorgio and his home began to change. Today I remember a long-ago summer we shared. And for the first time, sorrow makes room for sweetness.

Profile

Cynthia J. Starks.

About two years ago I got married in a hurry. Not that my man and I were fleeing the law, but, after ten years, it was time. Unfortunately, my family did not attend. Since we were pulling the wedding together with literally nothing, I needed help—more than just holding my bouquet while we put on our rings.

Cindy Starks had been my friend for only a short time, but on the day of the wedding she arrived two hours early, worked with the caterers, even sent the florist back for the comb he'd forgotten—the comb that matched the flowers in my hair. The wedding was short and sweet, only ten guests. In many ways it was a sad day. But it was also a time of great blessing to be sharing it with a friend like Cindy.

Cindy left her job as an IBM speechwriter in 1993. Today, she works from her home in Trumbull, Connecticut. Her writing explores childhood, heritage, faith, and the role of family in community. She's currently working on a screenplay, *No Time for Charm,* and a set of personal essays called *The Eczema Kid,* about growing up in the 1950s.

—Deborah DiSesa Hirsch

Bio

Cynthia J. Starks
Place of residence: Trumbull, Connecticut.
Birthplace: New Haven, Connecticut.
Grew up in: Working-class Italian-American family.
Day job: Creative writer.
Education: B.A. in English, Albertus Magnus College.
Serial publication: *New Haven Register.*
Awards: Most Cheerful Girl, Eighth Grade Class, Lovell School, 1964.
Current projects: Trying to adopt a baby. Writing a screenplay.
Favorite book: *Pride and Prejudice* by Jane Austen.
Belief: Joyful Catholic.
Craving: Chocolate!

❖

"PORTRAIT OF JOHN STENZEL"

© JOSEPH BRANCHCOMBE 1996

© 1996 Joseph Mack Branchcombe

John Stenzel

Improvisations on a Paceline

I am sixty miles into my first 100-mile bicycle ride, the Chico Century. I have finished the hilly section and enter the windswept flatlands of California's northern Central Valley. Against a quartering headwind—not quite in my face, but more in the face than at the side—I begin to crank my gears lower and lower, even though the countryside is table-top flat. Four hours earlier, several thousand riders had started out, snaking through the cool morning air like a neon-hued Spandex worm, climbing into the foothills from the little university town of Chico.

Ahead of me I can see dots in the distance. I am alone with my self-imposed sentence, my speedometer-battery dead, my gut cramping and growling from too much rest-stop fruit juice. My car is waiting for me forty upwind miles away. How the heck am I going to make it?

From behind I hear the smooth whir of riders, and my pace increases automatically, even though I have been passed many times already by lines going several miles an hour faster than I want to. This group hasn't closed in too quickly. Can I ride their slipstream? A few minutes later I have joined a quartet of gray-haired riders wearing Sacramento Wheelmen jerseys. I am about to get a lesson in the impromptu jam session known as paceline riding.

My newfound mentor, Gordon, drops his left hand down and edges toward the traffic lane. My front wheel is spinning slightly behind his and to the side, and I have been enjoying an eerily quiet pocket of calmer air amidst the methodical north wind. I hear someone call out "Clear," signaling that Gordon can safely sag back to the rear of the line. Just behind me is the metallic, free wheel hum of another rider following closely. As soon as I lose the comfort of Gordon's slipstream, the resistance increases on my pedals, and I must fight the urge to press too hard. Five minutes earlier I was warned not to speed up when my turn came "at the point," the head of the paceline, and here I am, trying to maintain a steady cadence. A good paceline is a smooth one, and seasoned riders have little patience with the dangerous "bungee-cord" style of inexperienced cyclists.

I'm determined not to rush, or slow down, or pull too long at the front. Gentle corrections waft up from behind me, just as I've requested: "That's a bit rich, ease off, fine, fine, anytime you're ready to come back, just let me know." Just as I do before a concert, I'm feeling my share of performance anxiety, though I don't fear judgment from this crew. Nevertheless, before I really need to, I'm pointing my finger down, easing to my left, and letting the group stream past my right hip. This way I'm the only rider exposed to traffic, and the new leader can smoothly begin his pull at the front. All I do is let up on my pedals—the wind does the rest. Gordon welcomes me back in with a grin, and for some reason I thank him: "Heck, I should thank you—that was fine, real steady."

Working together this way, sharing the wind load, we move several miles an hour faster than a solo cyclist. The teamwork turns work to pleasure. Gordon's helmet mirror lets him spot cars before I do, calling out "Car back," and "Clear," but the group keeps up a lighthearted banter even as they clip along. Within a few minutes he's up front again, and I've gotten a few more bits of advice: never touch the brake; find a tandem going your speed and stay with 'em all day; focus on the seat-post of the guy ahead, not the wheel; stay aware of what's coming; don't zone out; ease off early, not late, before you get tired. I'm a sponge for this basic knowledge, and learning it makes me forget the soreness in my seat and the tightness in my gut.

After several more exchanges we pull into the last rest stop, stretch our legs, and fill water bottles. We agree to keep together for the final run into Chico, straight into the wind. I feel almost no fatigue, I'm floating with a rhythm and harmony that I don't experience in my rides alone. Even as I enter this new world, I'm aware of the next level and the next, of racing packs and the thirty-five mph *peloton* of the great European races. Yet here, in miniature, is my fantasy camp, my master class, and I buzz with the collective energy of the group and the moment.

I've experienced this feeling before, in team sports like basketball and rowing—yet my mind is drawn, oddly, to music. I think of a chorus blending disparate voices, of a small group playing sonatas with tight agility. A few years back I'd played recorder sonatas and studied Baroque performance style at a music camp run by my older brother, a cellist, and his harpsichordist partner. By the second summer I had caught the magic from these professionals and moved through technique into the next level of teamwork. With complete trust we passed melody lines back and forth, completing harmonies, articulating lines, adding ornamentation, listening and responding as we maintained pulse and spirit. Now I was feeling the same joy, riding a bike instead of playing a recorder.

Our paceline turns north and hooks up with the section-line roads into town. We have attracted a pack of thirty tired riders who are glad for the windbreak. The five of us smoothly exchange stints at the front, with hardly a word spoken. In the confusion of the finish-zone parking area I lose track of my teachers, the quartet that had absorbed me, so I load up my bike and drive away. On the freeway a truck passes me, and I unconsciously slide in behind it. The wind-noise falls once I enter its slipstream.

Profile

John Stenzel brings music to everything he does, whether it be row, row, rowing his boat or ride, ride, riding his bike.

An accomplished linguist, he moves easily through the world's many accents, skipping with astonishing ease from Etonian English (he did study at Oxford), to Sid Caesar German, to shopkeeper East Indian, to California Surfer Dude. He likes to ski too fast, which brings him pleasure, but also brings other things (his wife, Amélie, just showed me the bruise on her thigh from their last ski trip). He sings around the office—Mozart or "Rubber Ducky" or whatever it is he is rehearsing at the moment. When I join in, he never seems to mind that I don't know the words or the tune. He is a good person and/or a good actor. He also plays recorder like a classically trained lark. Indeed, everything he does is like a lark to him, seemingly effortless, but graceful and beautiful. This is especially so for his writing.

—John Boe

Bio

John Stenzel

Place of residence: Berkeley.

Birthplace: Richmond, Virginia.

Grew up in: San Jose, when there were still orchards.

Day job: Lecturer, English department.

Education: B.A., Pomona College. M. Philosophy, Oxford University. Ph.D., University of California at Davis.

Serial publications: *American Rowing*—essay.

Current projects: Anthology of essays and poems about rowing. Critique of computer-assisted writing.

Craving: Quality—in people and practice. In the Robert Pirsig sense, not Donald Trump's!

Favorite Bach cantata: BWV 106, "Actus Tragicus."

Favorite books that I can't re-read for fear of spoiling the pleasurable memory: Robert Heinlein's juvenile science-fiction.

Favorite easy rock climb in a stunning setting: Snake Dike, Half Dome.

Runner-up: South East Buttress of Cathedral Peak.

Favorite student question: "Do we need to know this?"

Favorite computer message: "The application 'unknown' has unexpectedly quit, because an error occurred."

Sharon Streeter

Coming of Age

Madame Vincent is ninety-two. She takes the stairs to the second floor, because once she was caught in an elevator for an entire day alone. She uses a cane and takes each step with caution. At the first-floor landing, she pauses and seems to lose her bearings. I think for a moment that she is almost blind, as she reaches for the wall, searching for a clue to her whereabouts.

"Ah," she says to no one in particular, "*C'est le premier.*"

I have just locked my door and am ready to go out. It is now that she notices me.

"*Bonjour, Madame.*" She greets me with a nod of her head.

"*Bonjour, Madame,*" I reply. "*Vous allez bien?*"

"I have just returned from mass at Salpetriere," she declares in French as she leans onto her cane. Madame Vincent does not speak English. My own has been left behind. But my French has not yet purged itself of its abrupt American style.

"How did you get there?" I ask. I don't mean to be disrespectful, but Salpetriere is a fair distance.

"The bus," she answers, as if it's of no concern. "They know me there."

Her delicate body is wrapped in a shabby tweed coat. Nylon stockings droop on tiny legs and twist around her ankles. She has pulled her thin, silver hair into a smooth bun, and finished it off with a black velvet hat that appears to have lived as long as Madame Vincent.

"After mass the priest asked a nice young man to accompany me to the bus." Her pale blue eyes become alive as she shares this act of friendship.

"*Mais c'est bien.*" I smile. I'm relieved that this woman is not alone in the world. She shuffles past me in the dark hallway. "*Au revoir, Madame,*" I say to her small, hunched back. I'm off to find a cafe for lunch where I can write in my journal.

I try to imagine Madame Vincent getting on and off the bus. "What must it be like?" I ask myself. I don't even use the bus at home in Portland. This is Paris. Everything goes fast, and the steps of a bus are high above the ground. People getting off are in the way of people getting on. Does she know immediately where to descend, or does she ask? I must give her credit.

I first met Madame Vincent a few days ago. She was ahead of me on the sidewalk. I watched her put all of her weight against the solid oak door to enter the building. I slowed my pace. It had been a long weekend—too many people and too little sleep. So I passed behind her and stood at the corner to wait a few minutes. I did not want to deal with this old woman.

Old woman.

"I, too, shall be an old woman one day," hissed the good woman of my conscience. "Relax," replied my demon, "you're allowed to be less than compassionate from time to time." But impatience joined forces with fatigue. I pushed my own weary body against the door and caught a glimpse of Madame Vincent's sleeve as she rounded the hall corner.

"*Me voici,*" she said, as though to warn me of her presence.

"*Bonjour, Madame.*" My voice seemed thin in the cool, stale air of the vestibule.

Madame Vincent had stopped at the foot of the stairs. I wasn't sure if she was resting or waiting for me.

"I have been to the Boulevard Arago for some bread," she offered. The corner *boulangerie* is not open on Thursdays.

"I understand they have to take a day off," she added, "but it makes it difficult to buy my bread." I nodded in sympathy.

She motioned for me to go ahead. "Unless," she suggested, "you will be taking the elevator." I reassured her that I could certainly use the stairs to get to the first floor. Climbing stairs was a novelty, actually. I wondered if she could even imagine my single-story ranch-style house in Oregon.

Up we went, in single file, my steps slower than usual. Madame Vincent spoke to me from behind, and told me of her harrowing experience with the lift.

"The door would not open. I knew that someone would arrive eventually," she said, "but it was a long wait. I was very tired. No place to sit down, you know."

"And such a tiny box," I thought. I remembered the day I tried to squeeze in with my suitcases. It was then that she cautioned me.

"Don't get old," she began, then added before I could reply, "particularly if you must get old alone. *Toute seule*," she affirmed with a shake of her head. We arrived at the door to my flat. As I turned the key, I asked Madame Vincent if she would like to come in for a rest.

"No, thank you," she responded. "I'm going to make myself a good, hot cup of tea. You're most gracious to ask."

My door stood open. I watched Madame Vincent as she rounded the bend and turned her back to continue to the second floor. She planted what seemed like enormous, heavy shoes firmly on each step, first one, then the other. I thought about my impending birthday and wondered how fifty had arrived so quickly. I felt the weight of my bags and watched a wisp of a woman climb alone to her flat, as she had done a thousand times.

Profile

Sharon Streeter is a French teacher, traveler, photographer, and a gourmet cook. She plays the piano, sings, and occasionally brings other amateur and professional musicians together for an evening of music-making.

Sharon spent eighteen years developing an ornamental garden with rare trees, shrubs, and perennials—carefully placed to provide interest throughout the four seasons. With her math-teacher husband as the photographer by her side, Sharon explored and studied French gardens. She has published articles on gardening for the *Pacific Horticulture* magazine and given slide presentations. As one of the founders and first president of the Hardy Plant Society of Oregon, she initiated and edited the semi-annual membership bulletin for five years.

In 1989 Sharon was catapulted from her world by the sudden, traumatic death of her husband. Her grief and new life alone have changed her. She left teaching and has begun to define and express herself as a writer.

—Nancy Travers

Bio

Sharon Streeter

Place of residence: Portland, Oregon.

Birthplace: Seattle.

Grew up in: Des Moines, Washington.

Day job: Writer. Retired French teacher.

Education: B.A., University of Washington. M.A.T., Lewis and Clark College.

Serial publications: *Pacific Horticulture. The Bulletin of the Hardy Plant Society of Oregon.*

Award: John Philip Sousa "Most Musical" Award, Federal Way High School.

Current projects: Volunteer for Multnomah County Library. Organizing another garden tour in France.

Favorite book: *Between Meals: An Appetite for Paris* by A.J. Liebling.

Belief: Non-practicing. I believe in using my talents and being an advocate for others.

Craving: Chocolate chip cookies.

Loathing: Giant shopping malls.

Lisa Teasley

Black Writer, Black Reader

A writer must read. She's got to know and experience the classics, the best stories that have come before her, as many as she can. She must continue her education.

But what happens when a writer is black and must read classics written predominately by white authors? Almost always it's a hurtful experience. "Nigger" this, "monkey" that—and/or "darkie" that. I'm not only talking about *Huckleberry Finn* or *Heart of Darkness*. Before I hurl a book across the room out of anger, I wonder how to work out my frustrations constructively.

In the book *High Cotton*, the African-American writer Darryl Pinckney describes his trials and tribulations while working for the writer Djuna Barnes, and how her many digs inspired him, at one point, to "get them all," to "expose . . . the sins of Western literature." He set out, as I have wanted to, and listed on index cards: the nigger box in Hemingway's *The Sun Also Rises*; the Cadillac of niggers in Fitzgerald's *The Great Gatsby*; the darkie towns of Dashiell Hammett; and the passage in D.H. Lawrence's *Lady Chatterley's Lover* where he likens sleeping with a black woman to mud. Pinckney finds, as I have found, "niggers" in Rimbaud, William Carlos Williams, Poe, Defoe, Katherine Mansfield, Shaw, Genet, and, of course, Céline. He found Virginia Woolf's comparisons of a black man to a monkey.

I needed only open the first page of Virginia Woolf's *Orlando* to find the hero "in the act of slicing at the head of a Moor . . . the colour of an old football, and more or less the shape of one, save for the sunken cheeks and a strand or two of coarse dry hair, like the hair on a coconut . . . who had started up under the moon in the barbarian fields of Africa." She goes on to add that Orlando's "enemy grinned at him through shrunk, black lips . . ." What hatred Woolf had! And I can't, for the life of me, figure out why. After thirty-three years, one might think that I had toughened myself to these blows. But I haven't. Every time I pick up a book by a white author, particularly one written before the 1970s, I am always shocked.

Even with Proust. I thought I had escaped unscathed, but halfway through the first volume of Proust's *Remembrance of Things Past*, the story is told of a minor character who "went the other day to the Zoo, where they have some blackamoors—Singhalese . . ." and this character, Madame Blatin, approaches one of the cages and says, "Good morning, nigger!"

Even Truman Capote's most beloved Holly Golightly failed to win me over. In fact, I hated her after her exclamation to her agent in *Breakfast at Tiffany's*: "You're such a slob. You always nigger-lip." Later she puts down the narrator's short story for being about "Brats and niggers . . . It doesn't *mean* anything." Still later, she imagines the babies that she and her Brazilian boyfriend would have: "I'm sure some of them will be rather dark—José has a trace of *le negre*. . . . What could be prettier than a quite coony baby with bright green beautiful eyes?" In still another scene, the narrator comes down to her level and describes those who goaded their horses through Central Park as "savage members of a jungle ambush, a band of Negro boys [who] leapt out of the shrubbery . . ." But does a writer hate a writer for his or her failed humanity, or does a writer look at a writer strictly for how he or she perceives and illustrates the world?

Should I pass on Henry Miller for his unfavorable sexual descriptions of women and miss out on his spiritual wisdom in *Big Sur and the Oranges of Hieronymous Bosch*? Should I be embarrassed by the fact that the amazing American writer Toni Morrison debuted with a tale of black incest and was awarded the Pulitzer Prize for Literature for her portrayal of a black slave mother who kills her child? Should I dismiss Gabriel Garcia Marquez for his numerous offensive portrayals of "mulattos," or Nabokov for also writing numerously on the love of a man for a prepubescent girl? Should I skip the precise first-person narratives of Knut Hamsun because he was a Nazi sympathizer?

The end result of Darryl Pinckney's exercise in exorcising racist classic authors was that he threw out the index cards. He said he realized the motive for his note-taking was "pretty sorry," since after leaving the employment of Djuna Barnes he had "fallen into the pit of trying to prove that there was more to me than she thought." His grandfather told him, "Let them talk. You know your name."

Just as I know mine. The stories I have to tell come from what I've perceived and need to express. Whatever limitations are exposed of my moral character, I will find out, when and if I am read. And as a reader I still have these many humps to get over—the psychological pain of an uncomprehended white racism. At some point, I hope, I will be over it. Besides Darryl Pinckney's tossing of the cards, there are other examples of transcendence. A writer friend of mine, who is Jewish, named his daughter Céline.

Profile

confession:
i like artistic people who dabble in the predictable:
touch football, romances in paris, long-distance fondling.
and none of the above.
perhaps.
should you be ashamed of who i am?
and i of you? nudity is nostalgic, beauty
buttresses the smile on your sepia frame. i dig
frames, especially if they encompass a picture
of dreadlocks jumping   one, two, three over
a prayer with apples.   in the garden the snakes
hiss at your ending, a beginning really as the
accordion stretches a latin-flavored coda. tobacco juice
chews the crust off your day, fortified with a glass
of wine. do i detect a slight speech impediment?
express yourself before the boogie-wo/man
cross-references those wings.

From the poem "she has many ancestors,"
for Lisa Teasley.
                                        —Kevin Powell

Bio

Lisa Teasley
Place of residence: New York.
Birthplace: Los Angeles.
Family: Husband, John Vlautin. Daughter, Imogen Teasley-Vlautin.
Day job: Writer/painter.
Education: B.A. in English, University of California at Los Angeles.
Anthologies: *In the Tradition: An Anthology of Young Black Writers.*
Serial publications: *Between C and D. Catalyst. Rampike. Los Angeles Times. LA Weekly. Details Magazine.* Fiction and articles.
Cover art: *Callalo,* Volume 17, Number 4. *Herstory,* Volume 1 (Spring 1992).
Awards: May Merrill Miller Award for Fiction. National Society of Arts and Letters Short Story Award. Amaranth Review Award for Short Fiction.
Current project: Historical novel on the West Indians who dug the Panama Canal.
Favorite animal: Iguana.

Holly L. Thomas

One More Woman with Her Bags Packed

There's a lot happening in New York City, but you pay a high price for it. In the fifteen years I've lived within a train commute of the place, I've done an excellent job of staying away, but now the city is coming to me. Here in insecure Poughkeepsie, seventy miles north of Times Square, people are starting to run red lights and stop signs just like they do "downstate." Bird-flipping is becoming standard practice on local highways, which are being widened and strip-malled, the better to serve those spun-out by Manhattan's centrifugal force. Worse, the accents are starting to change. I hear more and more women saying "coffee" through their noses. "Off" has become a two syllable word—"ooh-wuf," accent on "ooh." It used to be that some people in New Jersey said "youse" when they should have said "you" and some multi-generational Hudson Valley folks did too, but there the similarity between the two accents stopped. No more.

My boyfriend is a minstrel raised in Southern California in the '60s and has lived more places than I've visited in the decades since, but has never spent more than three consecutive nights in the five boroughs. Yet even he is starting to sound like a Brooklyn truant, a waitress in some diner off ("ooh-wuf") exit twelve of the Jersey Turnpike, and a bag boy in the Bronx. He's a musician and a natural mimic so he can't help it, he says. I say ("I sez," if we stay here much longer) it's time to run.

We live in the Mid-Hudson Valley, a complicated, beautiful, and historic region of Washington Irving tales, Dutch barns, tribal place-names, and Rockefeller money. Still full of farms and country estates, it's also a place IBM made cocky with suburban prosperity until the company's three largest plants here imploded a few years back. Now we lure New Yorkers northward to buy our farms and homes, and to shop in our outlet centers. We invite them instead of resisting them.

Understand that I'm no urbanophobe. I love the Met—both the opera and the museum. It's a groove to walk down Fifth Avenue on a spring day when the cameras outnumber the tourists, and I can go two crowded blocks without overhearing a conversation in American English. Central Park on a summer afternoon has a thousand different impromptu concerts and roller-blade demonstrations to choose from, and a bazillion dog, human, and sportswear fashion combos to observe. It's one of the places that gives me hope that we all might one day learn to get along with one another. And the unsung places I won't identify never stop working to rejuvenate the city and the people who care about it. Still, if I wanted to live with the pressure New Yorkers accept—if I wanted to adopt the attitude with the accents—I'd already be there.

Instead, I've kept my distance, always exhausted by a day's visit to the concrete canyons, and eager to get back home. I have turned down great jobs that would have made me a commuter, one of the growing crowd that buys strong coffee and the *Daily News* at the Poughkeepsie train station in time for the 6:20 express to Grand Central every morning. The New York license plates on my ten-year-old Honda have rolled past stop signs in nearly every coastal state and maritime province, but they have never accompanied me onto Manhattan Island. I've stayed away from Times Square for fifteen New Year's Eves in a row. Although I have been to Yankee Stadium, I have managed to avoid concerts at Madison Square Garden, and I have never carried a Bloomies bag.

My relationship with New York City has always seemed balanced. The pendulum has predictably swung between love and hate without getting stuck at either end of the arc or pausing too long in the center. I've lived just close enough to enjoy an occasional dose of the place, but not too close. Yet now the attitudes and the accents are spreading northward into the fringe of farm country. IBM's void is being filled by anything we can attract. And houses whose values went down with Big Blue's work force are being marketed to people willing to sleep here and work in the metropolis. It's time to move on while we still love this area, to give the newcomers a little more room. Before my sweetheart can teasingly slip into a "Yo! You gunna knock ooh-wuf the typin' an eat wit' me, o' whut?" without even making me wince.

Profile

Holly L. Thomas arrived at the potluck with Tony. I'd never seen him in a tweed jacket before. Holly was beautiful. Beaming, glasses sparkling. Clutching her stories and poems. We sat on a bed piled high with overcoats. She read. I listened, oblivious to the clamor and buzz of painters, models, art directors who crowded my Highland, New York apartment. Stomachs growling, they waited, while we stuffed ourselves on hard-to-resist prose and verse.

At that point Holly was still a high-profile land use planner. At work you'd glimpse a woman who'd outgrown a carefully built career, still doing her stint for Dutchess County. Camouflaged in business attire, pacing, she'd speak in low, flat tones. Spare sentences that gave nothing away. Inside she was raring to break loose. Through the 1990s I sketched, painted, and wrote with Holly. I heard her pass, ruminating, through seasons of speculation, her heart in West Coast cafes. Curled on the deck on sunny winter days, or down at The Balancing Act deli pouring tea, she'd laugh aloud, writing. Or grumble, pen wiggling furiously. She pieced out plans, and, between notebooks and pages, packed her pine cone collection and tub toys, and consoled her cats. Crossed off the lists on her fridge. Finally, blotting lots of spattered ink with soggy Kleenex, came "This is the Last Time" poems, and the Westward Ho theme for her moving sale. In '96, her staid stint in New York over, she set out, without her business suits, for Seattle.

Her work is about changes, omens, and renewals, the pitfalls of deadening and questionable security, the humor and sanity in seeing blessed, beckoning risks. I just received a card she sent me while traveling cross-country. It shows a man who threw a line into the night sky and walked out onto it.

—Annie LaBarge

Bio

Holly L. Thomas
Place of residence: Seattle.
Birthplace: Schenectady, New York.
Grew up in: Albany, New York and New Brunswick, New Jersey.
Day job: Former land use planner out East. Now freelance writer, poet, and student of my new surroundings.
Education: B.A., Dartmouth College.
Serial publications: Government documents related to land use and environmental issues. Local news and reviews for the *Harvard Common Press*.
Awards: For creative writing? Ask me again in five years.
Current project: A collection of poems.
Favorite book this year: *The Little Notebook* by Nicole Gausseron.
Belief: Non-denominational Christian.
Craving: Time within earshot and sight of big surf.
Favorite radio station: It's a toss-up between KPLU and KUOW, local NPR affiliates.
Preferred music: I'm a jazzaholic, at least I listen to a lot of jazz.

Margaret Thompson

Still Life: Cache Creek, B.C.

Only when I came to Canada did I realize how European I am. I left an old world, where history is measured in millennia, where humans burrow comfortably in the sedimentary layers of the past, nonchalant about continuity. I came to British Columbia, where people gasp in amazement at any building more than a hundred years old. I found myself craving longevity—the mark of an alien. As a result I fell in love with the ancient natural landscape, and my foreign eyes could not help seeing the little towns of this province as puny, ephemeral things, unlikely to endure in this iron country, like smears of dirt on the skin.

Take Cache Creek, for instance. I stay here often, one of its many impermanent residents. It is halfway between my home in Fort St. James, another small town to the north, and the Lower Mainland—a convenient place to break a journey. It is typical small-town B.C., a place that people go through, not to. It clutters a junction of highways that dip and swoop by without a second thought, hurrying off again into the bare brown hills.

Cache Creek always feels temporary, as insubstantial as a movie set. The buildings give me the impression that there is nothing behind their facades, that they are all, somehow, pretending to be real. Gas stations and motels jostle for position on the main street. Wander Inns and Slumberlodges all promise Good Eats and oblivion. One motel would have us believe it is a castle, the usual clapboard crowned by a fringe of plywood battlements.

By day, the town seems to be populated entirely by greasy men tending gas pumps and fast food outlets. They minister to tired travelers like me who browse apathetically among the tawdry souvenirs or slump against cracked vinyl, uncritically consuming plates of fries and giant hamburgers oozing ketchup. The smell of hot oil taints the air. In the evening, people vanish to their motel rooms—to listen to their air conditioners if they are lucky, to sweat listlessly in front of the cable TV if they are not.

The streets empty at night. The side roads off the highway soon bump into naked hills or swallow their own tails. In the older part of town, small, dispirited houses sag and crack side by side, held up by dried vine-tendrils. Recently, houses have begun a creeping advance up the hillsides; some stand alone, high up, raw on their dusty lots.

There is a creek. It threads its way through the town, keeping its head down, intent on its own business. It ignores the tires and broken slabs of concrete, the rusty iron, beer bottles snapped off at the neck, sodden cardboard, plastic, wire, and scum that clots its banks. It veers away from the wood chip plant that is steadily chewing unprofitable trees, and the landfill opposite that is holding a non-stop funeral for big-city garbage behind tasteful screens of earth.

Whenever I arrive in Cache Creek, I take a room, lay claim to it by dropping off my suitcase, then leave the motel and walk uphill. I soon outstrip the paths and dirt-bike tracks and climb the runnels scoured by ancient rains, dust puffing around my feet like talcum, until it is too steep to go any further and I sink onto the coarse, brown grass. Up here the wind always blows, the smell of sage is strong, and the hawks wheel silently overhead. The hills heave into the distance, soft and placid, loose folds of dusty hide draped over bone and sinew.

The antiquity I crave is here, in the land itself. The hills endure. From this vantage point Cache Creek is muted, no more than a blemish. The town is an irrelevance, a temporary excrescence which could easily be scraped away. Cache Creek and all the little towns of B.C. mutely repeat the basic truth of this country: they and their inhabitants are here on sufferance. Only human will keeps the wilderness at bay; patiently, the land waits for that will to falter, to reclaim what belongs to it by ancient right. It has always been ready. Just let people turn their backs for an instant, and the gimcrack houses will fall as the ancient hills stealthily creep back, and at their feet, the creek will dash unheeding down its winding, rocky bed.

Profile

Margaret Thompson has lived in Canada for thirty years, but no one will ever mistake her for a Canuck—her British reserve is legendary in our small northern town. Still, I know the Margaret who gladly shares a bottle of wine and turns into a dancing fool whenever we listen to Paul Simon's music.

Her love of language has affected many people—the kids at the Speech Arts festival who wait nervously for her adjudication, the teenagers in her high school English classes, and the adults in her evening courses. Yet most of our time together is spent walking in the woods, watching for eagles, or picking fiddleheads—we both love the hunting-and-gathering thing.

Her years in the North have honed her ability to see ordinary things in extraordinary ways. We spend hours in her backyard, surrounded by her flower gardens and her bird feeders, feeling a bit like ladies of the manor. Our conversations drift toward the mundane, and we commiserate about raising children—we each have three. Sometimes Margaret hands me a poem or a short story, and I have no words to describe the *rightness* of her language. I simply read, and am moved.

—Carolyne Kennedy

Bio

Margaret Thompson
Place of residence: Fort St. James, British Columbia, Canada.
Birthplace: Surbiton, Surrey England.
Education: B.A., University of London. Diploma of Education, University of Exeter. M.A., San Diego State.
Books: *Squaring the Round*—self published prose and poetry about the early days of Fort St. James. *Hide and Seek* (Caitlin Press)—short stories.
Serial Publication: *Amethyst Review*—poetry.
Awards: Central Interior Writing Competition—three-time winner. Stephen Leacock Poetry Competition—four runner-up prizes.
Favorite book: *A House for Mr. Biswas* by V.S. Naipaul.

Kyoko Uchida

Elsewhere

Every place I've lived has been a temporary arrangement: I've always known that I'd leave. My father's work took him from Japan across oceans, and he carried us with him, back and forth. Believing that we would learn to assimilate more quickly, he chose neighborhoods with few other Japanese families, schools where I was among few Asian children. We were to remember that we were merely visiting and to behave accordingly. What I learned was how to leave places. I've come to inhabit a landscape of displacement—of arrivals and departures. I had already lost each place we lived years before I ever saw it.

In the mythical America, however, immigrants from the world over can find a place and become anything they want if they work hard enough, if they want badly enough to be American. Or if you at least look like some people's idea of an American. Third-generation and fourth-generation Asian-Americans are still asked, "Where are you from? No, where are you from *really*?" Or "How long have you been here? You speak such good English!" Other people tell me that I'm American because I sound like one, though the passport I carry is Japanese. This is a country where you're assigned a place to "be from," whether you ever belonged there or not. Most Asian-Americans never belonged in the countries their grandparents came from; most have never seen that faraway place assigned to them by others. Their place is here, in America. Yet, in the real America, they're often robbed of this claim. It is a country where everyone is supposed to *arrive* from elsewhere, as if to a final destination. I myself have never truly belonged here. I know I have no tangible claim to this place, that I'll leave it again. The more I'm told I fit in, the more I become uprooted, a foreigner.

In Japan, where I was born and where I look like I belong, I'm expected to think and act like everyone else. It's the superficial similarities that bring out the profound differences in the way we see things: we have so little in common that we speak only in sharp silences. I've become a stranger, among childhood friends and family, in what's supposed to be my native home. Each landscape I enter is as familiar and as distant and inaccessible as the last. In either country, I feel like an impostor, half native, half foreigner, pretending to belong. This feeling of displacement is an intimate part of me, as well-known to me as my own body. It's the only constant I can claim.

One year in college, I ran away from the places I'd known and went to France. I felt at ease in being foreign without question, in speaking bad French. I was allowed to feel out of place, being from elsewhere. Where that *elsewhere* was was another question. It was the year of the Gulf War and later the Rodney King beating. My American friends stuck together under an identity forced onto them by events, and, while I was often seen as an American, I saw myself apart.

Four years ago, I drove with a friend across the United States from a southern Californian "planned community" to a college town in upstate New York. We traversed the crayon-colored deserts, the blood mountains, a two-day stretch of plain. In Iowa, where I nearly drove into the river, six boys and a girl circled the stalled car and asked, "You came all the way from *California?*"

I live now in Ithaca, the kind of town where people end up staying without meaning to, buying a house to fix up out by Route 366, raising children on organic vegetables from the Farmers Market, growing old. The frost jewels my windows early in winter, which is bitterly wet and sunless. People joke that we have only two seasons: the Fourth of July and winter. Still, the summers are lush and ringing with lilac and children's voices by the willowy lake. Small shops and galleries on The Commons turn over as fast as the undergraduates; the restaurants close and open again. It is a place that sees thousands of arrivals and departures each year, while the shoe store has been here forever, the deli, the Ph.D.s. Here in this town, someone also from elsewhere told me, "The more difficult and necessary task is staying home—making that place where you're misunderstood your own."

Maybe it's true that we are all from elsewhere or going elsewhere; maybe no one belongs anywhere anymore. Listen. I listen to my voice, and it says I am here now.

Profile

Kyoko Uchida.

The trick to not getting seasick, travelers will tell you, is to focus on some fixed point on the horizon. At parties, where people adopt varied and unnatural attitudes, Kyoko Uchida reminds me of such a steadying point. It is not that she is motionless or distant, but that the gravity which she recognizes is not that which governs the bodies moving around her. She'll sit with me over a defeat I took at the grocery store on an expired coupon, without losing her ground in the post-grad high talk about Hollywood men that's going on at her other shoulder.

Her poems are of geographical and emotional displacement, haunting self-portraits accumulated by a Japanese woman attaining and securing her adulthood in countries not her own. They are appearing here and there, eking their way into print, like persons who once shared a journey going off to their various destinations.

—Mario Hernandez

Bio

Kyoko Uchida
Place of residence: Ithaca, New York.
Birthplace: Hiroshima.
Grew up in: Hiroshima. Houston. Vancouver, BC. Toronto. Orange County. Bordeaux.
Education: B.A., University of California at Irvine. M.F.A., Cornell University.
Serial publications: *Northwest Review. Quarterly West. Phoebe*—Poetry.
Current projects: Prose poem sequence. Finding a job.
Favorite book: *Letters to a Young Poet* by R.M. Rilke.

David L. Ulin

Going Underground

I'm from New York. After I moved to Los Angeles a couple of years ago, I discovered that I missed one thing in particular about my hometown—the marvel of modern urban life known as the subway. Whenever I look out at the sprawl of LA, I think, "What this city really needs is an underground railway."

That's why I went downtown on Saturday along with 50,000 or so of my fellow Angelenos to inaugurate the first leg of the Metro Red Line. This 4.4 mile, five-stop subterranean jog from Union Station to MacArthur Park had the city fathers—and mothers—clapping each other on the back in a frenzy of self-congratulation. The Rapid Transit District's publicity flacks had taken great pains to point out that this wasn't the first subway ever to roll beneath the streets of LA. The Hollywood subway ran a whopping one-mile route along Glendale Boulevard from 1925 to 1955, and the Blue Line, when not crushing hapless drivers at crossings throughout the Southland, also goes underground for a brief stretch downtown. Still, the hoopla surrounding the Red Line's opening stressed the historic nature of the event, an irony in a town where history is just another word for last year's news. And for the budget-conscious, the price was right—free for the opening weekend, and only a quarter for the first month of operation.

Although ex-Mayor Tom Bradley, Governor Pete Wilson, and other luminaries attended a special 11:30 AM. ceremony at the Civic Center Station, the system didn't officially open until one o'clock. Of course, only in LA would you have to *drive* to the subway. I showed up at Union Station about a quarter to one and, after parking my car, was surprised to discover a long line. I wandered over to the Plaza at Olvera Street, where there were dancers and tables set up to distribute various opening-day giveaways. The lines were shorter here, and after five or ten minutes I came away with an official Metro shopping bag full of goodies, including a Red Line refrigerator magnet and a cardboard replica of a subway car.

Inside, the line moved slowly. One of the things that had made me skeptical about the Red Line were claims that it would not be like New York's subway. Yet the Red Line publicists had been right. Thus far, passengers were behaving like suitably laid-back Southern Californians. In New York, a wait of an hour or more to ride the subway would be enough to incite a riot, but here, the atmosphere was festive—as though we were spending a day at the beach or at Disneyland. That's the way one of the new RTD transit cops put it: "Disneyland at a price that everyone can afford."

Once underground I could see that this *was* Disneyland, or at least a theme park. Coming off the escalator, I was confronted—not by graffiti and the acrid stench of urine—but by . . . art? Yes, a mural tracing the history of Los Angeles. The whole thing reminded me of the ride at Universal Studios where they fake the giant earthquake. "There should be a big banner," I thought, "Subwayland: The Adventure Begins." It couldn't be more absurd. The ride would take seven minutes and drop us at a station located nowhere that we wanted to go. This being LA, we'd all have to wait in line on the other end, just so we could take the train back to Union Station, pick up our cars, and drive home.

On the platform, transit workers kept everyone several feet back from the tracks. Even so, when the horn blast of an approaching train filled the station, we all pushed forward to see. The tunnel filled with light, and the train pulled in. It was a subway, all right—curved chrome and flat windows—but spotless. Then the doors opened, the people crushed forward, and for the first time in Los Angeles, I felt at home. I elbowed my way to a seat, glad I'd had years of experience in subway etiquette. The novices whom I left in my wake looked insulted. "How long," I wondered, "will it take them to learn?"

Inside, the first thing I noticed was the smell. A clean smell, like a new car. Or not quite a new car, but a new Band-Aid—the way the gauze smells when you peel back the wrapper. Then I noticed that the seats were upholstered, which was why the smell was so strong. Upholstered? I laughed to myself. "We'll see how long that lasts. Wait until people start living down here."

After the train was full and we had jolted into motion, I found myself happy to be on a subway again, enjoying the people around me as they oohed and aah-ed. The ride was quiet, the result of "rubber-like pads under the trackbed," according to an RTD brochure, and, when we pulled into the Civic Center Station, people started chattering like birds. They were black, white, Latino, Asian. They were young, they were old. They were all together: a glorious mosaic of city life. Most had never ridden a subway before. We went through Pershing Square, and on to Metro Center Station, disembarking at MacArthur Park.

Back at Union Station, the crowds were as thick as they'd been when I arrived. For days I'd been laughing at what I saw as flaws in the system—the 7 PM closing time; the fact that there were no turnstiles, just an "honor system" in which tickets were bought but not collected; my own suspicions that one good seismic jolt would crush these manmade tunnels. But, standing in the waiting room, clutching my refrigerator magnet and cardboard subway car, I had to admit I was impressed. Sure, it was a train to nowhere; sure, it would have little impact on my life. Still, it was a start.

I thought about this when I went to retrieve my car from the park 'n' ride outside. At the bottom of the ramp, a parking attendant asked for my ticket.

"That'll be $5.50," he said.

Profile

David L. Ulin may be the only writer in the world who didn't move to Los Angeles to get into the movies. He's lived here for five years and hasn't written one script. Or even seriously thought about it.

Not that David has anything against movies. It's just that his interests turn more towards books. Reading them, writing about them. And writing them. He's working on one now, trying to decode the Jack Kerouac mystique and place it in a context that will make sense of Kerouac as a real person who once existed in the world.

David didn't like LA much when he first got here, but he's getting used to it now. He likes the space of it, the fact that, out in California, he's got room to breathe. At his home in the Fairfax District, he writes in a tower, a tall cylindrical room with twenty-foot-high ceilings and a wall of slanting, translucent windows that color his desk with morning light. On certain days, at certain times, he says, it's like working inside a cathedral. What this means, David still hasn't figured out, but he *does* know he likes the way it feels.

—Peter Schramm

Bio

David L. Ulin

Place of residence: Los Angeles.

Birthplace: New York.

Day job: Freelance writer.

Education: B.A., University of Pennsylvania.

Books: *Cape Cod Blues: Poems* (Red Dust, 1992).

Serial publications: *Los Angeles Times. Newsday. The Nation.*

Current project: A book about Jack Kerouac for the University of California Press.

Favorite book: *Stop-Time* by Frank Conroy.

Membership: National Book Critics Circle.

Favorite music: Rock 'n' roll.

Favorite sport: Baseball.

My team: The Yankees. I'm a hard-core fan, born and bred.

Food: I eat whatever's put in front of me.

Dan Watkins

Ramumu Hoolihoo, Incorporated

The slender volume rested flat against the back of the library shelf behind two Balzacs. How did it get there? Probably slipped or pushed back. How long had it been there? Probably a long time; who reads Balzac nowadays?

It was really more of a pamphlet than a book, old, dusty-gray cardboard cover, no title on the front, self-published probably, three staples for a spine. Inside the front cover, from the yellowed pouch stamped "Seattle Public Library," I slipped out the due date card. The last time the book had been checked out. . . . It had never been checked out.

The Economy of Appetite:
A Study of the Anthropology and Pathology
of Pygmy Capitalists of Western New Guinea
by
Sir Hoyle Raiburne, Ph.D.

It had no table of contents, no publisher, but it had a publishing date (1952), and it had a foreword:

Words cannot express my eternal gratitude to the dozens of scientists and dreamers who bravely journeyed into the jungles of Western New Guinea in search of mankind's barbaric past, and found it. . . . I would also like to thank the Ramumu Hoolihoo pygmee [sic] tribe, those little, brown people whom I was fortu-

nate enough to discover and whom, after many trials and tribulations, I have learned to love. . . .

It was signed, "Sir Hoyle Raiburne, Ph.D., London, England, 1952." On
the next page was the dedication: "In Memorium: Greteline Bottoms-
Raiburne (1895-1951) Who Gave Much More Than I In The Name Of Science." On the facing page it began:

> Off the southern coast of Western New Guinea, on a remote is-
> land surrounded by a cobalt ocean and aeons of unrecorded time,
> there exists a race of men: tiny, savage, white-collared. . . .

I didn't read any farther. It didn't really catch my attention. So I wandered the library as I'm wont to do. I'm unemployed, looking for work.
Honestly I am. I'm wandering the library, looking for work. I held onto the
book, however. I don't know why. When I returned to it several hours later
(after a nap, a game of chess, another nap), I haphazardly flipped to the
back of the book where a grainy, off-kilter, black and white photograph of
the author accosted me. I grimaced, and tittered, and immediately returned
to the beginning of the book. I read straight through to the end, without
stopping, without looking up. Thirty-seven double-spaced, typo-ridden
pages in forty-five minutes. It was astonishing, disgusting, and oddly con-
soling, given my present situation, "between opportunities," as they say.

It seems that Sir Hoyle Raiburne, Ph.D. (A Ph.D. of what? From where?
Never says, which casts considerable doubt on the authenticity of his knight-
hood as well), along with his wife Greteline, stumbled upon a primitive
culture practicing peculiar rituals that curiously reminded Sir Hoyle, although in a twisted fashion, of capitalism. After many "personal sacrifices"
in the summer and fall of 1951, the Raiburnes finally gained the pygmy
tribe's trust. In ritual dances around a great fire, the pygmies recounted
their incredible history.

The Ramumu Hoolihoos' Western New Guinea pygmy ancestors were a
warrior tribe. They killed and ate their enemies. But, seeking greater privacy, the tribe left the mainland and settled on an uninhabited island off the
southern coast of Western New Guinea, now simply called Ramumu Island. Lacking rivals to kill and eat, the pygmies became pacifists and vege-
tarians. They remained totally unspoiled by the modern world until, one

day, Raymond Hoolihan, a New York stockbroker, appeared and promptly spoiled them. Apparently, Hoolihan had gone completely mad following the stock market crash of 1929, and vanished from sight. His subsequent movements are shrouded in mystery until, sometime in the mid 1930s, he materialized on the island one sweltering summer night, saw the pygmies, and wanted to be Chairman of the Board once again. So he became Chairman: he was white and very, very tall; that was good enough for the pygmies. (By the family photograph—wife, two kids—found in the leather wallet that the pygmies kept for religious purposes, Sir Hoyle estimates Hoolihan at five foot six, whereas pygmies rarely grew beyond five feet in stature.)

Using his "business sense" (Raiburne's words), Hoolihan organized, re-structured, fired off memos ("charcoal on palm tree leaves"), and instituted company policies and dress codes ("sun-dried seaweed," writes Sir Hoyle, "painted with white chalk and worn like a collar round the neck"). The product: coconuts. Raymond Hoolihan, CEO of Raymond Hoolihan Incorporated was bastardized to Ramumu Hoolihoo, Inc. for easier pronunciation.

> In his sickness and dementia, [Sir Hoyle speculates] Mr. Hoolihan thought he had cornered the market on coconuts. It is not hard to imagine that, after a few short months, Mr. Hoolihan fancied himself a powerful conglomerate.

The Ramumus, honest, hard working hunter-gatherers to begin with, enjoyed working for Hoolihan at first. They wanted to please the "Big Ramumu," as Raymond had come to be called. But soon Hoolihan, in his lunacy and megalomania, became suspicious and overbearing toward his pygmy workers. He spied on them constantly, from the trees, the bushes, the spear-like high grass. At staff meetings he reviled them with unrealistic deadlines, impossible productivity levels, and dreadful threats; if a certain fathomless profit margin was not reached, *kwali teekee nik! nik!*—which, roughly translated, means "heads will roll." Although nearly a god in their eyes, the Big Ramumu's tedious managerial style ate away at the Ramumus. Frustrated and grumpy, the pygmies rebelled against Hoolihan's authority. Sir Hoyle states:

> Worker subversion took many forms. The more timid Ramumus ate the coconuts that they gathered and murmured hateful

curses about Mr. Hoolihan to the gods. Bolder workers conspired to pierce his fleshy, drinker's nose with an especially long quill from a bird of paradise and, when their plans failed, settled on secretly bedding Mr. Hoolihan's many mistresses. And the most audacious Ramumus embezzled large amounts of coconuts in pouches hidden under their grass skirts and tried to escape the island on rickety, ill-designed rafts fashioned from bamboo shoots and hollowed-out coconuts.

Raymond Hoolihan bitterly noted the obvious decline in productivity; the daily piles of coconuts were getting smaller and smaller. One day he strapped himself to the belly of a lumbering ox in an effort to catch the pygmies red-handed. It worked. He finally caught them stealing; the paranoid knew it was going on all along, and he fired off a memo. The Ramumus preserved the actual document ("a nipa palm leaf," notes Sir Hoyle) in clay. It reads:

> From: Big Ramumu
> To: All little employees
> Managmint regretz to unform You that do to
> uniVoidabul Corprit DownSizing your Jobs have
> been alim elinim Turminated.

Although their English was spotty at best, the Ramumus understood the terminology well enough; they had been laid off. They were no longer wanted. They felt used, taken advantage of, depressed, and angry. Raymond feared that they might try to organize, unionize, maybe form a rival company. But he was mistaken. In a mad frenzy the pygmies revolted, stoned the Big Ramumu to death with coconuts, and ate him. The Ramumus felt lost, however, without Hoolihan's guidance, misdirected though it was. So they recreated Raymond's business philosophy as they perceived it, a philosophy that stressed, above all else, "self-sacrifice for the good of the company." That moment proved decisive in the evolution of the Ramumu Hoolihoos as they reverted to ritualized cannibalism, or *anthropophogy*, man eating man.

> Over the course of our stay, [recounts Sir Hoyle] my wife and I witnessed and, after a time participated in, the strangest, most barbaric ritual, I daresay, cilivized [sic] man has ever seen. On pre-designated nights roughly equivalent to the start of each fi-

nancial quarter, as pygmies danced and beat their drums round a blazing fire, the little Ramumus offered up to the current Big Ramumu (in memory of Mr. Hoolihan always the tallest pygmy in the tribe) their flesh for consumption. I will not trouble you gentle readers, especially the delicate constitutions of the fairer sex, with the horrific details. Suffice it to say that the menu featured the entire human anatomy. During the feast, the little Ramumus let out blood-curdling wails and screeches, but they never drew back their arms and legs. After the ritual had ended, however, the next tallest pygmy crept up to the Big Ramumu sleeping off his gluttony and dispatched him with a large, ritually blessed coconut. As the pygmies roasted their dead leader, that tallest pygmy assumed the role of the Big Ramumu, and the cycle continued anew . . . .

In a postscript to the book, Sir Hoyle writes, "Irrespective of the opposition to my findings voiced by the scientific community, perhaps, above all, one should leave this strange, fascinating tale with the knowledge that we so-called civilized men live in a society not far from the barbarism of primitive man—with its hope and fear and cannibalism." As I turned to the back page, to the photograph of Sir Hoyle, I found myself nodding in agreement. America was, indeed, not far away.

Sir Hoyle Raiburne, Ph.D. smiled up at me from the page. I now understood why he had published the book by himself, likely with his own money, and in spite of the probable ridicule and disbelief of his colleagues. He had to publish, to justify his own sacrifice, to justify the price he paid for his research. The tall, thin Englishman, circa 1952, mustached, goateed, widowed, wore a pith helmet and many-pocketed khakis. But, despite that gleaming, toothy, indomitable British grin, there seemed to be a glassiness, a touch of sadness, even despair, about the eyes, as he leaned on a crutch under his left arm—for he had no right; and stood on his right leg—for he had no left.

Profile

As I swim through the night at 13 Coins, a restaurant in Seattle down near the Terry Avenue freight yard, I consider the man next to me at the bar and conclude: There really isn't much I *can* say about Dan Watkins as a writer or a friend. I just met the guy.

Dan says he doesn't talk to many people. Somehow I believe him. When he asked me to write about him—he said he doesn't know any other writers—I said, "Well, shouldn't I know what kind of writer you are? How about letting me read something you wrote?" He replied by saying, "Sorry, I don't have anything with me." He *says* he's a writer. He *says* he's trying to get his novel *The Autobiography of Riley Prancer* published. At this hour I'm willing to believe anything.

This is what I know about Dan Watkins: rather odd-looking, a little sad, and a little pissed off— "generally," he says. I can sympathize. All in all not a bad guy, as far as I can tell.

He said that if I wrote this thing for him that he'd buy the next round. In this instance, anyway, he's a man of his word.

—James Robb

Bio
Dan Watkins
Place of residence: Seattle.
Birthplace: San Francisco.
Grew up in: Sebastopol, California.
Day job: Temp.
Education: B.A. in English, University of California at Los Angeles.
Award: Most Improved Player, Sebastopol Little League Soccer, 1978.
Current project: *Drohns Smoking Their Brains Out*—a novel.
Favorite book: *Catcher in the Rye* by J. D. Salinger.
Philosophy:
    1. World peace will occur only when everyone takes off their clothes.
    2. People look silly without their clothes.
    3. People would rather be cruel to each other than look ridiculous.
More info: I was unemployed for a period of ten months and wrote "Ramumu Hoolihoo, Incorporated" at the height of that misery.

❖

Joey Kay Wauters

Spirits of the Season: Alaska

He stands in my doorway, tall and imposing, wearing Carhartts and Sorrels. His sturdy bulk makes it hard to tell where muscle and man stop, and the layers of leather and flannel begin.

"I'm so glad you came," I say.

"You don't have me for long," he replies in a husky voice, glancing at his watch. It is three o'clock, dusk on this December day in southeast Juneau.

The alcohol on his breath knocks me back, but I bite my lip and invite him in. I am lucky he showed up at all, and I feel guilty for my pleading tone on the phone when I told him my husband was gone on a business trip.

"Well, let's see what I can do in a half hour." He coughs, unleashing more toxic fumes. It's one of those liquors I can't stand, gin or vodka—clear stuff that smells like lighter fluid. Taking off his wool cap, he reveals a head of gray curls. He is older than I expected. This does not look promising. But what choice do I have? There is no one else I can call. Reluctantly I lead him to the bedroom, opening the closet door.

"There." I point in accusation at the water pressure tank inside. To examine it, he drops to his knees awkwardly, his tool box clattering at his side. Is his clumsiness due to arthritis or inebriation? I offer coffee.

"Nah," he grunts. "People been givin' me coffee all day." His wrinkled face looks still ruddier under the naked bulb hanging in the closet. After finishing inside, he even trudges up the steep, icy slope to check the water lines from our well, but this Eighty-Proof Plumber is unable to work a thirty-minute miracle. "Don't expect any water soon. It's frozen *way* down deep. You've got great heat tape," he says, praising my husband's handiwork. "But it isn't working. Plug out there is dead as a doornail. Call an electrician."

The electrician is out. His wife says he will call back. As my next telephone vigil begins, I suddenly am aware that the only males I am willing to wait by the phone for these days are repairmen. The glacial Taku winds howl, and I cry as I picture multiple pipes bursting during the frigid night. Careful not to waste a drop of precious liquid, I direct my tears into the dog's empty water dish. They barely cover the bottom of the bowl, but the dog slurps them up anyway. I know then I must get a grip on the situation. I decide to do what any sensible person would under the circumstances: *throw a party*.

"It's a Frozen Pipe Party," I tell my friends. "Bring a gallon of water and something to eat. I can't cook here."

"We're going to drink water?" Catherine asks incredulously.

"No, silly, the water is to flush the toilet." The perfect hostess always plans ahead for her guests' sanitation needs.

Down the sixty-four snowy stairs to my cliff-hanging house, Catherine hauls a chafing dish and spicy meatballs. Sara brings steamed broccoli and a "chick flick," a sappy movie our husbands would gag on. The house soon overflows with hearty laughter and gallons of water. I feel better even before I pour the Margaritas over snow that I scooped up far from the dog's territory. We dine on finger foods. Then I serve dessert in the bedroom, where the women are piled on the waterbed, watching the video. Kleenex is passed around as we sniffle in unison during the mushy scenes. We memorize romantic lines to practice later on our unsuspecting husbands.

My friends commiserate over my primitive living conditions. "Why didn't we take Basic Wiring and Plumbing in college?" one asks.

"We were too busy studying feminist theory," another laments.

I hug them good-night at the door. There were no preparations or cleanup for this evening, thanks to paper plates, plastic silverware, and the food they brought. I realize I have discovered how to give the perfect party.

The electrician shows up early the next morning. I give him a merry greeting, feeling almost civilized now that I have had a sponge bath. The electrician phones my red-cheeked plumber, a buddy of his. They confer over possible cures, like consulting physicians, agreeing that since the heat tape is now working, the plumber should come back to witch for water. I must leave for work before the plumber returns. Should I have insisted on a different one this time? My friends asked how I could trust an elderly plumber under the influence. Yet it doesn't seem right to switch plumbers in mid-thaw. I leave my front door unlocked and pray for the best.

My faith in the plumbers union is restored when I read the note fluttering on my door that evening: "Water working now. Took two of us three hours. Merry Christmas."

I mentally calculate the cost of the bill as I head toward the kitchen, drawn by the faint sound of a trickle of water. It would not be heard by most ears, but to mine each drop pinging into the metal sink is a musical note. I forget about the bill as I turn the faucet on full force and let the melody of water roar. What to do first? The range of choices dazzles me: run the dishwasher, scrub the kitchen floor, wash clothes? I linger over each option, knowing all along I will choose the steamy waterfall of a shower.

I pour myself a glass of water from the faucet, raising a silent toast to the hardy professionals who risked icy pathways, frostbite, hypothermia, and my barking dog—all in order to restore this liquid gold to me. So what if the plumber's Happy Hour began a little early? Mine might too if I worked ten-hour days in sub-zero temperatures for an endless list of cold customers. Was it vodka or gin on the plumber's breath? No matter. I will buy a bottle of both to drop off at the shop tomorrow, with red ribbons attached for my slightly soused Santa and his helper. I look into the refrigerator and see small mountains of food left by caring friends. Maybe I'll call more friends tonight. Another Frozen Pipes Party. Why not? It'll be easy—all I have to do is shut off the water again.

But first, my shower.

Profile

Joey Kay Wauters and I met at a Maxine Hong Kingston reading at San Diego State University in 1989, when Joey was on sabbatical. We had a mutual friend, the poet Sandra Alcosser, who was teaching at State and who had invited us both to dinner and to the reading. We ate close to the university at a Chinese restaurant in one of those horrible little California shopping centers comprised of six or seven struggling shops, smudged plate-glass windows and doors, all of which look out over an immense, oil-stained parking lot. What the dinner lacked in atmosphere was made up for by the company and the conversation. A native Californian, I was fascinated with Joey's stories of the frozen north. We were geographical opposites—and, as you know, opposites attract.

Many of Joey's stories tell of her life up north—what seems like a foreign land to me. And I finally got to read Joey's work-in-progress: a comic novel that begins in San Diego with two women leaving behind hilariously misfit men and taking off on a wild car trip to Alaska—all kinds of interesting adventures stopping them along the way.

—Bonnie ZoBell

Bio

Joey Kay Wauters
Places of residence: Southeast Alaska. Northern California.
Birthplace: Auburn, California.
Grew up in: Rural areas.
Day job: Professor of English, University of Alaska Southeast.
Education: B.A., University of the Pacific. M.A., University of San Francisco. D.A., University of Michigan.
Serial publications: *Redbook. Dominion Review. Poet.*
Awards: First Place, *Redbook* Short Story Contest. Pacific Northwest Writers Literary Contest. National League of PEN Women. *Writer's Digest.* American Chapbook.
Current project: Novel set in Alaska.
Favorite book: *Middlemarch* by George Eliot.
Belief: A Pacific Northwest climate keeps your skin looking young.
Craving: More sunshine (despite the above belief).

John Milton Wesley

The Final Days of Emmett Till:
Legacy of a Lynching in Our Little Mississippi Town

The building still stands at the intersection of Weber Street and Highway 49 West in Ruleville, Mississippi. The gas pumps are gone, and so is the red kerosene tank from which we pumped a quarter's worth of coal oil for wood stoves, barbecue pits, and lamps. The old occupants are gone, too, along with any sign of how, forty years ago this weekend, they damaged the psyche of every young African-American male in the nation.

The current residents of what was once Michelle's Grocery are African-American. That would not be so surprising, were it not for the tenants who once lived above the store. The Michelles treated African-Americans with respect and fairness. Their children played with us. During the early 1950s we shared birthday parties and make-believe swims in shallow plastic pools in the store's backyard. All the while Mrs. Michelle cranked out home-made ice cream, popped popcorn, and kept an eye out for bad guys who might suddenly come upon children of different colors innocently enjoying being children.

After old man Jack Michelle died, the store changed hands. To us—the children of that sleepy town north of Jackson—it was the closing of a safe port in a sea of bigotry, racism, apartheid, segregation, and cotton. For nothing had prepared us for the characters who would somehow come to life in our midst.

The new owners were J.W. Milam and his half-brother, Roy Bryant.

Milam had admitted that he and Roy had lynched Emmett Till, the four-teen-year-old black youth from Chicago who was accused of whistling at a white female.

Only a few of us had ever seen Emmett Till. He was one of those kids who came from "up North" every summer to join us in the cotton fields. Not because they had to, or needed the money or the grass sacks filled with government-issue cheese, powdered milk, meal, and flour, but because they needed a break from the hustle and bustle of urban life.

Emmett stood out among the Chicago boys because he talked continu-ously, seemed mature for his age, wore a straw hat, had funny-looking, light-colored eyes, and all the girls thought he was cute. Like other black boys who came from up North, he could keep us spellbound with stories of white girlfriends, the forbidden fruit. After all, they were our masters because they were white, regardless of their ages. Even our parents and grandparents called white children mister and miss. It was custom. In our minds, the thought of referring to a white kid in Mississippi as a girlfriend or boyfriend could mark a black child or his family for retaliation from the Ku Klux Klan, or from anyone who was white and aware of the thought, comment, or rumor.

Yet we were always intrigued by wallet-size photographs from *Life* or *Look* magazine that the Chicago boys carried in cheap plastic wallets. We believed they were real photos of girlfriends, and that up North you could have a white girlfriend and it was OK. We imagined racial bliss and integrat-ed movies where blacks didn't have to sit in the balcony. We imagined danc-ing to the 1950s equivalents of Little Anthony and the Imperials singing "Shimmy, Shimmy, Coco Bop," and Smokey Robinson and the Miracles crooning, "You Really Got a Hold On Me."

We believed that up North there was no color line. We believed that blacks only had to stay in their place in the South, in Mississippi. After all, we had our stories, too. Our stories were of people who left the fields on Friday and disappeared without a trace by Monday morning. Somehow we knew that if they didn't show up in jail, they would surface in Chicago. We also knew they would return one day talking "proper," the men with processed hair-dos, loud-colored suits, and pointed-toed shoes. If they made it real big, they would be driving Cadillacs. Such was the mystique of the flight north; the myth of the black exodus to the promised land.

Chicago boys like Emmett Till relished their ability to dazzle us with their lack of fear of white people. It never occurred to us at the time that they always made these boasts when there were no white folks around to challenge them. We could only marvel at what we imagined their lives must be like in a place where your seat on the bus was determined not by the color of your skin but by the availability of a vacant seat. To the children of the Mississippi Delta, Emmett Till was Marco Polo, who had gone to the New World and returned in August to let us know what to expect. But in August things would change forever, and this Marco Polo would never return alive, and no black boy would ever think of his world the same way again.

We had heard rumors of black men being beaten and even lynched for reasons most people would think absurd. Still, we were beguiled by stories of black boys with white girlfriends. Real or imagined, the notion of a white female speaking intimately to a black man was a fantasy. The more stories we heard from Chicago boys, the more we believed that maybe we were reading the signals wrong. Perhaps white females really did want to be with us intimately. Perhaps all girls were the same, regardless of color. Maybe, if we acted a little less scared, we too could have white girlfriends and earn bragging rights. Never mind the admonition always present in our minds, that in Mississippi such an offense was punishable by death.

We had no idea that four days later, on August 28, 1955, Emmett Till would come face to face with this horrible truth.

It all began at a general store in Money, a one-horse town not far from the Tallahatchie River. This general store was frequented by bus loads of cotton choppers and pickers. We went there for lunch at noontime to buy pork 'n' beans, sardines, cinnamon rolls, and RC colas. Often we stopped there on the trip home from the fields in the evenings. It was a place of alcohol, tobacco, gossip, rumors, and pathos.

On this particular weekend, rumors were afoot that Emmett Till had entered the store on a dare from some of his young friends and begun a conversation with Roy Bryant's wife, who was behind the counter. While his friends peeped in from the outside, Emmett talked freely with the woman. Though it was never proven, one account has it that he "wolf-whistled" and inadvertently touched her in a "non-sexual" way. At this point Emmett's friends became frightened and warned him that they should all run away.

As rumors of the incident spread, Emmett began to share his friends' concern. He talked of cutting short his stay and returning to Chicago. His aunt felt the incident would blow over if he kept quiet and out of sight. Sometime in the wee morning hours of the following Sunday, two white men went to the home of Emmett's aunt and uncle and took Emmett.

When Emmett's savagely beaten and decomposing body was found eight days later, he had been bound with barbed wire, shot in the head and thrown or rolled into the Tallahatchie River, weighed down by a seventy-four-pound fan used to draw hot air out of a cotton gin.

Immediately, Milam and Bryant were suspects, at least in our minds. Reluctantly—these were, of course, "upstanding" white citizens of our community—they were arrested by local authorities. They admitted abducting and beating Emmett but said they did not kill him. Five white lawyers volunteered to represent the brothers, and an all-white jury acquitted them.

Later, in a paid interview with the novelist and journalist William Bradford Huie, Milam acknowledged the murder. "The killing was justified," he said in the *Look* article. "Well, what else could we do? He [Emmett] was hopeless. I'm no bully; I never hurt a nigger in my life. I like niggers—in their place. I know how to work them. But I just decided it was time a few people got put on notice."

"As long as I live and can do anything about it, niggers are gonna stay in their place. Niggers ain't gonna vote where I live. If they did, they'd control the government. They ain't gonna go to school with my kids. And when a nigger even gets close to mentioning sex with a white woman, he's tired of living. I'm likely to kill him. . . .I stood there and listened to that nigger throw that poison at me, and I just made up my mind. 'Chicago boy,' I said, 'I'm tired of them sending your kind down here to stir up trouble. Goddamn you, I'm going to make an example out of you—just so everybody can know how me and my folks stand.'"

By the time this article appeared in 1956, I was eight years old. I was well aware of how J.W. Milam and his folks stood. In their minds they lived in a society in which blacks were believed to be genetically inferior to whites. Theirs was a climate widely accepted by most segments of the white community, and now even sanctioned by law, or so it seemed to us. The court verdict was not what made this so evident at the time. It was the presence of the local police, state police, sheriffs, deputies, and constables who joined the Milams' weekend beer crowd on Saturdays at the store some 200 yards from our front door. By now the corner of Weber street and 49 West had become a gathering place for bigots.

Often when word reached the store of an escape from the State Penitentiary at Parchman, the penal farm a few miles to the north, an instant posse was formed. Without warning, dozens of armed, intoxicated white men would set out, often stopping home long enough to pick up their bloodhounds. Many times, when the hunt was over, they returned to the store in a caravan. They often signaled their arrival and success by firing into the air.

If the death of a peer brings with it a sudden sense of mortality, especially to a child, then the presence of the killers in our midst as neighbors and free men not only confirmed the obvious, but bordered on the absurd. Only the children really knew the impact of the arrival of this family on the deepest of levels, in those places which, once changed, remain forever changed.

Soon the parties at the store became a little rowdier and were no longer confined to weekends. Soon the Shoemakers, a white family who lived on county property adjacent to our small plot of land, forbid their daughter, Angie, to play with me or any of the black kids in the neighborhood. She could no longer come over to our house to practice her lessons on our piano, even though her family did not own one. Angie's father, who drove a bulldozer for the county road department, came home one afternoon and proceeded to bulldoze a makeshift playhouse he had constructed for us earlier. Her mother later explained that the family had been warned that Angie and I should no longer be allowed to play together.

The psychological impact served only to further confuse and lower our self-esteem and deepen the age-old notion of white supremacy. It already seemed odd to us that when we were in the fields chopping and picking cotton, white children were home playing or involved in some organized community activity to which we had no access. To us, if black and white children could no longer play together, not because of something we had done but because of some inherent dark stain on our souls only visible to whites, then just maybe to be white was better.

It was now obvious that to survive the physical threat of white suprema-cy, one had to consciously avoid certain types of environments and people. We knew—though there were no words in our young vocabularies to ex-press the thought—that the more sinister threat was the possibility that we would come to believe that we, as African-Americans, were inferior to whites simply because of our color.

In the days that followed, my life and that of my friends changed, and so did our community. We mapped out routes to town which took us away from and around the store. We were warned not to look at white women at all, and to speak with them only when spoken to and when absolutely nec-essary. We were warned not to look white men in the eye. We were told there would be no more birthday parties in the backyard of Michelle's Gro-cery. We were told to keep our oatmeal cookies to ourselves. By then it didn't matter. For us the age of innocence was already dead.

Profile

I met John Milton Wesley during the 1994 Unity Conference in Atlanta, a first-time official gathering of African-American, Asian, native American, and Latino journalists.

John, who was an exhibitor at the conference, had introduced himself as a "senior social marketing specialist" for the National Clearinghouse for Alcohol and Drug Information. So I thought he was some type of market-ing guy with a long title.

But during a reception at the Carter Center, John and I walked for two hours among the center's paneled walls, viewed former President Jimmy Carter's photographs and documents, and we talked—about everything under the sun.

I shivered when he described his childhood in the South during segrega-tion, and was surprised to learn that his godmother was Fannie Lou Hamer, the late, famed Civil Rights leader.

John, I realized, was an unusual marketing guy, one who loved writing, and was a writer himself. But I still thought he was just a marketing type with a long title.

Then, about a year later, I read an essay John wrote about the Civil Rights struggle in the 1960s in the Mississippi Delta where he grew up. I read it once. I read it twice. Then I put it down and thought, "Wow! This marketing guy really is a writer."

—Donald Blount

Bio

John Milton Wesley
Place of residence: Ellicott City, Maryland.
Birthplace: Ruleville, Mississippi.
Grew up in: Delta of Mississippi. Moved to Jackson on June 12, 1963, the night Medgar Evers was gunned down in his driveway.
Day job: Partnership development, marketing, media and idea development, consulting.
Education: Tougaloo College, Mississippi. Yale University. Columbia University Graduate School of Journalism.
Anthologies: *Black Southern Voices. Mississippi Writers, Volume III.*
Serial publications: *Essence Magazine. Prevention. Pipeland Magazine.*
Awards: *Reader's Digest* United Negro College Fund First Place Award for Poetry, 1968. Maryland Department of Health and Mental Hygiene Outstanding Community Service Award, 1988. National Conference of Blacks in Government.
Current project: Novel and screenplay set in 1957 Mississippi.
Favorite book: *Living Well is the Best Revenge* by Calvin Tomkins.
Belief: Despite fame, weather will determine the attendance at your funeral.

Nancy W. Woods

Perfecting One's Body Parts

Before getting on with my life, I needed just one thing. I needed to get my hands on a Wonder Bra. It was hot, it was English, and it could create cleavage where before none existed. In Portland, Oregon, the only place you could get a Wonder Bra was at Saks Fifth Avenue, where there was a waiting list 200 names long.

I gave Saks a jingle, then waited my turn. Several weeks later, a cardboard box appeared on my front step. I grabbed it and ran upstairs to the bedroom, where I ripped it open. Inside was another box, this one shiny and red.

"Take the plunge," the label read. "Nothing gives your bust or your confidence such a superb boost as the Gossard Super-Uplift." The undergarment boasted forty-six separate components and twenty-eight distinct sewing stages.

I pulled it out. What I held in my hand was stiff and bulky, not a piece of underwear so much as an appliance. Though covered with ribbons and lace, it was one serious piece of equipment.

What did I have to lose? I put the Wonder Bra on. At first I thought there must be some mistake—it was way too narrow across the front. But after I wiggled it into position, I could see what Gossard was up to. Without any visible winches or pulleys, the bra somehow took the body fat under my arms and corralled it up front, where it could do some good.

The effect was startling. When I looked in the mirror, not only did I have cleavage, but I felt like I had a tummy tuck as well. And there were other benefits. Inside each cup was a secret pocket and inside each pocket was a padded insert. What a great place to store a spare house key. With the Wonder Bra I could avoid breast enlargement and the risk of waking up one morning to find both saline implants down around my knees.

But the transformation didn't come without a price, $39.50 to be exact. And while wearing it I did notice a certain difficulty in breathing. Like all shows, this one eventually came to a close. I removed the bra and put it back in the red box.

My body immediately sank back to its original shape, bringing relief. I felt less self-conscious, less aware of my body, and more aware of the need to accept myself.

I buried the box under a pile of socks, in the far corner of a dresser drawer, then walked back downstairs. Then it hit me. My problem wasn't too-small breasts. It was too-big feet. What I needed was Wonder Shoes. If I could just get my hands on a pair, my body would finally be perfect, and I could actually live the rest of my life.

Profile

When I spotted her, Nancy W. Woods was sitting in the Coffee Cow—a restaurant in northeast Portland with a stuffed cow sitting on a bike above the tables. I sat down beside her. She gulped down a double-tall latte while describing her next essay, "In Defense of the Afternoon Nap."

"As a society, we need to sleep more," Woods insisted. "Think of all the crime that could be avoided if people would just go home and go to bed."

Woods should know. She comes from a long line of nap takers, people who fall asleep at the drop of a hat. Which should explain why she came to writing so late in life. For years she slept, when she wasn't delivering mail, shooting wedding photos, or selling prescription drugs. Only recently did she dust off the portable Olivetti her parents gave her for leaving home. She's been writing between naps ever since.

Today she lives in Portland's Hollywood district—which means that she gets to call herself a "Hollywood writer" without actually living in LA.

—Twyla Jasperson

Bio

Nancy W. Woods
Place of residence: Portland, Oregon.
Birthplace: Fairbanks, Alaska.
Grew up in: Fairbanks, where infected mosquito bites and frostbite are chronic childhood ailments.
Day job: Avoiding one so far.
Anthology: *Common Journeys*.
Serial publications: *The Oregonian. Heartland.*
Broadcast: Oregon Public Radio.
Award: A rejection letter signed by Robert Gottlieb.
Current project: Columnist for *The Woman's Journal* in Portland.
Favorite book: *Trees to Know in Oregon* by Charles R. Ross (available free or very cheap through the Oregon State University Extension Service).
Belief: "Hell is other people."—T.S. Eliot.

Afterword

Grassroots Publishing or Why I Started Cune Press

"You've got a finite number of seats on the plane," Juris said. "If you can double the amount of money you charge for each seat, you double your income."

Juris Jurjevics of Soho Press was giving me a lesson in economics. It was March 1994, we were sitting in a yuppie bistro in Manhattan's Soho district, and Juris wasn't referring to the airline industry. He was talking about trade publishing: poems, novels, stories, memoirs, histories—the life blood of our culture. Like most literary writers, I was spending years finding publishers for my work. Submitting manuscripts is expensive. I spent more on postage, phone calls, copying, and in time lost from work than it would have cost to print my books myself.

"So the large shops," Juris continued, "have decided to maximize their income. They aren't looking for good books, per se, but for books that sell."

I talked with other independent publishers: Shirley Cloyes at Lawrence Hill; Nick Lyons at Lyons & Burford; John Oakes at Four Walls, Eight Windows; André Schiffrin at The New Press; Philip Turner at Kodansha. I also talked to insiders at Knopf and Penguin, to literary agents, and to editors at *Publishers Weekly* and *The New York Times Book Review*.

My informants were angry over the direction publishing was taking. They were ashamed of the hundreds of poor quality books that the conglomerate-owned presses were churning out. Those who worked at the large houses fantasized about escaping to Seattle or Taos to start presses of their own. The people I talked to convinced me that the current publishing machine had little or no need for manuscripts from the provinces. "If you write for the large presses," said one Manhattan writer, "you write their book. They design it, you color between the lines."

In April, back home in Seattle, I sifted through my notes. I began to see patterns. Then it struck me: the old publishing system was dead.

Since the acquisition of Knopf in 1960, publishing companies had been acquired by ever larger corporate entities, and their lists had become more and more commercial. With the most recent wave of acquisitions, however, the trend had escalated. As André Schiffrin points out (in *The Nation*, 6/3/96), the traditional yearly profit of 4% after taxes could not satisfy new owners who required 12% to 15%. To meet these goals, publishers were forced to remake their businesses. And, although a few imprints would continue to publish thoughtful books, these exceptions proved the rule. In the first months of 1994 a thirty-year-old trend reached critical mass. Our largest publishers, in an informal partnership with chain bookstores, completed their transformation into giant factories devoted to "bestsellers."

A shift, a juncture, a turn in the path. The change was marked by extraordinary publishing events:

1. The week of January 10, three well-known literary publishing entities (Ticknor & Fields, Atheneum, and Harcourt Brace Trade Books) were eliminated or severly reduced. Cork Smith and other revered editors were laid off. *New York Magazine* collected the gory details. (The *New York Magazine* article appeared 2/28.)

2. On January 30, *The New York Times Book Review* ran the first installment of a two-part "Fishboy" article about Mark Richard, a typical young novelist who went hungry in Manhattan while searching for a publisher. "Fishboy" painted a picture of an industry ruled by greed and cynicism.

3. On February 14, *Publishers Weekly* responded to "Fishboy" with an angry editorial that accused the *Times* of "simplistic finger-wagging."

4. On February 28, the PEN writers group called a meeting (To protest? To mourn?) in the McGraw-Hill auditorium. Harry Evans of Random House made the startling admission that their award-winning books lost money.

In Seattle in mid-April, the sun was out but I was broke. I am a building contractor and I had no work. While I waited for my phone to ring, I wrote several articles about publishing. The new system, I realized, has two tracks: Conglomerate-owned presses publish whatever will sell in large quantities; and grassroots presses are left to publish thoughtful, whimsical, insightful books, writing by new authors, original work that stretches and revitalizes.

Grassroots publishers include mid-sized independent presses, traditional small presses, and what I call "micro-presses"—new one-person and two-person publishing houses which rely on desktop technology and are formed by artists and writers themselves. This latter group is the most quickly growing branch of the publishing industry and largely accounts for the enormous increase in the number of new publishers (39% in 1995 alone). The heroes of grassroots publishing are renaissance women and men who are writers, have market savvy, typically know their way around the World Wide Web, and use their skills to bring their work before the public.

These new author/publishers are not all that different from our literary pioneers—women and men who got ink on their hands or, at the least, were deeply involved with financing, designing, distributing, and promoting their work. I am thinking of Walt Whitman, Virginia and Leonard Woolf, Carl Sandburg, Ezra Pound, James Joyce, D. H. Lawrence, Anaïs Nin.

By now it was the end of May. I resented the effort of sending paper through the mail for harried editors to praise but almost never to publish. No matter how good my writing, I knew, it still would take years to find a publisher. I was spending my life in perpetual adolescence.

I was ready to start my own press. Why not? I decided to establish an imprint, to use it for my own writing, and to make it available to a few other writers in whom I believed. "I'm free," I thought. "Now I can hold up my writing to the 'clear Sophoclean light.' No more contortions to satisfy the taste of a particular editor who is herself guessing about public taste." I was overcome by bliss. I recommended this therapy to friends. And now, 30 months later, deep in debt, just completing an eight-month-long night-and-day work jag, I still believe that I did the right thing.

To put it plainly: Cune Press and *An Ear to the Ground* are part of the grassroots publishing movement. The "authors" of this book consist of more than 200 people: essayists, profile writers, artists, and volunteer publicists and sales reps. *An Ear to the Ground* announces to writers that it no longer is enough to send manuscripts to New York and wait for rejection. Now, those who are writing to be read need to select their very best unpublished work and find a way to bring it before the public.

Why? Because writing is not simply self-expression, it is public service. *An Ear to the Ground* embodies a concept of literature that places good writing at the center of civilized life. In these times of rapid change we should not be surprised that our families and communities are suffering. The symptoms of social fragmentation are reported on the six o'clock news.

We hear almost nothing, however, about the antidote.

Imagination has the power to heal. Our ideas give us light. The stories we tell bring alive the spiritual maps of previous generations, the routes that our forebears have devised to link everyday life to what is vital and true. Our literature—our imagination, ideas, stories—develops the elasticity of character that makes it possible for us to live together. It brings forth our reason, our humanity.

Literature is useful, even essential. But it is not the sort of thing that should be justified by its utility. Our literature is the highest articulation of who we are as a people. It is what we have accomplished as a civilization.

Two years ago, here in Seattle, I met a woman from Tunisia who paints and makes films and writes poetry. She has lived here for many years, yet she still receives small checks from the country of her birth. "For my poetry," she explained.

Tunisia is very small, yet it has found a way to help its poets. Our economy is enormous. Why can't we be equally wise?

Instead we abandon good books to the marketplace. We expect literary works to support their authors and their publishers by sales to individuals. Does any other "entertainment product" succeed in this approach? Pro sports could not survive on ticket sales to individuals. Neither could television, movies, theatre, ballet, or the symphony. Why should thoughtful books?

I have spoken about literature and read my essays before public groups. I've found a hunger for good writing and an eagerness to purchase books. The flame is alive and well, but the publicity and distribution apparatus has broken down. It's difficult for readers to learn about books that they will enjoy. It's hard to purchase books. Public demand for literature is waiting to be cultivated. But up-to-date business arrangements will be necessary for sales to increase. At present, especially for our smallest presses, the vast majority of literary books fail to break even.

An Ear to the Ground speaks to those who care about the fate of our culture. Isn't it clear that we need a renaissance of imagination, thinking, and writing from all levels of society? Such rebirth will not come from a centralized publishing system fixated on profits. It depends upon the spirit, insight, and energy of women and men at the grassroots.

—Scott C. Davis

Acknowledgments

An Ear to the Ground is a cooperative publishing venture. Artists and writers have donated the use of their work. My wife and I and the Portland writer Steven Schlesser have provided most of the money required to produce the book and to pay for the first print run. (For other financial support, see "Donations.") Bjorn Benson, Holly L. Thomas, and I have worked long hours to produce this book. We are grateful for the crunch-time help of Neal Bastek, Danielle Bennett, Mari Lynch Dehmler, Doug Nathan, Steven Schlesser, Diane Sepanski, and Marietta Szubski.

We also have been assisted by a devoted cadre of proofreaders, bookfair staff, envelope stuffers, and other volunteers or part-time staff (apologies to those we've inadvertently omitted). Thanks to Penny and Pat Barrett, Bill Boyd, Dave Calfee, Kit Camp, Gene Cubbison, Katie Davis, Lisa Ede, Grover Ellis, Cathryn Epley, Tom D'Evelyn, Reuben Green, Ruth Hatfield, Janet Louvau Holt, Jan Hudson, Lynn Kohner, Jill A. Malat, Elizabeth Marouk-Coe, Alan Marts, Sally Marts, Marc Messing, Andy Rutten, Ephraim Swanson Dusenbury, Martti Vallila, Helena Maria Viramontes, Greg Wood.

Artists and writers and a group of volunteers (see bios that follow) are acting as sales reps and publicists for *An Ear to the Ground*. Many are also holding readings and asking for financial support to help pay our printer's bill. We are donating sample copies of this book to teachers and students who wish to use *An Ear to the Ground* in English, history, creative writing, and communications classes. We hope that these classes will find *An Ear to the Ground* useful.

Without the assistance of our volunteers, this book could not have become a reality. For more information about the writing, visual art, and other products and services of these volunteers, please contact Cune Press.

Biographies

Paul Aaron, mentor. Paul is a Ph.D. in history who works for Brandeis University and the Benton Foundation in Washington. He is creating a video archive that documents the refugee experience in the former Yugoslavia.

Kathi Allen, writer/publicist. Kathi is a freelance writer and research consultant based in Issaquah, Washington. In the wake of the Jack-in-the-Box ecoli hamburger controversy, she testified before Congress and the Senate and founded a national food safety organization (STOP, Safe Tables Our Priority) which succeeded in getting an overhaul of the USDA's food safety regulations—the first since Upton Sinclair wrote *The Jungle* in 1906. Her work-in-progress: a docu-novel on the control of moneyed interests on government food safety policy. Working title: *Acceptable Risk.*

John Anderson, fund raiser. John has degrees in Art History, Business Administration, and Arts Administration. He has run a gallery and frame shop, is an investment consultant, and has worked in several museums and for the Arts Alliance, a state-wide council of arts groups. John has served on umpteen boards of arts and educational organizations.

Randy Attwood, writer/publicist. Randy is a veteran newspaperman and essayist who lives in Kansas City. His fiction and non-fiction work is finding increased publication on the Internet. Two short stories have recently been accepted for print publication. An agent has accepted three of his novels for representation. "Although I have turned my recent attention to fiction, the art of the essay remains an integral part of that fiction. I used to love John D. MacDonald's Travis McGee series for the essay/harrangues Travis gave us about these United States. Many of the characters I create have opinions to express. The art of the essay brings to fiction an important voice and prose element. I developed my own fiction voice by first creating a prose voice for columns and editorials. Essays remain a writer's first line of expression."

Judith E. Avery, writer. Profile of Laura L. Post. Judith is a divorced mother of two sons who traces her lineage back to the Mayflower. She is the Director of Nursing at the Gladman Psychiatric Health Facility in Oakland, California.

Beth Balderston, writer. Profile of Anson Laytner. Beth was an intern with the Multi-faith AIDS Projects (MAPS) in Seattle. She edited the newsletter and worked in a home for people living with AIDS. Art, writing, and exercise are hobbies important to her well-being. She is currently living and working with a Quaker family in Costa Rica.

Eric Bashor, supporting artist. Eric is a visual artist who specializes in contemporary abstract paintings as well as a variety of print media. Eric spends time in Seattle, Kansas City, and Sacramento. He has studied at Cornish College of the Arts and, in 1995, was listed in *Who's Who in American Colleges and Universities.* He is represented by Gallery V in Kansas City. (Contact Jerry Vegder, Gallery V and Associates 5 East Gregory Kansas City, MO 64114 816-523-4488).

Neal Bastek, editor. Neal is a freelance writer and editor who recently moved to Seattle from Virginia. He is turning the mounds of paper in the Cune offices into computer database entries.

Bjorn Benson, editor. Bjorn is a freelance writer and editor in the Seattle area. He is part of the team that produced *An Ear to the Ground.*

Joy Benzaquen, writer. Profile of Sylvia Benzaquen. Joy lives in Oceanside, Long Island, and works in the printing industry.

Donald Blount, writer. Profile of John Milton Wesley. Donald is a journalist for a Times Mirror newspaper in Allentown, Pennsylvania. He is writing a novel and lives in Bethlehem with his children and fellow journalist Teresa.

John Boe, writer. Profile of John Stenzel. John teaches English at the University of California at Davis.

Jill Bossert, writer. Profile of Hillary Rollins. Jill is a freelance fiction writer based in Manhattan who is currently working on a novel. She has worked as a writer and editor of trade books about art and illustration and holds a B.A. from NYU and an M.F.A. in creative writing from Columbia. She also has training as an artist and has worked for the American Society of Illustrators.

Carol Bowers, writer. Profile of Claire Simons. Carol owns Tecolote Publications, which she operates from her garage in Ocean Beach, a dropout seaside community at the end of Interstate Eight. She writes occasional articles for local publications, runs a weekly writers workshop, and is president of the Ocean Beach Historical Society.

Bron Bradshaw, writer/publicist. Bron has been interested in classical music, classic literature, and European culture since early childhood. She majored in European history at both the undergraduate and graduate levels as a means of uniting those interests in a disciplined academic pursuit. Currently she works as a departmental administrator in a major academic medical center, endeavoring to work in as many literary allusions as possible in the course of business! Her favorite literary period is the nineteenth century. She marvels at the recent conversion of many favorite novels to the silver screen.

Joseph Mack Branchcombe, artist. Portraits of Kenneth Carroll, Mari Lynch Dehmler, James Hall, Arthur Quinn, John Stenzel, and Sharon Streeter. Prior to becoming a professional artist, Joseph worked as a cook, warehouseman, gardener, and contractor's assistant. Disabled as a youth from rheumatic fever, and without formal education, Joseph produces paintings, photography, and videos that draw in part from his Blackfoot Indian and African-American heritage. His work has been exhibited in San Francisco and Crete. He lives in San Francisco.

Annye Brown, writer. Profile of Donna Clovis. Annye is a school nurse in New Jersey. She has a Master's Degree in nursing from Jersey City State College and serves on various state committees for nurses. Her hobbies include gardening and listening to jazz and folk music.

Paul Brown, artist. Portraits of Jocelyn M. Ajami, Sean Bentley, Nathalie Handal, Brad Knickerbocker, Krista Koontz, Lisa Suhair Majaj, and Jerry Reid. Paul is a twenty-three year old illustration student at the Art Center College of Design in Pasadena, California. When not making art he runs a small clothing label geared toward casual wear.

Vanessa V. Brown, writer/publicist. Vanessa is a writer who has produced an as yet unpublished trilogy of environmental fiction. She has a B.A. in English from the University of Washington, has studied with Nelson Bentley, Coleen McElroy, Charles Johnson, and Roger Sale. She has taught creative writing, works as a real estate agent and considers herself a sculptor, photographer, writer, Democrat, and environmentalist.

Melissa A. Burke, writer/publicist. Melissa is freelance writer who lives in a loft in the bowels of downtown Los Angeles. When she is not writing and editing she works at a south central Los Angeles high school. Much of her writing is based on her experiences in the classroom. Interesting facts: in 1987, at age 16, Melissa traveled to India; in 1994 she visited Cuernevaca, Mexico, where she lived with nuns and helped to organize the barrios. Works-in-progress: yes.

Jean Burpee, hostess. Jean lives in Douglas County, Oregon. She has recently sent the youngest of her three children off to college. Jean serves on the boards of several service organizations including Western Rivers Girl Scout Council and Douglas County Museum Foundation. She raises vegetables all year long (favorites are leeks and Brussels sprouts in the winter months) and watches her big leaf maples grow (she has what may be the second and third largest trees in the world ?? sitting in her yard).

Geoff Cahoon, computer support. Geoff is a jazz musician (Be-bop in the style of Charlie "Bird" Parker and Post-bop in the style of Julian "Cannonball" Adderly) who works as a carpenter and music teacher. He lives with his wife, son, and pet goose in Seattle.

Alisa Caratozzolo, writer/publicist. Alisa is

a graduate of the Creative Writing program at U.C. Davis. She lives in San Francisco where she writes short stories and occasional articles. Her cats are named Zita and Izzy.

Victor W. Chapman, writer. Profile of James Bash. Victor is a writer in Portland, Oregon.

Tavis Cockburn, artist. Portraits of Barbara Miriam Frances Abety, Nimri Aziz, Sylvia Benzaquen, Adrian Castro, Sara Nadia Rashad, Sande Smith, and Margaret Thompson. Tavis has been drawing as long as he can remember—muscle-bound super heroes, fantastic vehicles, and planets. A native of Ontario, Canada, he attended a regional arts high school and one semester at the Ontario College of Art before moving to Los Angeles to continue his training at the Art Center of Design, where he is in fifth term studies, majoring in illustration.

Cathy A. Colman, writer. Profile of Kathryn Flynn Galán. Cathy is a poet and journalist based in southern California who teaches private workshops in writing and last year won the A.A. Montandon Award for Poetry from *Hyper Age Magazine.* Her poetry has appeared in many publications including *The Southern Poetry Review, The Spoon River Review, Rohwedder,* and *The George Washington Review.* She has served as a book critic for *The New York Times Book Review* for nine years. Of her many credits, one of the most interesting: she has written a text in celebration of the fall of the Berlin Wall that was performed at the Kennedy Center. She holds a Masters Degree in creative writing from San Francisco State University.

Sybilla A. "Billy" Cook, writer. Profile of Russell DeGroat. Billy is a freelance writer based in Douglas County, Oregon. She is a mainstay of the writers' group, An Association of Writers. (P.O. Box 1101 Winchester, OR 97495.)

Candace Crossley, writer. Profile of Doris Colmes. Ex-Midwestern cheerleader, ex-Lutheran, ex-Chicago model, ex-Miami dope dealer, ex-Cranbrook Academy and Brooklyn art student, ex-Long Island Sound boatbuilder, ex-cross-country truck driver, ex-Sports Illustrated photographer's assistant, ex-San Francisco homeowner, ex-singer, ex-wife, explosive, exemplary, excessive, sucker, seeker, languishing in some dogforsaken paradigm shift. And that's not the hundredth of it.

Doug Dahl, writer/publicist. Doug is a freelance writer based in Vancouver, Washington. He escaped the Navy with his sense of humor intact and wins the "most creative manuscript submission" award every time he sends out customized coffee mugs along with his *Letters to Grandma* work-in-progress.

Roz Davidson, writer/publicist. Roz has recently completed *Sleuth-Lets,* a one-hour book of thirty-second mystery stories, with Rikki-Roz Productions, her own label. She is currently at work on a screenplay and poetry anthology. Her work has appeared in numerous publications.

Scott C. Davis, writer. Profiles of Barbara Nimri Aziz, Katherine Burger, Lance Carden, John Felstiner, Horton Foote, Jerome Gold, Cy Keener, Zoë Landale, Sara Nadia Rashad; "Afterword"; "Calling on Writers, Publishers, Booklovers." Scott is a freelance writer based in Seattle. He served as editor for *An Ear to the Ground* and founded Cune Press in 1994.

Julie Finnin Day, writer. Profile of Krista Koontz. Julie is the former editor of *The Portland Alliance,* a left-wing community newspaper. After a stint of working in the Department of Corrections and administering urine analyses, she is now an overqualified copy aide at *The Oregonian.* Julie and her husband are building a straw-bale house in Portland. She is also a master of Indian cooking.

Wendy Deeley, writer. Profile of William I. Lengeman III.

Paul Dusenbury, artist. Portraits of John Felstiner, Jerome Gold, Zoë Landale, and Jody Seay. Paul has been an art teacher in Seattle Public Schools for over twenty years. His "muscular impressionistic" work, balancing emptiness and air, has been displayed in numerous exhibitions. He received his education in art at Hampton University in Virginia and the University of Washington.

Omar Eby, writer. Profile of Bruce Duane Martin. Omar teaches British fiction and advanced writing. He lives in the Shenandoah Valley of Virginia.

Colleen Adair Fliedner, writer. Profile of Cheryl L. Schuck. Colleen is the author of *Stories in Stone: Park City, Utah. Miners and Madams, Merchants and Murderers* (1995). In addition to lecturing and public relations for various organizations, she is writing a historical novel. She was recently named outstanding alumna of California State University, Long Beach. (To purchase her book contact Flair Publishing 4141 Ball Rd. #446 Cypress, CA 90630.)

Stephen C. Frederick, writer/publicist. Stephen describes himself as a true book lover who likes to be surrounded by books—"especially old, well-used hardbacks." Favorite reading includes the Bible, *Science and Health,* and the *World Almanac.* He also loves trees, cats, and ferns, and appreciates the Beatles, Joan Baez, and Bach. He is "somewhat suspicious" of the entire computer culture and feels that about three hours of TV per week is plenty. He is a native of Eastern Washington and stays close to his family.

Gabriela Fried, writer/publicist. Gabriela is a freelance writer, translator, interpreter, and social psychologist from Montevideo, Uruguay. She is currently based in Los Angeles where she is pursuing a Ph.D. program in Sociology at UCLA and serves as a foreign correspondent for *Posdata* magazine. (email: gfrieda@ucla.edu)

William Goldsby, writer/publicist. William is the Executive Director of Reconstruction Inc., a program designed to provide housing, employment, and support to men who have been convicted of two violent crimes.

He is an ex-offender and veteran and served in the Peace Corps in Guatemala and Honduras as a youth developer and nutritionist. As a consultant for the Pennsylvania Prison Society, he interviewed prisoners in Philadelphia county jail who accused correctional officers of abuse. William also serves on the Pennsylvania Futures Commission on Justice in the Twenty-first Century. He graduated from Western Washington University with a degree in conflict resolution.

Steve Grace, artist. Portraits of Lance Carden, José Casarez, Donna Clovis, Kurt Hoelting, Cy Keener, Joan Piper, Vada Russell, and Shauna Somers. Steve left northern California for Seattle in 1992. A self-taught watercolorist, Steve plans to enter Cornish College of the Arts. He currently cooks at a local pizzeria and practices two forms of martial arts: Non-classical Wing Chung (empty hand), and Cabales Serrada Eskrima (using sticks). Look for his paintings, but watch his hands.

Janne Graham, writer. Profile of Vada Russell. Janne writes for nonprofit organizations. A former metropolitan resident, she now lives in a rural community.

Natalie Greenberg, editorial consultant. Natalie served as Managing Editor with Atlantic Monthly Press for fifteen years.

Ben Grevstad, gaffer. Ben is a woodworker, tilesetter, and remodeling contractor based in Seattle. He runs long distance for fun. (Contact Front Office Construction at 206-364-6288.)

Kris Grevstad, staff. Kris plays mbira and studies logic. When his bank account gets low he works as a carpenter.

Jef Gunn, artist. Portraits in woodcut of Hanna Eady, Horton Foote, Arun Gandhi, Frederic Hunter, Steven Schlesser, and Dan Watkins. Jef is an artist living in Seattle. He works in woodcut, encaustic, collage, and drawing. (Contact him in Seattle at his studio 206-789-7867 or through Quartersaw Gallery in Portland 503-223-2264.)

Miyo Hall, writer/publicist. Miyo is a San

Francisco Bay Area native who works as an EEG and bio feedback technician. She enjoys creative weaving, cooking, and walking her dog and husband in the woods.

Dale Hamilton, artist. Frontispiece. Dale is an artist based in Vancouver, B.C. He specializes in landscapes.

Lisbeth Hamlin, artist. Portraits of jonetta rose barras, Peter Galperin, Jan Haag, Cheryl L. Schuck, Holly L. Thomas, and Kyoko Uchida. Lisbeth's focus on art as an appreciation of cultural diversity has taken her to India, Kenya, and Namibia. Her etchings, paper collages, and watercolors form an ethnological record of traditional life. She was commissioned to paint for a resident of Saint Eustatius and illustrate a multimedia book of songs in France. Her work has been exhibited in Saint Louis, Washington, D.C., New York, and Kenya. Lisbeth received her B.A. in art from Principia College and her MA from New York University. She currently lives in New Jersey.

Diane R. Hanover, writer. Profile of Catherine Foster. Diane is a freelance writer and editor living in Boston.

Marianne Hanson, artist. Portraits of Lucy Aron, Kathy Connor, Grace Druyor, Kathryn Flynn Galán, and Cynthia J. Starks. Marianne has worked as a theater costume designer, art gallery owner, graphic and advertising designer, and literacy specialist. She describes her home in Seattle as "live-in sculpture," gardens as "hieroglyphic inspiration," and time as "life-long learning." She works for church outreach and is currently exploring drawing, painting, sculpture, writing, and illustration in a variety of media.

Katharina Harlow, writer/publicist. Katharina lives with her 12-year-old son in Carmel, California where she teaches calligraphy and grows roses.

Joyce Hart, writer/publicist. Joyce is a freelance writer living in Minnesota.

Mandy Helseth, computer application consultant. Mandy works for Polestar, an information systems company specializing in information systems technology for small businesses. (Contact Polestar at 360-892-8549 voice, 360-892-0655 fax, or Mandy@MatrixTrim.com e-mail.)

Eleanor Hernandez, writer/publicist. Eleanor is a healer who focuses on mind, body, and spirit. She is establishing a private practice based in Kitsap County. She currently works to register Latino voters in King County. "We've lost focus," Eleanor says, "how to treat and respect each other. How to work together."

Mario Hernandez, writer. Profile of Kyoko Uchida. Mario is a writer in Ithaca, New York. His poetry has appeared in *Prairie Schooner*.

Deborah DiSesa Hirsch, writer. Profile of Cynthia J. Starks. Deborah has won numerous awards for her essays, articles, and fiction. She runs a marketing communications firm in Stamford, Connecticut, and specializes in placing stories about computers and the Internet in the media.

Sunny Hobbs, writer. Profile of Jerry Reid. Sunny is 26 years old, a graduate of American University in International Relations, and a resident of Richmond, Virginia. Currently she is racing in a Pro Supertruck at Southern National Speedway in North Carolina. She is a member of the Lyn St. James Automotive Team, which recently participated in the debut of the Mercury Mountaineer for Ford.

Bill Hudson, host. Bill is a screenwriter living in Los Angeles. He enjoys film noir and is a fan of Howard Hawks, and Billy Wilder.

David Hughes, writer. Profile of Scott Richmond. David is the author of *Big Indian Creek*. (Available from Stackpole Books at 1-800-Read-Now. $19.95, hardcover.)

Bonita Hurd, editor. Bonita works as a freelance copy editor in Santa Cruz, Ca. (408-425-1303, voice. bonhurd@cruzio.com, email.)

Yuki Inoue, artist. Portraits of Peggy Bird, Reba Owen, and Claire Simons. Yuki was born in Kamakura City, Japan. In 1984 she attended college in the United States, earning degrees in Fine Arts and Graphics. She lives in southern California where she works as an illustrator and occasional translator.

Bert Jackson, Jr., writer/publicist. Bert is a resident of Spokane, Washington with degrees in physics, human resource management, and land use planning. He is married and has one teenage daughter. He and his family enjoy singing and acting in local community theatre productions.

Twyla Jasperson, writer. Profile of Nancy W. Woods. Twyla is the pseudonym for an Oregon writer. She chooses to remain anonymous so she can more easily eavesdrop on private conversations while walking down city streets.

La'Chris Jordan, writer. Profile of Jamal Gabobe. La'Chris is a freelance writer based in Seattle.

Mohja Kahf, writer/publicist. A poet and fiction writer, Mohja is a first generation immigrant of Syrian origin who grew up in Utah, Indiana, and New Jersey. Active in the Muslim-American community, Mohja currently is a professor in the English Department and the Middle East Studies Program at the University of Arkansas. She works on the literary history of Arab women and on Muslim women's interpretations of Islam. She received her B.A. and Ph.D. from Rutgers University. Her poetry has been published in *The Exquisite Corpse, Visions International,* and other journals.

Drew Kampion, writer. Profile of Kurt Hoelting. Drew is the author of *The Book of Waves.* He has been editor of *The Island Independent, Surfer, Surfing, Wind Surf,* and *New Age* magazines, as well as editorial director of Patagonia, a clothing company. His current projects include freelance features, several books, and extensive home improvements. He lives on Whidbey Island. *(Book of Waves,* which has sold out two editions, will be available from *Surfer Magazine.*

Readers may contact Denise Bashem at 714-496-5922.)

Carolyne Kennedy, writer. Profile of Margaret Thompson. Carolyne comes from New Brunswick and has lived in British Columbia for many years. She is a single mother of three boys and a teacher of grades 5 and 6 in a local Fort St. James elementary school. She does not think of herself as a writer, but is an avid reader who is highly articulate and very funny.

J. Spencer King, computer support. Spencer is a high school student in Seattle who loves computers and serves as a reporter for Kidstar Radio (part of the Kidstar Interactive Media Network). In this capacity he has interviewed high level Chinese officials and traveled to Japan. Spencer maintains an email correspondence with Nicholas Negreponte.

Toby Judith Klayman, mentor. Toby has had a long, distinguished career as a visual artist, an advocate for artists, and a teacher of art. She lives in San Francisco and is the author of *The Artists' Survival Manual.* Her work-in-progress with Cune Press is *Klayman's Crete,* text and images from a small village overlooking the Libyan Sea. (*Artists' Survival Manual.* Scribners 1984, 1987; now published by the author, 1996. 8.5 x 11. 259 pages. $25.00. Available from Toby Judith Klayman email Tobykcrete@AOL.com or snailmail 515 Prentiss St. San Francisco, CA 94110 or voice 415-285-7987.)

Krista Koontz, writer. Profile of Václav Havel. Krista is a freelance writer based in Portland whose work has appeared in *The Oregonian, The Christian Science Monitor,* and other publications. She is also an essayist in *An Ear to the Ground.*

Jeffrey Knapp, writer. Profile of Adrian Castro. Jeffrey teaches English at Florida International University. (For poems, bios, and sound files of Castro, Philp, Sebon, and Knapp, try http://www.paradise.net/encounter and click on "poetry.")

Brad Knickerbocker, writer. Profile of Arun

Gandhi. Brad is a senior writer for *The Christian Science Monitor*. Based in Ashland, Oregon, he travels widely throughout the West covering political, economic, social, and cultural issues with an emphasis on the environment. He has reported from West Africa, Europe, the Middle East, and Panama. Brad is also an essayist in *An Ear to the Ground*.

Scott Knickerbocker, writer. Profile of Brad Knickerbocker. Scott is a student at Principia College in Elsah, Illinois. In the spring of 1996 he and several fellow students created *Soulbook,* a collection of poetry, short prose, and visual art. They raised funds, designed and laid out the book using PageMaker and Photoshop, and produced it in Xerox with a plastic spiral binding. (*Soulbook.* 8.5 x 11. 100 pages. 25 drawings and photographs. $10.00; add $2.50 shipping and handling. Send orders to: *Soulbook,* 188 Scenic Drive, Ashland, OR 97520.)

Annie LaBarge, writer. Profile of Holly L. Thomas. Annie, a former college art instructor and teacher of the disabled, is now a writer, artist, and disabled teacher. She lives in Highland, New York.

Heidi Lane, writer/publicist. Heidi is a freelance writer living in West Point, New York.

Merrily Cordova Laytner, artist. Portraits of Katherine Burger, Linda H. Elegant, and Anson Laytner. Merrily received her M.F.A. at Otis Institute. Her work is widely exhibited.

Beck Lee, writer. Profile of Peter Galperin. Beck is a native New Yorker and graduate of Wesleyan University. Beck runs a public relations/marketing company specializing in the entertainment industry.

Wooten Lee, writer. Profile of Shauna Somers. Wooten is a screenwriter living in Los Angeles. She makes her living as a publicist and freelance writer.

Kym R. Lindsey, writer/publicist. Kym, an avid reader, teacher, bookseller, and writer, has spent her life involved with words. She lives in the San Francisco Bay area, where she

also enjoys "most" sports, walking—especially at night, and music.

Kealy Connor Lonning, writer. Profile of Kathy Connor. Kealy—a reading teacher, wife to Greg, and mother of two—lives in LaCrosse, Wisconsin.

Peter Malarkey, artist. Portraits of Jamal Gabobe, Gary Lilley, and David L. Ulin. Peter is an oil painter living in Seattle. He is represented by the Martin Zambito gallery in Seattle. (Martin-Zambito Fine Art 206-726-9509.)

Mary Ann Marger, writer. Profile of Grace Druyor. Mary Ann has published two adolescent novels and numerous articles and poems. She graduated from the University of North Carolina and is art critic for *The Saint Petersburg Times.*

William J. Martin, writer. Profile of Jocelyn Ajami. William is a Boston resident who used to direct programs for people with severe disabilities and now works as an entrepreneur in the energy business. He also writes short stories, plays, and novels.

Susan Chernak McElroy, writer. Profile of Jody Seay. Susan lives on a small farm in western Oregon. She is the author of *Animals as Teachers and Healers: True Stories and Reflections* (New Sage Press, 1996).

Cydney Brooke McIntyre, artist. Portraits of Russell DeGroat, Václav Havel, and Hillary Rollins. Cydney has studied at the California Institute of the Arts and has a B.A. in Studio Art from Cal State Hayward. She lives in Seattle where she creates visual art and works as an independent producer for public radio. Her programs on Celtic culture and other subjects have aired on KBCS in Bellevue, Washington; WBUR in Boston; and KVMR in Nevada City, California; and have been distributed to other stations on the American Public Radio Network.

Ann Melone, writer/publicist. Ann studied history in the midwest previous to becoming an anti-poverty advocate and volunteer in Seattle. Her writing has been published in

The Eliot Review and *The Carolina Quarterly*, as well as in the anarchofeminist 'zine she co-writes, *Presently Out of Product*.

LaDonna Meredith, writer/publicist. LaDonna writes poetry, short fiction, and has plans for a book. Her interests include Scottish history and folklore, particularly the early 1300s. She lives with her husband in Springdale, Arkansas.

E. Ethelbert Miller, mentor. Profile of Kenneth Carroll. Ethelbert is a widely recognized poet who serves as director of the African-American Resource Center at Howard University. His most recent books are *First Light: Selected and New Poems* (Black Classic Press, 1994) and *In Search of Color Everywhere* (Stewart, Tabori & Chang, 1994).

Lorraine Millings, writer/publicist. Although Lorraine has had over 30 poems published in 38 publications, and another 21 upcoming in small presses, she considers herself a "maverick" poet. Her work concerns global awareness—humanity, ecology, and "sociological/cultural oneness of ethereal fantasy." She is a member of Antelope Valley Writers, the American Academy of Poets, and will be listed in the next edition of *Poets and Writers*. She also finished the L.A. Marathon in 1994. Millings lives in Lancaster, California.

S.P. Miskowski, writer. Profile of Hanna Eady. S.P. is a dramatist/director based in Seattle. Her recent works include *The Red Room, Duende,* and *Feasting*.

Brian Moss, gaffer. Brian is a booklover and psychotherapist who lives and practices in Seattle. In an earlier life Brian worked as a carpenter and, for fun, restored pianos.

Stuart Mozel, gaffer. Stuart recently sold his '63 Impala—the first car he fell in love with. His hobby is repairing miscellaneous devices.

D.A. Murray, writer. Profile of Joan Piper. D.A. works for Homestead Books in Seattle. She is a painter and published cartoonist, whose work appeared in the 1994 anthology *Seattle Laughs*.

Kay Nelsen, writer/publicist. Kay has published stories in *Renovated Lighthouse, The Strain, Supernatural Magazine* on Audiobook, and *Street Beat Quarterly*. She is currently working on a middle-grade novel for children and a fantasy novel for adults. She lives in Denver, Colorado, with her husband, Doug. Kay sees a great future for the small press. "It's been simmering there, barely bubbling, unnoticeable and is now ready to explode. Freedom of thought and expression reside there, the future of the written word, the unfolding of honest composition, revolving into an underground revolution attacking the parched wasteland of what we know as traditional publishing."

Dudley W. Nelson, writer. Profile of Reba Owen. Dudley is a poet and writer and has been a state game warden in Oregon for twenty-eight years.

Nancy Neyenhouse, writer/publicist. Having lived throughout the United States, Nancy has made her home in Puyallup, Washington. After graduating from California State Polytechnic University with a degree in biology, she entertained a desire to follow her zoology professor to Yellowstone National Park and radio-tag grizzlies. Instead she married her high school sweetheart, settled down, and raised two children. Gardening and exploring Mount Rainier National Park and its wildflowers support her love of the outdoors and all of its wild things. She has honed her editing and proofreading skills as an executive-level secretary for the past ten years.

William O'Daly, writer. Profile of Doug Nathan. William is the translator of six books, published with Copper Canyon Press, by Chilean Nobel laureate Pablo Neruda. He has published a chapbook of his own poetry, *The Whale in the Web* (1979), also with Copper Canyon Press.

Terry O'Donnell, writer. Profile of Steven Schlesser. Author and lecturer, Terence served on the staff of the Oregon Historical Society for nearly two decades. His memoir of his years in Iran, *Garden of the Brave in War,* is now in its third printing and will be translated into French. In addition, he has written *Portland: An Informal History and Guide; That Balance So Rare: The Story of Oregon;* and most recently, *An Arrow in the Earth: General Joel Palmer and the Indians of Oregon.* When not lecturing, he divides his time between Portland and the Oregon coast.

Sandi Griffiths O'Neil, writer. Profile of Mari Lynch Dehmler. Birthplace, Shanghai, China; present residence, Elkhorn, California. Artist, musician, traveler, film aficionada, avid reader, former marine biology librarian.

Anna Ostapiw, artist. Portraits of Elizabeth Woodroof Cogar, M. Cassandra Cossitt, William I. Lengeman III, Bruce Duane Martin, Scott Richmond, Ronnie Ritts, and Carol Schirmer. Anna is an artist who lives in Pennsylvania and specializes in pastel landscape paintings in an impressionistic style. Her work has been widely exhibited and her national juried shows include the Catharine Lorillard Wolfe Exhibition in New York and the Maryland Pastel Society in Baltimore. (Contact Joe Gibbons, the Gibbons Company, 2104 N. Washington Avenue Scranton, PA 18509, 717-348-2750 ph, 717-348-0552 fax.)

Herb Payton, writer. Profile of Sean Bentley. Herb, an English major, manages electronic media for CD-ROM projects at Microsoft. His spare time is taken with reading, growing herbs and tomatoes, cooking, collecting wine, and "making a real effort to try every single malt scotch known to man and beast."

Robin Parker, writer/publicist. Robin lives and writes in La Porte, Texas. Her main focus is her husband, three kids, and two cocker spaniels. But when all are fed and the laundry's caught up, she works on her novels and short stories. She also has produced "submission logs" which writers use to keep track of submissions to publishers. (Submission logs. A pad of 25 is $3.00 plus $1.00 shipping and handling. 10315 Carlow La Porte, TX 77571.)

Sowmya Parthasarathy, hostess. Sowmya is a New Delhi native who has a Master's in Architecture from M.I.T. and works as a planner for a San Francisco urban design firm. Her interests are reading and water color painting.

Kevin Powell, writer. Profile of Lisa Teasley. Kevin is the author of *recognize* (Harlem River Press, 1995) in which "she has many ancestors" appears, and co-editor of *In the Tradition: An Anthology of Young Black Writers* (Harlem River Press, 1992). He was in the original cast of MTV's *Real World* and is a staff writer for *VIBE* magazine. He lives in New York City.

Chris Cocklin Ray, writer. Profile of Carol Schirmer. Chris is a jeweler and metal worker and is determined to create outrageous, unsaleable pieces of metal work combined with beading. She lives in the Seattle area and is the mother of two children.

Tiffani Raimondi, writer/publicist. Tiffani is a poet currently based in Venice Beach, California. Her work-in-progress: a narrative poem on Haiti that's 4,000 pages long. Tiffani is a Portland-Seattle native who has served as bosun's mate in the Coast Guard and has lived in Manhattan for five years.

Shane Reiswig, artist. Portraits of James Bash, Robert J. Brake, Doris Colmes, Catherine Foster, Doug Nathan, Laura L. Post, Joey Kay Wauters, John Milton Wesley, and Nancy W. Woods. Shane is a visual artist based in Seattle who works in many mediums, including gouache. Recently he has completed illustrations for *Fly, Rod, and Reel.* He graduated from Art Center College of Design in 1992 and has exhibited his work in Los Angeles, Juneau, Tacoma, and Seattle. (Contact Shane at 206-523-9579.) ·

James Robb, writer. Profile of Dan Watkins. James lives in Seattle.

Lynne B. Robertson, writer. Profile of Elizabeth Woodroof Cogar. Lynne is a freelance writer and editor based in Richmond, Virginia, who has twenty-seven years' experience in journalism and advertising. Her travels have taken her to Russia, Australia, and points in between. Her current devotion is to her "baby" dog, a ninety-pound Golden Retriever named Savannah.

Max Rodriguez, writer. Profile of jonetta rose barras. Max publishes *The Quarterly Black Review of Books (QBR).* (625 Broadway, 10th Floor, New York, NY 10012; 212-475-1010.)

Steve Rowse, staff artist. Photoshop collages of portraits of John Felstiner, Jerome Gold, Zoë Landale. A native of Canada, Steve is a student at the Art Institute of Seattle, where his focus is illustration and video aspects of computer animation. His goal is building clientele for his graphic and design and video company, Spilt Milk. (Reach him at 206-632-2086.)

Mamoun Sakkal, art director. Mamoun hails from the ancient Syrian city of Aleppo, has a Masters in Architecture from the University of Washington, and lives in Bothell, Washington. He is a licensed architect, an award-winning interior designer, and an accomplished illustrator. His father was a teacher who published the first children's books in Syria. Mamoun's love is graphic design and, especially, the design of Arabic typefaces. Mamoun recently won first prize in an international Arabic calligraphy competition. He is also a scholar who has achieved international recognition for his research into medieval Islamic domes and *muqarnas* (a decorative feature of medieval Arabic architecture). (Contact Mamoun at Sakkal Design 206-483-8830.)

Peter Schramm, writer. Profile of David L. Ulin. Peter has known David for years.

Macaria Cossitt Scott, writer. Profile of M. Cassandra Cossitt.

Sourav Sen, host. Sourav is a New Delhi native who recently received a Master's in City Planning from U. C. Berkeley. His hobbies: landscape photography and sailing.

Janice Sethne, writer. Profile of Robert J. Brake. Janice is a graphic designer, teacher, and writer. She owns a Website production

company in Portland, Oregon. She is also the proud owner of a peach-faced lovebird named Freits, a "cut-up when it comes to index cards or other nest-building material," and co-owner of Skippy, "a wire fox terrier named after the dog who played Asta in Dashiell Hammett's *Thin Man* series." She says even her "pets have a literary inclination."

Aishah Shahidah Simmons, writer. Profile of Sande Smith. Aishah is an *Afrolesfemcentric* film maker/writer/activist who is based in Philadelphia. She is currently writing, directing, and producing *NO!* an experimental narrative documentary about rape in the black community. (Contact Afrolez Productions, P. O. Box 58085, Philadelphia, PA 19102-8085.)

Bruce Smith, writer. Profile of Linda H. Elegant. Bruce is the author of *The Common Wages* (Sheep Meadow), *Silver and Information* (University of Georgia, National Poetry Series Selection), *Mercy Seat* (University of Chicago), and two forthcoming volumes: *To the Executive Director of the Fallen World* and *New and Selected Poems.*

Sabrina Smith, writer. Profile of James Hall. Sabrina is a full-time mother of two boys, part-time travel agent, assists her husband's musical career, and edits the Dominican College newsletter, *Pathways.* She lives in Anselmo, California.

Diane Solvang-Angell, graphic arts consultant. Diane has had a long career as a freelance graphic designer and a teacher of graphic design. She has mastered the arcana of corporate marketing in her current position as Communications Manager at SAFECO Insurance Corporation. In her spare time she creates clay portraits and studies screenwriting.

Les Standiford, mentor. Les directs the Creative Writing Program at Florida International University. He is a recipient of fellowships in fiction from the National Endowment of the Arts and the Florida Arts Council and is the author of five novels, including *Spill* (Atlantic Monthly, 1991) and

Deal to Die For (HarperCollins, 1995).

Len Stevens, writer/publicist. Len lives in Portland with his wife, Kathleen, and three children Sarah, Hart and Ethel Elizabeth. He graduated from Lewis and Clark College and then obtained what he was assured would be a valuable degree from University of Puget Sound Law School which subsequently folded. A lawyer for several years in Portland and Micronesia, he now dabbles in a number of dubious business schemes—and writes. From his love of story-telling, he has written four novels and is working on a fifth. Len is a regular contributor to *Cune* magazine.

Renée Stout, writer. Profile of Gary Lilley. Renée was the first American sculptor to exhibit at the National Museum of African Art, Smithsonian Institute. In 1993 she was awarded a Tiffany Fellowship. Her work has been exhibited nationally and internationally and is in several collections, including the National Museum of American Art and the Dallas Museum of Art. She lives in Washington, D.C.

Seth Stroh, computer support. Seth is a Senior Systems Engineer for Specialized Communications in Bellevue, Washington where he designs Internet information distribution devices and FM radio subcarrier systems.

Marietta A. Szubski, writer/publicist. Marietta has a thing for islands. She was born on Key West, "did time" on Manhattan Island with a New York ad agency, and has resided on various islands of the Bahamas. She is now based on Bainbridge Island, near Seattle, Washington, where she is earning a living as a poet, freelance copywriter, and Internet content provider. She is a "motion junkie" who enjoys sailing, flying, cycling, and rock climbing. Marietta has a B.A. in creative writing from Miami University, Oxford, Ohio.

Lisa Teasley, artist. Self-portrait. Lisa is an accomplished visual artist who has exhibited and published widely. She lives with her husband and daughter in Manhattan.

Amy Thornberry, writer. Profile of José Casarez. Amy is a scenic artist based in Los Angeles. Her credits include *Fargo* and *The Mighty Ducks III*. She attends print and sculpting classes at the Burnsdall Art College and is also in the teacher training program at Iyengar Yoga Institute.

Linda Thornton, hostess. Linda lives in Portland, Oregon where she works as a Christian Science Practitioner and helps to nurture the family recording company (Cocoa Mill Music) and the singing career of daughter Dawn-joy.

Lina Tibi, writer. Profile of Nathalie Handal. Lina is a Syrian poet living in London and is one of the most prominent contemporary Arabic poets. She has published three collections of poetry, including *A Sun in the Closet* (1989) and *Self-Portrait* (1994). Her latest is *Here She Lives* (1996). She is also co-editor of *Al-Katiba*, a literary journal featuring Arab women.

Sallie Tisdale, writer. Profile of Peggy Bird. Sallie is the winner of several literary awards, the author of five nonfiction books, most recently *Talk Dirty to Me*, and a contributing editor of *Harper's*. Her work has also appeared in *The New Republic, The New Yorker, Outside,* and other magazines. She lives in the Pacific Northwest.

José Toledo, writer. Profile of Miriam Frances Abety. Cuban born José is a writer who currently makes his living as a social worker in Miami. A member of *Café-con-leche* Writer's Group, Toledo is working on *A Way to the World*, a novel set in revolutionary Cuba of the 1960s.

Nancy Travers, writer. Profile of Sharon Streeter. Nancy is a visual artist who taught at Clackamas Community College for twenty-five years. She is now retired and devotes time to her own work.

Barbara Sachs Turner, writer. Profile of Lucy Aron. Barbara has published a novel, short stories, and several magazine articles. She has received awards from the Individual Arts Fund of Santa Barbara and the James Kirk-

wood Fund at the UCLA Writer's Program.
Laurie Vette, graphic arts consultant. Laurie works for Tim Girvin Design in Seattle. In her spare time she raises Rachel, currently four and one half years old, and climbs mountains. Most memorable climbs: the northwest face of Half Dome and Liberty Ridge on Mt. Rainier.

Patricia Vineski, writer/publicist. Patricia is a freelance writer and booklover based in Parishville, New York. She is currently pursuing an M.F.A. in Poetry at Vermont College and spends her free time herb gardening and rehabilitating wildlife.

Constance Warloe, writer. Profile of Jan Haag. Constance is the author of the novel *The Legend of Olivia Cosmos Montevideo* (Atlantic Monthly Press, 1994) and editor of *I've Always Meant to Tell You: Letters to Our Mothers, An Anthology of 80 Women Writers* (Pocket Books, 1997).

Barbara Weston, writer. Profile of Ronnie Ritts. Barbara's articles and short stories have appeared in magazines including *Writer's Market, Earthwise Review, ByLine, Minnesota Ink, and Wellspring.* Her reviews and profiles of writers have been featured in *The Bloomsbury Review, New Letters Review of Books,* and *Inside Books,* and her interviews with writers are regularly seen on television. A member of National League of American Pen Women, she has won numerous awards for her writing.

David Williams, writer. Profile of Lisa Suhair Majaj. David is the author of *Traveling Mercies* (Alice James Books, 1993), a collection of poems. (Available from Alice James Books, 98 Main Street, Farmington, ME, 04938; 207-778-7071.)

Gail Williams, artist. Cover illustration. Gail is a visual artist and art teacher currently studying at the California Institute of Integral Studies in the Women's Spirituality program. Focusing on integrating the personal, political, and spiritual, she uses mixed media to make sacred containers: images, ob-jects, altars, figures, and clay pots. Gail lives in San Francisco. She also leads support groups and workshops in the national networking organization No Limits for Women in the Arts. (415-648-1637.)

Bonnie ZoBell, writer. Profile of Joey Kay Wauters. Bonnie was awarded a National Endowment for the Arts Fellowship in Fiction for 1995–1996 and is a previous recipient of a PEN Syndicated Fiction Award. She is currently on sabbatical from Mesa College in San Diego. Her fiction has appeared or is forthcoming in *The Greensboro Review, The Cimarron Review, Gulf Stream Magazine,* and other publications.

Calling on:
Writers, Publishers, and Booklovers

We believe that ordinary people can bring change to enormous institutions and industries. Cune Press is calling on writers, publishers, and booklovers to do their part to protect the environment, to reform the publishing industry, and to support individual literary presses.

Writers: The Environment

Al Wong of Arbokem, Inc. has donated agri-pulp paper for the initial press run *of An Ear to the Ground.* Currently many rural communities suffer from air pollution caused by the burning of excess wheat straw. Wong's company takes wheat straw and turns it into paper. The beauty of Wong's system is that the potassium byproduct can be sold as fertilizer—no need to dump poison into our rivers. *An Ear to the Ground* will be the first trade book produced on agri-pulp paper.

Cune Press calls upon writers to require that their books be printed on this type of agriwaste paper, other non-tree paper, or on non-clearcut paper.

Publishers: Returns Policy

The book industry has long been plagued by an open returns policy. Publishers give bookstores a 40% discount, plus the right to return the book for credit at any time. How did this policy begin? Dennis Stovall of Portland's Blue Heron Press likes to repeat a story that circulates among publishers: At the onset of the Great Depression, when small, independent bookstores were struggling, a generous large press(Putnam, as the story goes) instituted a returns policy to help these independents survive.

The depression is long gone yet the policy remains. Only it's been twisted to accomplish the opposite of the originally intended effect. Now the policy forces struggling small presses to subsidize the rapid expansion of chain super-bookstores. It is also used by large publishers as a device for aiding the chain bookstores in their efforts to take market share from independent bookstores. The large presses give discounts to chain bookstores for ordering in large quantities, even though the chains also *return* books in large quantities. These so-called "quantity discounts" are not available to small, struggling independent bookstores who lack the financing to pay for large quantities of books, even if the money later comes back in credit for returns.

Just as the returns practice is now detrimental to independent bookstores, for many more years it has been abused in ways which harm publishers. One example is called the "float-game." A chain bookstore or a wholesaler returns books after eighty-eight days and then reorders them four days later. The idea is to avoid paying bills that are due in ninety days. The publisher bears the expense of shipping, plus labor to unpack and repack. The effect is for the publisher to finance the bookstore's inventory for an indefinite length of time. Since chain superstores have the largest inventory, they receive the largest subsidy—money which allows them to sink millions into aggressive expansion efforts.

Another example is "hurt-theft." To save packing labor, many bookstores have begun shipping returns loose in boxes. These books arrive in damaged condition, and yet publishers are expected to give full credit. Returns are running so high that publishers are unable to use pre-publication order figures to determine the size of their print runs. And small, struggling publishing houses find themselves paying $300 or $400 per month for books that they cannot resell.

A third example is "remainder roulette." Publishers sometimes find themselves paying for returns of more books than they originally printed. How is this possible? They ship books to the wholesaler, who sends them to the bookstores. The bookstores fail to sell the books and send them back to the wholesaler as returns. Then the wholesalers, with the publisher's permission, sell them back to the bookstores for pennies on the dollar as "remainders" to be retailed at steep discounts. Instead of selling the remaindered titles, however, some bookstores return them for full credit. In this way a single book can be returned for credit more than once. Individual books do not have serial numbers. The wholesaler's paperwork can't hope to detect the switch. And even if the wholesaler did have precise paperwork, nothing can stop bookstores from returning remainders for credit in the place of copies that actually sold to the public.

Cune calls on publishers to institute a "no returns" policy: Publishers will offer a 50% discount to retailers. If the merchandise does not sell, retailers will mark it down and move it—as it's done in other industries.

Booklovers: Support a Press

As explained in the "Afterword," good writers and the small publishing operations that put them into print are having a difficult time surviving. Who will pay the cost of bringing new ideas into our culture?

In some cases foundations and large corporations have been willing to support medium-sized literary presses with grants. The difficulty with such grants is that they are very difficult to get, especially when foundations and corporations are under pressure to pay for human services previously provided by government. Grant money could stretch much farther, however, if it could be used to enable the thousands of authors who are starting their own publishing operations each year to publish, along with their own work, the work of other writers.

Ideally, the IRS would approve an umbrella concept whereby an author could organize a 501(c)(3) charitable, non-profit corporation with an independent board, could herself be hired as director, and could produce her own books and the books of other authors in co-publishing arrangements. Tax-deductible donations would pay startup costs and overhead, including a portion of the director's salary. Individual authors would find investors to cover the cash costs of publishing their books. The organization's staff would design and lay out the books, supervise print runs, and do promotion for the imprint. Income from books would be split between the press and the author. At present, the IRS would likely judge such an arrangement to be "self-dealing"—an author's scam to enrich herself. The reality, however, is that literary publishing is almost never a money-making business. Such an effort actually would be an author's attempt to benefit other writers. Cune calls on booklovers who have legal and accounting skills to explore and develop this and other innovative forms of business organization.

In the end, the best solution is for the public to value good writing and to support it with their book purchases. Cune calls on booklovers to sponsor parties for local authors, to attend bookfairs, to purchase good writing from independent presses.

For Teachers

In the hope that teachers will find *An Ear to the Ground* a useful classroom resource, we are providing an index to genres or categories of writing. All *An Ear to the Ground* essays are first-person or "personal" essays. They are thus in the same genre. Yet, within this genre, many different kinds of literature are invoked. For example, Adrian Castro's essay, "Ofun Twice, Again," which deals with Lukumi culture (brought to America by the Yoruba tribe of West Africa), may be considered an anthropological narrative, as well as an example of traditional *griot* storytelling. It also contains spoken word poetry. It is our intention to revise and refine this index in later editions—we welcome your suggestions.

Indexes

For the convenience of readers we have included the following indexes: Favorite books; Places; Proper Names; Subjects. For an index of genres or styles, see "For Teachers."

Favorite Books

Looking for a good book? We have asked essayists from *An Ear to the Ground* to tell us their "favorite books," i.e., books that they would recommend to friends. These books are listed in "Bios" following each essay. And we have collected them below. (Curious about which *An Ear to the Ground* essayist picked a given book? Refer to the page number following the title.)

Places

The entries in this index are taken from *An Ear to the Ground* essays, author profiles, author bios, and the "Afterword."

Proper Names

The entries in this index are taken from the essays, author profiles, and "Afterword." One asterisk indicates an essay author; two, a profile author. Page numbers refer to the first page of the essay, profile, or article of the back matter in which the name appears.

More Copyright

Donations

Special thanks to PhotoLab, Inc. (PLI) in Cincinnati for two oversized estat posters from our electronic originals for use in our tradeshow display. Thanks to Arbokem, Inc. for the donation of the agriwaste paper on which *An Ear to the Ground* is printed. Thanks to Seattle's Lasergraphics/Books A to Z for production assistance and consulting. We are also grateful for support from the individuals and companies listed below.

Angel ($2,000 and over)

Hignell Printing, Winnipeg, Manitoba
The Schlesser Company, Portland, Oregon

Mentor ($1,000 to $1,999)

Anonymous
Microsoft Corporation
Individuals:
Sean and Robin Bentley

Benefactor ($500 to $999)

Companies:
Barrett Business Services
Columbia Consulting Group
Contact International
Continental Hardwoods
Digicolor, Seattle
Emerson Hardwoods
The Grout Company
Hardwoods, Inc.
KAYU International
Lasergraphics (Books A to Z), Seattle
Lumber Products
North Pacific Lumber Company
PLI (Photo Lab, Inc.), Cincinnatti
Weyerhauser
Wolfe Manufacturing
Woods Plus
Individuals:
Lenhardt S. Stevens

Partner ($250 to $499)

Peter Davis and Kristiann Schoening
Mrs. Edward Schlesser

Colleague ($100 to $199)

Companies:
Concordia College, Portland
Frank Lau Jewelry, Seattle
Literacy Unlimited, Bellevue, Washington
Individuals:
Dottie and Eli Ashley
John and Susan Anderson
Robert J. Brake
Ann Graves Davis and Don P. Davis, Jr.
Mary Lowenthal Felstiner and John Felstiner
Calvin A. Ginsberg
Lynn and Timothy Harmon
Kip Keener
Sue Menke
Barbara and Lawrence Reineke

Participant ($50 to 99)

Gary D. Cole
Page Knudsen Cowles
Juliet Jansen Schlesser
Thomas A. Wiley
Harry and Krista Koontz
Sharon Streeter

Cune wishes to thank the King County Arts Commission for financial support drawn from its Hotel/Motel Tax Fund. Cune is sponsored by the Allied Arts Foundation. Make tax-deductible contributions to the Cune Project/Allied Arts and mail to Cune at P.O. Box 31024, Seattle, WA 98103.

Colophon

This book was composed in Microsoft Word. It was typeset in
Pagemaker 6.0 by Adobe Systems. The cover was composed in
Macromedia FreeHand. We used Photoshop by Adobe Systems to
scan and balance the artwork and to compose collages. Typefaces are
Adobe Type 1 PostScript fonts: Minion for body text. ITC Franklin
Gothic for subheads; and Galahad for heads. This book was printed
on 60# agriwaste paper.

Like many independent publishers who utilize desktop technology, Cune is learning the ins
and outs of printing—far more difficult than we ever had imagined. One of the more difficult
and arcane problems is that of "dot gain." An image on the computer screen and a proof on
a laser printer do not accurately reflect the printed final output. That's because dots of ink
have a way of becoming larger when they are placed on paper. The only real way to get a
handle on the problem is to develop a profile for each type of paper and each press (and each
pressman?).

In the interest of furthering our knowledge and yours, Cune Press offers the following
density chart. On our computer each square has the assigned percentage of black. Printed
on 60 lb paper by a sheetfed press, some squares are blown out (no dots at all), some are
pure black, and the density of squares between has shifted (7%? 10%?) to dark. By identifying
which densities on the computer yield on paper 25%, 50%, and 75% densities, we can create
a Photoshop curve to lighten our original the appropriate amount. It should give us greater
control for subsequent printings—if we use the same paper, the same sheetfed press, and the
pressman supplies ink at the same levels.

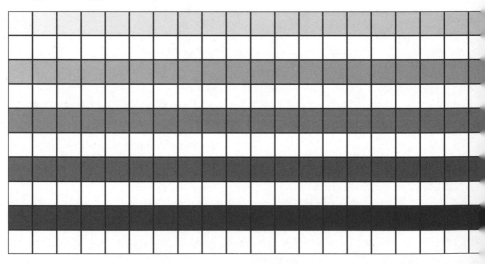